Recordings of use - Loans have their due back date stamped
by staff, but to help us manage the bookstock and its display
to best advantage, would you **please record your consul-**
tations of books **within the library by initialling** below the
latest 'due back date' or last initials.

30. SEP 1977 CANCELLED		
18. SEP. 1978 CANCELLED		
DEC 81		
1988 E		
CANCELLED		
2 CANCELLED		
CANCELLED 1994 / WITHDRAWN		
from STIRLING UNIVERSITY LIBRARY		
31 MAY 1995 A CANCELLED		

THEATRE, DRAMA AND AUDIENCE
IN GOETHE'S GERMANY

THEATRE
DRAMA AND AUDIENCE
IN
GOETHE'S GERMANY

by

W. H. BRUFORD, M.A.
Professor of German, University of Edinburgh

GREENWOOD PRESS, PUBLISHERS
WESTPORT, CONNECTICUT

Library of Congress Cataloging in Publication Data

Bruford, Walter Horace, 1894–
    Theatre, drama, and audience in Goethe's Germany.

    Reprint of the 1950 ed. published by Routledge &
Paul, London.
    Bibliography: p.
    1. Theater—Germany—History. 2. German drama—
18th century—History and criticism. I. Title.
PN2652.B7 1974   792'.0943   73-10579
ISBN 0-8371-7016-8

First published in 1950 by Routledge & Kegan Paul Ltd.,
London

Reprinted with the permission of Routledge & Kegan Paul

Reprinted by Greenwood Press,
a division of Williamhouse-Regency Inc.

First Greenwood Reprinting 1974
Second Greenwood Reprinting 1975

Library of Congress Catalog Card Number 73-10579

ISBN 0-8371-7016-8

Printed in the United States of America

CONTENTS

v

Contents

Contents

Contents

ERRATA

Page 60, line 3: *For* Le Grans *read* Le Grand
Page 181, line 7 from bottom: *For* Falvaire's *read* Falbaire's
Page 182, line 3: *For* Monvol's *read* Monvel's
Page 239, line 12: *For* hyprocritical *read* hypocritical
Page 248, line 22: *For* omitted *read* toned down
Page 249, line 2: *For* fahionable *read* fashionable
Page 254, line 17: *For* new *read* now
Page 255, line 4 from bottom: *For* omitted *read* blunted
Page 290, line 18: *For* Amelia *read* Amalia
Page 315, line 13: *For* over twenty *read* thirteen
Page 335, line 11: *For* as it made clear *read* as is made clear
        line 16: For *Orestria* read *Oresteia*
Page 356, line 24 forward: *For* the plays of the Leipzig school of
    Lessing and his imitators *read* the plays of the Leipzig school,
    those of Lessing and his imitators
Page 362, footnote 1: For *Notes to a Traveller* read *Notes of a
    Traveller*

PREFACE

THE last section of my *Germany in the Eighteenth Century* (Cambridge, 1935) examined in a general way the effects of the political, economic and social condition of Germany on her literature in the eighteenth century. The present work, the appearance of which has been much delayed by the war, is a continuation of the earlier book, a study of one literary genre, the drama, in this same period, both in its passive and active relations with the life of the time and with the theatre, the medium without the aid of which the possibilities of the drama as an art form remain only half realised, like a musical score which is never performed. Once a play is acted, however, it affects those who see it in quite a different way from a printed book, for in what Friedrich Schlegel called 'the most social of the arts' author, actor and audience must necessarily collaborate. If the theatre is brought into such a study, not only plays of high literary value have to be considered, but also the much larger number of entertainments which hardly count as literature, but may be intimately linked up with contemporary life.

This is, of course, a big subject, but it seemed to me manageable if interest could be focused on interrelations in typical instances, no attempt being made to treat drama or theatre in the detail which would be expected in a history of either taken separately. As to the life and manners of those who made up the audiences, the reader is referred to the earlier volume. The sections concerned with the theatre deal mainly with the development of the repertoire. Good or bad German plays, and translations or adaptations of foreign works, if known to have been performed, may all throw light on the tastes and interests of the audience, so that in this respect our survey is more catholic than the ordinary history of the drama. Not much space can be given to the achievements of individual actors or to technical questions of production, but as there is very little to be had in English on German theatrical history, the more important developments, the achievements of the Neubers, of Schröder in Hamburg and Goethe in Weimar are treated fairly fully. The Hamburg National Theatre on the other hand could be passed over more rapidly because there is an excellent study of it available in English by the late Professor J. G. Robertson.

As a history of the German drama, this book is, for the reasons explained, in some respects wider and in some narrower in its scope than the usual histories. The evolution of the genre is described and the more important plays are considered individually, but always with the special aim of this study in view. Plot and character have to be summarily handled and little biographical information can be given. On the other hand, the fate of the plays in the actual theatre is followed, and it may surprise some readers to find how small a part some of the best of them, such as *Nathan der Weise, Iphigenie* or *Faust* played on the stage, though many made a triumphal return later, when firmly established as literary classics. In general we shall find that the better authors have seldom had as good a sense of the theatre as the leading playwrights of France or England, so that 'good' German drama tends to be book-drama, rather overloaded with ideas. The general background of thought had therefore to be kept in view, especially the process by which originally religious ideas were secularised under the influence of the Enlightenment and Sentimentalism. Finally, dramatic theory could not be neglected, because in the drama, as elsewhere, there had been little practice in Germany which has not been guided by a deal of theory.

While observing the interaction in the theatre of author, actor and man in the street, one is brought up against basic habits of German thought, in trying to account for the rapid growth of public interest in literature and the theatre in the later eighteenth century, and in tracing the effect of this rather one-sided aesthetic and intellectual development on the political and social views of the intelligent minority for long after 1800. It seems clear that for many, art became a kind of buffer against the impact of reality, and we are reminded of the two characteristics which

Preface

Thomas Mann, thirty years ago, when he was still 'unpolitical' himself, considered to be outstanding in the Germans, their passion for personal culture (Bildung) and their pride and delight in obedience. That the two are closely connected is suggested when we look at England through the eyes of Matthew Arnold and find an opposite one-sidedness. We are reminded of the truth in Goethe's saying, that a country's literature cannot be understood unless one calls to mind the whole state of its life. It is only when approached in this way that literature and the arts are a key to national character.

In sending this book to press I recall with gratitude the stimulus I received in the study of theatrical history from Robert Stumpfl, whose untimely death was a great loss to scholarship, and I wish to thank the librarians and staff of the Edinburgh University Library, the National Library of Scotland and the Hamburg Stadtbibliothek for unfailing helpfulness.

W. H. BRUFORD

EDINBURGH
August, 1949

I

THE SITUATION IN 1700

IN a country without political, social, religious or cultural
unity such as Germany at the end of the seventeenth century,
it could not be expected that the arts should display a unified
style, least of all an art so inescapably social as that of the theatre.
There was as yet no accepted type of German drama, as there was
a French tragedy and comedy, still less was there an accepted
tradition in the production and acting of plays. The modest
beginnings of a drama and a theatre existed, but each type of play
or performance known to us bears the marks of having been
exclusively designed for one or other of the sharply marked
classes, or rather estates, of society, and of having been the product of a particular geographical region. Even by the close of
the eighteenth century no classical type comparable in stability
and representativeness with the French classics had emerged, but
if we take Schiller's later plays as performed in Weimar as the
nearest approach to a classical German drama, we may say that
this drama was in the main evolved from elements already present
in one form or another at the beginning of the century. It is true
that important impulses were still to be received from without.
But the contemporary appeal of Schiller was not due so much
to what he had learnt from Shakespeare, the Greeks and the
French as to his power of expressing the thought and emotions
of his German public in a form adapted to their theatre in his
own time, and the general tendency throughout the century had
always been towards the same kind of higher synthesis which he
finally achieved of artistic and cultural elements derived from
many classes of society.

Neglecting for the moment regional differences, except to
point out that in a mainly agrarian country, with few large and

no very large centres of population, there were extensive areas where to most people the art of the theatre was quite unknown, while to the majority everywhere it was still a rare experience to see a play, we may note three possible but very different starting-points for a native German drama, which all existed at the beginning of our period. It was naturally at the courts, among the pleasure-loving aristocracy, that dramatic performances took place most frequently and on the most elaborate scale, performances of opera above all, chiefly by Italians in Italian, and of French plays, by French troupes of actors. Though little but the patronage was German here, these performances cannot be neglected in any history of the German drama, still less of the German theatre; the courts furnished in this art, as in architecture and many other things, the models and the standards for the middle class. For the mass of the people the chance of seeing a play acted was much smaller, but since the first tours of the English Players in Germany in late Elizabethan times, there had been travelling troupes who, in the absence of a princely patron, offered their entertainments in the most promising centres available, generally in towns at fair-time, to all who could pay a few groschen for a ticket. These strolling players were ready to put on anything that would draw a good audience, but they usually gave spoken plays in German.

Both court theatre and popular theatre were completely in the hands of professionals, chiefly permanent or semi-permanent troupes of foreigners in the one case, and wandering troupes of Germans in the other. There was another possible, though less likely, growing point for a German drama among certain groups of well-educated amateurs, who had behind them a well-established tradition of which the outstanding feature was a markedly didactic aim. Their didacticism was the forerunner of that striving after 'Bildung' which was to be one of the characteristics of the German literary drama throughout the century. Since the Renaissance the learned had attempted in Germany, as elsewhere, to imitate every kind of Latin poetry, including drama, both in Latin and in the vernacular. When to be able to speak Latin freely was the mark of an educated man, learning Terence by heart and sometimes acting him had an obvious educational value and was recommended or even prescribed by school authorities. A few scholars attempted original plays, or rather dialogues in Latin on similar lines, even before the Reformation, but they became particularly common with the great develop, ment of the schools which the Reformation brought about. The result was the (Protestant) School Drama, which flourished from about 1530, and was followed from about 1550 by the Jesuit (School) Drama, vhen its mis. onary possibilities in the new catholic gymnasia of the Counter-Reformation were realised by the great teaching order.

Both Protestants and Catholics valued performances by schoolboys before an audience of parents and other towns, people as an aid to Latin eloquence, a training in deportment and a form of school advertisement. The limited number of suitable plays by Terence and Plautus available, and a natural striving after originality, led to the composition of new Latin plays by schoolmasters. In protestant lands, though individual performances in Latin continued into the nineteenth century, the general protestant tendency towards bringing truth home to the masses in the vernacular soon led schoolmasters also, rather shamefacedly, to prefer German, and by the seventeenth century this was the rule, whereas the Jesuits held firm to Latin until very near the end (in 1772), and aimed at attracting the higher ranks of society. Even in German, these school performances were held to be good for the young and a useful means of spreading the true doctrine among their elders. Scores of them were pro, duced in the protestant states in the century following the Refor, mation and inflicted on patient audiences, often at Shrovetide, in place of the less godly plays which were traditional at that time of year. They dealt with all manner of subjects, the parables from the New Testament, Old Testament stories, or themes from classical antiquity, sometimes with a little comic relief but never with much art. They lost their importance with the rise of the wandering players, after the Thirty Years' War, but the schools threw up one last dramatist, the best of all, in Christian Weise, the Rector of the Zittau Grammar School for thirty years from

1678, who sometimes draws scenes from contemporary life with convincing realism, though with the same firm conviction, which Lessing still shared, that comedy has a moral aim.

In spite of the basic similarity between the protestant school drama and the Jesuit drama, in that both were acted by school-boys as an educational exercise, there were several differences between them. The pupils of the Jesuit gymnasia came from aristocratic circles, and this partly explains the close link that existed from the beginning between the Jesuit performances and the catholic courts. Though Biblical subjects were common, they were taken only from the Old Testament, except for a few special plays performed in church, and still more use was made of legends of the saints and episodes from church and local history, which gave scope for the propaganda of the faith as well as for effective conflicts between the saints and their persecutors, in scenes of horror and mystery. Apart from dialogues acted in church, the early performances took place in the open, con-tinuing in some respects the traditions of the medieval passion play, in a colourful but highly allegorical style, but as school buildings improved from about 1600, they were given in school halls and followed in their methods of staging every advance made by the professional court theatres, with their Italian picture-frame stage and movable scenery. Increasingly lavish use was made of elaborate costumes and scenic effects, as well as of choral and instrumental music and ballet, in fact in some southern capitals the boy players, upwards of a hundred in one perform-ance, with perhaps one or two students or masters in leading parts, attracted so much attention at certain periods as almost to constitute a kind of court theatre in themselves, in Munich for instance in the earlier seventeenth century, and in Vienna after 1640. Though the words were in Latin, a programme was printed with a synopsis in German, and there might be comic interludes in German too, while every effort was made in the choice of subjects and in their presentation to make a direct appeal which was almost independent of the words. Yet these plays always remained, as Flemming says,[1] 'Kunstgewerbe', applied

---

[1] *Geschichte des Jesuitentheaters*, introduction.

art, rather than real works of art, for the whole aim was to bring home a lesson to as large an audience as possible. That was also the purpose of the allegorical choruses or ballets which marked the end of each act and formed a sort of parallel action on the same moral theme, the nature of which was often indicated also in the sub-title of the play. Tableaux were sometimes used for a similar purpose, like those from the Old Testament which, accompanied by explanatory verses, foreshadow the content of each main episode in the action of the Oberammergau Passion Play, mainly written under Jesuit influence in the seventeenth century.

Interesting as this Jesuit drama is, we should not forget that each school normally produced only one play in public in a year, at the prize-giving (very like our own 'speech-day') in September, though it was often repeated two or three times. It formed such an important part of the school curriculum however that there were monthly practice shows for the school only, so that the boys could be called upon at short notice for a performance to mark a prince's visit or the like. Still, it was an occasional theatre of amateurs, and though it had some influence on other forms of drama, particularly the protestant school drama, it could not rival the professional stage in its effect on the dramatic tradition.

Its influence is clear in the learned drama of the Silesian School, of Gryphius, Lohenstein and Hallmann, which was book drama except in so far as it was acted by the protestant grammar schools, and is best considered along with the school drama. It was the work not of schoolmasters, but of officials of good education, who had come under the influence of the school drama in their youth and were glad to see their plays performed by boys before the only audiences of that day which could be expected to appreciate them. Their chief models, in addition to the Ancients, were Vondel, the Dutch classic, and the Jesuits. The sung choruses they introduced between acts show a curious compound of all three influences, as well as that of the opera. These are about the only plays among all those discussed so far which have any literary merit, except some of Christian Weise's, but though they are often on a high level of ethical thought in their stoical resignation to inevitable evils, and display wide culture and careful craftsmanship in their style, they are too hopelessly long-winded, clumsily constructed and dull to have deserved any success on the stage except the *succès d'estime* they enjoyed in Silesia and the neighbouring states, and except for an odd play, like the *Papinianus* or *Cardenio und Celinde* of Gryphius, taken over in a debased form by the wandering players, they left hardly a trace on the living theatre in 1700. Even the two very readable prose comedies of Gryphius, *Herr Peter Squentz* and *Horribilicribrifax,* 'the best German dramas of the seventeenth century' (J. G. Robertson), were by now quite forgotten.

The drama and theatre fostered by protestant and catholic schools in the sixteenth and seventeenth centuries and the work of the Silesians are interesting revelations of the attitude of the educated middle class to the theatre, one which had changed little, as we shall see, by Gottsched's time, but it is to the professional theatres that we must look for the main source of later developments. Before studying the itinerant stage in some detail, as the only true German professional theatre of the day, a little more attention must be given to the theatres which, though usually run by foreigners, benefited by all the wealth and social prestige of the courts.

In an age when all the arts looked principally to the courts for patronage, court influence was naturally very marked on their form and content, and on the lives of those who practised them. It was natural that of the various forms of the art of the theatre, the one most favoured at court should be opera, for it enjoyed supreme social and artistic prestige in western Europe, and already aimed at achieving that synthesis within itself of all the arts which Richard Wagner later so vigorously championed. It laid claim to the highest literary ancestry, for the Florentine 'camerata' out of which it had developed towards the end of the sixteenth century had been a Renaissance attempt to revive Greek tragedy. By 1700 opera had been the special plaything of the courts for a century, first in Florence, Rome and Mantua, then in the Paris of the *grand siècle*, where it became still more an entertainment for great court occasions, linked with the dance in the form of the ballet, and employing poets like Quinault, with his libretti in the grand style of Cornelian tragedy, and musicians like the great Lulli. This was grand opera, essentially in entertain-ment 'de luxe' for court circles, and reserved in Germany at first for festive occasions, the birthday of a member of the ruling family, a notable anniversary, a welcome home. A new work was often specially composed for such an occasion, or an old one might have a special introduction or finale adapted to the circumstances. In every respect opera fitted in perfectly with the baroque palaces, with their ornate and spacious apartments, their formal gardens and broad flights of stairs, the whole setting in which a prince of that age performed the drama of his daily life, from the 'lever' to the audience, the banquet and concert or ball, all of which had a semi-public and representative character, as visible symbols of supreme power. It was an entertainment on which quite dis-proportionate sums were lavished in Germany because it was the habit of German princes to try to make up in external pomp for what they lacked in real power, but it is interesting to note that even modern Russia does not despise such tokens of national greatness, and produces its ballet and opera stars at state ban-quets with exactly the same aim of impressing the visitors as generations of autocrats in earlier days.

The first operatic performance on German soil of which we hear was at Salzburg in 1618, at the court of the Archbishop and in the presence of an Austrian archduke. Like most of the operas of the southern courts later it was given in Italian. In most cases opera remained a purely Italian product, text, music, cast and conductor, though the orchestra would be the court one, for even the pettiest of seventeenth-century princes maintained an orchestra of some kind. Vienna began in a small way with short operas, or pastorals ending in ballets, from 1631, but from ten years later, and especially during the reign of Leopold I (1658–1705), most elaborate operas were regularly performed by Italian troupes conducted by famous Italian composers like Cesti and Draghi. By this time a lighter type of opera had developed, influenced by the popular Italian theatre, especially in Venice, where middle-class taste had to be considered, but Imperial

7

Vienna preferred a more formal type, and evolved one of its own which outdid even that of the French court in ceremonious grandeur. It had had a small theatre in the Hofburg since 1626, followed by a court theatre in 1652, and a still more elaborate one in 1667. Bavaria did not lag far behind. At the Munich opera house, designed by an Italian and opened in 1657, several notable composers were active, particularly the Venetian Agostino Steffani. From Munich Steffani passed on to Hanover (1688) and through his work for these two courts and Düsseldorf he exercised a great influence on German operatic music. Dresden similarly favoured Italian opera from the 1660's, and other courts employed Italians for shorter periods.

At the smaller central German courts, with their limited means, German composers and librettists were favoured. The most famous combination was perhaps the first, in 1627, when Heinrich Schütz composed the music and Martin Opitz made a German adaptation of the text of Rinuccini's *Dafne*, one of the early Florentine operas, for the wedding of a Saxon princess at Schloss Hartenfels near Torgau. In Silesia Gryphius wrote a short opera *Majuma* in three scenes for Frederick IV's coronation in 1653, and many other poets followed with German allegories, pastorals, etc., in dramatic form, to be sung at some similar celebration. In the latter part of the seventeenth century unpretentious works of this kind, in which songs, taking the place of the Italian 'arias', came to play a more important part than recitative, were produced in considerable numbers at many centres, anticipating in some respects the 'Singspiel', which in the following century, with the growth of the parodistic 'opera buffa' in Italy and ballad opera in England, was to become immensely popular with all classes and to culminate in some of the finest work of Mozart.

The bourgeoisie of the bigger towns followed the cultural lead of the courts and wanted opera too, but only two or three towns could afford anything better than an occasional visit at fair time by a troupe from a neighbouring capital. In Brunswick the opera founded in 1690 by Duke Anton Ulrich, himself an author of novels and libretti, relied to a great extent on the paying public provided for short periods twice a year by the visitors to the fair. They would not all be of the merchant class by any means, for fair time in all the big centres attracted the country gentry from miles around and provided a kind of town 'season' for them. But it was an audience that preferred opera in German, and a number of adapted and original works were produced, many by German composers, in addition to Italian operas.

The only purely trading towns to establish independent operas of their own in the seventeenth century were the two largest, Hamburg and Leipzig. Hamburg's first theatre was built in 1677 by a number of citizens, mostly patricians of the town and consuls of foreign states, along with the exiled Duke of Holstein. The initiative, it will be seen, did not come from the middle class. They formed a limited company to raise the capital necessary and were able to do things on a lavish scale. One of their best sets of scenery, for instance, a Solomon's Temple, cost 15,000 taler and later went to London. The singers at first were mainly 'arme studiosi', young men who were glad to accept this alternative to 'giving music-lessons, helping undertakers or sing-ing in church choirs' as a means of saving money for their future studies. There were apparently no women in the company at this time, but in spite of this, and in spite of the tactful production of a large number of Biblical and allegorical operas to pave the way for more worldly entertainments, there was soon much opposition from certain pietistic ministers, and a fierce controversy developed. The general public took little interest except in novelties, tickets were too expensive no doubt for most of them at half a taler each, and it was only the enthusiasm of the consular colony, men of birth and wealth, that kept the enterprise going.[1] Libretti in German were adapted or written by local talent, young lawyers for instance like Postel and Feind, and much of the music was composed by successive conductors, such as J. S. Kusser, R. Keiser (who was responsible for over a hundred operas), and the young Händel, who composed his first four operas there be-tween 1703 and 1706, before going on to Hanover and London. Many concessions were made to popular taste, comic scenes,

[1] See J. Geffken in *Zeitschrift für Hamburgische Geschichte*, III, 1851, 1-55.

increasing realism, and as elsewhere ballet and spectacle were perhaps more important attractions than music and drama. The Hamburg opera lasted from 1678 to 1738. Leipzig's did not last half as long (1693–1720). Like that of Brunswick it owed its existence mainly to the fairs, and had an even stronger rival in the neighbouring court of Dresden than Brunswick had in Hanover.

Important as the contributions were which the forms of theatre considered so far were to make to German dramatic art in the eighteenth century, its main source was the theatre of professional actors which had existed since the Thirty Years' War, in the form of very miscellaneous touring companies, lineal descendants of the troupes of English Players called over in the first instance by princes in late Elizabethan times for the entertainment of their courts. It was naturally only in the absence of court patronage that actors faced the hazards of the road, and they still sought eagerly after any support that court circles might give them, arming themselves in the first place, if possible, with a so-called 'Privilegium' from the prince of some state, which, if it did not usually give them a monopoly in that state, at least assured them of a certain status both there and elsewhere, and enabled them to style themselves on their play-bills the 'court troupe' of such and such a state. From the history of the Neuber troupe one may see what battles were waged in petition and counter-petition for such privileges, and at the same time how limited their value was, except in the most efficiently policed states. The ideal sought by all was still to become a standing troupe, backed for as long a period as possible by some prince or aristocrat, but this ambition was not realised by any eighteenth-century 'principal' until after mid-century, and in the meantime touring was an economic necessity.

It is surprising that a sufficient number of men and women should have been ready to follow a calling so uncertain, ill-rewarded and little esteemed by respectable citizens. Few of those who did so seem, by all accounts, to have been Ekhofs, filled with such a passion for the theatre that no other kind of life would have satisfied them. Many of the best certainly had 'theatre blood in their veins', as is still the case to-day, and had lived among actors since childhood, but the majority took to the stage simply for lack of a more attractive career. Sometimes a love affair brought a troupe a new recruit, but most frequently we hear of beginners who tried acting as a temporary expedient, if they were within the orbit of some existing troupe, as a last desperate means of keeping their heads above water. No previous training was demanded, so that anyone with a good presence, especially if it was backed by a little education, could be sure at least of being given a trial. We must remember how few alternatives were open to people with no social connections, no skill in a craft, no particular education and no desire for hard physical work. If they were not children of actors or showmen, they were usually people who had somehow strayed from the course normal in their caste—for it was almost a caste system that prevailed in Germany at that time—perhaps through some accident, or some weakness of character, or simply because the vague prompting of an artistic temperament led them towards the one free profession which called for no specialised training. We hear from the earliest days of students taking to the stage, perhaps only for a time, like the Hamburg opera singers mentioned above, and usually from lack of means to continue their studies. Some experience of a school theatre might have helped to turn their thoughts that way, instead of towards tutoring or, last resort, the army. In the seventeenth century several of the earliest German troupes had consisted wholly or mainly of students, and in the eighteenth there was always a fair sprinkling of ex-students to be found among the actors, like Neuber, Koch, Döbbelin and many others.

The earnings of actors, depending as they did on so many variables, fluctuated even more violently than those in other free professions, and at their best they were scanty. It was only towards the end of the century, with standing theatres, that a few principals of companies made fortunes; most of the touring princi-pals were buried in a pauper's grave. The limiting factors were the difficulty of attracting an audience night after night in the small towns of that day, and the waste of time and money in-volved in travelling, when towns of any size were so far apart and communications so bad. The aim was from economic necessity to attract a large audience for as many nights as possible in the same place. Only a few enthusiasts among the actor-managers attempted, for brief periods, to educate the taste of their audiences. Normally they had to give their public what it wanted, and to vary their repertoire to the limit of their capacity. In this latter respect the touring companies, from the English Players on, displayed considerable energy and resource. Green, in 1626, had a repertoire of nearly thirty plays, and the later seventeenth-century troupes usually kept up to this standard. Some managers, like Velten, went far beyond it, though it is hard to know how many of his eighty-seven plays and afterpieces he was really capable of performing, and had not named, on the lists from which our information is derived, for the purpose of making a favourable impression on some town council. We have more detailed knowledge of the eighteenth-century troupes. The Neuber company, in the course of two-hundred-and-three performances in Hamburg in 1735, extending over eight months, put on seventy-five different plays and ninety-three one-acters as afterpieces, so that the full-length plays were not given on the average more than three times each. Half of them were only acted once or twice, and only eight on five or more occasions.[1] The figures for Schönemann's troupe seem to have been comparable with this great record. In the first two difficult years of his company's touring it gave about sixty-two plays and afterpieces.[2]

It was only an exceptionally popular play like Borkenstein's 'local' comedy *Der Bookesbeutel* that could be given repeatedly (sixteen times in Hamburg in 1741, according to Schütze); usually a play could only be safely repeated two or three times in the one town, for instead of the millions who make long runs possible in London to-day, the towns visited by these German players had populations of some twenty to thirty thousand in the more favourable cases and in the vast majority under ten thousand. One can well understand the Neubers' complaint to Gottsched

[1] F. J. von Reden-Esbeck, *Caroline Neuber*, pp. 107 ff.
[2] Hans Devrient, *J. F. Schönemann*, pp. 316 ff.

of the great labour involved in writing out, learning and rehears´
ing new parts, and at the same time changing almost daily the
plays from their old repertoire which they present to the public,
and one appreciates the attraction for the actor of plays that were
at any rate partly improvised.

If we attempt to assess the economic position of the wandering
players more precisely, and ask ourselves for example what
profits the managers earned, and what they were able to pay their
actors, the evidence is scanty before the time of standing theatres,
and difficult to interpret because of the multiplicity of currencies
in Germany and the difference in the value of money between
that age and our own.

Perhaps the salaries paid to actors and actresses are the best
guide, because they can be compared with those earned in other
professions. We are told that in the Neuber troupe 'the highest
weekly wage paid was (normally) five gulden (nominally ten
shillings). A beginner received only two gulden.'[1] The actor
Koch, it is true, was paid five gulden from the beginning, and
finally nine, because of his exceptional services. But there were
several married couples in the troupe, man and wife both earning
a salary, and the young unmarried people were provided with
free meals by Frau Neuber. The young actresses lodged with her
too, and she made herself responsible for their physical and moral
welfare, as any guild master did for his apprentices. When
Schönemann set up his troupe in 1740 he paid Mme Schröder,
Ackermann and Heyderich the equivalent of six shillings a week
and Ekhof, then a beginner, five shillings. The value of this
sum is roughly indicated by a further entry in the same account
book, of a pair of shoes for the manager at three shillings and
sixpence. The total wage´bill was under two pounds ten
shillings for eight men and three women. Even eight years later,
when the troupe was well established, the wage´bill had only
slightly more than doubled (£5 8s.).[2] The salaries paid in the
standing theatres in the last quarter of the century show clearly
how much higher the value had become which was set on an

---

[1] Reden Esbeck, *op. cit.*, p. 57.

[2] Devrient-Stuhlfeld, *Geschichte der deutschen Schauspielkunst*, Ber., 1929,
p. 111, H. Devrient, *op. cit.*, p. 140.

actor's services. In Vienna in 1781, for instance, the normal top salary was the equivalent of £160 a year, and Schröder and his wife received £400 between them, at Mannheim in 1790 it was £156, and at the small court theatre in Weimar it was over £90 for a prima donna. Of course all these figures must be multiplied by five at the very least to arrive at something like the equiva-lent in present values. An actor in Weimar, for instance, at the end of the century, paid about four shillings and sixpence a week for board and lodgings, and another in Potsdam very little more.[1]

Of the other charges that an actor-manager had to meet besides wages the most considerable was travelling expenses, which often swallowed up more than a third of the takings, in spite of the use of the cheapest modes of conveyance. The troupes naturally toured by preference districts where fair-sized towns were not too far apart, the region round Hamburg, for instance (with Lübeck, Hanover, Hildesheim, Celle, Brunswick, Lüne-burg, Schwerin, Rostock, as possible places of call), or round Leipzig (with Halle, Dresden, Breslau and some smaller towns), but even the better companies had often to make long journeys. The Neubers alternated for years between Leipzig and Ham-burg, with perhaps a call or two in between, and on one occasion they went as far afield as St. Petersburg. Schönemann, when he had the 'Privilegium' or licence for Prussia, went as far south as Breslau and occasionally as far north as Königsberg, Danzig or Stettin. Ackermann touched points as far apart as St. Petersburg and Berne within a decade before settling down in the Hamburg region. Smaller companies toured occasionally even the remotest corners of German-speaking territory, and visited Denmark, Holland and Russia. No wonder that the memoirs of actors of that day are full of the hazards and hardships of the road. It is brought home to us how much time and money such journeys consumed when we read that even in 1792 it took an actor three days to get from Lübeck to Brunswick, now half a day's journey by train.

To help to cover their travelling expenses troupes would

[1] For the value of money see *Germany in the Eighteenth Century*. Appendix 1.

sometimes give a performance in quite small places. They might be invited occasionally to play to some exalted personage's house-party in the country, as the Neubers did before the Elector of Saxony at Hubertusburg, or Schönemann before George II of England 'auf der Göhrde' near Hanover, driving five miles across the moor from the village where he had to stay, and back the same evening. We are reminded by this of the third book of *Wilhelm Meisters Lehrjahre,* with its vivid picture of a travelling German troupe engaged, for lack of a French one, to entertain a house-party, and treated with disdain by their noble patrons unless, like the fair Philine, or the gifted dilettante Wilhelm, they had special personal attractions for some of them. Even the gross flattery paid to the visiting prince in an allegorical scene had been paralleled by Schönemann in a specially composed curtain-raiser, entitled *Hermann's Wish,* in which George II had been styled 'the protecting divinity of the Germans' and Schönemann had ended with the hope that he might soon be one of George's subjects.

The next big item in a company's expenditure was the hire of a theatre and the payment of the dues demanded by the town authorities. Down to the end of the century there were few buildings specially designed as permanent theatres except court theatres and opera houses, which were not available to German touring companies. We find the Neubers, Schönemann, Ackermann, making shift with whatever buildings they could hire, putting up a temporary stage if necessary in a hall or large attic, or even erecting a wooden booth on a vacant space, perhaps outside the city walls. In Leipzig, for instance, the Neubers first adapted the space above the meat-market for their purpose. They leased it for about three years at a time at a rent of twenty taler, left their stage and properties there during their absence and paid an additional rent of two taler for every day on which they acted.[1] When they were ousted from this by J. F. Müller's troupe they had a temporary wooden theatre, about forty yards by twenty, specially built for themselves outside the Grimmaisches Tor,[2] and used it until they were able to make a theatre out of an old riding-school in Zotens (later 'Quandts') Hof, where there were

[1] Reden-Esbeck, *op. cit.*, pp. 125, 274.   [2] *Ibid.*, p. 209.

apparently no seats except in the gallery.[1] Here after some years, being 800 taler in debt to the town, they had to give way to Schönemann, and built their last stage in a disused dyer's loft. During this same period of twenty odd years they had similar difficulties to contend with in many other towns where they made shorter stays.

The ideal of every 'principal' was to have his headquarters in some good-sized town where he would build a theatre for himself and act most of the year. It was with such an aim in view that Ackermann built a theatre, with borrowed money, in Königs-berg, only to be driven south by the threat of a Russian invasion at the outbreak of the Seven Years' War. After an Odyssey of nearly ten years he raised 20,000 taler to build the wooden theatre in the Opernhof in Hamburg which he leased after two years to the short-lived Hamburg National Theatre, and which was later the scene of the triumphs of his step-son, F. L. Schröder. But few were so bold, and most managers either hired what hall they could or, like the Direktor in the *Prelude on the stage* in *Faust*, put up a rough wooden structure, probably open to the sky. To be sure of daylight they began their performances early, so that if they were popular the crowd would be queueing up at the box-office 'even before four o'clock'.[2] It was one of the grounds of complaint of the enemies of the theatre that it interfered with work, and with attendance at church services. In Hamburg no per-formances were allowed on Saturdays, Sundays or public holi-days, and until nearly the end of the century no theatres were open there in Lent or in Advent. From 1787 Schröder was allowed to play for half of Lent and Advent, but still not on Sundays and Feast Days, as the Neubers had wished to do forty years before. Five years later Sunday evening concerts were allowed in aid of the theatre pension fund, then plays, in winter only (1798) and finally in summer too (1803). It was thus, by easy stages, that Hamburg introduced the 'Continental Sunday'. Some other places had done so earlier, but not very many,[3] though in the

---

[1] Reden-Esbeck, *op. cit.*, pp. 270, 307.
[2] Hours of beginning: English Players, 2 to 3; Neuber, 4 or 4.30; Schröder, 5 (till 1792), then 5.30, in 1810 still at 6. Weimar, 5.30.
[3] F. L. Schmidt, *Denkwürdigkeiten*, I, 24.

early days the English Players had often been allowed to play on Sundays.[1]

The number of performances, the days and times when they took place, the prices of admission, the repertoire and even the private lives of the actors and actresses were all strictly regulated by town councils from the time of the English Players, in accord-ance with the general policy of the well-policed states and towns of that age. From an early date the towns claimed a share of the takings, often a very large share, up to a quarter, and to be sure of their due, some town councils insisted on having their own official in the box-office. But in the very considerable sums recorded as having been paid by various troupes to town authori-ties, it is frequently impossible to say how much represented the rent of the theatre. How high the town-tax could be is seen from the example of Stranitzky, who paid 2,000 gulden a year rent for the Kärntnertor Theatre in Vienna (1712–15), and 1,300 gulden a year tax to the poor-house.[2] The money raised from the comedians, after the deduction of expenses and tips, was in most towns applied, as it was in many other countries, to charitable purposes, perhaps to salve the consciences of the town councillors for accepting money from so tainted a source, and to appease the clergy. The councillors usually accepted however, or demanded, a number of complimentary tickets. Sometimes a special per-formance was given in their honour, which attracted a large audience.

In addition to wages, travelling expenses, rent and dues, a principal had to meet several regular minor expenses, such as costumes (though for the most part the actors provided their own), scenery and properties, lighting, printing, the services of a musician or two, of various casual workers and perhaps of a sentry or a fire-watchman, if the town required it. The sentry was considered necessary to keep order in the theatre, and survived into court theatre days and later. At Weimar for instance an officer and two men of the Hussars were on duty at each

[1] Creizenach, *Die Schauspiele der englischen Komödianten*, xxiii. This is explained as due to the survival in some places of the freer medieval views about the theatre.
[2] W. Flemming, *Das Schauspiel der Wanderbühne*, p. 7.

performance. According to a statement by Schönemann (1748), these odd items added up to more than his wage bill (£1 10s. a day, compared with £5 8s. a week), or his travelling expenses. He claimed that his income for a season of thirteen weeks in Breslau had been only three-quarters of his expenditure.[1] Even allowing for some exaggeration in view of the purpose for which this return was made, the reduction of his debt to the town, these figures indicate why theatre principals were so often in difficulties, and why payments to authors were kept as low as possible or avoided altogether.

The strolling players naturally did not neglect to advertise their performances, but in the absence as yet of cheap local news-papers with a wide circulation they had to fall back on other methods than those familiar to us. Two forms of advertisement in particular were constantly used by them from the days of the English Players onwards, and by their successors the marionette players in some instances down to 1914. They distributed play-bills, and they attracted the attention of the townsfolk by loud trumpeting or drumming, combined perhaps with a procession through the streets. They sent a man ahead of them if possible with the play-bills, to stick them up in prominent places and deliver them by hand in people's houses. When they arrived themselves, the less dignified troupes at least might go round the town as Italian players had done since the sixteenth century, dressed in gay costume and headed by a drummer or trumpeter. Every now and then they would halt and be their own town criers, while the clown and perhaps a tumbler gave exhibitions of their skill. It was like the first act of *Pagliacci,* or the chapter in *Wilhelm Meisters Lehrjahre* (II, 4) describing the arrival of tight-rope-walkers in a small town. When the players came to have pretensions to culture, and wished to mark themselves off from the common run of itinerant entertainers, they naturally aban-doned the more showy method, and it was often forbidden by the authorities. Schönemann did not beat the traditional drum for instance when he visited the court town Schwerin in the first year of his principalship (1740), but he took care to draw

[1] Hans Devrient, *op. cit.*, p. 140.

attention to his 'well-bred behaviour' in a note printed on his play-bills, and he is said to have returned to the old practice two years later in Berlin.

When J. C. Brandes wrote *Die Komödianten in Quirlequitsch* in 1770, he made his players 'trumpet themselves' in the old style, but stated in the preface that the custom was now out of date. In his comedy a third-rate company of actors and marionette-players arrives in a village, arousing the ire of the local baron when he learns they are not French or Italian but merely German. We see the principal in the costume of harlequin following a hired drummer, and reading in a loud voice from a large play-bill whenever he sees a few people approach. The play-bill is a mild parody of the kind of thing that was quite common for the best troupes in the 'forties and 'fifties, and continued in use among Bavarian marionette players into our own time.[1] It runs: 'With the permission of the High Authorities, the High German well-studied players recently arrived will perform, in their theatre, with their specially large and artistic marionettes, *The Hapless Princess Amanda,* as played before Emperors, Kings, Princes, Counts and innumerable high personages. The entertainment will end with a horrifying Duodrama by three living people, *The Fair Melusina.* Beginning at five o'clock sharp, in the barn beside the Swedish Cat inn. Price of admission, front seats two groschen. Persons of rank pay what they think fit, and are requested to bring their own chairs. Servants are not admitted free. Season tickets available. This week positively the last appearance.'

The crudeness of the processions, the rodomontade of the play-bills, the association of actors in people's minds with mounte-banks and all the fun of the fair, the low social origin of many of them and their not infrequent irregularities of conduct, all made it impossible for people of taste and education to take the strolling players seriously. The fare they provided was, moreover, exactly what one would expect from such companies playing to such audiences. It was a completely low-brow entertainment,

---

[1] See e.g. Reden-Esbeck, *op. cit.*, for the Neubers' play-bills, and Netzle, *Das süddeutsche Wandermarionettentheater.*

aiming at an immediate appeal by the readiest means to hand, mimicry and slap-stick farce, crude emotionalism, the physical attractions—agility, strength, lung power, sex appeal—of the actors and actresses, and spectacular stage effects of every kind. Since Hermann Reich's *Mimus* (1903), German scholars have been accustomed to distinguish between pure 'theatre' of this kind, which Reich called 'Mimus' and had no difficulty in find-ing represented throughout the ages since classical antiquity, and 'drama' in the full sense of the word,[1] which makes use of some of these primitive elements, but only for the material em-bodiment of an imaginative creation, a unified whole, 'some possibility of life seized on by the poet's mind, and imagined as a single movement of events . . . an idea shaping itself forth in the action of life', to quote Lascelles Abercrombie's formulation of his very similar conception.[2] It is more usual in this country to think of the true actable drama as intermediate between the two extremes of pure theatre (Mimus) and merely literary play or book-drama. It is a form of art only to be achieved in the theatre itself by a difficult feat of co-operation between actor, author and, to some extent, audience. The appeal of the purely theatrical is comparable perhaps with the beauty of the material in archi-tecture and the plastic arts, book-drama with the interest of the underlying idea. Drama proper, like any true work of art, communicates a spiritual whole to the imagination through the senses.

The usual performance of the travelling players at the beginning of our period consisted of a more or less serious play, the Hauptak-tion, followed by a farce, the Nachspiel. The 'Hauptaktion' came to be called 'Haupt- und Staatsaktion', because it was full of 'state scenes' introducing people of rank and consequence, princes, noblemen and illustrious persons, in a court setting. 'The splendour of which the masses caught glimpses in real life, and which they painted in still brighter colours in their envious day-dreams',[3] and the freer and more exciting lives led by the

---

[1] See e.g. A. Kutscher, *Die Elemente des Theaters*, 1932; R. Petsch, *Zwei Pole des Dramas*, 1924, and his *Gehalt und Form*, 1925.

[2] "Principles of literary criticism", in *Outline of modern knowledge*, London, 1931.

[3] Carl Heine, *Das Schauspiel der deutschen Wanderbühne vor Gottsched.*

great were the favourite themes. 'Just as every master tailor longed for the title of "court tailor", and was proud if his son-in-law was the court chimney-sweep; just as the lower middle class thronged eagerly to see the processions of the mighty, and swelled their ruler's consciousness of his power by their acclamations, so they asked that their theatre should be concerned with the court world. Politically powerless themselves, they wanted to imagine what it was like to be a ruler, and to feast their eyes on the fate of princely personages. . . . The *Prodigal Son* can no longer be a middle-class boy as in the age of the Reformation; he must be a cavalier with a servant, and ride off on a grand tour to see the world. . . . How characteristic is the re-modelling of the *Merchant of Venice*. The hero now has to be a prince, and his beloved is the daughter of an aristocrat, who sits in judgment together with the Duke.'[1]

It is clear that these plays reflect the idle fancies of the lower ranks in a society with well-marked classes or estates, their dreams of luxury and power. They differ chiefly from the novelettes and cinema films on similar themes to-day perhaps in that class barriers were too high for wish-fulfilling elevations of a hero or heroine, as in old fairy tales or modern success stories. There is no patriotic note and no appeal to historical feeling. The aristo-cratic world portrayed is quite unreal and exotic. Fantastic loves and hates, ambition and crime, are given rhetorical expression, but merely to furnish purple patches for the actors, without any consistency in the characters presented or in the interpretation of human destiny. They do not rise to genuine tragedy, but ruin old tragic themes with happy endings and poetic justice. Lear and Cordelia are not allowed to die, any more than in Schröder's later version. They are freed from prison by Cornwall, and the last scene in the 1692 performance at Breslau was summarised as follows on the programme:[2] 'Kent in fair clothing, with Lear, Cordelia and Gloucester, mourning his son Edgard. Edgard makes himself known. The father dies of joy. Regina (Regan) comes out with a dagger, and stabs herself. Lear orders the wicked

---

[1] W. Flemming, *Das Schauspiel der Wanderbühne*, p. 16.
[2] Creizenach, *op. cit.*, p. 352.

son to be hanged in four chains, and so to end his life. He rejoices over his daughter Cordelia's obedience, and so this play ends.'

For a century and a half, as Devrient says, from the English Players to the last burlesque plays in Vienna, and even beyond them in many respects to the popular theatre of later days, drama written purely for the stage remained essentially unchanged. 'It was enriched by the Jesuit and protestant school drama and the opera and went to extravagant lengths in imitation of them, but its main characteristics were still the same. The inseparable connection of time and place (in plays of the "chronicle" type), the intermingling of the serious and the farcical, the use of music, the love of the surprising and prodigious, the accumulation of outward incidents and the weakness in characterisation, pretentious attempts to be political and learned, courtly, over-refined and precious side by side with comedy of the lowest order, all this is to be found in the first English comedies and tragedies, with which the 'Haupt- und Staatsaktionen' really constitute one and the same genre.'[1]

It is not surprising that an olla podrida of this kind should arouse disgust in any admirer of French classicism, with its good sense and restraint, its carefully distinguished kinds and severely pruned forms, but a sufficient number of texts have survived to indicate how effective the plays could be, given competent acting, as pure entertainment. They were almost completely unliterary, in that their effectiveness depended little on the sensitive use of words but greatly on visible action and stage-play. Realising afresh the merits of pure theatre, in the light of the distinction between the two 'poles' of the drama, recent German criticism has drawn attention to the suitability for their particular purpose of many of the adaptations of older plays made by the English Players and their successors.[2]

The acting versions were almost always made by members of the company, with little feeling for the beauty of words but a good sense of the theatre. The poetry, the tragedy and the humour,

[1] Creizenach, *op. cit.*, p. 65.
[2] See W. Flemming, *op. cit.*, and Anna Baesecke, *Das Schauspiel der englischen Komödianten in Deutschland.*

all the higher literary qualities of Shakespeare and his contemporaries evaporated in translation and might be replaced by something affected or banal, yet some borrowed plays show distinct improvements on their source as regards stage effectiveness with an uncultivated audience, like slick Hollywood films of great novels, and the technique is the peculiarly English one brought over by the professional actors of Shakespeare's age. Its two main features are just those which differentiate typically English drama from French, namely that the events of the dramatic plot are as far as possible presented in action on the stage in the order of their happening, not reported in the dialogue later, and that startling contrasts are not avoided but purposely sought, especially the contrast between tragic and comic elements within the one play. Anna Baesecke for instance illustrates from the surviving text how differently the theme of the prodigal son was treated by Hans Sachs and by the English Players. Instead of someone talking about what will happen or has happened, the incidents are brought on to the stage as if they were happening before the eyes of the spectator. 'He wasted his substance with riotous living' becomes a lively scene in an inn, with wine, women and cards and a double-dealing innkeeper, a scene in which 'speech is only one of the less important means of expression'. It is true that the School Dramatists had already attempted something of the kind with the scene, but they had failed to give it a dramatic climax. In the later version we see the Prodigal, after ordering a banquet and making rash wagers, feel in vain for his money, while in the background the innkeeper makes off with his victim's purse, stolen by his daughter in the night.

What applies to individual situations is true of the plot as a whole. It is made clear and lively, full of visible action, if lacking in ideas and character interest. The motivation is made as direct as possible, full use is made of expressive movement and pantomime, and of the simple properties available, especially of changes of costume—hence the attention paid to stage directions, as Creizenach pointed out, in the surviving plays—dancing and ballet are freely introduced and music is employed to reinforce the emotional tone. At the same time the principle of contrast is never forgotten, the contrast of things as they seem and as they are, as in the *Prodigal Son*, contrasting attitudes of different social estates in similar situations, and the mingling of tragic and comic features, the traditional stumbling-block of French critics of Shakespeare.

Through the English Players the association of tragic with comic scenes in the same play came to be part of the tradition of the German popular stage. There was a special reason why the clown should play a particularly prominent part in their early productions, namely that he could keep the German audience amused with little or bad German, the worse the better, whereas the serious scenes had to be played at first in English and would be imperfectly followed, in spite of the externalisation of the action and the exploitation of every device of the theatre. He was probably put on at first between the acts, without a real share in the action. In some surviving plays he still appears merely as a very *terre à terre* commentator on the tragic scenes, but in the popular plays of the successors of the English Players, for a generation before and after 1700, there was very often a secondary plot, in which the funny man parodied the hero of the serious scenes. This is so for instance in the late version of *The Merchant of Venice* (*Der Jude von Venetien*), edited by an actor who had been to the university, perhaps about 1670, and it is a regular feature in the productions of Stranitzky and his successors in Vienna, who continued the tradition of the strolling players, though themselves now settled at the Kärntnertor Theatre, at a time when farther north Gottsched and the Neubers were attempting to reform the old tradition out of existence.

In *Der Jude von Venetien* the prince who replaces Shakespeare's Antonio falls in love at first sight with a lady in Venice, the counterpart of Portia. So does his servant Pickelhäring with her maid. From the first the Prince and Anciletta act and talk in the style considered fitting for courtly lovers on the baroque stage, masking their feelings in highly decorous and mannered language, while the plebeian pair are unashamedly sensual and brutally direct. 'O heaven, what a lady!' cries the prince, and Pickel-häring: 'O hell, what a pretty wench!' and the comic contrast is fully exploited, with rather wearisome iteration but sometimes with effects that must have been very telling on the stage, especially in the declaration scene, where the attendant couple, reproved for their immodesty and made to keep their distance by the principals, are kissing again as soon as the others take their eyes off them. Similarly in Stranitzky, 'The comedy in Stranitzky's Haupt- und Staatsaktionen is based on the primal incongruity between man's spiritual desires and his physical needs. The grandiose language, the noble sentiments, and the exaggerated idealism of the tragic characters are countered by the baseness, the lewdness and the downright materialism of Hans Wurst. The function of the comic interludes has been described by Madame de Staël, in her phrase: "Le comique exprime l'empire de l'instinct physique sur l'existence morale." In this continual parallel between the two elements in the drama the very words of the serious persons are echoed on a lower plane. There is a constant descent from the sublime to the ridiculous, from the decorous to the obscene.'[1] 'I never laughed so much in my life', Lady Mary Wortley Montagu wrote to Pope from Vienna in 1716 after seeing such a play, in company with many of the court. The popular theatre might be indecent and extremely vulgar, but it was undeniably funny, as even Gottsched had to admit.

It is not surprising that the productions of Stranitzky and his successors were popular in Vienna with all classes, including the aristocracy. The Bavarians and Austrians, who are from the same basic stock, were already, as they are still to-day, the best natural actors among the German-speaking peoples, and it went along with this that the appreciation of good acting was wide spread amongst them. 'It is here', as Kutscher says, 'that most folk and national dances have survived, that the seasons of the year are most often celebrated in different forms of mime, this is the region *par excellence* for folk acting by the people themselves. Their delight in it is closely connected with their race, their temperament, in fact with their whole intellectual, social, religious, political life, a clear expression of national character. In Bavaria,

---

[1] B. Aikin-Sneath, *Comedy in Germany in the first half of the eighteenth century*, p. 47.

Tirol, Salzburg, Upper and Lower Austria, Styria there are districts in which one in every five or six has a talent for acting.'[1] They had the southerner's gregariousness too, which made even aristocrats, or spiritual aristocrats like Faust, find pleasure in popular festivals, where

> Zufrieden jauchzet Gross und Klein:
> Hier bin ich Mensch, hier darf ich's sein![2]

They all shared the same taste for good-humoured mockery of their neighbours' foibles, the Austrian and Bavarian 'frozzeln', expressed in racy dialect, and for drastic naturalism in word and gesture. *Naturalia* were certainly not *turpia* for an audience which laughed unrestrainedly when, to the English visitor's disgust, the two Sosias in *Amphytryon* 'very fairly let down their breeches in the direct view of the boxes, which were full of people of the first rank'.

Furthermore, the contents of these plays were not so very different from those of the operas which were, as we have seen, the characteristic form of entertainment for court circles, in fact they were for the most past adaptations of old operas, or of the Jesuit dramas which had much in common with these. The actor-authors of the plays of the popular theatre had always borrowed from any available source. When English actors were succeeded by native Germans, the new accessions to their repertoire came from many countries of Europe. Very few came from literary dramas in Germany itself in the seventeenth century, only one or two plays of Gryphius in a debased form (*Papinianus, Cardenio und Celinde, Herr Peter Squentz*). Plays from Elizabethan originals became less and less numerous as time went on, being replaced mainly from the Romance countries, Spain, France and above all, Italy. There are four plays at least of Calderon, two of Lope de Vega, and several other Spanish plays, some of them through French or Dutch translations, which are known to have been adapted for various touring companies. The best of the later seventeenth-century companies, that of

---

[1] Kutscher, *op. cit.*, p. 41.
[2] The south German in Goethe is well brought out by Viktor Hehn in his *Gedanken über Goethe* (1887).

Johannes Velten, staged a large number of French and Dutch plays (Molière, Pierre Corneille, Vondel and others), but with the vogue of Italian opera at the German courts, more and more plays came to be constructed from operas.[1]

The relationship between some of these later plays, the texts of which happen to have survived in manuscript, and their originals, has been carefully studied. One that like several others was first adapted from the Italian to become a German opera in Hamburg, and then turned into a Haupt- und Staatsaktion by some strolling player, is *Atis*.[2] The original, with an Italian libretto by Minato and music by Draghi, was first performed under the title *Creso* in Vienna in 1678. It was translated and adapted by Bostel for Hamburg six years later, and was being acted by the troupe of Hofmann, the one which so much disgusted Gottsched with its performances when he arrived in Leipzig, at least forty years later still. Venetian opera was better suited than most as a foundation for such a play, because it had already been influenced by the *commedia dell' arte* and contained comic scenes with a satirical tendency. In Hamburg these were 'naturalised' with realistic detail and local allusions, and they were taken over, in a shorter form, into the popular play, while the text of the serious scenes was put into prose, the arias remaining as spoken verses. Stranitzky's plays were rough-hewn in exactly the same way from Viennese operas of Italian origin, and sometimes from other plays, such as religious verse dramas.[3]

'The clown', it has been well said, 'embodies the spirit of the English Comedians' play. He is the vital centre of their theatre, the root from which it draws its sap.'[4] Under varying comic names, Bouset (posset), Stockfisch, and finally Pickelhäring, he was always the leader in the early troupes,[5] and he remained the central figure all through. It is with good reason that Goethe chose the Merry Andrew to represent the actors in the *Prelude on the Stage* in *Faust*, for it was the strolling players he had in mind

[1] Carl Heine, *J. Velten*, 1887; *Das Schauspiel der deutschen Wanderbühne vor Gottsched*, 1889. W. Flemming, *op. cit.*
[2] Mary Beare, *The German popular play Atis and the Venetian opera*, 1938.
[3] F. Homeyer, *Stranitzky's Drama vom 'Heiligen Nepomuk'*, 1907.
[4] Anna Baesecke, *op. cit.*, p. 68.
[5] See Creizenach, *op. cit.*, introduction, pp. xciii ff.

in the setting of the scene, and no one has better expressed the essential point of view of the actor. All the favourites of the Viennese popular theatre 'saw their whole art in extemporising; the playwright—and he was, of course, usually one of the troupe —had only written out a scenario, that was pinned up in the wings during the performance. Everyone extemporised as well as he could within this given framework, the junior actors adapting themselves of course to whatever the inspiration of the moment suggested to the seniors of the company. The scenario was a combination of the old Italian *commedia dell' arte* with the French, English, Spanish and Italian repertoire; Harlequin, Columbine, Pantaloon were the heroes, who played their traditional parts in pieces that might in outline recall some work of Molière, Shakespeare, Calderon or Lope de Vega. But Harlequin was always the central figure, everything centred round Hanswurst, he bore the whole play on his shoulders. Naturally the extemporising actor looked down with contempt on all those who memorised their parts and thus made themselves into the slaves of a writer.'[1]

To judge by the manuscripts that have come down to us, there is some exaggeration in Lothar's description of the extent to which improvisation was carried in the Haupt‑ und Staats‑ aktionen. Things may usually have been as he says in the earlier days, and with some companies later, but the text of the serious scenes was certainly often written out in full, though how well the actors conned their parts it is impossible to say. There were constant complaints in the days of the regular theatre of their shortcomings in this respect. It is equally certain that the all‑ important comic scenes were always at least in part improvised, their success depending largely on the mood of the chief comedian and of his audience, fresh gags being constantly introduced, so that plays could be seen repeatedly with pleasure. F. L. Schröder, who had acted in them with a famous Viennese principal, tells us that in his youth the comic scenes were spoken extempore, but he does not say this of the more serious parts. Perhaps the nearest analogy to these plays that we can think of in this country is the

[1] R. Lothar, *Das Wiener Burgtheater*, p. 6.

curious production that we call a Christmas pantomime. Here we have the chief comedian as the life and soul of the entertain‑ ment, in scenes where the gags have a topical and local flavour, and are often changed by the actors, sometimes no doubt extem‑ pore. And we have in the burlesque fairy‑tale scenes, with the emphasis that is laid in them on stage spectacle, gay costumes, transformations and so on, something not altogether unlike the elements derived from opera in the German popular plays. There are standing characters, such as the principal boy or the ugly stepmother, as in the Italian comedy, and our pantomimes used often to end with a regular harlequinade.

It has been mentioned that after the main play of the evening, which was usually in three acts, there was almost always a light one‑act 'Nachspiel', a farcical afterpiece improvised by a few actors following a brief outline, that might even merely be explained verbally before they began. J. C. Brandes tells us for instance in his memoirs how, about 1760, when he was with Franz Schuch, a Viennese principal who was an artist in improvisation, he had often to change costume to appear in a Nachspiel, because a play had turned out shorter than had been expected. When the curtain went up he would not know what the play was to be. 'When I asked Schuch his answer often was: "Just gag about love, and you will find out the rest all right." So I would begin the scene confidently with general reflections about the joys and tortures of love, or something of that kind. Schuch would then join me as Hanswurst, my man‑servant, and I immediately sought his help as my faithful counsellor. He sketched the exposition, and now I had the thread of the play.' We shall see in the next chapter how important these Nachspiele continued to be even after the introduction of the regular play, and the discussion of their debt to the Italian *commedia dell' arte,* and of the protracted controversy to which Gottsched's attempt to drive Harlequin and his improvisations from the German stage gave rise, will best find its place there.

The great actor Ekhof, who himself did so much to raise the level of his profession, sums up the situation on the German stage in his youth in the following words. It must be remembered

that his experience was of north and central Germany, not of
Austria, where there was a flourishing popular theatre in Vienna,
and that some degree of exaggeration would be natural in such a
witness. 'Travelling troupes of mountebanks, going from one
fair to another all over Germany, amused the mob with low farces.
The main defect of the theatre of those days was the lack of good
plays; the performance of the plays staged was just as ridiculous
as their plots. One very frequently put on everywhere was entitled: *Adam and Eve, or the Fall of the First Men.* It is not yet completely banished from the stage, and I remember seeing it acted
in Strassburg. You saw a fat Eve, in tights made of coarse,
flesh-coloured linen, to which a narrow girdle of fig-leaves was
attached. The costume of Adam was equally ridiculous, while
God the Father appeared in an old dressing-gown, with an
enormous wig and a long white beard. The comic element was
provided by the devils. Another defect of the old German plays
was that most of them were not written out in full. The actors
usually had just a scenario and played everything extempore.
Hanswurst above all found abundant scope for his sallies. Everything was on the same low level. A miserable wooden hut served
as playhouse; the scenery was lamentable; the actors, dressed in
rags and with wretched old wigs on their heads, looked like
cabbies disguised as heroes. In a word, the theatre was an amusement for the mob.'[1]

Yet contemptible as the strolling troupes might seem to later
generations of actors, they contrived to maintain themselves, and
so to keep alive the tradition of professional acting, without which
the standing theatres of Ekhof's maturity could not have been
founded. It may be convenient to mention here in order the
names of some of those who built up this tradition, a kind of
genealogy of the popular theatre.

It began, as we have seen, with the English Players, the first
of whom began to try their luck in Germany, when their profession had grown overcrowded in Elizabethan England, in
1586. There are records still earlier (from 1556) of English
musicians at a German court, for this was the great age of

[1] Quoted by Reden-Esbeck, *op. cit.*, p. 37.

English music, and even the five who were engaged in 1586 by the Elector of Saxony were listed as musicians in the court records. They were no doubt versatile entertainers, ready to provide 'clown scenes with acrobatic displays and comic dialogue, songs and dancing'.[1] They had come to the Elector from the court of his uncle, the King of Denmark, and seem to have been recommended to him by the Earl of Leicester. In 1592 a troupe under Robert Brown appeared in Frankfort-on-Main after touring Holland, and for fifteen years offshoots from this troupe, soon combined with Germans and acting in German, though usually under Brown's management, can be traced, sometimes established for a time at a court, sometimes touring the larger towns. Heinrich Julius, Duke of Brunswick was one of their principal patrons in the 'nineties, and was stimulated by their presence to write plays in the manner of those they had produced before him, to be acted by some of Brown's company under Thomas Sackeville, and by Germans whom they had trained.[2] The other important early centre was Cassel. John Green took Brown's place in 1607, and continued to tour in Germany and Austria until 1628 with a company that was no doubt always changing, but maintained an unbroken tradition. Next came Robert Renolds, then W. Roe, who between them kept up the tradition without a break right through the Thirty Years' War, either in Germany or in neighbouring countries, Denmark, the Netherlands and Poland. The last in this succession was Joris Jolliphus, active from about the end of the war (1648) to about 1660. His company seems to have made history by being the first to include women (from 1654). At least one other quite distinct troupe of considerable size is known, led by J. Spencer between 1604 and 1623,[3] and active in Brandenburg and elsewhere.

The later of these troupes had been almost wholly German, and from the middle of the seventeenth century purely German companies existed, with a similar repertoire and technique, all no doubt ultimately linked up with the English Players through

[1] Creizenach, *op. cit.*, iv.
[2] See A. H. J. Knight, *Heinrich Julius, Duke of Brunswick*, Oxford, 1948.
[3] Creizenach, *op. cit.* A. Cohn, *Shakespeare in Germany*. W. Flemming, *op. cit.* and article 'Englische Komödianten' in *Reallexikon*.

some members who had been trained in the older companies. By degrees the style and content of the plays offered had been adapted to German audiences and influenced by native German traditions, as can be seen from the versions of *Faust*, known to us only through marionette plays, but ultimately derived from Marlowe's *Dr. Faustus*. The most notable of the German 'principals' of the seventeenth century, Johannes Velten, was born in 1640, flourished in the 'seventies and 'eighties and died in 1692. Velten, a master of arts of Leipzig, had married the daughter of the actor-manager, C. A. Paul, after distinguishing himself in amateur performances in his university—we hear in particular of his playing in the *Polyeucte* produced by a younger fellow-graduate, Christoph Kormart, the published text of which shows an attempt to combine French classicism with the English tradition, in the resolution of narration into action and so on. Velten made a reputation for himself which lasted well into the eighteenth century. For seven years he was in the pay of the Elector of Saxony, but after giving a season in Dresden during Carnival he was allowed to tour each year, not only in Saxony, but in south Germany and occasionally in the north, in Berlin and Hamburg, where he died. His well-organised company is said to have consisted largely of university men like himself, and he certainly improved the current repertoire, adding adapted translations of ten of Molière's comedies, and of one or two other French classics, to the stock inherited from his predecessors. He regularly employed actresses for women's parts and seems to have aimed at greater realism generally.[1]

Between Velten and the Neubers the leading managers had all been members of his company or that of his widow, who carried it on for twenty years after his death, Julius Elenson, L. A. Denner and J. C. Spiegelberg, for example. Elenson's widow married first an actor in the company, Haack, and on his death another called Hofmann, who had been with Velten's widow, and who has already claimed our attention. This was the Haack-Hofmann company with which the Neubers received most of their training, and first acted at any rate occasionally in

[1] Carl Heine, *J. Velten*, 1887.

'regular' plays. They had served their first apprenticeship with the above-mentioned Spiegelberg, along with another actor who became a manager later, J. G. Förster, and in his turn trained J. F. Schönemann. The Neubers and Schönemann will require fuller study in later chapters.

When the Neubers formed a company of their own in 1727, they took with them some of the best of the very good actors of the Elenson-Haack-Hofmann troupe, such as Herr Kohlhardt and Herr and Frau Lorenz, and after a year they engaged a young man, G. H. Koch who, like Neuber himself and so many others, had had at least the beginnings of a university education, but found himself in financial straits. A little later J. F. Schöne-mann, who had been a medical student, came to them from Förster. Both Schönemann and Koch later became independent, the one in 1740 and the other in 1750, and were amongst the leading Principals of their day. In the last years of the Neuber company another of the best-known managers of the second half of the century, K. T. Döbbelin, made his début with Frau Neuber (1750). After a few years with Ackermann and others, he won a large sum at cards and set up a company of his own. From 1775 he was the provider of theatrical fare of a sort in Berlin for about twenty years.

In Schönemann's first company we find Ackermann, Frau Schröder, Ekhof, and the widow of J. C. Spiegelberg, herself the daughter of his colleague Denner. Her daughter later married Ekhof. Frau Schröder and Ackermann branched off from this company and started a short-lived troupe of their own (1742–44). It was revived in 1746, after the birth of F. L. Schröder and the death of his father, an organist in Berlin, and Ackermann married Frau Schröder while the company was in Russia (1749). After long wanderings Ackermann ended up, as we have seen, in Hamburg, built a theatre, and leased it after a year or two to the Hamburg 'Enterprise' or National Theatre, entering the new company with most of his best actors, but not his stepson, the young F. L. Schröder. When the National Theatre failed, half the company, led by Seyler, went on tour in north-west Germany until in 1771 it became the court-troupe in Weimar, and acted in the small theatre in the Wilhelmsburg until the whole castle was destroyed by fire in 1774. A year later the company became the nucleus of the new Gotha Court Theatre. It still included some of the best actors of the day, in particular Konrad Ekhof, and here Iffland, who had run away from a good home to become an actor, was trained. When the Gotha theatre was wound up in 1779, after the death of Ekhof, its best actors were engaged by the newly founded National Theatre at Mannheim. Meanwhile Ackermann and his family has re-established a company in Hamburg, which under F. L. Schröder went from strength to strength. Schröder's four years in Vienna at the Burgtheater (1781–85), after other members of his company had already gone there, brought the Hamburg realistic style to the best-endowed stage in German-speaking lands, and through his guest performances Schröder exercised considerable influence in Mannheim and elsewhere. From Mannheim Iffland carried a modified form of this style to Berlin, when he became the head of the Court Theatre there in 1796, and strongly influenced Weimar and other leading theatres through his guest performances.

This bald outline will at least indicate how it was possible for a living tradition of acting to grow up in Germany during the eighteenth century, as one company grew out of another and as more and more personal links were forged, first between the various touring companies, and then in the second half of the century between the standing theatres which developed, with members of the old touring companies as their first personnel. Great changes took place, both in the repertoire and in the style of acting and production, but through the family connections between successive generations of actors, and the strong guild spirit which existed among them, which put beginners in the relationship of apprentices to their seniors, continuity was preserved, in fact the chief complaint of young enthusiasts was of the conservatism and exclusiveness of the old stagers.

In Austria the theatre seemed, as we have seen, to be a more natural creation of the spirit of the people. A series of excellent comic actors made Vienna the theatrical centre of German-speaking lands, with a number of subsidiary centres in the south, which together formed a relatively closed system. Actors were certainly exchanged with the north, and Viennese principals sometimes toured there, but they were rather loth to leave their home for regions where the appreciation of their art was less spontaneous. The first permanent popular theatre in Vienna was the Kärntnertor Theatre, made famous for its improvised comedies and sensational tragi-comedies (derived, as described above, largely from court operas) by J. A. Stranitzky. It had long been usual for travelling quacks and dentists to attract crowds at fairs by providing some kind of entertainment, so that it is not surprising to find that Stranitzky had both qualified as a dentist and given marionette shows, as well as comedies with living actors, before he became the first tenant, in 1710, of the theatre built by the town council of Vienna near the 'Carinthian Gate'. He created the character of the Viennese Hanswurst out of the Pickelhäring of the older troupes, and the Harlequin of the Italian comedy, making him into a stocky Salzburg peasant, wearing a peasant's red jacket and long trousers, both braided, a white ruffle under his little pointed beard, and a conical green felt hat, whose jests were as broad as his dialect. Gottfried Prehauser carried on the tradition, toning down some of the crudity, for some forty-five years after Stranitzky's retirement in 1725, and he was joined in 1737, the year in which Caroline Neuber 'banished' Harlequin, by Stranitzky's godson, J. J. F. von Kurz (Kurz-Bernardon), who brought the extemporised burlesque to perfection in Vienna, while in the north the regular play was gaining ground. In the 'sixties and 'seventies, when the French type of play was establishing itself in Vienna too, under the patronage of Maria Theresa, Kurz went on tour in Germany, and F. L. Schröder gained valuable experience as a comic actor by joining his troupe in 1767, while the National Theatre was running in Hamburg. Another Viennese principal who toured Germany for many years was the already mentioned Franz Schuch (1716–64), a rival of the Neubers and of Schönemann in the 'forties, and a popular entertainer in Breslau during the Seven Years' War. 'He had only to show himself on the stage,' says Flögel, 'and everyone began to laugh. Off the stage he was a gloomy, serious man, who said little. As soon as he put on Hanswurst's jacket, he used to say, it seemed just as if the devil had come into him.'[1]

Such then was the popular theatre which Gottsched set out to re-model. It was clearly open to criticism on many counts, and Gottsched was only the most determined of its opponents. Long before his day its representatives had called down upon themselves the condemnation on moral grounds which had been the lot of professional players in every country in turn, from the mimes of ancient Rome to the Comici of sixteenth-century Italy and seventeenth-century France and England. In the resulting controversies, learned arguments based on quotations from the Fathers had everywhere been used to support objections which were in reality evoked by profound moral and social sentiments. It is just because the theatre is the most social of the arts, and because the personality of the actor is such an all-important factor in it, that, as Devrient pointed out, it has so often been subjected to more sweeping condemnation than painting, sculpture or literature, even though these have not escaped moral criticism. Behind the opposition, as he says, is the kind of feeling which made Plato exclude the theatre from his Republic. 'Drama arouses the passions, especially sexual love, since this is usually the main interest in plays. It induces an excited, indulgent and restless mood in the spectator, makes him indifferent to everyday reality and puts him all the more at the mercy of his wishes and desires. For only passion pleases on the stage, and the poet adorns it to increase its attractions, giving it an appearance of greatness and nobility.'[2] Moreover, actors in the old days, as was urged for instance by Cardinal Paleotti in Bologna, were for the most part 'notorious vagabonds accompanied by women of a like reputation'.[3]

These and similar moral criticisms of the theatre and of actors were raised, in a narrow puritanical spirit, in Hamburg towards the end of the seventeenth century, in the course of the 'Theater-streit', lasting several years, occasioned by the establishment of the

[1] *Geschichte des Groteskekomischen*, 1788, p. 140.
[2] *Deutsche Theatergeschichte* (ed. Stuhlfeld), p. 86.
[3] Lea, *op. cit.*, I, p. 311.

German opera. The leader of the opposition was a respected pietistic minister, Anton Reiser. His *Theatromania* (1681) used much the same arguments as had been put forward so vehemently by Prynne in England fifty years before.[1] The dispute continued to break out in different towns for the next century and more. In Hamburg it became heated again just after the failure of the National Theatre, with Lessing's theological opponent Goeze in the forefront of the battle, which was occasioned this time, characteristically enough, by the indignation aroused among the orthodox by a local minister who himself wrote for the stage. This wordy warfare was of course only the climax of a series of minor clashes between the players and a strictly orthodox section of the public. The players themselves could not treat such opposition with indifference. It seriously threatened their livelihood, it undermined all their attempts to attain to higher social status and it occasioned some of the best of them much searching of conscience, for they were often believers, and not by any means indifferent to the refusal of the clergy in many places to admit them to communion or to give them Christian burial. From the time of Frau Velten onwards they wrote, or had written, pamphlets and so forth in their own defence.

One of the most elaborate of these documents is the series of prefaces to Schönemann's published version of his repertoire.[2] In spite of his attempts, following Gottsched and Frau Neuber, to purify the stage, respected theologians still regarded plays as sinful amusements, he tells us, and young people who took to the stage as a career were cruelly persecuted and despised by their friends and relations. He had found people in every class in fact who thought it a good deed to cheat a comedian. He admitted that actors had many personal failings, that many of them had only adopted this profession because of difficulties caused by their youthful transgressions, and that even in maturity they too often regarded themselves as licensed libertines. Extravagance, laziness, loose living, dishonesty, ingratitude and vanity were according to him their typical vices. Yet he claimed that the chief aim of the

---

[1] J. Geffken, *loc. cit.*; Devrient, p. 88.
[2] *Die Schönemannsche Schaubühne*, vol. 2, 1748, and later volumes.

theatre was to moderate and purify the passions. Surely all pleasures were not to be condemned? And did not the theatre perhaps divert people from grosser pleasures?

Caroline Neuber had claimed already in 1734 that her aim had always been 'to observe the strictest morality in her performances', and in fact 'not so much to amuse the spectators as to improve them'. A few years later, in an appeal to the Hamburg Senate for a licence, she claimed in effect that the stage would make people exactly as the Senate would want them to be, namely orderly and docile. She pointed to the example of Greece and Rome and brought forward some of the debased moralistic versions of Aristotle's catharsis theory then current. Comedy helps us to distinguish virtue from vice and to realise their consequences—*castigat ridendo mores*—and tragedy 'teaches us the most sublime notions of virtue' and fills us with respect for the laws and love for those in authority.[1] Similar moralistic defences of the theatre were to be made by Gottsched and all the friends of the theatre down to Schiller.[2]

Looking back on the history of the German theatre when writing his autobiography, Goethe summed up these controversies and drew attention to their lasting effect on the German drama and theatre of his time. The Germans, he said, had involuntarily fashioned their theatre according to the demands of the clergy. It would have developed healthily if left to itself in south Germany, where it was really at home, but 'the first step towards reforming, but not improving it, was taken in north Germany by undistinguished people with no artistic capacity'. Gottsched's efforts already tended to make the German actor a tame creature (we shall see later that Goethe saw much to deplore in the decline of improvised comedy), but soon the Hamburg clergy began a general offensive against the theatre. The friends of the theatre were compelled to defend it as serving the purposes of morality, thus obscuring its true *raison d'être*, which is aesthetic, connected with what Goethe calls 'höhere Sinnlichkeit'. They stressed its ethical and social utility, not its appeal to eye and ear,

---

[1] Reden-Esbeck, *op. cit.*, p. 205.
[2] For the earlier theorists see B. Aikin-Sneath, *op. cit.*

and being good middle-class Germans themselves, even the literary men came to take the same point of view and did not notice that they were perpetuating 'Gottschedian mediocrity'.

A third factor working in the same direction was the influence of three actors who, being men of character, 'could not lay aside their sense of dignity even on the stage and therefore favoured in their dramatic art everything that tended towards morality and respectability, towards what was socially approved and good at any rate in appearance. Ekhof, Schröder and Iffland were helped in this by the general tendency of the time to break down the barriers between different classes and occupations in its enthusiasm for a common humanity.' The result was the sentimentality and the moralising of such plays as *La Brouette du Vinaigrier* and *Le Philosophe sans le savoir*, typical domestic dramas of the 'seventies in their German adaptations. The fragment breaks off with the observation that developments such as these might well have had the effect of preventing for ever the growth of a German theatre, though Goethe (in 1813) apparently does not think that this has happened.[1] Perhaps the drift of Goethe's criticism may be brought out by a quotation from Mr. Santayana's *The Genteel Tradition at Bay*: 'We exist by distinction, by integration round a specific nucleus according to a particular pattern. Life demands a great insensibility, as well as a great sensibility. If the humanist could really live up to his ancient maxim, *humani nil a me alienum puto*, he would sink into moral anarchy and artistic impotence—the very things from which our liberal, romantic world is so greatly suffering.' The everyday German theatre had become for Goethe what at one time he even called his own *Iphigenie*, too humane for words, 'verflucht human'.

[1] 'Deutsches Theater', in *Werke*, Jubiläumsausgabe, vol. 37.

II

GOTTSCHED AND THE REGULAR THEATRE

GOTTSCHED is probably best known to posterity through Lessing's hostile criticism and Goethe's description in *Dichtung und Wahrheit* of his visit to the old man when he himself was a student in Leipzig. He tells us how Gottsched, when his man-servant was late with his master's wig, was seen by his two visitors to swing the wig on to his head with one hand, and box the servant's ears with the other. It is like a scene from one of his wife's comedies, and reminds us that he was a man of fiery temperament, who lived in the days when professors wore perukes and had men-servants who could be treated not unlike Russian serfs. He was a Prussian from Königsberg, which he had left hurriedly as a young graduate because, being over six feet tall, he was in danger of being forcibly recruited for Frederick William I's guard of 'lange Kerle', as he wrote in the wordy elegy which this event immediately inspired (in 1724):

O Schrecken! welches mir die Geister eingenommen,
O Schrecken! das mir Mars durch seine Wut erweckt.
Von Dir ist der Entschluss von meiner Flucht gekommen.

It throws a vivid light on the social standing of a professor in Prussia to learn that even when he was thinking of accepting a call to Frankfort-on-Oder in 1739, he was warned by his patron, Count Ernst Christian von Manteuffel, that he still might not be safe there from the attentions of Prussian recruiting sergeants, and this warning is an indication too, that, in spite of what E. Reichel says, Gottsched's explanation of his flight from Königsberg is perfectly genuine. He was born nine years earlier than Dr. Johnson, in 1700, and like him had to make his own way in the world, but he had few of the Doctor's great gifts of mind and character, and was far less fortunate in his literary inheritance. As the son of a clergyman he was able to acquire a learned education at Königsberg, it is true, without suffering the humilia, tions that were the lot of a sizar at Oxford, and by journalism, by lectures on poetry and philosophy, the publication of one or two compendia and bold leadership of the 'German Society' of Leipzig, he raised himself, apparently without much difficulty, so high in the esteem of 'Klein Paris' that he was elected Lecturer on Philosophy and Poetry there at the age of thirty, and Pro, fessor of Logic and Metaphysics four years later. But the Spensers, Shakespeares and Miltons of Germany had still to come. There was little in the way of a literary tradition, and the language, not ordered and enriched by the best minds of many generations, like English, was vigorous but crude. The cultural differences between the two countries were of course closely connected with their varying political, economic and social development. The millions whose native speech was German were not yet sufficiently united politically to provide a solid basis for a unified literary language, and the rich and powerful classes of society tended to despise German and to import their literature, as if it were just another luxury, from France.

Lessing, a generation later, was already a little more fortunate, largely through Gottsched's efforts, though he was too close to him to realise it. It is easier for us now to see how much, in spite of the change in literary fashions, Lessing and his contemporaries had in common with Gottsched. For what he had been seeking in his blundering, thick,skinned way was the rehabilitation and improvement of German as the literary medium for Germans, instead of the Latin of the scholars and the French of the courts, and the fullest use of German to further the spread of that way of life and thought which seemed to him natural and reasonable. It was an aim comparable in some respects with that of Luther, who had roughed out a first version of a literary language and gained wide acceptance for it through his translation of the Bible, but Gottsched aimed at secular culture and sound morals, not the salvation of souls. We shall find that although, as the century wore on, many more things were seen in heaven and earth than had been dreamt of in Gottsched's philosophy, his first principle, that of the freedom and self-sufficiency of the human mind, was by no means rejected, but only differently interpreted, with a fuller understanding of the intuitive, imaginative approach to experience, for Gottsched was followed by genuine poets. He himself had no creative gifts of that kind, and did not really know what poetry meant. As Max Koch says, his motto might fittingly have been 'Invitis Musis', and one might think that Pope, who himself did not think any rules binding, had him in mind when he wrote the lines:

> Some drily plain, without invention's aid
> Write dull Receits how Poems may be made.

He had, however, one of those vigorous, single-track minds, not uncommon in the history of the country which has produced the 'leadership principle', which by sheer persistence and painstaking organisation can get things done. What he did was to make a good many Germans take their own language, and certain literary genres, especially the drama, seriously. At the same time however he greatly over-stressed the moral content of the drama and made it so literary, in a narrow conventional sense, that given his own way he might have killed it as an entertainment. Even corrected as his influence was by the instinct and tradition of the stage, it went far towards giving a permanent twist to the German drama, so that almost every German play with artistic pretensions since his time has been more or less of a book-drama.

Gottsched then was a populariser and organiser, not a thinker or poet. His philosophy was that of Christian Wolff, which in its turn had only been Leibniz and water, but he expressed his second-hand views with an air of conviction, in a language closer than Wolff's to that of the man in the street, so that it was in his formulation (in his *Weltweisheit*, 1734) that the philosophy of Enlightenment gained the widest currency. Kant's later formulation of Aufklärung (in *What is Enlightenment?* 1784) as 'the emergence of man from his self-imposed tutelage' through daring to think for himself, could in certain important respects be applied to Gottsched. He felt himself to be a modern man, who accepted the results of scientific discovery, not caring how far they might lead him away from the views of the church in which he was brought up. But for the protection of Count Manteuffel, a fellow-Wolffian, he would have been hounded out of Leipzig by the Dresden court preachers, Catholic and Protestant alike, as Wolff had been from Halle. There was even a certain strain of anti-clericalism perhaps in his willingness to consort with the players. But he did so with a good conscience because of his conviction that they could be made to exert a highly moral influence on society, and that no means of spreading enlighten-ment and virtue should be neglected. He and his allies in the theatre always claimed, as we have seen, that their aim was to edify as well as to entertain. The stage was to become a rival of the pulpit or a substitute for it. But it was definitely a lay pulpit that Gottsched had in mind, preaching the same 'useful know-ledge' as those 'moral weeklies', the *Vernünftige Tadlerinnen* (1725–26) and the *Biedermann* (1727–28) which he was editing at the same time, and the more learned periodicals and manuals with which he followed them up.[1] A certain missionary zeal which it is hard for us now to appreciate sought an outlet both through the spoken and the written word.

The essence of this gospel was that men should be reasonable, and therefore natural, for the two conceptions were synonymous for him, as they had been for the French classics. But his notions of the reasonable were as usual determined, as it seems to us now, by certain axiomatic beliefs which were only partly rational. There was a good deal in them which seems for instance to have been conditioned by the form of German society in his age, as it affected his personal life. As an academic teacher of middle-class origin he instinctively rejected the idleness and the love of luxury he found in court circles in Dresden, their gallantries and their gaming, their German larded with French, their notions of honour and their conventions of politeness. In his writings he praises instead the industry, orderliness and simplicity dear to the middle class, and celebrates in the manner of the *Spectator* the

---

[1] *Kritische Beiträge* (1731–44), *Neuer Büchersaal* (1745–50), *Das Neueste aus der anmutigen Gelehrsamkeit* (1751–62). He translated the arch-sceptic Pierre Bayle (1741–44) and brought out the first German encyclopedia (1760).

benefits that society owes to trade and industry. On the other hand he does not approve of the slovenly conceited pedant with his mere book-learning, or of any kind of superstition. It is the *honnête homme* who is his ideal, the educated professional man not ignorant of the world.

His views on aesthetics were of a piece with his general philosophy. Here, too, he liked things to be neat and tidy, made with an obvious purpose and attaining it by economical, logical means. Even in Lessing's time it was still a commonplace that art had a moral purpose. 'In poetry all genres should make us better men; it is deplorable if we have to begin by proving this, and still more so if there are poets who themselves doubt it.'[1] There is a difference of course between Lessing's subtle, though doubtless mistaken, moralistic interpretation of the Aristotelian 'catharsis' and the pathetic *naïveté* with which Gottsched states current doctrine in his *Kritische Dichtkunst* (1730), a kind of manual intended in the first instance for the dilettantes of the Leipzig 'Deutsch-übende Gesellschaft', the university men, mostly quite young, with a taste for versifying who, as Lessing says, were not yet distinguished from poets. 'The poet chooses a moral thesis, which he wishes to impress on the spectators in a concrete manner. He invents a general story to illustrate the truth of his thesis. Next he searches in history for famous people, to whom something similar once happened, and borrows their names for the characters of his story, to lend it dignity. He devises accompanying circumstances to make the main plot seem as probable as possible—these are the sub-plots or episodes. This whole he now divides into five portions of about equal length and arranges them in such a way that the later parts follow from the earlier, but he does not trouble to enquire whether everything happened in just this way in history, or whether all the subsidiary characters had the same names as he has given them.' The moral which Sophocles wished to illustrate in *Œdipus Rex*, for instance, is that God does not let even those sins that are unwittingly committed go unpunished. One cannot think of any work that Gottsched was less fitted to expound than *Œdipus*,

[1] *Hamburgische Dramaturgie*, 77. Stück.

but this is only an example of the unbounded self-confidence and ineptitude with which he rode roughshod over the creations of Homer, Shakespeare, Milton and most of the world's master-pieces.

He had not studied poetry under Pietsch in Königsberg for nothing, nor spent years in reading Dacier and all the current French theorists, when he had once realised, after seeing some of the better performances of a touring company in Leipzig, especially Corneille's *Le Cid* in German translation, that a play could be a fit spectacle for an intelligent man. He was captivated by French good sense and clarity, and by the ideals of *bienséance* and *vraisemblance*. The Unities became an absolute necessity for him, not only the unity of action, which followed, he thought, from the necessity that the whole play should illustrate a single moral—though episodes might bring home other moral truths by the way—but also the unities of time and place as then under-stood in France. He singled out for ridicule a 'School Comedy' he had seen, in which episodes from the *Æneid* had appeared alongside others from Luther's Reformation. It had evidently been a play in the baroque tradition, in which the purification of the Church by Luther had been prefigured symbolically in the foundation of Rome by Æneas, and the Whore of Babylon by Dido, just as in the Oberammergau Passion Play tableaux from the Old Testament reinforce the meaning of episodes from the passion. There was a unifying principle in this kind of play, though for Gottsched a much more obvious kind of unity was necessary. 'For where is the probability', he asks (as Cervantes had done), 'if in the first act the hero is seen in the cradle, then later as a boy, youth, man, old man and finally in his coffin?'

Gottsched held in fact the 'imitation' theory in its crudest form. He had not learnt to distinguish between the laws of the imagina-tion and those of real life, or understood that the dramatist uses actors, speaking and moving figures, to body forth a vision, which must indeed have unity, in order to be as convincing and pleasing as possible, but not a unity based on the theory that what happens on the stage must produce in the spectator the complete illusion that it is real life he is beholding, any more than a painter should aim at deceiving the beholder into taking a painted landscape for a real one. It is an essential part of the attraction of the picture that it is known not to be 'real' in this literal sense, but paint on canvas in a frame, holding fast something shaped by an artist's imagination and so removed from time and space. But Gottsched was nothing if not literal. 'Or is it probable', he asks, 'if we see it become evening several times on the stage, and we ourselves remain sitting there in the same place, neither eating nor drinking nor sleeping? The best plots are those which did not require more time to happen in reality than they need in the theatrical performance, that is, three or four hours.'

Of course these views were not original in Gottsched. They represent the last stage in the development of the poetic theory of the Renaissance, itself abstracted uncritically from Aristotle by humanist poets, eager for technical recipes for the rapid production of works to rival those of the Ancients. The very special conditions under which Aristotle's *Poetics* had come into existence were not understood in Germany until Herder's time. The Renaissance theorists and later the French accepted what they took to be his 'rules', together with contributions from Horace, Longinus, Cicero, etc., as applicable to any age or clime, but whereas in Italy and France the pseudoclassical tradition proved readily assimilable, and did not prevent genuine talents from expressing freely the thought and feeling of their own age and society, Gottsched, with the pedantry of a German rationalist, seized on the formalism of the French theorists and produced, with his ungifted followers, nothing but dead imitations of the French classics, from which all the passion and grace and wit of his models had completely evaporated. There is nothing new either in his rules about the social rank that is most fitting in the heroes of various dramatic genres, famous historical personages in tragedy, and 'honest citizens or people of moderate rank, such as barons, marquises and counts at the highest', in comedy. All that is original is the crudity of expression. Most of the Renaissance and classical French theorists from Scaliger (1561) onwards maintain a similar doctrine, which has been traced back, not to Aristotle, but to the Greek grammarian Diomedes, from whom it was taken over in medieval compilations and then by the Humanists from the Scholastics,[1] though there are hints in Aristotle which might be taken to support it. But it needed a Gottsched to claim that it is not fitting to make people of high rank ridiculous in comedy, because that would be 'contrary to the respect that we owe them'. Here he' strikes the note which is so familiar in the sycophantic court poets of his day, like his friend, J. U. von König at Dresden. Gottsched himself did not fail to inform the reader that the first book of his Odes consisted of those on 'hohe Häupter'.

Gottsched's dramatic theory is clearly only of interest now for the light it throws on his time and on his own mind. Reading the following passage, for instance, we cannot help applying it to the author's own efforts to turn the German theatre into an instrument for good. 'What had been satirical jesting became something noble and edifying, so that the most highly respected people were no longer ashamed to be amongst the audience. The Athenians were such enthusiasts for the theatre, that they made it almost an obligation to attend performances of tragedies. In fact, since the poets made their work conform in every respect to religion, and frequently introduced excellent moral teaching and ethical maxims into their plays, this type of performance became a kind of religious service, one much more edifying for the people at large than all the sacrifices and other ceremonies of heathen religion.'[2] Gottsched must surely have been thinking when he wrote this of the efforts he himself was making to turn the German popular stage into just such a 'moral institution' as he imagined the Greek theatre to have been, and it is clear that Greek example, as well as French, played a part even as early as Gottsched in the fashioning of classical German drama.

Gottsched's reform efforts had begun soon after his arrival in Leipzig early in 1724. In Königsberg, he tells us, he had had no opportunity of seeing professional acting, though he speaks of a school performance at which he had been present when he was seventeen. But in Leipzig at fair-time the Haack-Hofmann

---

[1] O. Walzel, 'Das bürgerliche Drama', in *Neue Jahrbücher für das klassische Altertum*, 1915.
[2] *Kritische Dichtkunst*, chap. 10.

company (see p. 32) duly appeared, and he missed none of their performances, such was their novelty for him, though, as he tells us in the preface to his *Sterbender Cato*, they 'played nothing but bombastic Haupt⁄ und Staatsaktionen enlivened by the antics of Harlequin, full of fantastic adventures and amorous imbroglios, low grotesque comedy and obscenities'. The only good play was *Roderich und Chimene*, a prose version of *Le Cid*.[1] When he asked Hofmann why he did not put on other good plays, such as those of Gryphius, he was told that this had been attempted by his troupe earlier (as earlier still, by Velten for example, as mentioned above), but now the public would not listen to verse, especially in serious plays without any clown scenes. Hof⁄mann would not risk staging an adaptation of Fontenelle's *Endymion,* a pastoral, made by Gottsched. The following year Gottsched saw the troupe again at the autumn fair and criticised their performances at some length in his *Vernünftige Tadlerinnen.*[2] He thought very highly of their acting, singling out for special praise an unnamed actress (Caroline Neuber) who played in man's clothes four different types of student in one comedy. He thought some of their plays were of a sort to do good, in correcting men's fault by acting them convincingly, but others were too Italian, full of Harlequin and Scaramouche with their suggestive jokes (i.e. improvised burlesques in the style of the *commedia dell' arte*) and others too Spanish (i.e. in the baroque tradition), full of bombast and unnatural flowers of speech. He praised a trans⁄lation of Pradon's tragedy *Regulus,* and three satirical German comedies by 'the German Molière at the Dresden court' (König), *Die verkehrte Welt, Der Dresdenische Schlendrian* and *Das Ge⁄spräch im Reiche der Toten.* Such authors were performing in his opinion exactly the same task as his moral weekly, 'the correction of coarse behaviour, foolish habits and low literary taste'.

At this time Gottsched had already come to believe that a reformed stage could do much for the spread of enlightenment and virtue, but it was the value of comedy that he particularly stressed, contrasting its realistic representation of vices and virtues

---

[1] Really Greflinger's translation in alexandrines (Hamburg, 1679), spoken as prose. See Waniek, *Gottsched,* p. 113.
[2] I. Stück, p. 44.

found in ordinary everyday life with the fantastic plots of the Haupt' und Staatsaktionen—or of opera, which he detested equally. He had not yet read the French theorists, Dacier in his translation of Aristotle's *Poetics*, d'Aubignac, Corneille and Voltaire in their prefaces and so on, whom he names as his teachers in the preface to *Cato*. His education had been theo' logical and philosophical to begin with, and though he had read some French his subsequent literary training had been based on Latin and recent German literature rather than French. It was, in fact, in the court atmosphere of Dresden, which extended its influence to Leipzig, that this new interest was aroused, and the reform of the theatre with which Gottsched's name is associated owed more than a little to court influence.

It was after all not to be expected that even the educated middle class would of its own accord demand a type of art so foreign to its own traditions as classical French drama, and tragedy in particular. Its conventions were too strange, its language and the habits of thought and feeling expressed in it too much the product of a particular age and class in a country with an entirely different history. What could a German who had not lived in Paris, or at least seen this drama performed by good French actors, make of 'the refinements of love and honour, the restrained passion, the elegance, of plays written in an age of great national achievements and in a language chastened by the Hôtel de Rambouillet for a few thousand noblemen and upper middle'class officials and lawyers in Paris?'[1] Molière was easier to appreciate. His pictures were drawn from ordinary life, he wrote for the sensible bour' geois rather than for the courtier, and there was always an element of pure 'theatre' in his work, as that of a professional actor with much experience of provincial audiences. Adaptations of some of his plays had been presented, as we have seen, by Velten towards the end of the seventeenth century. But it was at Bruns' wick, a court with a dramatic tradition going back to the English Players, that at about the same time plans had been made for the performance of French tragedies in German, and Duke Anton

---

[1] W. H. Bruford, 'Actor and public in Gottsched's time', in *German Studies presented to H. G. Fiedler*, Oxford, 1938.

Ulrich had had some verse translations made by the librettist, F. C. Bressand. A quarter of a century later the manuscripts of these translations were dug out by the Duke's son and successor, August Wilhelm, when the Haack-Hofmann troupe visited his capital at fair-time, and he asked this rather talented company to attempt a performance of them, which they did. Hofmann, the Neubers and Kohlhardt in this troupe were not only good actors but people of some literary cultivation, and they apparently gave satisfaction with performances of Pradon's *Regulus,* Racine's *Alexandre le grand,* Corneille's *Brutus,* all in Bressand's translations, and *Le Cid* in the still older translation, also in alexandrines, made by Greflinger in Hamburg.[1]

This was in the early 'twenties (the troupe visited Brunswick every year from 1722 to 1726), and in 1725, on their annual visit to Dresden, König got them to give *Regulus,* which he apparently revised for them, and three of his own comedies. This was the repertoire Gottsched saw later in the same year in Leipzig, as described above. He had seen them in *Le Cid* the year before. He had, of course, had nothing to do with these performances, the credit for which is due to the Brunswick court and to König. König had made a first attempt at raising the literary level of Hofmann's performances in Dresden a year before this, when he persuaded him to stage two of his own comedies.[2] Gottsched only comes into the story in 1727, by which time the Haack-Hofmann troupe had broken up, on the death of its much-married Prinzipalin, and the Neubers had just formed from some of its members and others their own company and obtained for it the licence for the Saxon circuit which Hofmann had held. König was interested also in this further attempt at improving the repertoire, though Gottsched was now the leading spirit. As master of ceremonies and court poet König was able to obtain for the new troupe the loan of rich dresses from the Dresden opera. The impression which resulted from this, that the new enterprise was favoured by court circles, must have materially assisted the Neubers. 'Nobody', as C. H. Schmidt says, 'dared to question the

[1] Gottsched, *Preface* to *Der sterbende Cato,* Waniek, *op. cit.,* pp. 113, 120; Esbeck, *op. cit.,* p. 51.
[2] Waniek, *Gottsched,* p. 104.

taste of the court.'[1] Moreover, it was to court circles in Dresden, Braunschweig-Blankenberg and Hanover, and to officials and scholars influenced by the prevailing court taste, that the Neubers looked in the first instance for support, as is seen from Neuber's letter to Gottsched from Hanover in 1730: 'Here in Hanover I have found more taste for German tragedies than I expected. The town has been visited by a good many troupes for some years, especially by the Brunswick company with the famous harlequin Müller. These have so much disgusted people that on our first arrival we had very poor audiences. These other companies had conducted themselves so badly too that no one would give us a taler's credit. But when we began our so-called verse plays, and put on the new costumes, things soon changed. The privy councillors of the Court of Appeal here were the first to come, and as they liked the performances the rest of the nobility and all the better-class people soon followed, and now everyone admits that they have never seen anything like it. But of course the mob who kept the earlier troupes going are not won over yet, because we don't give them enough opportunities of playing the fool.'[2] The letter from Nürnberg (1731) is in a similar strain, while from Hamburg he writes (1732) rather less cheerfully: 'There are a few people of rank here who come regularly.'

The reform of the repertoire owed a good deal then to the ruling class, but of course still more to Gottsched and the Neubers and their sustained efforts to bring about a change which some of the nobility regarded with mild benevolence but probably would not have stirred a finger to effect of their own accord. Gottsched's own motives, in so far as they proceeded from his general philosophy and ethical aims, have been discussed above. We shall probably not go far wrong in ascribing his action also in part to a certain eagerness to be in the limelight. At any rate his inordinate vanity soon revealed itself. Unless his protégés were willing to do everything to the greater glory of Gottsched and his wife, they soon lost favour.

Friederica Carolina Neuber, at the time when Gottsched,

---

[1] *Chronologie des deutschen Theaters,* 1775 (ed. Legband), p. 43.
[2] Reden-Esbeck, *op. cit.,* p. 96.

supported by the 'German Society' of Leipzig, made his first approaches to the newly formed Neuber troupe, was a woman of thirty, with ten years' experience of acting behind her and a considerable reputation both in serious and comic parts. She was, above all, a woman of impressive strength of character—a character formed on the basis of a passionate nature by much suffering. She was the only child of a Zwickau advocate, a martyr to gout, who vented his spleen with brutal cruelty on his wife and daughter. He was capable of throwing a hammer at his wife and striking his daughter in the face with a bunch of keys. Caroline lost her mother when she was eight, and found life with her bed-ridden tyrant of a father so intolerable that she had left home twice before she was fifteen, the second time with an assistant of her father's ten years older than herself, to whom she claimed to have been promised in marriage. The pair were brought back ignominiously in a cart under escort (like Melina and his wife in *Wilhelm Meister*) and spent some months in semi-starvation in prison before being acquitted in view of the father's cruelty. Caroline had to return home, but she escaped finally at twenty by jumping out of the window into a hedge and running off with a young student, Johann Neuber. They joined the Spiegelberg company of actors in the neighbouring town of Weissenfels, and were married in Brunswick in the following spring, already apparently members of another company, the Haack-Elenson (later Haack-Hofmann) Company, in which, as we have seen, there was a relatively good tradition and a number of good actors, so that they sometimes rose above the usual theatrical fare of the day. It was immediately after the Neubers had raised a new company of their own out of the ruins of the old, in 1727, that Gottsched entered into negotiations with them, or rather with Herr Neuber, for in the early stages only his name is mentioned by Gottsched, and it is he who reports on the progress made. Gottsched speaks of Frau Neuber just as 'a good actress'. Naturally Gottsched would deal with the official head of the troupe and would find it easier to approach a man, especially one with some academic training. It may have helped that there were two or three more former students in the company.

We still have some sixteen of the letters addressed to Gottsched by the Neubers, and they are the best key to the understanding of their relationship. Herr Neuber always adopts a most respectful tone. He addresses Gottsched as 'Hoch Edler Hochgelahrter Inbesonders HochgeEhrtester Hr. Professor und besonders werther Freund und Gönner!'—which is a little superlative even for those days, and signs himself, 'Your most obedient servant'. He frequently expresses gratitude to Gottsched and the German Society for their help, and disappointment that they cannot make more rapid progress with their plans, because of lack of support from the public, difficulties with rival troupes in Leipzig and the absence of a sufficient number of good plays in the new style. The two surviving letters from Frau Neuber to Gottsched are also very respectful but decidedly livelier in tone. They reveal her as a woman of character and originality, warm and impulsive, idealistic and devoted to Leipzig and the aims of the German Society. The style is clear and vivid, but the punctuation over-economical. In a typical letter of February 1735[1] she says that her husband is to come to Leipzig to find a new theatre for them, and goes on: 'I am of little or no use in such matters. I am too impulsive (zu huy) and often make more mistakes in my haste than can be made good afterwards. In a word, I have not enough understanding or patience for business negotiations and building operations. Up till now I have not been able to do much that satisfies me, but I assure you that on this occasion I shall think of the advancement of the aims and credit of the whole German Society in all my plays, whatever their titles may be, and will never pursue my own advantage without at the same time furthering the Society's ends, especially as I see here, if only dimly, an opportunity of being considered worthy of accomplishing something useful and creditable. Leipzig and my personal advantage shall be nothing to me, unless a firm foundation can at the same time be laid for the German Society. It may still seem too bold of me to bind myself in this way, and who can say whether I shall have the good fortune to accomplish it, but there is nothing else I want if that cannot

[1] Reden-Esbeck, *op. cit.*, p. 171.

be done. It is sometimes a good thing to have a bee in one's bonnet. I simply must go on to another sheet for I have a lot more to write about.'

Next time she sees Gottsched, she continues, she will need a full day to tell him all the news. She describes the preparations for the morrow's gala performance of *Der sterbende Cato* in the opera house at Brunswick in honour of the Prince of Bernburg. There were to be wax candles throughout the house, the ducal orchestra was to provide incidental music, and the adjutant-general to send soldiers as supers, for Cato's and Caesar's armies, 'all of the same height, and accompanied by their non-commissioned officers. They are to be as smartly turned out, head and foot, as if they were to be given away to a foreign master' —a vivid eighteenth-century touch, reminding us of the trade in soldiers, and bringing out clearly, as does the whole paragraph, the company's eager desire for the favour of aristocratic circles. The letter throws some light too on the relative importance of Herr and Frau Neuber in the management of the company, about which opinions have differed. It seems that Herr Neuber was not a nonentity, but that he was much inferior to his wife as actor and writer and as a personality. On one occasion she repudiated an arrangement made by her too easy-going husband and claimed not to be bound by it, as she had not signed it, and in general she showed greater shrewdness and tenacity.

One can see that though her education must have been scrappy —at fifteen she wrote like a servant-girl, even if she did know some French and Latin, as has been stated—she had a lively wit and a ready pen in her maturity. It was she who composed most of their many petitions to town councils and ministers of state in the course of their struggles for the Saxon and others licences, and the use of Leipzig theatres, sometimes addressing long verse epistles to high personages in the hope of gaining their attention. For special occasions, 'town council performances', a prince's birthday and the like, she wrote allegorical verse prologues and poems of congratulation. On the birthday of the Duke of Schleswig-Holstein in 1738, she composed for instance a prologue called *The Origins of the Drama*, containing two dozen allegorical personages. The front stage, we see from the printed programme,[1] represented a fair garden, where the action symbolised the moder/ ate enjoyment of the good things of life. 'The inner stage', the programme continues, 'shows the temple of Reason, illuminated by the sun (Aufklärung!). Reason and Virtue meet one another. Reason is preceded by Truth, Piety, Work, and Virtue by Hope, Love and Pleasure. The following form pairs: Truth and Serious/ ness, Piety and Industry, Work and Obedience, Hope and Trade, Love and Prosperity, Pleasure and Usefulness. Reason reproves the uninvited guests (Impudence, Ingratitude, etc.) for their free behaviour and has them conducted away by the Guardian Spirit, to celebrate their feast in peace and virtue.' The exact connection with the drama is not very evident, but it is clearly associated with everything that is good. Lessing said of her dramatic sketches that they showed a complete knowledge of the theatre, but relied too much on dressing up and a festive atmosphere of unreal pomp. 'Perhaps she knew her Leipzig audience,' he adds, 'and what I consider a weakness was only evidence of her shrewdness.'[2]

The aims of the reformers are frequently defined by Frau Neuber in her appeals to official bodies, as in the passages quoted earlier (p. 38). Besides providing a moral form of entertainment, she tried to raise the status and improve the reputation of actors and actresses as a class by insisting on a higher standard of per/ sonal behaviour than was usual among them. They had to learn their parts and be punctual and tidy, and she kept a motherly eye on their private life, making unmarried actresses live and take their meals with her, and providing some meals for the bachelors too. All had to lend a hand at any work that was required, the women at making costumes, for instance, and the men at hand/ ling and painting scenery, copying out parts, even adapting or translating plays if they had the ability. Some, like the future manager, G. H. Koch, were extraordinarily versatile. There was thus something patriarchal about the life of her company, as in that of any master/craftsman with his apprentices, and all

[1] Reden-Esbeck, *op. cit.*, p. 228.
[2] Reden-Esbeck prints a dozen of her programmes, and Seuffert in *Deutsche Literaturdenkmale*, No. 63, her prologue, *Ein deutsches Vorspiel*.

this tended to bring actors into better relations with ordinary respectable society, especially as her example was followed in all the better troupes later in the century.

But however high they might aim and however willing they might be to make sacrifices for their art, the Neubers remained professional actors and had somehow to earn a living for them-selves and their troupe. They could not therefore neglect the taste of the public, which was still deplorably low. Their second difficulty was the lack of good German plays. They had to begin with the repertoire of the Haack-Hofmann company, with slight improvements. We have seen Gottsched's description of this in 1725. There were so few translations of French tragedies available that, in Devrient's words, the tragedies in alexandrines on the Neubers' repertoire too stood out like white crows. They had already Bressand's versions of *Regulus, Brutus* and *Alexandre le grand*, and apparently two translations of *Le Cid*, Greflinger's and a more recent one, made for the Brunswick court about 1710, by G. Lange, the mayor of Leipzig to whom Gottsched dedicated his *Cato*. Corneille's *Cinna*, translated by a patrician of Nürn-berg, Herr von Führer, was soon added, being already in existence, but it was three years before they could stage the first fruits of the translating activities of Gottsched and his friends, in *Bérénice* (Racine) by the Silesian pastor, A. B. Pantke, the continuation of *Le Cid*, by Magister Heynitz, and *Iphigénie* (Racine) by the professor himself. The translations were found rather wooden even by contemporaries. Of *Bérénice* Neuber writes that people complain of 'a certain inexplicable obscurity, which prevents the hearer from understanding immediately what is spoken' and adds the advice of a 'Swedish cavalier' to the translators, to try first to make the French thoughts their own and then to express them in free and natural German.

To this original stock of eight regular plays mentioned in Gottsched's preface to his *Cato* some score of other plays were added in the following ten years. In 1731 came the professor's 'original', *Der sterbende Cato*. The author, to do him justice, is very modest about it himself, admitting in his preface his debt to Addison and Deschamps (about four-fifths of the text is translated matter) and explaining that his aim had been to provide a version of Addison's play which should be free from the irregularities of the English stage, to re-write it, in fact, as Dryden re-wrote *Antony and Cleopatra* in his *All for Love*. He had considerably less to do than Dryden, dealing as he was with a classicistic play, already more than sufficiently pruned and polished, but he objected to the subsidiary plots, the lack of logical sequence, and the marriages arranged by the dying hero. The result of his labours was a play without action, passion or eloquence, colder even than Addison and lacking the distinction, visible even in this cramping form, of Addison's use of language. It says much for the acting of the Neuber troupe, especially of Kohlhardt in the title part, that the play was usually well received. As a book it went through ten editions in twenty-five years. The subject was evidently one that appealed to the educated middle class, indicating the same kind of taste as the preference of Corneille to Racine for translation. They were enthusiasts for patriotism and freedom in the abstract, and especially for that stoic heroism which proclaims the inviolability of the human will, the 'kein Mensch muss müssen' attitude still exalted by Lessing in *Nathan der Weise,* as previously in *Minna von Barnhelm* (in Tellheim) and *Emilia Galotti* (in Odoardo and Emilia). This, as Unger points out, was one of the two leading themes of the literature of the Enlightenment. Their fondness for it can perhaps be understood as a psychological compensation, required by the better citizens of little despotic states to maintain their self-esteem in the face of repeated humiliations from superiors. They were all Catos at heart, but it was enough to feel that their minds were free, and they were content to do as they were told. *Cato* must also have attracted attention through the prestige of Gottsched, as author of the *Kritische Dichtkunst,* a professor of Leipzig, and 'Senior' of the German Society, which was linked up with similar literary and patriotic societies—for all such societies combined cultural patriotism with literary enthusiasm—in other towns. It must also have helped that this kind of play was approved of by the highest circles and that its Roman subject would appeal to every educated man.

Meanwhile the versatile G. H. Koch was not only acting and painting scenery for the Neubers, but diligently translating and adapting plays. One which remained a favourite with Frau Neuber was the tragedy he made out of an opera by König, *Sancio und Sinilde,* and he did several others. More ambitious and impressive were two plays by a wealthy Hamburg merchant, G. Behrmann, who was one of the Neubers' most generous supporters. *Die Horazier* (acted first in June, 1733) is based on Corneille, a rehandling of part of the theme of *Horace,* and decidedly more original than *Der sterbende Cato.* Through aiming at the unity which Corneille himself missed in his own play, and therefore restricting the scope of the action, Behrmann makes it a series of debates on the relative claims of family and country, in war-time, on those bound by ties of marriage to members of a hostile state. The pathetic rather than the heroic aspect is stressed, and there is a distinctly pacifistic strain in the speeches of the women, especially of Camilla, in her insistence on the inhumanity of war. 'Auf, widersetze dich der Römer Tyranney!' she cries to her sister-in-law, 'Sonst dürften ihr einmal auch wir zum Opfer dienen. Was Menschenliebe heischt, weiss keiner unter ihnen.' If the characters here are made more credible for a Hamburg audience by being given some of their own humanity, in *Timoleon,* Behrmann's second play, first performed in 1735, also by the Neubers, the most effective 'tirades' are on the theme of political liberty, the democracy of 'council and citizens' as opposed to the tyranny of an individual ruler. The main theme is again the conflict between family and patriotic ties. Timoleon, the 'citizens' friend', to preserve the liberties of his republican fellow-countrymen, goes to the length of having his own brother, the would-be tyrant, put to death. The most striking passage (I, 3) runs:

> Was, soll ich meiner schonen?
> Da Bürger von Corinth für ihn nicht sicher wohnen?
> Ich gönne der Gewalt nun ferner keinen Platz,
> Die Freyheit ist gewiss der Bürger grösster Schatz.
> Ist sie einmal dahin, so ist sie stets verlohren.
> Zur Knechtschaft sind wir nicht, nein wir sind frei gebohren.
> Wir kennen keinen Herrn, als Pflicht und Vaterland,

Als Rath und Bürgerschaft, als Weisheit und Verstand,
Als Recht und Billigkeit, als Redlichkeit und Treue;
Wer uns die Freyheit raubt, der stirbt mit Furcht und Reue.

It is a long way from such sentiments to the *Führerprinzip*, and Schütze and Frl. Mentzel, historians of the Hamburg and Frankfort-on-Main theatres respectively, agree in thinking that it was the republican sentiments of this work which made it so popular in Free Towns like these two, though it was less popular, to judge by the number of performances, in Leipzig, on which the neighbouring capital, Dresden, cast its shadow. The same cause contributed to the interest taken in the many Roman subjects amongst the plays already discussed, especially the translations of Corneille, and some minor ones like Koch's *Titus Manlius* and *Der Tod Cäsars,* or *Cajus Fabritius,* adapted from an Italian opera by a Leipzig professor of medicine, C. G. Ludwig, who also wrote a play for the Neubers on *Ulysses von Ithaka.* When German regular plays came to be produced in greater numbers, in the 'forties and 'fifties, they revealed still more plainly, as we shall see, a middle-class point of view in both authors and public.

In what year the Neubers began to produce translations of post-classical French comedies is difficult to determine, but the first translation of a Destouches play was made by Koch in 1732 (*Le Philosophe Marié*). By 1740 Gottsched had realised how much better suited they were than tragedies to the average German audience, but there is no mention of them in Neuber's correspondence with him, which goes down to 1736, and it seems possible that the introduction of them may have been due to Frau Neuber herself, with her superior sense of the theatre. Later Frau Gottsched translated and adapted many French comedies, but Gottsched did not marry his 'geschickte Freundin' until 1735, and in that year we already find a considerable number of French comedies in the Neubers' repertoire during their long stay in Hamburg. They were mostly translated, no doubt, by Koch, Türpe or others in the troupe, probably into prose.

For this Hamburg season of eight months in 1735, during which the company seems to have given six performances a week, over thirty comedies from the French were acted, and not a third of their number of French tragedies. A good many are light one-acters by Le Grans, Boissy, Delisle and others, but there are three by Molière, one each by Corneille and Voltaire, two by Regnard, five by Marivaux and three by Destouches. That these plays were far more popular than the tragedies is seen by the number of performances. Many of the comedies were given four or five times, *L'Avare* as many as eight times, whereas only half of the French tragedies could be acted more than once or twice, and only three out of eleven reached four or more performances. The German tragedies were even less popular. The importance of post-classical and even contemporary French comedy, the *comédie larmoyante,* in the repertoire of the Neubers has not usually been stressed enough in histories of literature, where their name is almost exclusively associated with the performance in German of classical French tragedy. The choice made even of the tragedies is, as we have seen, significant. They did not act simply the best, but those which would go down best with their public, and they soon became aware of the attractions that sentimental comedy could hold for German audiences as well as French. Schönemann followed them in the same direction, and gradually moved on in the mid-fifties from French sentimental comedy to sentimental 'domestic drama' of the English type. The development right down to Lessing's time was therefore fairly continuous as regards the content of the plays produced, which tended throughout to reflect more and more closely the ways of thought and feeling of the average German audience.

While constantly on the look-out for literary plays which would be better adapted than classical tragedy to the tastes of the more progressive and intelligent elements in their audiences, the Neubers could not afford to neglect the almost universal demand for pure entertainment. Their repertoire therefore shows a skilful dove-tailing of the new into the old. In Hamburg in 1735 they gave an afterpiece at more than half of their performances which was entirely in the old tradition of the itinerant stage, pure *commedia dell' arte.* Harlequin figures by name in many of those to

which a title was given on the programme, as 'clumsy philosopher', 'living clock', 'dancing-master', 'cobbler and advocate',
'marquis Mascarilias', and the fact that for sixty-two afterpieces
no title at all was announced beforehand is probably just as
clear an indication that they also were improvised, following a
scenario. Gottsched certainly did not approve of this compromise, but he could not provide the troupe with its bread and
butter. The Neubers were however well aware of the incongruity between the two halves of their programmes, and partly
because of this and pressure by Gottsched, and partly for more
personal reasons, the bitter struggle in Leipzig with their rival,
J. F. Müller, a specialist in harlequinades, who succeeded in
wresting their Saxon licence from them and preventing them
from returning in 1737 to their old theatre, they staged a demon-
stration in Leipzig in that year against harlequin and his devotees.
In a characteristic short curtain-raiser by Frau Neuber, acted in
the wooden booth outside the Grimma Gate to which they had
themselves been banished through Müller's machinations, harlequin was solemnly banished from the German stage—banished,
not burnt, as has often been stated through the confusion of
'verbrannt' with 'verbannt'. The banishment of harlequin is
rightly regarded as a turning-point, but the battle against him
was naturally not won in a day, and even the Neubers, for
economic reasons, could not live up to their literary pretensions.
As Lessing put it, in his caustic way, in the *Hamburgische Dramaturgie*, 'they had got rid of the party-coloured jacket and the name,
but the clown remained. The Neuberin herself played many
pieces, in which harlequin was the chief character. But harlequin was christened Hänschen, and dressed in white instead of
in checks. Truly, a great triumph for good taste!'

That this is literally true can be seen from a study of the
repertoire of the Neuber troupe in Leipzig in 1741, recorded in a
contemporary periodical.[1] They were there from June till
November, acting daily in fair-time and twice a week out of
fair-time, and it is interesting to see what the most enlightened of
German publics would accept fourteen years after the first attempts

[1] See Reden-Esbeck, *op. cit.*, p. 259.

at the reform of the theatre. It is true that by this time the Neubers had quarrelled with Gottsched, in 1739, refusing to act Frau Gottsched's version of *Alzire* instead of Stüve's, which they had already memorised and used, and they had antagonised the Hamburg public by Frau Neuber's over-frank farewell speech from the stage after an unsuccessful season in 1740. The company had gone to Russia from Hamburg, invited by the Empress Anna, who was, by marriage, Duchess of Courland, and surrounded herself with German favourites, but the adventure, though it had for the moment relieved the Neubers of their debts, had turned out badly, because of the sudden death of the Empress six months after their arrival. Gottsched had meanwhile begun to publish the translations and original plays composed under his direction in a new periodical, *Die deutsche Schaubühne*, believing that Germany had lost 'the only troupe that had a healthy and reasonable repertoire', though Schönemann, who left the Neubers at this time and set up a troupe of his own, soon sought and obtained Gottsched's support. The Neubers had now three serious rivals in Leipzig and Saxony, Schönemann, J. F. Müller, and Schuch. Their idealistic policy of 'opposing the majority' (Devrient) had been anything but a success financially, and they had always had to live from hand to mouth. Increasing difficulties were to lead to a temporary break-up of the company in 1743, but a comparison of the 1741 Leipzig repertoire with the Hamburg one of 1735 shows that there had been no change in the policy of the management. In their sixty performances the company performed a surprisingly large number of plays, forty-three of full length, and thirty-three one-acters. Of the former only sixteen were repeated, each once only, and of the latter four were given twice and three on three occasions. Twenty-nine of the plays and fourteen of the one-acters figure in the repertoire of 1735, already mentioned. But nine full-length plays and four one-acters are marked as first performances, as well as five original 'preludes', all from Frau Neuber's pen.

The lack of good German plays is still very noticeable. Of the full-length plays, three-quarters were translated from the French, half of them being comedies and half tragedies. The

French tragedies were: four by Pierre Corneille (*Le Cid, Horace, Cinna, Polyeucte*), one by his brother Thomas (*Essex*), two by Racine (*Iphigénie, Phèdre*), and five by Voltaire (*Brutus, Zaïre, Alzire, L'Enfant Prodigue, Le Festin de Don Pierre*). The French comedies were: two by Molière (*L'Avare*, played three times, and *Le Malade Imaginaire*), three by Regnard (*Démocrite, Le Distrait, Le Joueur*), four by Marivaux (*Le Dédain Affecté, Le Jeu de l'Amour et du Hasard, La Double Inconstance, L'Île des Esclaves*), four by Destouches (*L'Irrésolu, Le Philosophe Marié, L'Obstacle Imprévu, Le Triple Mariage*), one by La Chaussée (*L'École des Mères*) and several by minor authors (Le Grand, Dancourt, Dové, Saint Jory, J. B. Rousseau, etc.).

The only German tragedy acted was Gottsched's *Sterbender Cato*, given once only, apart from the performance in which the last act was played in more or less Roman costume, to turn to ridicule Gottsched's ideas about historical costume. Koch's *Sancio und Sinilde* (from König's opera) was another serious play. The comedies are mostly one-acters and a good many are of the semi-improvised type. König's *Der Dresdenische Schlendrian* (see p. 48) was still being given because of its local interest. The rest are even lighter fare of very mixed origin. One at least, *Die närrische Wette,* from the Dutch, can be traced back to the seventeenth century, when it figured on Velten's programmes. It was still a favourite, one of the few to be repeated. It is true that when possible Frau Neuber seems to have presented a one-act comedy by a known author, usually from the French, 'instead of an afterpiece', as the programme would announce, but at one-quarter of the performances at least she gave anonymous farces, five of which are identical in title with those played in Hamburg, except that in one of them, in which harlequin had figured, his name is now omitted from the title (*The living clock*). Other farces already acted in Hamburg are: *The four love-sick spirits, Love-sick Lizzy, the cobbler's daughter* and *The bearded woman*. The new ones have titles which are equally low-brow, such as: *The frigid maiden, The merry postman,* or *The unseemly and ridiculous love affair* (from the Dutch). The proportion of farces to regular plays is however decidedly lower in Leipzig, less than a third, instead of over a half, an index no doubt to the superior taste of Leipzig, but in the preponderance of sentimental over classical comedy the same tendency is to be seen as in Hamburg. The only classical comedies are two of Molière's, but another play of Destouches is added to the repertoire, and La Chaussée makes his first appearance, with *L'École des Mères*. Marivaux, who had apparently been one of the big hits in Hamburg (*Le Jeu de l'Amour et du Hasard*, five times; *La Double Inconstance*, four; *L'Île des Esclaves*, three, and two others twice each) does not seem to have gone down so well in Leipzig, only four plays being tried once each, whereas those of Destouches and La Chaussée were all given a repeat.

Sentimental drama, it is clear, was in the ascendant, but improvised farce died hard, and before turning to the continuation by Schönemann and others of Frau Neuber's pioneer work, it may be well to discuss more fully at this point the lively controversy about the relative merits of improvised and regular performances to which the combined action of Gottsched and the Neubers gave rise later in the century, for when the abuses to which improvisation led were no longer clearly before men's eyes, they remembered the attractions of Harlequin, or what they had heard about them, and began to wonder whether his banishment had after all been justified. In practice, as we have seen, improvisation lingered on for a considerable time, in Austria well into the nineteenth century, so that there were many even in the later eighteenth century who had seen improvised plays, and many actors who had taken part in them. Several well-known actors are among the later defenders of Harlequin. Schröder, as we have seen, had some experience of improvisation with the Viennese Kurz, and his biographer is expressing the great actor's own views when he writes: 'I am far from wishing to decry the merits of Gottsched, Sonnenfels and Gebler in their attempts to make the theatre more regular and moral. I know what sort of farces they wanted to banish from the stage . . . but I am just as sure of this, that no one can claim to have shared in a feast of mirth at its liveliest and most infectious who has only heard prescribed phrases recited from the book, however wittily written and naturally spoken, who has not seen what effect the impromptu sallies of the actors can have on the audience, and the ready response of the audience can have on the actors. It is like drinking champagne; the effect quickly wears off, but there is nothing like it.'[1] F. L. Schmidt too, who knew many actors in his youth who had acted in extempore comedy, says that they all spoke of it with the greatest enthusiasm, and felt that with it, true comedy had disappeared.[2]

One or two leading writers also had something to say in favour of Harlequin and the extemporised play. The first was Justus Möser, the author of *Osnabrückische Geschichte* and *Patriotische Phantasien,* an enthusiast for local history, inherited ways of life and everything that was home-grown and deeply rooted, but a broad-minded, independent thinker, who reminds us sometimes of Burke, sometimes of Cobbett. In 1761 he published his essay, *Harlequin, or a Defence of the Grotesque-Comic,* a well-written counterblast to the narrowly rationalistic and moralistic views of Gottsched and his like, 'the stern scholar in his inherited armchair' trying to discover by formal reasoning whether harlequin pleases or not. It is a fact of experience that he does, though his is only one kind of comedy. There are many kinds, just as there are many kinds of picture. A Teniers is none the less pleasing because you would not hang it beside a Michelangelo. The reader is asked to confess that he doesn't often go to the theatre to be improved. There is a place for pure entertainment, for the fooling and caricatures of Harlequin, as well as for serious plays. He does not want the kind of mixture found in the Haupt- und Staatsaktionen, nor defend the vulgarity and indecency of some of those who have deceived the world under Harlequin's name, but the comedy of types has its own laws and its own kind of unity. He evidently thinks of the fixed types as a sort of shorthand device, enabling the actors to make their effects quickly and surely. An interesting letter of 1761 from Möser to Abbt[3] throws light on this point. One of the chief difficulties encountered by comedy in Germany, Möser says, is

---

[1] F. L. Meyer, *Schröder,* I, p. 179.
[2] *Denkwürdigkeiten,* I, p. 12.
[3] *Vermischte Schriften,* ed. Nicolai, 1797, II, p. 216.

the lack of a central capital, where in time a number of typical characters immediately apprehensible by the whole country would be conceived, 'as Herr Lessing, who was the first to notice the advantage brought to the fable by fixed characters, will con- firm. Harlequin is in fact like such an animal in fable, and so are most of the characters used by authors of this kind of comedy. The common man knows them as well as the fox and the lion. And perhaps you, sir, know Tyburn and La Grève, though you will not be able to name the place where thieves are hanged in Berlin or Vienna.'

Lessing praises Möser's essay very warmly in the number of the *Hamburgische Dramaturgie* (18) from which the passage about Frau Neuber and the Harlequin was quoted above. In his usual way, he finds a counterpart to Harlequin in antiquity, in the Parasite of Attic and Roman comedy, and pleads for his re-instatement, in his traditional costume, but he says nothing directly about improvisation. The only other German writers quoted by C. F. Flögel in his still valuable *Geschichte des Groteskekomischen* (1788) in defence of Harlequin are Wieland in his *Agathon,* an ironical passage, and a writer in the *Literatur- briefe* (No. 204). Flögel gives a history of the *commedia dell' arte,* its influence in various countries, and what seem to him parallels in antiquity and in Spain. He was interested in every aspect of the comic as a cultural phenomenon, and is a mine of information on comic festivals and the like.

But the most eloquent apology for extemporised comedy is that which was put by Goethe in the first, unpublished, version of *Wilhelm Meisters Lehrjahre,* which he called *Wilhelm Meisters Theatralische Sendung* (Book 3, Chapter 8) into the mouth of the 'Prinzipalin' Mme de Retti, who is clearly based on Frau Neuber. Goethe represents her as regretting in later years the banishment of Harlequin for which she had been responsible, and attempting in vain to reintroduce a modified form of extemporised play. She would have purged the older plays of their indecency and acted regular plays alongside them, but she would have liked to see an extempore performance say once a week, to keep her actors in practice. 'For extemporising', she is made to say, 'was the school and the touchstone of the actor. It was not enough to memorize a rôle and then imagine one could play it. The actor's intelligence, imagination, dexterity, knowledge of the theatre, presence of mind were clearly revealed at every step; he was forced to acquaint himself with all the resources of the theatre, he became as much at home on the stage as a fish in water, and a poet who could have used these instruments properly could have made a great impression on the public.' She had been over-awed by the critics, German playwrights had provided her only with literary but unstageworthy plays to replace the old ones, and but for the translations of Molière (and, we may add, the *comédie larmoyante*) her plight would have been a hopeless one.

Mme dè Retti's arguments are very much those of L. Riccoboni (*Réflexions Historiques et Critiques sur les Différents Théâtres de l'Europe*, Paris, 1738). But we have seen already that there is another side to this question, if it is viewed from the angle of the moralist and social reformer, and the triumph of the regular play was principally due to these non-aesthetic considerations.

REGULAR TRAGEDY AND COMEDY

Although Gottsched's reform of the theatre had by no means completely transformed the repertoire of the Neuber troupe even after more than ten years, as is clear from the obstinate survival of popular low-brow afterpieces and from the evidence of the public's preference of sentimental comedy to tragedy in the grand style, it was nevertheless obvious by the 1740's that the literary play had come to stay, and one touring company after another began to introduce 'regular pieces' into its repertoire. By 1748 even Franz Schuch, one of the best exponents of extemporised comedy, is found thanking Gottsched for 'laying the foundations' of the new type of theatre,[1] though as we have seen he put on afterpieces of the old type for a long time afterwards. In 1751 he even entertained for a time the extravagant idea of taking his troupe, via Strassburg, where he had held his own for nearly a year against the French Comedians, to Paris itself.[2] The

---

[1] Danzel, *Gottsched*, 2nd ed., p. 163.   [2] *Ibid.*

supply of new German plays unfortunately did not come near to meeting this growing demand, though such as there were followed Gottsched's lead for some time unquestioningly.

Regular tragedy in particular continued to be a very rare commodity. The only German tragic author who gave real promise before Lessing was in fact Johann Elias Schlegel, and like so many German writers, he was far more advanced in his theory than in his practice. It has recently been claimed for him with justice that he was a pioneer in aesthetics, anticipating the attitude to art which prevailed at the end of the century.[1] In spite of the imitation theory which held the field in his time, he understood the nature of dramatic conventions, and defended the use of verse in comedies because it reminded the audience that they were witnessing something that was not nature, but art. He has long been acknowledged as a pioneer in his appreciation of Shakespeare. The same translation in alexandrines of *Julius Caesar* (by C. W. von Borck, 1741), which gave rise to Gott-sched's condemnation of the play as more full of 'elementary blunders in regard to the rules of the theatre and of common-sense' than the worst of Haupt- und Staatsaktionen, evoked from the twenty-two-year-old student a warm appreciation of Shake-speare's bold and original creation of characters and deep know-ledge of human nature. He already saw a general difference between the English dramatic tradition and that of the French classics, in that the one stressed character, and the other a logically constructed plot, but he saw merits in both, and did not, like Gottsched, dogmatically reject Shakespeare because of his neglect of the rules. At twenty-four Schlegel went to Denmark as private secretary to the Saxon minister in Copenhagen, and there he wrote down, still in his twenties, for he died at the age of thirty, judgments not published till 1764, which revealed a complete break with Gottsched, as when he said, in effect, that dramatic conventions ('rules') differed in different nations, accord-ing to the taste and manners of each. The French and the English theatres were equally fine, each in its own way, and his countrymen had made the mistake of turning their theatre into

---

[1] Elizabeth M. Wilkinson, *J.E.S.*, 1945.

a German-speaking French one.[1] In some passages he pours scorn on Gottsched's narrowly rationalistic interpretation of the moral aim of the theatre. His last two essays were occasioned by the proposal to establish a theatre in Copenhagen, and Schlegel's enlightened ideas about an endowed Danish theatre were not without importance, when published in the 'sixties, in the movement to establish the first German National Theatre in Hamburg.

In spite of his catholic power of appreciation and his high intelligence, Schlegel as a playwright is disappointing, though he gave far more promise than any of his contemporaries. As a Saxon growing to maturity in the 1730's, he could not escape the impact of Gottsched's ideas, and as a boy at Schulpforta he already tried his hand at regular tragedies on classical themes. One, *Die Geschwister in Taurien* (originally *Orest und Pylades*), was performed by the Neubers in 1739 at Leipzig, soon after Schlegel had become a student there. The other two, *Die Trojanerinnen* (originally *Hekuba,* written at sixteen), and *Dido,* were revised and published later. They are technical exercises, alexandrine dramas in the French tradition, but novel among German products in that they were based on a direct study of the Greeks. In the year of his Shakespeare essay, Schlegel tackled a German theme, though he went back to Tacitus and the mists of antiquity for it. *Hermann* (1741), is the first patriotic drama in German, but patriotic only in a cultural sense. Its characters are shadowy figures, built round one or two general traits, the Romans corrupted by civilisation, though this is before Rousseau, and the Germans happy in their primitive innocence, unless led astray, like Hermann's brother Flavius, by the example of Roman neighbours. 'Rom lehrt uns Kunst und Witz, und zähmt die wilden Sitten', says Flavius, to which his father replies: 'Rom jagt die Unschuld weg aus den beglückten Hütten.' Hermann, trained in Rome, turns the Romans' own military art against them and frees his people, we are to understand, but there is no fighting and no dramatic tension in the play whatever. A simple love intrigue in the French manner gives the plot what little shape

---

[1] *Gedanken zur Aufnahme des dänischen Theaters,* 1747.

it has. Yet *Hermann* was still being performed twenty-five years later, when Goethe saw Koch's new Leipzig theatre opened with it.

In Denmark in 1746 Schlegel wrote a second 'historical' play, *Canut*[1] for the opening of the national theatre. It is a great improvement on *Hermann*. It is already a study of an 'immoralist', to use a modern term, in the person of Ulfo, Canut's brother-in-law, who, once his personal ambition is involved, is incapable of loyalty to his friends, his wife or his king, yet through his fire and outspoken audacity certainly holds our attention. It is clearly the creation of the character of Ulfo that has called out the best in Schlegel as an artist. He is meant as the villain of the piece, but like Milton's Satan he steals all the thunder, in this case from Canut, who is compact of mercy and magnanimity in the Stoic tradition, morally admirable but aesthetically lifeless.

Schlegel's early comedies too are concerned with characters, but rather in the sense of La Bruyère's 'caractères', or what in England we called 'humours'. The moral weeklies are full of such studies, following the immediate example of the *Spectator* and the *Guardian*, both translated by Frau Gottsched, and French comedy had excelled in the dramatisation of similar types since Molière. But the models preferred to Molière by the Gottsched school were the shallower studies of Regnard, whose *Jean de France* was translated by Detharding in Hamburg as early as 1740, and was followed by others, or of Destouches, or the 'Danish Molière' Holberg. In these later writers there was nothing of Molière's awareness of depths of character eluding rational analysis. The Neubers staged translations of *L'Avare*, *Le Distrait*, *Le Joueur*, *L'Irrésolu*, as we have seen, and Schlegel's prose comedies *Der geschäftige Müssiggänger* (1741) and *Der Geheimnisvolle* (1747) follow in the same tradition. The former, an early work, was said by Lessing never to have been performed, to his knowledge, and he thought that with the dull 'Alltagsgewäsche' of its dialogue it never would be. The second, developed from a hint he found in Molière, is a picture of 'un homme tout mystère',

---

[1] Edited by Brüggemann in D. L., Reihe Aufklärung, VI.

but in spite of Schlegel's theoretical aim of winning the sympathy of the audience for his characters, his pedlar of secrets entirely lacks human interest. Lessing considered *Der Triumph der guten Frauen,* a comedy of intrigue, which was still being acted at the Hamburg National Theatre, to be the best of these prose comedies, but by French and English standards it cannot be rated very highly. The dialogue is natural, but it is hard to find the wit which Mendelssohn praised in it. Two husbands, one a bully and one a rake, are both persuaded to make a fresh start with their devoted wives, after one of the wives, in man's clothes, has pretended to be her own husband's rival in an intrigue with the other wife. She is not recognised by her husband whether she appears in male or female attire, even when he is making love to her as a supposed stranger. The women, even the lively maid, are all virtuous, but the wives are revoltingly tolerant of the mis-behaviour of their husbands. If the tone here is really, as Mendels-sohn said, that of cultivated people, Saxon society must have been most demoralising for men, but it is safer to conclude that the piece was entirely literary in inspiration. The other work of Schlegel's that was acted at the Hamburg National Theatre was *Die stumme Schönheit,* a one-act play in alexandrines which Lessing held to be the best original verse comedy in German. It is, however, a light-weight affair. The action is highly im-probable and rather farcical, but it moves quickly and furnishes amusing situations, and Schlegel shows considerable skill in keeping the dialogue entirely natural in his neatly turned verses.

Besides three volumes almost entirely devoted to the transla-tions from the French, the principal fare offered by the Neubers in the early years of their troupe, Gottsched's *Deutsche Schau-bühne* contained in its six volumes two translations from Holberg, three of Schlegel's plays, three tragedies by Gottsched himself (*Der sterbende Cato, Agis* and *Die Parisische Bluthochzeit*) and two comedies and an afterpiece by his wife. There are a few minor pieces by Quistorp, Krüger, Uhlich and Grimm.

Of Gottsched's two tragedies after *Cato,* both 'Staatsaktionen', *Agis* might have been expected to interest the middle class, with its picture of a plain-living Spartan king who tried to carry out a revolution from above, and to reintroduce the communism of the days of Lycurgus, but only one performance can be traced and it was never reprinted.[1] *Cato* however, as we saw, went through ten editions in fifteen years and was acted repeatedly all over Germany.

The comedies were rather better than the tragedies. Frau Gottsched did free adaptations of Molière and Holberg, trans/ ferring the scene to Germany and introducing an obvious moral. What is astonishing in one who was the most cultivated German woman of her time, who shared in all her husband's literary work for the spread of enlightenment and found in that activity some consolation for childlessness, is an occasional crudity of feeling and expression which did not escape Lessing's criticism. Of *Die Hausfranzösin* he wrote: 'It is not only vulgar and commonplace and cold, but in addition dirty, disgusting and extremely offen/ sive.' Her *Testament* has more claims to originality. It is a pure comedy of intrigue, not without some amusing satirical touches, as when an extravagant nobleman, announcing that he is to entertain his best friends, 'the only people in the world who have true German blood in their veins', invites the tradesmen to whom he owes money, and two Jewish moneylenders. They all consort together because they are freemasons like himself, 'and in our order we do not pay much attention to rank'. Her anonymous *Pietisterei im Fischbeinrocke* (1737) had introduced into a trans/ plantation of a French play to Königsberg so many local hits and so much criticism of the Pietists that it was banned.[2] It contains a scene in dialect written with much verve. Her *Un/ gleiche Heirat* too is interesting still as a social document, with its contrast of the hardworking, sensible middle class with the vain, self/seeking aristocracy. It takes sides with the former much more uncompromisingly than Molière had done in *Georges Dandin,* thus anticipating a host of domestic dramas of the second half of the century. The learned professions too were obvious subjects for satirical comedy, in Germany as elsewhere. One of J. C. Quistorp's comedies, *Der Bock im Prozesse,* is meant to be

---

[1] Until 1935, in D.L., Reihe Aufklärung, III.
[2] Reprint in D.L., Aufklärung III.

funny about his own profession, the law, with its jargon and formalities, but it is merely tedious. The other comedy of his in the *Schaubühne* is a comedy of humours, *Der Unempfindliche*. J. C. Krüger, an actor in Schönemann's troupe, who had stage experience and a more genuine comic vein than any of the Gottsched circle proper, attacked the clergy so bitterly in his anonymous *Die Geistlichen auf dem Lande* (1743) that the play was immediately banned. It was partly founded on his own experience as a student of theology at Halle, but it is also dependent on *Tartuffe*, as *Der Bock im Prozesse* is on Racine's *Les Plaideurs*. He followed it up with *Die Kandidaten* (1747), which again anticipates a SturmundDrang theme, that of Lenz's *Der Hofmeister*, at least in that it is highly critical of the attitude of the aristocracy to their tutors. Krüger translated and adapted many plays by Marivaux for his troupe. *Der Bauer mit der Erbschaft* (*L'héritier de village*), in which he makes effective use of Hamburg Plattdeutsch, furnished Ekhof with one of his best rôles. It was low comedy in which Krüger excelled, as Lessing said, and his eminently actable plays naturally had far more success on the stage than those of the more gifted Schlegel. His satire of the clergy evoked a pendant, *Die Ärzte*, a crude and indecent comedy by Lessing's journalist friend and distant relation, C. Mylius, who had studied medicine.

All these writers at least began their careers as disciples of Gottsched, though some gradually emancipated themselves from his influence, and Schlegel in particular seems just as much concerned in his later work with presenting virtue in a sympathetic light as he is with the traditional aim of comedy, ridiculing vice. Gottsched considered pastoral plays, like his *Atalanta*, the proper genre for the former purpose, and also as a substitute for opera, but they were never very popular. The change of emphasis in Schlegel reflects the general development which was taking place in the French theatre, in Destouches, Marivaux and especially Nivelle de la Chaussée, the emergence of *comédie larmoyante*. The German writer who showed this influence most clearly was C. F. Gellert, another product of a Saxon Klosterschule, who at the university of Leipzig had been in close touch with Schlegel and his friends, all contributors to the *Neue Bey-träge* that appeared in Bremen from 1744–48, and struck a more popular note of sincere feeling than the earlier Gottsched school. Gellert, delicate, gentle, pious, inclined to melancholia, who in all his teaching and writing wished to improve as well as to please, was in character the very antithesis of Nivelle de la Chaussée, the Parisian man of letters and salon hero, in his personal life and loves a heartless egoist with a mordant wit. Sentiment, which La Chaussée cunningly exploited as a novelty to please the Parisian public, seems to have been regarded by Gellert, quite sincerely, as the root of all virtue. He founded his moral philosophy lectures on the teaching of the Scottish followers of Shaftesbury and his 'moral sense' theory. His fables, letters and comedies, all alike, aimed at 'pleasing good hearts as much as men of wit'. The ethical confusion everywhere produced by this tendency to subordinate sense to sensibility, to regard virtue as needing no conscious guidance, is occasionally apparent in some otherwise inexplicable lapses, particularly in his Richard-sonian novel, *Die schwedische Gräfin*. In his comedies, he set out to evoke 'tears of pity rather than joyous laughter'. There is always a rather grotesque figure or two to laugh at—the female Tartuffe in the *Betschwester* (1745), the miserly Damon, the envious Orgon and the free-thinking Simon in *Das Loos in der Lotterie* (1746), the pedantic Magister in *Die zärtlichen Schwestern* (1747). But the real interest is focused in the first play on the two girls who, out of mutual affection, vie with each other in renouncing the same suitor. Apart from this they are very like the pair in *Die stumme Schönheit,* which was no doubt influenced by this play—or is *La Fausse Agnés* of Destouches perhaps behind them both? In the second play the penniless lovers, Carolinchen and Anton, are in the limelight, neither of whom desires any-thing but the happiness of the other. 'Providence provides for a virtuous love' by making them win the first prize in the lottery. In the third play it is again two girls who are held up for admira-tion, sisters this time, the elder of whom gives all her thought to making the younger one realise that she really loves her devoted suitor, breaking off her own engagement when she discovers that

her Siegmund is out for money, though she promises him a
sufficient share of the fortune she has inherited to put him out of
the way of temptation a second time. Lessing calls Gellert's plays
genuinely German, 'true family pictures, in which one immediately feels at home', from which we gather that good middle-
class circles in Saxony did think and feel like this and were
interested in the same kind of thing as Gellert's characters. His
biographer Cramer says that the plays were written not so much
for the world of fashion as for the middle ranks of society, because
there were no German theatres at the courts. One thing such
circles were interested in was evidently material comforts, but they
feel sure they can attain them without risk to their souls. There
is much talk of capital and interest and valuable legacies. The
company is always being summoned to tea or coffee, new luxuries
then, and they drink them out of porcelain cups that are just
beginning to have handles. A good father does not force his
daughter to marry the man of his choice, nor do young people
marry for money, if we are to approve of them. Prosperity nevertheless comes their way, for those who follow the dictates of their
hearts, the virtuous, in his view, are kind heaven's special care.
This brings sentimental tears to the eyes of the audience, just
because they know it is too good to be true.

Gellert's poem on Richardson's portrait ends with the lines:

> Die Worte, die er schuf, wird keine Zeit verwüsten,
> Sie sind Natur, Geschmack, Religion.
> Unsterblich ist Homer, unsterblicher bei Christen
> Der Britte Richardson.

The tone of Gellert's comedies is almost perfectly described by
the words which Richardson used of his own intentions in his
Familiar Letters, out of which the novels grew: 'He has endeavoured
to point out the duty of a servant, not a slave; the duty of a master,
not a tyrant; that of the parent, not as a person morose and sour,
and hard to be pleased, but mild, indulgent, kind, and such an
one as would rather govern by persuasion, than force.'

One has only to compare a play of La Chaussée with one of
Gellert, or those of Destouches or Marivaux with the prose

adaptations made of them in Germany, to see that most of the characteristics which, in the view of French literary historians, distinguish the 'drame' from the 'comédie larmoyante' are to be found on the German stage even before Lessing's *Miss Sara Sampson*, the first German domestic tragedy, although the drame did not begin its triumphal career in France until 1757, two years after *Miss Sara*. The reason is no doubt that these German plays of the 1740's were already being written mainly with a middle-class public in view, whereas in France, especially in Paris, there was an aristocracy which retained considerable influence on taste. The fact that these German comedies were in everyday prose gave them a different colouring from that of La Chaussée's verse comedies, with their alexandrines and their 'style noble'. There were no German counterparts to expressions such as 'hymen' and 'transport', 'temples' and 'tribuneaux', with their suggestion of a heightened existence. The German plays were frequently, if derived from the French, brought down to a lower social level in the process of naturalisation, and the influence of Richardson and other earlier English models, the 'moral weeklies' in particular, worked in the same direction. Gellert himself provided a theoretical justification for the 'intermediate genre' of which both the *comédie larmoyante* and English domestic tragedy in the manner of Lillo were different varieties. Characteristically enough it was written in Latin, as a sort of inaugural lecture when he became a professor in Leipzig in 1751. Lessing translated it in 1754 for his *Theatralische Bibliothek,* and with his *Miss Sara Sampson* in the following year he came down on the side of the English variety of middle-class play, which came now to be all-important for the further development of the German drama. Lillo and Moore found, in fact, incomparably more imitators in Germany than in their own country.

At the beginning of his career, however, Lessing, together with his college friend Weisse, was quite clearly of the school of Gottsched, for he grew up in the atmosphere of Leipzig, and could not but follow the lead of his predecessors when he was learning his art. He rapidly outgrew Gottsched's influence, whereas Weisse, as a typical product of the Saxon school, with little originality, remained particularly susceptible to French influence and produced nothing of lasting value.

Young Lessing, the schoolboy who needed twice as much work as his fellows, 'doppeltes Futter', had evidently a fairly wide acquaintance with ancient and modern European comedy when, at his Meissen Klosterschule and at the University of Leipzig, he wrote his own first attempts. He and Klopstock were both, no doubt, spurred on by the sight of J. E. Schlegel's early triumphs, and in Lessing's last years at school he must have read Gellert's comedies as they came out in the *Bremer Beiträge,* for his earliest completed comedy, *Damon,* shows the familiar characteristics of sentimental comedy, the 'rührendes Lustspiel'. It is a study of two contrasted friends, one false and one true, and the magnanimous friend is duly rewarded by Providence in gaining the hand of a rich widow. The honourable man and the selfish schemer are contrasted as in the later domestic drama, but they are not yet the representatives of the middle class and the aristocracy respectively. The technique is elementary, but there is occasionally a trenchant remark in Lessing's manly style, as when Damon points out to Leander how much harder it is to 'practise the duty of friendship than to talk about it in glowing terms', an anticipation of Nathan's words to Recha about good actions and pious sentiments.

Der junge Gelehrte, begun at school, remodelled at Leipzig, and performed in January 1748 by the Neuberin, is not quite so purely literary in inspiration, though Holberg and several others are laid under contribution. Lessing as a student was much concerned with the conflict between the learned and the worldly way of life, as the famous letter home makes clear, in which he explains how acutely conscious he had become on arriving in Leipzig of his boorish awkwardness and monkish ignorance of the world, and how he had taken himself in hand by learning to dance and attending the theatre. He was adapting himself, as Goethe did later, to the atmosphere of 'Klein Paris,' which made newcomers feel like country cousins, and like Goethe in *Die Mitschuldigen,* but not quite so unreservedly, he gives too many points to the man of the world, and is inclined to be cynical, for fear of appearing naive. *Der junge Gelehrte* is a product of the head, not of the heart, and its point of view is only in part middle-class. It is life in good society that is praised as an educative influence, but the father, a well-to-do citizen, is presented in an unfavourable light, as he might have been by Gellert, being ready to force his ward to marry his pedantic son, merely because he has hopes of her gaining a fortune for the family. The technique is purely French, though the unity of place is treated with a certain irony, in that the characters themselves comment on the extraordinary way in which all seem to be drawn towards the study of Damis.

Der Misogyne and *Die alte Jungfer* are pure farce, designed as afterpieces for the amusement of a public accustomed to the mixed fare provided by the Neubers. The characters, the situations and the jokes are put together from Italian, French and even English sources, to judge by names like Wumshäter (from Beaumont and Fletcher's 'Woman-hater')—some characters have even more obvious labels—and although Harlequin is not there under his old name, Peter, the pastrycook's boy in *Die alte Jungfer,* has exactly his old function. There is even a rôle provided in *Der Misogyne* for an actress like Frau Neuber, who delighted in appearing in the same play first as a man and then as a woman.

There are some bad lapses in *Die Juden* and *Der Freigeist* (both 1749), but in both plays the central ideas are recognisably of a piece with Lessing's later religious writings and his *Nathan.* The worst moment in *Die Juden* is when the Baron, out of gratitude to the stranger who has saved him from highway-robbers, offers him his daughter's hand after a few hours of acquaintanceship, though with her full consent, certainly, for like some more famous 'naïve girls' in later dramas, she is supposed to be 'nature left to itself'. But the whole tissue of improbabilities is only designed to suggest that the Jews are a much-maligned race who, if the Germans consider it a point of religion to persecute them, can hardly be expected to refrain from occasionally getting their own back, though there are also among them admirable men like the good Samaritan in this play. The baron's own bailiff and village elder, who like the baron himself have been so free with accusations against the Jews, turn out to be the real culprits, and it is the noble stranger who is a Jew, with a straight nose and the manners and education of a gentleman. He is the first idealised Jew in German literature, and though the play aroused the indignation of at least one reviewer, as we know by Lessing's discussion with him (*Theatralische Bibliothek*, 16), and was probably never acted, it evidently met with the approval of many cultivated readers. A few years after writing it Lessing became acquainted in Berlin with the first Jew who made a name for himself in German literature, Moses Mendelssohn, and when he came to make a Jew the hero of his last play, he wrote not merely from a humanitarian impulse, but from the experience of years of close friendship with one of the finest men of his age.

In *Der Freigeist*, which is only interesting for the light it throws on the development of Lessing's thought, we know from a letter that one of his aims was to reconcile his father to his play-writing, no easy task, we realise, when we remember what most ministers of religion thought about the theatre. He undertook to make a free-thinker look ridiculous, thus illustrating the effectiveness of comedy in conveying moral lessons. He hoped at the same time to counter his father's disapproval of his association with the black sheep Mylius, who vaunted his free-thinking in the title of a journal he edited. But the edge is taken off the conflict between Adrast, the free-thinker, and Theophan, a young theologian, who are about to marry two sisters, because Theophan is the model of a tolerant and understanding clergyman, and Adrast, though, as an intolerant rationalist, he has the strongest suspicions of his future brother-in-law's cloth, is himself 'full of virtuous principles', as Theophan and their genial future father-in-law both realise. The latter believes that Adrast and Theophan will in time come closer and closer to each other, that is, that the fundamental beliefs which govern their actions are really very much the same, in spite of the difference between their creeds. This implies that creeds do not very much matter, or at least that morality is not indissolubly linked with positive religion, as Gellert, for instance, would have held. His free-thinker, Simon

(*Das Loos in der Lotterie*) is a very different figure, a thoroughly self-indulgent man with no principles, and that is how Adrast's man-servant, Johann, a caricature of his master, thinks of atheists, so he boasts to Theophan's man, Martin, of the fine times they have, while the ignorant Martin imagines free-thinkers as monsters, who might very well have tails and horns. Between them they thus lend some support to Adrast's view that religion is good for the plebs, to keep them in check: he also finds it very becoming in women. With Theophan he never has any serious discussion, but he is put to shame by one example after another of Theophan's goodwill to him, and at last has to admit that it is genuine. The play is spun out to five acts by these incidents and by a love intrigue, borrowed from Delisle, which results in an exchange of brides between the two men, for like does not attract like. The serious sister, we feel, will soon have Adrast going to church again, and the gay one will not allow Theophan to become too ascetic. That they all, as in *Nathan* later, become members of one family is no doubt to be taken symbolically, as an expression of the author's ideal of a tolerant community.

It is convenient to mention at this point some dramatists whose names are familiar to every reader of the *Hamburgische Drama-turgie,* writers all influenced by Lessing at a time when he was gradually emancipating himself from the Gottsched tradition. Lessing's fellow-student of Leipzig days, C. F. Weisse (1726–1804), wrote with a fatal facility, without having anything personal to say, but he performed a useful function in his day in supplying the stage with actable plays not without literary polish. His work is probably a more reliable index to public taste just because of his lack of originality, than that of any other dramatic author of the time. He began, like Lessing, by writing translations and so forth for Frau Neuber, and his first original play, a one-act verse comedy on the old story of the *Matron of Ephesus,* was acted by her in the same year as *Der junge Gelehrte.* While earning his living as tutor to a young count he wrote a number of comedies for Koch's new theatre from 1750, not all of which were published. They were character comedies of the type discussed above. Weisse still followed the lead of the Gottsched school when he began to try his hand at tragedies in 1758, stimulated by Nicolai's offer of a prize. At the same time he remained on good terms with the group who gradually broke away from Gott-sched, the 'Bremer Beiträger', and even opposed the master's taste completely by adapting an English ballad-opera, Coffey's *The Devil to Pay*, in 1752. We shall see later how successful Weisse was with comic opera when it eventually established itself.

Weisse's early tragedies are in alexandrines, in the orthodox French style. The dominant themes are love and ambition, the plots are taken from remote ages and countries and the characters are completely without subtlety, studies in black-and-white. His attention was then drawn by Lessing to English subjects, and in the same 'regular' form he treated two subjects from English history, *Eduard III* (1758) and *Richard III* (1759), the latter of which is still remembered because of Lessing's use of it in the *Dramaturgie* as a peg on which to hang much of his inter-pretation of Aristotle. Lessing will not allow the play the merits of a true tragedy, chiefly because of the unrelieved villainy of the hero, though much of his criticism would apply equally well to Shakespeare's tragedy. He calls it a dramatic poem, but what strikes us most of all if we compare Weisse with Shakespeare is the absence of anything that can be called poetry in the German drama, and the substitution of crude moralising for character interest. Soon Weisse, still following Lessing, introduced English blank verse and a wider range of emotions, though he still kept strictly to the unities and chose for his experiments subjects from the Greek such as *Atreus und Thyest* (1766), the second German play in blank verse to be acted (ten years after Wieland's *Johanna Gray* in Zürich, 1757). In his handling of a confessedly Shakespearian subject, *Romeo und Julie*, in 1767 (for he claimed to have written *Richard III* before reading Shake-speare's play), Weisse showed the same lack of appreciation of Shakespeare's unique quality and the same eagerness to assimi-late him to the style to which the audience was accustomed. The prose domestic drama was now establishing itself in Ger-many, after Lessing's *Miss Sara Sampson* in 1755. *Romeo und*

Julie is in rather flowery prose and the pathos of the situations is exploited to the uttermost, to such good effect that the play had an immediate and unprecedented success, at the Hamburg National Theatre, for instance. In form however, apart from the use of prose, it was a perfectly regular tragedy, pruned of all episodic scenes and comic relief and introducing only eight speaking characters. Of course all Shakespeare's entrancing lyricism had completely vanished.

Only a little less popular were the two sentimental comedies in prose which Weisse had written a year or two before this, dealing with family subjects in an 'English' setting like *Miss Sara Sampson*, but with a happy ending. *Amalia* introduces, like Schlegel's *Triumph der guten Frauen*, a woman dressed as a man who sorts out a matrimonial entanglement, but like Gellert's heroines she is compounded of altruism and touchingly renounces her own claims because, as she is made to tell us just before the curtain falls, 'actions by which we bring about the happiness of others are a source of inexpressible joy'. The title of the second play, *Grossmut um Grossmut,* in itself indicates that these comedies form a link in the chain connecting Gellert's plays with the family pieces of Iffland and Schröder in the 'eighties, with their inevitable parade of good hearts. It is not surprising that when Weisse had attained a position of security, as a collector of taxes, and married, he came to rival the popularity which Gellert had enjoyed before him as a universal adviser in family and literary matters, the editor of an old-fashioned literary periodical (Nicolai's *Bibliothek der schönen Wissenschaften*) and of the first children's paper, *Der Kinderfreund* (from 1775).

Weisse lived to a ripe old age, but the two tragic dramatists who came to the fore at the time of Nicolai's first prize competition in 1756 both died young, like J. E. Schlegel before them. They were both noblemen, educated in Saxony and influenced by the Saxon literary tradition. J. F. von Cronegk (1731–57), received a careful education from tutors and at the Universities of Halle and Leipzig, travelled in Italy and France, and showed early promise of literary powers in various genres. He was encouraged in his dramatic attempts by Koch's troupe and later by Weisse, and passed on in the usual way from character comedy to tragedy. His second tragedy was unfinished when he died at the age of twenty-six. Both are exceedingly dull and completely regular plays in alexandrines, full of declamation and noble sentiments but weak as regards action and character interest. *Codrus* won Nicolai's prize against Brawe's *Freigeist*. *Olint und Sophronia* is only known because it happened to be the play with which the Hamburg National Theatre opened and which Lessing discussed in his first number of the *Dramaturgie*, with very little enthusiasm, but as much as it deserves. The indifference to suffering displayed by the good characters in such dramas of martyrdom, he rightly says, takes all the passion out of tragedy. What tension can there be in a play where 'there is not a single Christian to whom martyrdom and death do not come as easily as drinking a glass of water?'

J. W. von Brawe (1738–58), who died even younger, had more native talent and vigour and gave greater promise as a dramatist. He also enjoyed the advantage of coming under Lessing's personal influence, so that from the first he was less hampered than Cronegk by the Gottsched tradition. After a thorough schooling at one of the well-endowed boarding schools in Saxony, Schulpforta, Brawe had been welcomed in Leipzig by Weisse, who was still living there with his young count, introduced to Lessing, Ewald von Kleist and their friends and infected with the common enthusiasm for tragedy. Gellert's lectures on moral philosophy also left their mark on his first play, for Gellert, unlike Lessing, held deists like this 'free-thinker' to be dangerous people who threatened to undermine all Christian principles of morality. *Der Freigeist* was the work of an ambitious young student, eager to win Nicolai's prize and led to attempt domestic tragedy by the example of *Miss Sara Sampson*. Among the English plays which the plot recalls the most obvious is Young's *Revenge*. Brüggemann's contention, that in the person of Henley, the villain of the piece, who attacks virtue as virtue, not out of self-interest, and calls his Satanism 'honour', we have a study in 'subjectivist' character, is surely an over-intellectual and Nietzschean interpretation of a thoroughly dull and immature play, which is only kept moving by clumsy monologues and scenes with confidants. August Sauer characterised it rightly long ago as a pure tragedy of intrigue.[1] Henley, a kind of super-Iago, lives only for a revenge which shall go on into eternity and to that end tempts his hated rival into unbelief and its accompanying excesses and crimes, for despite all his free-thinking, he cannot but believe, like Franz in *Die Räuber* later, in God and eternal punishment. The play was not acted for ten years and only achieved some success on the stage in the 'seventies, when Henley passed as a good stage villain no cruder than many a Storm and Stress hero.

In his third year at Leipzig Brawe wrote a second tragedy, *Brutus,* on the same theme of revenge, a play more obviously influenced by Lessing. Like so many tragedies of the time, from Gottsched's *Cato* onwards, it is full of stoic sentiment, and like Lessing's *Philotas,* and Ewald von Kleist's *Cissides und Paches,* it reflects the Spartan spirit with which Frederick's example infected his admirers in the early days of the Seven Years' War, being entirely without a love interest. Brawe follows Lessing in treating history simply as a 'repertory of names', for almost the whole of the action is invented. A personal enemy of Brutus brings up the latter's son as his own and through him causes the defeat and death of Brutus at Philippi. The play recalls Lessing's study of the Ancients at this time and his experiments with fate-drama such as the fragment *Das Horoskop,* for a prophetic dream informs Brutus that his doom will come to pass 'through his own blood' and the chief interest of the play is its handling of the conflict in the mind of the son Marcius, thought by Brutus to be dead, when he is brought, rather too ingeniously, into a position resembling that of Œdipus, and in his attempt to avoid patricide comes ever nearer to it. Even before Weisse, Brawe imitated the blank verse with which Lessing was experimenting in the fragment *Cleonnis,* in which every line ends in a stressed syllable. This was too much of a novelty for the theatre of the day, so that in spite of its merits, *Brutus* was only acted once, at Vienna in 1770.

[1] *J. W. v. Brawe,* Strassburg, 1878.

Looking back over the contribution made to the German theatre down to the time of the *Hamburgische Dramaturgie* by educated playwrights, as distinguished from the actor-adapter, who in every troupe provided a large proportion of the repertoire, we are struck by the preponderance of Leipzig writers. There were in fact hardly any elsewhere except three or four in Hamburg, and of the few outside Leipzig most had either come from there or were in personal touch with Gottsched. As Jakob Minor says, 'Germany has never again had an intellectual centre in as full a sense as Leipzig was one in the eighteenth century, down to the 'seventies. Literary groups of influence and importance existed here, one succeeding the other, throughout the century. In the centre of the German book trade and one of the leading German universities, in this market where learning was bought and sold there was no lack of resident literary celebrities, who, as older groups broke up, continually stimulated the formation of new ones. From here Gottsched, Gellert, and for a time, Weisse, dominated German literature and the German theatre. It was here that Goethe was made into a poet and that Schiller was at least introduced for the first time into literary circles.'[1] Although Leipzig was of no political importance, it was intellectually a more important centre than the capital of any of Germany's states, large or small, and everything favoured the growth there of a free intelligentsia. The large crowds it attracted twice a year at fair-time, not only of merchants but of gentlefolk from miles around, with money to spend and time on their hands, made it, as we have seen, the Mecca of travelling players and one of the first commercial towns to have a permanent theatre. Culturally it felt itself to be a 'little Paris', and although the kind of dramatic literature produced in Leipzig is not to be explained from these facts, it would have been very surprising if a Saxon school had not come into being and drawn to itself writers of distinction.[2]

[1] *Lessings Jugendfreunde*, D.N.L., Bd. 72, Einleitung.
[2] For Leipzig as a commercial and cultural centre see *Germany in the 18th century*, pp. 182 ff., 288 ff.

III

THEATRE AND THEORY IN THE AGE OF LESSING

LESSING was born in 1729, when the Neubers were making their first experiments with literary drama, and he only knew the company when he was a student in Leipzig, and Caroline Neuber was playing to audiences which often consisted of a few students. Two years after Lessing had seen the first of his plays staged by her the company was finally dispersed, and Caroline herself, after unsuccessful appearances in Vienna and a miserable old age spent in Saxony, died in 1760. At her funeral the minister refused to let the coffin be carried through the churchyard gate, and it had to be lifted over the wall, so strong was the prejudice, in spite of all her efforts, against a woman who had devoted her whole life to the stage.

The next turning-point in the history of the German theatre and drama came in the 'sixties, with the mature Lessing's creation of plays which were both literary masterpieces and eminently stageworthy, and with the first attempts to found so-called 'National Theatres'. Though Lessing produced comparatively little, his plays were so much superior to those of any contemporary that they set the tone for almost a generation and were imitated by a host of minor writers. At the same time his critical writings opened up wider horizons. In particular, the attention of German dramatists was directed to English drama, as more akin than French to their national genius. Shakespeare came to the knowledge first of a few in the study, and then of many from the stage, while English domestic drama found a welcome which it had not received at home. Most of the remainder of this history will be concerned with the working out of these influences.

But there were many minor figures, actors and dramatists, whose efforts contributed something to the general upward movement in the generation following the Gottsched reforms. To appreciate Lessing's achievement correctly we must follow the career of some of these men, and also keep in mind the general movement of ideas, in the period between the accession of Frederick the Great (1740) and the decade which saw the end of the Seven Years' War, in their relation to social and political developments in Germany.

To begin with the more technical matter of the history of the stage, there are two or three troupes which may be taken as typical representatives of the much larger number about which little is known. It is only in the last quarter of the century with the growth of periodicals devoted to the theatre like Reichard's *Theaterkalender* that we can obtain a bird's-eye view of the theatrical world. We learn from him that in 1776, for instance, more than fourteen German companies were active, some in standing theatres and some on tour. We are probably safe in assuming that at no time since the Neubers had there been less than half a dozen German troupes at work simultaneously, though some of them may have been short-lived and some have appeared only in out-of-the-way corners of the large area where German was spoken.

The most notable principal in the first twenty years of Frederick's reign was J. F. Schönemann, who, as we have seen, sought and obtained Gottsched's patronage on leaving the Neubers. He was a man of some education, seven years younger than Frau Neuber (born in 1704 at Krossen on the Oder). He is said to have attended the Graues Kloster in Berlin and to have studied medicine at Frankfort-on-the-Oder and Halle. Why he took to the stage is not known. As mentioned earlier, he was first with the Förster company, acting the usual trash, then from 1730 to 1739 with Caroline Neuber in her best period. When he set up a company of his own at Lüneburg, his wife's home, in January 1740, he had amongst its eight men and three women three beginners who were all to make a name for themselves, Konrad Ackermann, Sophie Schröder and Konrad Ekhof. He had two other Neuber troupe actors with him (Heyderich and Uhlich), and at first played hardly anything that is not to be found in her repertoire. He began for instance in his Lüneburg barn with Racine's *Mithridate,* translated by Professor Witter of Strassburg, which she had presented in Hamburg two years earlier, and of the fifteen full-length plays he is known to have given in the first year, nine at least were from her repertoire. They consisted of *Der sterbende Cato* and various translations of the French classics. They met with some success, especially where the court circles whose patronage he too aimed at could be interested in them, at Schwerin for instance on his first tour, and he tells us how much he was helped by letters of recommendation from people of rank to friends in his places of call.

There are characteristic novelties however already in the first year. They include two tragedies, the work of the young J. E. Schlegel, soon to prove the most promising German dramatist of his day, and a comedy by Holberg, translated by the Hamburger Detharding. Schönemann continued to give special attention to new German dramatists, and to cultivate the character comedy of the Holberg type, which represents a further step towards the domestic drama, making a far less formal and foreign impression on a German audience than the French classics, even the comedies of Molière which were Holberg's model. But though Schönemann's ambition from the outset was to outdo Caroline Neuber in educating the public up to literary drama, he had to make the same sort of concessions to public taste as she had found necessary. In his six months' season in Hamburg he even gave a few of the old Haupt- und Staatsaktionen enlivened by Harlequin scenes, the type of play in which he had learnt his craft and which still affected his style of acting. He never came to be quite at home in classical tragedy, and the critics speak of the 'affectation and unnaturalness' of the Schönemann school. He found that the Hamburg public at any rate had lost its taste now for strong meat of this sort, but it still demanded comic after-pieces, and Schönemann continued to supply them, here and elsewhere, for many years after this, often farces without a title that must have been largely improvised. Those with titles are frequently from Frau Neuber's repertoire. He also gave a good deal of ballet and of burlesque pantomime.

French sentimental comedy continued to be very popular. New translations were constantly being added to his repertoire, and his company acted in all a dozen plays of Destouches, seven of Marivaux, five of La Chaussée, and many by minor French contemporaries like Le Grand, Delisle, Saint Foix and Boissy. Molière was acted occasionally, some ten plays in all, but the classical tragedies of Corneille and Racine steadily lost favour, though Voltaire, as a contemporary celebrity, still made an appeal, ten plays of his being acted.

The outstanding successes in the early 'forties were the character comedies, owing particularly to the acting of Ekhof and Ackermann. Ackermann of course soon became independent, but Ekhof stayed with Schönemann till the end, in 1757. He was the particular star of the troupe and its virtual head in the later years. The greatest attraction of all among these comedies was provided by the Hamburg bookkeeper Borkenstein in *Der Bookesbeutel,* a comedy of Hamburg life. Its strong local appeal combined with the new level of natural acting attained by the company—Ekhof as a Hamburg man spoke Plattdeutsch, and in the later performances of the play at any rate three rôles were acted in dialect—to make this play quite extraordinarily popular. It was acted sixteen times to full houses, says Schütze, in the first season.

It is not difficult even for a modern reader to understand the appeal this play had for Hamburg audiences. For the first time they saw unmistakable citizens of Hamburg on the stage in a fulllength prose comedy. There had been realism in some of the operas earlier in the century, but nothing so convincing as this. It is a comedy of manners rather than of character, full of homely touches. The opening scene shows us mother and daughter, one knitting, one sewing, while their two maids spin, and all sing in chorus from a new songbook decidedly free 'lay songs'. We are not surprised after this to learn that the daughter has had no education and behaves like a servant girl herself, though her father is a welltodo rentier. He is too mean and the mother too ignorant to bring up their daughter better, so she finds no favour in the eyes of the young Leipzig merchant, a friend of her brother's, who before seeing her had thought of her as a possible match for himself, and he proposes to her poor but better educated friend instead. The introduction of refined visitors from 'Klein Paris' into an old-fashioned Hamburg household gives the author many opportunities of poking fun at the 'Schlendrian', the ignorant conservatism, of some of his fellow-townsmen. That is what the title itself means, the 'book-purse', in which women in earlier days had carried their prayer-book, having become a symbol for everything out of date.

The chief characters, the offensively rude and miserly Grobian and his wife and daughter, are types such as the local 'moral weekly', *Der Patriot*, had been satirising for years, but the well-observed detail of their everyday life made them live for con-temporaries, and for us now has a period interest, as when Frau Grobian, hearing that the strangers have been invited to stay to dinner, exclaims: 'What, must I lay a clean tablecloth and pewter plates (instead of wooden platters) in the middle of the week?' —for no one in their circle thought of inviting anyone to a meal except on Sundays. The Hamburg dishes that are mentioned by name, like 'Plücktefinken' and 'Bunkenknochen', the description of table manners and of marriage customs, or of the monosyllabic conversation and uninhibited behaviour of young men and women in the merchant class, and a dozen other similar details are quite clearly drawn from life, whereas the fashion-plate figures of the polite Leipzigers with whom the rude natives are con-trasted never come to life at all. The play is rather clumsily constructed by an obvious amateur who has read his Gottsched, and makes all the action take place in a few hours in the 'Saal' of Grobian's house. The moral of the work, too, is one that the master would approve, namely that the education of children, especially of girls, and Hamburg manners in general, were in sad need of improvement, though the humour is more boisterous and genuine than in most of the comedies of his school. The drastic nature of the language, imitated perhaps, like the descrip-tive names (Grobian, Gutherz, Sittenreich) from Holberg, anticipates the boldness of *Götz von Berlichingen*, but would not shock a generation accustomed to Hanswurst.

Borkenstein's comedy was frequently imitated. It was the earliest ancestor of the Hamburg 'local comedy' which retained its popularity with small suburban theatres down to the present century.[1] A curious link between the generations is the fact that Borkenstein's daughter Susanna (he married very late, when he had made a fortune) became the wife of the Frankfort banker Gontard, and was celebrated by Hölderlin as 'Diotima'—a very different Susanna from the one in the play.

Schönemann had enjoyed a certain measure of success in Hamburg. He had for some months attracted good audiences to the opera house, the only good theatre in Hamburg, which had been let to the Neubers for the first time two years earlier, German opera being now quite dead in the city. He had improved on the Neubers' performances of French classics, especially in the matter of costume, and scored a hit with character comedy, as well as with pastoral plays like Rost's *Gelernte Liebe* and Gottsched's *Atalanta*. These pastorals, in which songs and dancing were important ingredients, were a popular and inexpensive substitute for opera until displaced by comic opera a few years later. They were cultivated particularly in Leipzig, and Goethe's *Laune des Verliebten*, written there, is in the same tradition. Schönemann had been taken up to some extent by literary circles. With some of his company he had been invited to the homes of Behrmann, the dramatist and patron of the Neubers, and Brockes, a poet with more than a local reputation. All this tended to raise the status of the profession, but Schönemann could not escape the necessity of moving on to new audiences. He tried, as the Neubers had done two years before him, to introduce a system of season tickets, but there was little response. Audiences grew smaller and smaller for lack of variety, and intrigues within the company led to the secession of Mme Schröder and Ackermann. The new company they founded obtained, after a lawsuit with Schönemann, the lease of the opera house from Easter 1742,

---

[1] See the reprint, ed. F. F. Heitmüller, in Sauer's *Deutsche Litteraturdenkmale*, and the same author's *Hamburgische Dramatiker zur Zeit Gottscheds*, Wandsbeck, 1890.

and Schönemann, who had been on tour in the north-west, was unable to return to Hamburg. He had again a promising reception in Schwerin, where the court had approved of him in 1740, but there was no sign yet of the permanent support he was to obtain here later, and he turned his eyes towards Berlin, a field to far entirely uncultivated by the exponents of regular drama.

The Berlin stage in 1742, in spite of the Philosopher on the Throne, presented a picture typical of German conditions at their worst. Frederick of course shared the admiration of most of his fellow-rulers for French literature and drama. It is well known how as Crown Prince he surrounded himself in Rheinsberg with French literary men, and seemed to have made the writing of good French prose one of his principal aims in life. In the year of his accession, 1740, though he displayed a very different sort of ambition in his immediate seizure of Silesia, he did not forget to foster the arts in Berlin, so greatly neglected in his father's time, though it was by the characteristic step of engaging a French troupe of actors for his private theatre, and sending his architect, Knobelsdorf, and his master of music, Graun, to study abroad. In 1741, in spite of the expense of the Silesian campaign, Prince Henry, in his name, laid the foundation-stone of Berlin's first opera house, and Italian singers and a French ballet were brought to the court. Meanwhile the licence of the notorious 'strong man', J. C. von Eckenberg, who had been entertaining Berlin at various times since 1717, but particularly in the early 'thirties, had been renewed, and the pantaloon of his troupe, Hilverding, had set up on his own and also been licensed. Eckenberg was a saddler's son who gave up his father's trade after marrying a tightrope-walker and took to the road in variety. He had been as far afield as Switzerland, Sweden and Denmark, had prospered at times and somehow added a 'von' to his name, perhaps by purchase of a title in Denmark. From an early date he had engaged actors to supplement the display of his own strength and his wife's agility, and given every kind of entertainment, from acrobatics and shadow-plays to miming and farcical comedy.

By 1742 Berlin was tired of this kind of thing and some few

were a little ashamed, so that there was a chance for Schönemann to try his luck, which he did, with the King's permission, from September 1742, opening with Gottsched's *Cato*, and Rost's pastoral, and continuing with the repertoire already described. As even this fare was a novelty for Berlin and had a certain prestige, Schönemann was so successful in the first few months that he applied for permission to build a theatre of his own, instead of continuing to use the improvised stage in the town hall that had sufficed till now for German companies. He was promised a site and even timber for the building by the King, but in the meantime Knobelsdorf had built the opera house and it had been opened in the King's presence with Graun's new opera, *Caesar and Cleopatra* (December 1742). This and other court entertainments put the German players, with their restricted repertoire, quite in the shade. Frederick could not be persuaded, as Schönemann wrote to Gottsched, that a German could write or German actors perform anything worth seeing on the stage, much less to go to see a German play for himself. The usual allegorical Vorspiele on the King's birthday and so on made no impression for all their fulsome flattery. In vain a twenty-year-old student, J. C. Krüger, who had just joined the troupe and became a productive theatre poet, brought together in his *Das beglückte Berlin* Justice, Truth, Reverence, Joy, The Golden Age and The Spirit of Providence to sing Frederick's praises; it all fell on deaf ears, and Schönemann, giving up the idea of settling in Berlin, applied for and obtained in August 1743 a licence to tour in Prussian lands. Uhlich, then in his troupe, wrote to Gottsched at Christmas 1743: 'We have been acting to empty benches, for as there are special festivities at court every day, which anyone can see for nothing, we have no hopes of good takings. Yesterday, for Christmas Eve, there was a masked ball. Operas are being produced with lavish splendour.' In the following May Frederick succeeded at last in acquiring the famous Italian dancer, Barbarina, for his capital, and established her in a palace in the Behrenstrasse, but by this time the unfortunate champion of the regular German drama had exchanged theatres with Franz Schuch in Breslau, the specialist in extempore farces, for despite the low opinion Frederick had had of the Breslau manager a year before, he was quite willing that the Berlin public should have what it liked in unimportant matters.

Schönemann seems to have made few additions to his reper-toire in Berlin. The biggest innovation, not a success at the time, but important as foreshadowing a new type of entertainment, the comic opera, was his performance in January 1743 of a transla-tion by C.W. von Borck of Coffey's *The Devil to Pay*, one of the successors of Gay's *Beggar's Opera*. The translator had witnessed the popularity of this new kind of opera in London, where he had been Prussian *chargé d'affaires*. He had also made the acquaint-ance of Shakespeare's plays—for all that German critics might say later about the neglect of Shakespeare in England, no intelli-gent foreigner who resided there could fail to see that his plays were very frequently performed, with some adaptation, both in London and the provinces. Herr von Borck was the first translator of a complete work of Shakespeare into German, with his version of *Julius Caesar* (1741), but the time was not ripe for its perform-ance, and Gottsched, as we saw, dismissed it with scorn. The Leipzig arbiter of taste certainly cannot have approved of *The Devil to Pay* either, but was probably not consulted, any more than about Schönemann's farces. The operette had some success in Hamburg, but it was only in Weisse's livelier version (see p. 81), with new German music, that it became all the rage nine years later, when Gottsched's opposition only made him ridiculous.

We need not accompany Schönemann on his later wanderings, with all their disappointments and occasional successes. His repertoire continued to be a mixture of classical French comedy, *comédie larmoyante* and Holberg, a steadily decreasing proportion of French tragedy, and an all too small number of original German plays, mostly comedies, provided by his theatre poets Krüger and Uhlich, by Frau Gottsched, Quistorp and Gellert in Leipzig, and by J. E. Schlegel. Sentimental comedy pre-dominated, in versions better adapted now to German audiences. We have seen that in Marivaux's *L'héritier de village* (*Der Bauer mit der Erbschaft*), for instance, Ekhof could speak Plattdeutsch, as in *Der Bookesbeutel*. Even after serious plays like Racine's *Iphigénie*

94

there was often a display of dancing by a few members of the company, sometimes two, sometimes as many as five, and a farcical afterplay was still almost a necessity. The very high proportion of translated plays performed is easily seen from the seven volumes of the *Schönemannsche Schaubühne* (1748–55) in which, following Gottsched's lead, the manager published the chief plays of his repertoire. Almost all their contents, apart from a few comedies by Krüger, are from the French.

Schönemann's prefaces to these volumes are all concerned with the difficulties he encountered as actor-manager. In Volume II, writing after nine years' experience, he says that he has been hampered particularly by three prejudices, that of the low-brows, as we should say, who reject anything they do not them-selves understand, that of the timid Francophiles, who, not content to learn from the French, think that the Germans will never come up to French standards, and that of the clergy, with their moral objections to the theatre. He claims, as was men-tioned above, a highly moral influence for the theatre, its chief aim being, he says, to temper the passions. J. C. Krüger went further, and soon after joining his troupe published anonymously the already mentioned comedy, *Die Geistlichen auf dem Lande*, his first and weakest play. Here he carried the war into the enemy's territory, representing the clergy as vicious hypocrites. The play was never acted. In his third volume Schönemann com-plains of the ignorance and pedantry he has found in aesthetic matters in universities, and of the disgraceful behaviour of well-dressed students in the theatre, where they puff clouds of tobacco smoke on to the stage itself. He makes however an honourable exception of Leipzig. In the fifth volume there is finally out-spoken criticism of the actors themselves, most of whom, he says, had only taken to the stage as a last resort when youthful mis-demeanours had brought them low in the world. No wonder if far too many of them have proved, in his experience, extrava-gant, lazy, loose-living, ungrateful and conceited.

By 1751, when this volume was published, Schönemann has clearly lost all his illusions about the theatre, yet it was in this same year that his ducal patron at Schwerin made him his

'Court Comedian' with a fixed salary, and he continued to enjoy this support until the Duke's death in 1756, playing for most of each year at Schwerin, though he was free to put in a four months' season in Hamburg. The effect on Schönemann was disastrous. He took life very easily now and indulged in extravagant hobbies like horse-dealing, while the troupe went steadily down, in spite of Ekhof's unflagging devotion to his art, which led to the foundation of a rather grandiloquently named 'Actors' Academy' in 1753. Ekhof wanted the actors themselves to take some of the responsibility for the company's productions, and got them for about a year to meet in council once a week, to discuss the principles of their art and current practical problems of production. It was clearly the idea of a serious-minded artist serving under a rather slack manager. This experiment in democracy was taken up later at several leading theatres, Vienna, Mannheim and Weimar, for instance, but it cannot be said to have been a great success anywhere, and it certainly did not hold Schönemann's troupe together for long. When the Academy had died a natural death Ekhof became the virtual manager, and when finally he left the company in 1757 Schönemann quickly found himself in an untenable position, however many farces and extemporised plays he might give to the Hamburg public. He closed down his theatre in December of this year and went back to his horses at Schwerin, where he lingered on, a typical decayed actor, sustained by the bottle and his memories, until 1782.

The second of the trio of successors to the Neubers, G. H. Koch (1703–75), did not start a company of his own until he was nearly fifty, after twenty-one years as actor and theatre-poet with the Neubers. He obtained the Saxon licence for a troupe which he brought together there in 1750, and for several years had a hard struggle in Saxony, interrupted by one not very successful visit to Hamburg in 1755. Harlequin had often to help him out. In 1758 he took over the Schönemann company, as joint manager with Ekhof, and for the rest of the war years, until 1763, he remained in Hamburg, occasionally paying a visit to Lübeck. This was a distinct approach to a permanent theatre.

No principal had maintained himself in Hamburg for such a long period before, and Koch only contrived to keep his theatre going by offering a most varied programme, a few tragedies, a great many comedies, including in the later years a few plays by Cibber and Colman, translated by Bode, comic operas, ballets, and of course the usual farcical afterpieces. He had been the first to stage Weisse's adaptation of Coffey's *The Devil to Pay* (Leipzig 1752) with new music by Standfuss, and he eventually made comic opera very popular. To make tragedy tolerable he had before this gone back to the practice of the previous century of introducing 'intermezzi' between the acts, miniature comic operas like *La serva padrona*, and in Hamburg he engaged Italians to sing in them. The public taste for these often charming trifles was shared, we may note, by Frederick the Great, who all through his reign maintained a small Italian troupe at Potsdam to play them for him. In tragedy Koch and his troupe, like the Neubers, still imitated the French style of acting, with the stiff and formal 'grace of a dancing-master' that Lessing still had to criticise in Hamburg (*Dramaturgie*, No. 4). He usually played them still in the traditional court dress, though sometimes a kind of classical costume was attempted. War conditions favoured him in Hamburg, where many strangers had taken refuge, but as soon as the war was over he returned to Leipzig. In 1764 Ekhof left his troupe to join Ackermann's. After a year in Dresden at the Court Theatre, which, though unsuccessful, was at least encouraging in that a leading court had at last shown some interest in a German company, Koch had the first proper theatre built which Leipzig had ever known, and opened it in October 1766 with Schlegel's *Hermann* and a Regnard comedy. It was an important innovation that in the costumes for *Hermann* some attempt was made to indicate the period. For reasons which will be discussed later, comic opera now became all the rage, and it was Koch's company, naturally enough, which started the fashion, with Weisse's revised version of *The Devil to Pay* (*Der Teufel ist los*), with music by Hiller. A long series of similar works, mostly by Weisse and Hiller, followed, and these too achieved great popularity all over the country. The lyrics in them became the best-known songs of the day, and mark an important stage in the history of the German 'lied'. These Leipzig productions were so attractive to students of the university that a professor started an agitation against the new theatre mania (his lecture hour was five o'clock, when the theatre opened), with the result that the number of performances permitted by the town council was reduced to two, and Koch was about to close down when he was invited to Weimar by the Duchess Anna Amalia. Between 1768 and 1771 he was subsidised by this court, only leaving Weimar to act in Leipzig at fair-time. New comic operas were written for him by Musäus and composed by Wolf —both residents of Weimar with court posts. In the last four years of his life Koch ran a troupe in Berlin (1771–75), where he was the first in Germany to perform *Götz* (1773), and *Clavigo* (1774).

Koch was a steadier character than Schönemann and well earned the respect of the public. An ingenious and economical manager, he did everything that could be done in his time to maintain a repertoire on a reasonably high level, but like the rest he was handicapped by the lack of suitable German plays and by the low taste of his audiences, to which he certainly made great concessions. One must remember that there was still a good deal of competition to be met from foreign troupes. He was already far from the strolling player, however, and had succeeded in maintaining in the same town for years at a time something like what we should now call a repertory theatre. This was the first step towards the later National Theatres. His Leipzig theatre evoked too the first German publication devoted entirely to theatrical criticism, in the *Schildereien der Koch'schen Bühne* (1755).

The third notable company was that of Konrad Ackermann, one of the original members of Schönemann's troupe, who left him with Sophie Schröder, as we have seen, in 1741. Ackermann was a north German of good education, born at Schwerin in 1712. Nothing definite is known about his early history, but he was a well-built man of soldierly bearing and hot temper, who had apparently seen service abroad. Sophie Schröder, having left her husband, an organist in Berlin, who was drinking himself to death, made a living by fine sewing till she joined Schöne/ mann's company in 1739. The first company she and Acker/ mann started, in her name, only lasted for two years, and its repertoire was on the same lines as Schönemann's. Character comedy, in which Ackermann had already distinguished him/ self, made up the greater part of it, tragedies were also attempted and harlequinades, before or after the main play, were not despised. Sophie Schröder's husband, hearing stories about her success, came to live on her for a time early in 1744, then returned to Berlin, where he soon afterwards died. But the company was not well supported, and before Friedrich Ludwig Schröder was born in Schwerin at the end of 1744, it had already been wound up, and his mother was again earning her living with em/ broidery. In 1746, however, Ackermann tried his luck again, in Danzig, and Sophie Schröder soon joined him, only to meet with failure again. With some colleagues they both joined a German troupe in Russia next year, and it was in St. Peters/ burg that the three/year/old F. L. Schröder made his first stage appearance, as an angel of innocence, with six words to say, a part which he played so well that the Empress Elisabeth took him on her knee and fondled him. This and the wedding of Ackermann with his mother in 1749 were among his earliest memories. While they were acting in Moscow he was sent to his first school. The family arrived back in Danzig in 1752, just before the birth of Dorothea Ackermann.

In the next year Ackermann conceived the bold plan of build/ ing himself a theatre in Königsberg, and started a new company, which played first in a hired hall there, and then, till the theatre was ready for them, went on tour to Warsaw, Breslau, Glogau, Frankfort/on/Oder, Halle, Magdeburg, Berlin, Frankfort again, Stettin and Danzig. In Warsaw young Schröder attended a Jesuit school for a month or two, and willingly fell in with the suggestion of one of the Fathers, that he should run away from his parents and join them, so neglected and unhappy was he at home, but he was soon found and brought back. Ackermann's new company made a name for itself in the performance of tragedy, old and new, especially the domestic tragedy just being imported in those years from England, and immediately recognised by Ackermann as promising from his professional point of view. They did *The Gamester,* for instance, at Breslau (1st Octover, 1754) three weeks before Schönemann staged *The London Merchant* at Hamburg, and they followed him with this play at Halle, so that when they were in Berlin on the same tour, Lessing made Ackermann's acquaintance and arranged to give him his new play, *Miss Sara Sampson.* It was performed for the first time, most successfully, on 10th July, 1755, at FrankfortonOder, in the presence of the author. Ackermann was the first Mellefont, his wife Lady Marwood, and little Arabella was played by the tenyearold Schröder. Though tragedy made up nearly half the company's repertoire at this time, what was called 'ballet', a sort of mime combined with dancing, on the lines of the old harlequinades, was already a specialty of theirs too, and it was in ballet that young Schröder was first trained.

At last, in November 1755, Ackermann could begin his performances in his own theatre in Königsberg. He was the first manager to take the bold step of borrowing money enough to build a permanent theatre, eleven years before Koch did the same in Leipzig, so that in a way, this is more of a turningpoint than the establishment of the socalled National Theatre, which developed out of his second venture of the same kind, at Hamburg, after the Seven Years' War. His first never came to much because of the war, for at the end of 1756, Ackermann felt so nervous about the Russian advance that he decided to abandon his theatre temporarily, and to take his company on tour outside the battle area. During the year in Königsberg, he had added twenty plays to his repertoire, one of the most popular being Pfeil's *Lucie Woodvil,* an imitation of *Miss Sara Sampson.*

When the Ackermanns went away, the only member of the family left behind was the boy Schröder, now twelve years old, and a boarder at the Königsberg Collegium Fridericianum. The lawyer who was supposed to be his guardian paid no attention to him, no money was sent for his school fees and he had therefore to leave the school in July 1757. He was not sorry to do so because of the pietistic narrowness and extremely harsh discipline of the establishment, where, as a high-spirited, carelessly brought-up child he was always in scrapes. For a year, living with the caretaker of the theatre, a cobbler, he had not even enough to eat, and was left to run completely wild, learning conjuring tricks from a mountebank who hired the theatre for a few months, and practising all kinds of risky acrobatic feats. He saw the Prussian army retreating before the Cossacks, and by the beginning of 1758 Russian troops were temporarily quartered in the theatre. Then a Scotch tight-rope walker called Stuart, and his charming young Danish wife, hired the theatre and began to look after the boy with the greatest kindness. The gentleman-vagabond Stuart declaimed Shakespeare to him in English, and his wife taught him French, English and music. He was about to sail with them to England when at last, early in 1759, he received a letter from his stepfather, now in Switzerland, telling him to go to a relative in Lübeck. After many adventures on the sea voyage he reached Lübeck and finally joined the troupe in Basel in April 1759, having been parted from them for over two years.

It was not until the end of the war that Ackermann settled down again, this time in Hamburg. The troupe toured until spring 1761, mainly in Switzerland and Alsace, making a precarious livelihood, welcomed in some places, but in others finding Swiss town councils very suspicious of strolling players, because they had seen so few. In Zürich Wieland was in the audience, and soon afterwards they performed his blank-verse tragedy *Johanna Gray* at Winterthur, in his presence, but although the verses were good, there was no dramatic life in the play. Apart from this there were few novelties in the repertoire of these years, though new translations were added, including in 1759 Diderot's *Fils Naturel* and *Père de Famille* and Lesage's *Turcaret*, the new French 'drames'. From summer 1761 Ackermann moved gradually farther north, from Freiburg and Karlsruhe to Frankfort-on-Main and Mainz, and on to Hanover, Göttingen and finally Hamburg, in the summer of 1764. As the prospects here pleased him at first, he gave up the idea of returning to Königsberg and prepared to play in Hamburg for an indefinite period, going to the length, as has been mentioned, of again building a theatre with borrowed money. When the National Theatre was set up three years later, the directors simply leased this building from him, took over his company, and added no more and no better works to the existing repertoire during their two years of management than had been usual under him in the preceding years. There had been twelve full-length plays added, or revived, in 1765, seventeen in 1766, and three before Easter 1767, when the new management came into action. After Easter there were ten more that year and thirteen again in the following year. 'There was no alteration at all in the quality of the repertory or in the manner in which plays were produced and acted. Indeed, if anything, the change was for the worse. The fact that Lessing was associated with the undertaking was purely adventitious and exerted no influence on the conduct of the theatre; and Lessing made no concealment of his powerlessness.'[1]

The story of the Hamburg National Theatre is clearly told in Professor J. G. Robertson's scholarly study of the *Hamburgische Dramaturgie*, the running commentary on the work of the theatre which Lessing was commissioned to write, and we may confine ourselves here to a bare outline. The moving spirit in the foundation of the theatre was J. F. Löwen, a secretary and literary man, forty years old, who had taken a special interest in theatrical matters since his student days, served as dramatic critic of a Hamburg newspaper and, coming into close touch with Schönemann's troupe in Hamburg, had married the daughter of the principal, herself an actress of talent in the troupe. On their moving to Schwerin he had joined them there, obtaining a small official post under the government which left him plenty of free time to spend in Hamburg whenever he could find any writing to do for the theatre, as he did for instance when Ackermann settled there. Ackermann evidently soon found him less of a help than a hindrance, and took on again as his hack writer a man who had in earlier years combined this post with that of tutor to young Schröder. It is no wonder if Löwen was offended at being rejected in favour of a drunken nonentity who was in

<hr>

[1] J. G. Robertson, *Lessing's Dramatic Theory*, p. 20.

the habit of going to bed in his boots, but even from his surviving writings we can see that he was himself an extremely conceited man, with a bee in his bonnet and a passion for intrigue. In his *History of the German Theatre* (1766), a pamphlet put together with the help of Ekhof, and chiefly concerned with the Neubers and their three successors, in the *Preliminary notice* about the coming national theatre, and in his *Address to the staff of the Hamburg Theatre on taking over its directorship*,[1] he deals with the present defects of the German theatre and his plans for its im-provement.

The main defects he sees are: that all existing troupes are touring companies run by uncultivated actor-managers for profit, that the actors are themselves uncultivated and lacking in self-respect, that they are not supported by princes or big towns, and are everywhere opposed by the clergy, and finally that there are not enough good dramatists to provide them with a German repertoire. As we have seen, this is all quite sound criticism, and Löwen strongly stresses the importance of the social back-ground in explaining this situation. The remedies are: (1) To establish in some large town, in Berlin for preference, or failing that, in Hamburg, a standing theatre not run for profit, and con-trolled by a salaried director—from the beginning he clearly thought of himself as the obvious choice for this post; (2) to set up a dramatic academy, where actors might be given cultural and technical education. In Hamburg he took this task upon himself; (3) to raise the status of actors, by paying them well, assuring them of pensions, and in return insisting on their good behaviour; (4) to encourage dramatists by the offer of prizes.

Some of these ideas were old projects of Ekhof's, as we have seen. Others, e.g. the suggestion of a subsidised theatre, with salaried actors, had been put forward in Denmark by J. E. Schlegel, and only recently published in his collected works. But the original source of all such plans was of course the French national theatre, the *Comédie-Française*, established in 1680.

In order to carry out his grandoise idea, Löwen needed financial support, and if possible an existing theatre, and he found both

[1] All reprinted and edited by H. Stümke, 1905.

in Hamburg. He gradually interested two business men in the project. One, Herr Bubbers, had once been an actor himself, and still kept open house for people of the theatre, and another, Abel Seyler, of whom a good deal will be heard in this history, was a Swiss of a type unusual in that country, rather like Thomas Mann's Christian Buddenbrook, who had made money in Hamburg but was rapidly losing it. He was readily persuaded to come in because his mistress was the leading actress in Ackermann's troupe, the redoubtable Sophie Hensel, who liked the notion of a theatre where she would have the management in her pocket. Seyler's business partner, Tillemann, was brought in too, and nine other Hamburg citizens, who however gave little active support. What is not quite clear is why Ackermann agreed to be bought out, when he was not in any greater financial straits than usual. But Löwen, out of spite, had organised hostile criticism of his theatre, which perhaps made him uncertain of the future, and at fifty-five he was losing his memory and his grip of business. The 'Consortium' offered him rather good terms, which, he thought, would allow him and his wife, who hardly acted at all now, to retire from active work, while still able to keep an eye on their young daughters, who both obtained contracts with the new company. F. L. Schröder refused to stay, and went off to the company of Kurz, at Mainz. Seyler became business manager and Löwen artistic director, but though Löwen made and published the already mentioned oration about the momentous nature of this new venture, he proved to have no personality and therefore no influence over the actors, who simply laughed at him. The Consortium allowed the leading actor of the troupe, Konrad Ekhof, to arrange the repertoire and do the casting, all on the same lines as before.

It might well be argued that this Hamburg 'Enterprise', due to the persistent intrigues of a 'Theaternarr' and an ambitious actress, and to the gullibility of a few business men, who soon saw that this theatre would prove too big a strain on their resources, does not deserve all the fuss that has been made about it, and would have been completely forgotten but for Lessing's *Hamburgische Dramaturgie*. But it was at any rate symptomatic, and it started a movement for which a good deal of backing proved to be available, so that the inference seems reasonable that some subsidised German theatre of this kind would have been attempted round about this time, if not in Hamburg, then in some other centre of population. There had been moves in the same direction in two court towns three years before this, in the tiny Hildburghausen, owing to the whim of a prince, and in Vienna, where the German theatre, though still in a poor way, was being referred to as a 'Nationalbühne' at any rate in 1766. The word 'national' could be more fittingly used of a theatre in the capital of the Holy Roman Empire of the German Nation than else-where.

After the Hamburg experiment, the term 'national theatre' came to mean, in the first place, a theatre which, unlike the court theatres or the touring companies, should appeal to the whole national community, not merely to a section of it. And in the second place it meant a non-commercial, permanent theatre, subsidised, like other institutions that already existed in the German states for educational and cultural purposes. The desire for it arose primarily out of the efforts made by Gottsched, and the actors and writers who took up his idea, to give Germany a drama and theatre comparable with those of the French. There was cultural nationalism in this, for many Germans had become conscious of the cultural backwardness of their country and were eager to overcome it. There was also in it the aim characteristic of the 'Enlightenment' everywhere, to raise the moral tone of society generally, and to combat prejudices, unworthy of reasonable men, associated with confessional, regional and class differences. A higher degree of cultural integration based on the national language, almost the only cultural possession that was common to the whole people, was what these enthusiasts were seeking, and there were good reasons why, in the Germany of that age, they should try to bring it about by enlisting the aid of the state, an idea which would not readily have occurred in that century to individualistic Englishmen. The champions of culture were eager to do what the churches had failed to do, but they were accustomed to a church that was state-protected, and they aspired to similar guarantees for their movement, especially as they had seen the rulers of all the larger German states establishing foreign operas and theatres, and training musicians, artists and craftsmen at the expense of the state—or the ruler, it came to the same thing —with some regard perhaps to the general good, but primarily for the pleasure of a small ruling class.

It is not only in this respect that German developments were intimately bound up with absolutism and 'Kleinstaaterei'. There was, as J. Petersen has pointed out,[1] no other forum, no parliament, for instance, where the unified language which Luther had brought into being could be heard by the whole nation. 'On the stage German art, reaching out towards the future, made for itself a "fatherland" that knew no internal divisions, but extended as far as the German language was heard', and he reminds us that even to-day, the German equivalent for 'the King's English' is 'the language of the stage'. If Burke had been born in Germany, Leslie Stephen once suggested, he might have been a Lessing. 'The English political order tended to divert literary merit into political channels.'[2] In Germany, on the other hand, we find among dramatists many who in England might have been politicians, and still more who, in an earlier age, would certainly have been preachers, but for the one career they were born too soon, and for the other too late. In the same way the educated public in Germany, in the late eighteenth century, seems to have obtained a similar satisfaction from seeing certain plays to that which an Englishman might feel at a political meeting, and certainly the greater popularity of the theatre, and of other forms of art, in Germany than in England at this time was due in part to the exclusion of the middle class from politics. The more serious-minded went to the theatre to be confirmed in their view of life, to have the pleasure of saying to themselves: 'That is just what I feel', though it would probably not be about any large public issue, but on some question of family life. It is probably not accidental that in Russia, over a hundred years later, we again find actors and public speaking of the theatre frequently as a

---

[1] *Das deutsche Nationaltheater*, Leipzig and Berlin, 1919.
[2] *English literature and society in the 18th century*, p. 197.

kind of holy place, a temple of art. Just as Löwen, in his grandilo-
quent inaugural address to the Hamburg actors, spoke to them
of the 'theatralisches Heiligtum', the temple in which they were
to serve, so we hear in the 1890's of an anecdote which Chekhov
liked to tell, about an actor who, after a rehearsal, refused to
whistle on the stage some tune that a lady friend had asked him
for, with the words: 'Would you whistle in church? And isn't
the theatre a church?'

LESSING AND THE ENLIGHTENMENT

To understand the wider implications of such a view of the
theatre, and to see the unity of intention behind the very diverse
writings of Lessing, we must stand a little farther back from the
subject for a moment and consider the movement of the Enlightenment in a rather more general way than was necessary
for the discussion of Gottsched's personality and writings. We
are primarily concerned here with Lessing as critic and dramatist,
but we shall find that the whole man entered into each of his
works, in which his developing philosophy of life found each
year a more adequate expression. Like every writer, he was concerned above all with just those problems which were felt to be
important by his age, and it is one of his great merits that his
mind was capable of assimilating so much of the best of what
had been thought and felt not only by his contemporaries, but by
their great predecessors since the Greeks. He had something
already of that 'panoramic ability' which was later to be a
characteristic of Goethe, and in a measure of all the greater
German writers. Lessing acknowledged freely that he had
'warmed himself at the fire of others', and his borrowings were
indeed innumerable, but he was no mere compiler or imitator.
With materials taken from many sources he built something truly
his own, stamped with his intellectual energy and tolerant
humanity, completely individual in style, and answering the
needs of his time. Even to appreciate the transformation which
he helped to bring about in the theatre we must ask ourselves
what these intellectual and spiritual needs were, and what

contributions were being made by other minds towards meeting them.

The name Enlightenment (Aufklärung) expresses 'the sense of relief and escape' that was everywhere in evidence among the enlightened few at having left the dark ages finally behind them. Emerging from tutelage, in Kant's famous words in his essay *What is Aufklärung?* and having at last the courage to think for themselves, they felt full of confidence in their power, as intelligent individual minds, to understand and re-shape their world. It was the same kind of feeling, of man's ability to become his own providence, as is widespread, we are told, in the Russia of our own day. In its more modest way, 'the eighteenth century', as A. N. Whitehead says, 'was a success. If you had asked one of the wisest and most typical of its ancestors, who just saw its commencement, John Locke, what he expected from it, he could hardly have pitched his hopes higher than its actual achieve-ments.'[1] These practical results were only possible because of the 'century of genius' which had preceded it, when by careful observation of the natural world, with the attention concentrated on those features of experience which could be weighed and measured, the founders of modern science had at the same time fundamentally changed man's outlook. They established a new kind of rationalism, with different first principles from that of the visionary Middle Ages, for they were intent on rationalising not the infinite, but everyday life.

In the ages of faith, men had started from a 'measure of proba-bility', to use Lecky's phrase, which was theological. From the seventeenth century, though still humanly credulous on occasion, they measured the probability of things by secular standards, so that they gradually ceased to believe, for instance, in magic and witchcraft, and at the same time the supernatural and historical side of Christianity began to lose its appeal. The religious con-flicts which were the consequence of the Reformation had ulti-mately the same effect of shaking belief in dogma as such. It had to be shown to be reasonable, by the new scientific standards, to be accepted, for instance, by the English deists, who prided

---

[1] *Science in the modern world*, p. 79.

themselves on consistency. Even leading churchmen showed no real interest in dogma, but like Archbishop Tillotson (died 1694) preached sermons whose content 'was little more than a prudential morality, based rather on reason than on revelation, and appealing deliberately to sober common sense'.[1]

In the time of Locke it was not difficult to bring religion, so understood, into harmony with science. The basic Christian notions of an all-good and all-powerful creator, supported by the tradition of centuries and by wide-spread agreement among contemporaries on what was good and valuable in life, seemed to be placed beyond doubt by the scientific discovery of design and order everywhere in nature. Bacon already had spoken of God's two scriptures, the Bible and the created universe. Now the book of nature came to be the form of revelation that was preferred, an incontrovertible proof of God's existence, and revelation in the other sense had to be tested by reason, it was thought, before we could know it to be genuine. In particular, the more orderly nature was seen to be, the more incredible miracles became.

The weakening of the belief in a special revelation, and the consequent displacement of the Bible from its position of central importance, had far-reaching effects in all protestant countries. The doctrines of original sin and grace took on milder forms under the influence of natural theology, and compromises became possible with various philosophies, ancient and modern, always with the general tendency to appeal to reason and common sense in all things and to concentrate attention on practical problems of life here below. What F. H. Bradley calls the 'Do it or be d—d' theory of morals came to be associated with 'theology of a somewhat coarse type', and men came to rely more and more on the rational powers of their own minds, without feeling the same need as earlier generations of support from a transcendent reality. The sense of mystery and of tragedy was weak in the eighteenth century, and an extremely optimistic view was taken of human nature and capacity, the remedy for acknowledged evils being

[1] Canon C. Smyth, quoted by G. M. Trevelyan, *Social History of England*, p. 357.

sought rather in an improvement of environment and education than in religious conversion. All varieties of Enlightenment united, as Cassirer says, in opposing the doctrine of original sin. Fundamentally, it was felt by all, man is good.

It followed naturally that protestant ministers of religion them/ selves gradually came to take a different view of their own function and duties, and that many idealistic young men, sons of the manse, for instance, who would a century before have been attracted to the church as a career, saw more promising opportunities of work in other spheres, while at the same time, in England, at least, the upper ranks of the hierarchy, through the practice of party patronage, were filled with men who above all sought leisure to pursue scholarly or scientific interests. In his important work, *Protestantism and Literature*, Herbert Schöffler has shown in detail, especially for England, how the study of the effects on the clergy of the general secularisation of aims and interests explains a number of leading features of eighteenth/ century developments in literature. In particular it throws new light on literature considered, as it had been already, most fruit/ fully, by Sir Leslie Stephen, 'as a particular function of the social organism'.

In sixteenth/ and seventeenth/century England, Schöffler says, the books most widely read had been the Bible and devotional works. The protestant churches had made good use of the in/ vention of printing, to bring home to any who could read, or be read to, the truths which all still felt to be supremely important for man, especially in times of acute religious controversy. Even of the early eighteenth century Leslie Stephen writes that the popular books were 'the directly religious books: Baxter's *Saint's Rest,* and the *Pilgrim's Progress*—despised by the polite but be/ loved by the popular class in spite of the critics; and among the dissenters such a work as Boston's *Fourfold State,* or in the Church, Law's *Serious Call*'. With the spread of rationalism, this didactic literature took on a new form, increasing all the time in popularity and reaching new types of reader. It became less dogmatic and more and more secular in its content. In *Clarissa,* Richardson claimed to have 'investigated the great doctrines of Christianity under the fashionable guise of an amusement'. Ministers of religion, and even strict calvinists and dissenters, were no longer, as formerly, prevented by their creed from publishing imaginative, as distinct from homiletic or scholarly works, and the fact of their active participation, Schöffler thinks, is as important as the social developments stressed by Stephen as an explanation of the moralising tendency of eighteenth-century English literature. It also helps to explain the popularity of certain specific themes, such as nature, night and the grave, loneliness, and subjects bringing in antiquarian interests and folklore. The rapidly increasing middle-class reading public still looked to books for guidance in the conduct of life, rather than for literary art or pure amusement. A surprisingly high proportion of writers were either ministers or sons of ministers, or they came from circles with strong religious interests like the dissenters. Accordingly they still had a 'message', but it took a palatable form. This secu-larised religious interest cannot therefore be neglected as a factor determining the content of widely read poetry and novels, and to a lesser extent of the drama.

'As a man is, so is his God' (Goethe). Ideas such as we find in the latitudinarian theology and natural morality of Augustan England are more readily understandable if we remember that those who developed them earliest belonged to the privileged classes in a society that felt itself, after the 1688 revolution, to be secure and stable. Lord Shaftesbury, the 'typical English moralist of the Enlightenment', called by Herder the 'virtuoso of humanity' who 'influenced the best minds of the eighteenth century', led the life of a scholarly country gentleman, and in his *Characteristics* he discussed moral and religious questions as they might have been discussed 'amongst Gentlemen and Friends, who know one another perfectly well'. He felt that anyone 'bred to a natural life, inured to honest industry and sobriety, and un-accustomed to anything immoderate or intemperate' would have acquired that 'good taste in the art of living' which he called the 'moral sense'. 'The "mere vulgar of mankind" may perhaps "often stand in need of such a rectifying Object as the Gallows before their Eyes" (just as they may need supernatural terrors to prevent them from defying the parson), but it is really only the enlightened few that Shaftesbury takes account of.'[1] There is some justification for trusting human nature which has had the right nurture, but this condition was not always remembered by Shaftesbury's disciples. What is really pre-supposed by them all is a settled and tolerably contented society, and they did not ask themselves whether their view of human life would have seemed as natural as it did to them if this well-ordered society were still in the making, or beginning to break down. Paul Valéry has put the point well in discussing Montesquieu. 'L'ordre bien assis,—c'est-à-dire la réalité assez déguisée et la bête assez affaiblie, —la liberté de l'esprit devient possible. L'oubli des conditions et des prémisses de l'ordre social est accompli; et cet effacement est presque toujours le plus rapide dans ceux mêmes que cet ordre a le plus servis ou favorisés.'[2]

Though in England the ruling class played an important part in the development of rationalism, the spread of Enlightenment encouraged everywhere the conception of an intellectual aristo-cracy, independent of the aristocracy of birth, but equally dis-tinguished from the vulgar, which maintained the international solidarity of science and art even amid political conflicts between the nations. The consciousness of the existence of this 'invisible church' (as Lessing called it in *Ernst und Falk*), made up of free minds in all nations, strengthened that confident belief in the steadily progressive character of civilisation, already aroused by the triumphs of experimental science, and the practical achieve-ments, in navigation, agriculture, medicine and so on, that had been based on science.

Although the wide-spread conviction that the methods of reason were generally applicable everywhere tended to make national boundaries unreal for the new 'clercs', the intellectuals, who were in this the heirs of the clerics of the Middle Ages, there were marked national differences to be found among the exponents of the new philosophy, differences largely due to historical forces hardly recognised yet for what they were. England was already

[1] B. Willey, *The 18th century background*, p. 75.
[2] 'Préface aux lettres persanes' in *Variété*, II.

distinguished by common sense, by a 'wait and see' reliance on individual experience, which distrusted bold theories through the conviction that real life is a complicated and incalculable affair. The empirical note found in British philosophy from Locke to Hume and beyond him is very different from the ready acceptance in France of ideas, derived by abstraction from complex reality, as the basis of whole systems of thought and of revolutionary action. The philosophers 'applied the seventeenthcentury group of scientific abstractions to the analysis of the unbounded universe. Their triumph, in respect to the circle of ideas mainly interesting to their contemporaries, was overwhelming; whatever did not fit into their scheme was ignored, derided, disbelieved. We cannot overrate the debt of gratitude which we owe to these men for their humanitarian achievements. Voltaire must have the credit, that he hated injustice, he hated cruelty, he hated senseless repression, and he hated hocuspocus.'[1]

The Aufklärung, as it had taken shape in Germany by about 1750, was still recognisably the same movement as what has been sketched above, but many ideas had been modified by German intellectual and social influences, as well as by the intermediaries in France and Holland, through whom most of these ideas were introduced into Germany. The aristocratic note of Augustan England, the graceful, leisurely style of a Shaftesbury or Hume, were lacking in Germany, where such ideas appealed in the first instance to academic teachers of philosophy and theology, then to scattered ministers and officials, and so gradually, especially through the 'moral weeklies', to a wider and wider public. The aristocracy was not nearly so active in the spread of enlightenment as in England. The court classes were naturally great readers of amusing French literature, and followed to some extent the movement of thought in Paris, so that religious scepticism and selfcentred hedonism were widespread in court circles, but the cultivated country gentleman with literary interests and activities was a much rarer figure than in England. The part played by the protestant clergy and their sons, on the other hand, was even greater than in Britain. 'This mysterious growth in importance

---

[1] Whitehead, *op. cit.*, p. 73.

of the protestant parsonage for secular literature is a by-product of the Enlightenment, common to all protestant countries. Ministers take an ever-increasing interest in general literature; young students of theology attract and hold the attention of their contemporaries by works on the border-line between the older devotional literature and literature proper; the sons of the clergy, like many of their fellow-students, abandon the study of theology with increasing frequency as Aufklärung spreads, or when they have finished their studies do not enter the church. From 1740, at all events, clergy, their sons and young theologians generally, come into literature in shoals, so that from the middle of the century its total aspect undergoes a great change. The consequences are similar to those already noted in English literature.'[1]

Schöffler gives in support of this statement a list of some one hundred and twenty German writers, excluding philosophers, born between 1676 and 1804, who either studied theology or were the sons of theologians. Over nine-tenths of them were born after 1720, so that they were at the university in 1740 or later, and the figures show that from the late 'sixties there was a steady stream of young university men with this theological stamp who played a part in literature. The better-known names, to the list of which even minor dramatists have been added for our present purpose, are: J. U. König, Gottsched, Gellert, J. C. Krüger, Melchior Grimm, J. A. Schlegel, Klopstock, Lessing, Hamann, Wieland, Musäus, Claudius, J. J. Engel, Lichtenberg, Eschenburg, Hölty, Miller, Salzmann, Herder, Bürger, Lenz, Klinger, Martini, K. P. Moritz, J. P. Richter, A. W. and Friedrich Schlegel, Arndt, Hölderlin, Jeremias Gotthelf, Mörike. One important cause of the enormous influence of English literature on German just at this time must have been, Schöffler suggests, not a racial affinity, but the attraction for each other of clerical or semi-clerical writers with a basically similar outlook of liberal protestantism. The German aristocracy, on the other hand, continued to lean towards the French, their rococo outlook lacking the deep seriousness of these other, exclusively middle-class circles, and the revolt against the French influence in

[1] Schöffler, *op. cit.*, p. 228.

literature in the 'seventies was, as we shall see, inspired not so much by national as by social and ethical sentiment. It was the protest of good pastors' and officials' sons against court frivolity and heartlessness. The catholic south kept aloof as long as possible from the whole movement initiated by the protestant north.

Once attracted by the rationalist outlook, Germans had more reason than Englishmen to desire a complete break with the church-centred past, for their country had suffered from religious wars to the point of complete exhaustion, and the only solution found had been a galling system of state-imposed religion. Though every variety of Christian belief found acceptance some-where in Germany, little toleration could be expected in any particular state, unless it were Prussia, for any but the official religion of that state, and conformity was usually enforced by law, much as under a theocratic government like that of Russia. Moreover, the wordy warfare of the protestant sects had wearied all reasonable men with its interminable hair-splitting. Yet there was, too, a deeply rooted mystical tendency in German religious thought, which had never disappeared since the Middle Ages, and was always cropping up in a new form. Although the critical zeal of the Aufklärung in Germany, once it had got under way, stopped at nothing in its search for truth, a series of profound and learned thinkers wrestled with the problem of reconciling science with religion, for them *the* problem of their day, and in the great period of German idealism, between Lessing and Hegel, went far towards reaching a synthesis which aimed at preserving the essential meaning of protestant Christianity, without doing violence to modern rational convictions. The highest merit of classical German literature lies in its expression in new symbols of this humanistic religion, which, though not finally satisfactory, proved an inspiration to serious cultivated men in Europe gener-ally until late in the following century, and made Germany their spiritual home.

The effort to modernise the essentials of Christianity began with Leibniz, who, while paying tribute to Luther as the 'libera-tor of half the human race', was at the same time, in Troeltsch's phrase, the first modern man on the grand scale in Germany, aware of the universe revealed by science in all its grandeur, beauty and harmony. His view of the world came from modern science, but his most serious thought was given to the attempt to reconcile this philosophy with the vital elements in Christianity. He saw in Christian dogma a core of meaning which could be expressed in forms capable of satisfying a modern intellect. The resulting system was 'a grandiose poem of logic . . . which, for all its one-sidedness and daring, kept men's minds open to the ideal values in their personal lives', and served for the following century as a link with the protestant piety of German popular tradition.[1]

The populariser of the ideas of Leibniz, Christian Wolff, observed his master's principles, never attacking revealed truths in his theological criticism, but treating revealed and natural religion as co-ordinated systems of truth. The 'neologists' who followed him went much further, accepting only those revealed truths which did not conflict with reason. This led to the dropping of one dogma after another, until they were left only with God, Freedom and Immortality. What was important in religion, they felt, was not so much doctrine in itself, but rather its effect on conduct and on man's peace of mind. Their ideal was the man who could prove in the battle of life the sustaining power of simple piety and trust in God's providence. Lessing and the thinkers and philosophical poets of the classical and romantic periods, with few exceptions, gave up the idea of a supernatural revelation altogether. For them the whole history of mankind was a divine revelation, and the notion of God's education of the human race became identical with that of the actual development of humanity, 'God' being simply another name for the immanent creative power in the universe.[2]

The effect of the new attitude to God, nature and morality, and of the growing belief in inevitable progress was much the same in German literature as earlier in England, a fair-weather philosophy of life, from which the tragic was banished, to make

[1] Troeltsch, 'Leibniz und die Anfänge des Pietismus', *Ges. Schriften*, IV, 508.
[2] E. Franz, *Deutsche Klassik und Reformation*, pp. 133f.

way for a rather sentimental belief in the innate goodness of man. 'Instead of being shaken to the depths by the fear of sin, men are filled with a quiet confidence as they perform the daily round, the common task. While a firm belief in the constant peaceful pro/ gress of the world takes the place of the glowing excitement aroused by eschatological hopes and fears, the element of un/ easiness, passion, tragic greatness is lacking. The poetry of the Aufklärung has a correspondingly shallow character. The demand of the Storm and Stress movement that these dangers should be recognised, and that great passion should be given its due, marks the transition from Aufklärung to the Idealism of the age of Goethe.'[1]

An equally important influence, working sometimes in alliance with Aufklärung, more often in opposition to it, in shaping the attitude to life of eighteenth/century Germany was the movement of religious revival known as Pietism, which had been spreading steadily since the last quarter of the previous century, after similar movements in Holland and England, for this too was a Euro/ pean movement, rooted in the same new modern world as Aufklärung. The new rationalist, unlike the medieval one, as we have seen, was an 'extravert', interested principally in explor/ ing and reducing to order the world without, finding God in nature and history. The pietist was essentially an 'introvert', interested in the mysterious world of his own soul. Like the rationalist, he tended to regard the state church and its forms as outworn. Religious knowledge and rites were of far less impor/ tance to him than personal religious experience in prayer and meditation. For the pietists conversion was the central event in life, and the important distinction between men was that be/ tween the converted and the worldly, not any difference of class or creed or sex. Like the Buchmannite movement of our day, pietism was an affair of groups small enough for brotherliness to be actually practised within them, and the touchstone of true Christian feeling was for them, as for the Aufklärer, its effect on conduct. But their appeal was not to intellect but to feeling, to introspective self/examination. The sentimentalism which was so

E. Franz, *op. cit.*, p. 135.

prominent in literature was an extension of this originally religious attitude to other objects. Instead of anxiously observing and, one may almost say, whipping up their feelings towards God, to the Saviour conceived as an intimate presence, many transferred their attention in a similar way to their friends and lovers, to nature and literature. Klopstock's *Messias,* Goethe's *Werther,* and Romantic masterpieces like *Hyperion* and the *Hymnen an die Nacht* are the literary fruits of this attitude in men of genius. At the other extreme are the family dramas and novels, with their faithful reflection of feeling in everyday life, mainly feeling enjoying social approval, a man's affection for his wife, his children, his dog, his old arm-chair. In other forms of writing, remoter and more abstract objects were found for these generous impulses, canalised by the gradual process of secularisation. Social and educational work in particular benefited enormously, stimulated first by Francke's pietistic foundations in Halle. It has been plausibly argued by K. S. Pinson[1] that the nationalistic ardour of the nineteenth century was fed by this same stream, and indeed no student of Fichte can fail to see how the nation becomes the object of his feeling for the transcendent and of his longing for immortality. What all these developments have in common is the primacy of feeling in human experience, increasing awareness of and pride in the capacity to feel as a distinctively human prerogative, parallel to the capacity to know.

The purely religious movement however became narrower and more hostile to knowledge with each generation. Leibniz, at first sympathetic, because of his friendship with Spener, was later repelled for this reason, and something similar happened in turn with Lessing, and with all who valued secular culture. For as Dilthey says: 'Those who see no value in the life of the world and reject its innocent joys always end up as enemies of culture, whether they begin as monks, or pietists, or writers like Tolstoy.'[2] A second danger was a lapse into superstition, for pietists were constantly on the look-out for modern miracles, for the direct intervention of the deity, and special guidance from

[1] *Pietism as a factor in the rise of German nationalism,* N.Y., 1934.
[2] Dilthey, *Ges. Schriften,* III, p. 75.

heaven in their everyday decisions. Jung-Stilling's autobio-
graphic novel is full of instances of 'däumeln', the use of a biblical
text chosen at random as an oracle, and similar practices. 'The
searching out of the ways of providence in petty personal affairs,
in the accidents of daily life, will never be reconcilable with a
conscious acceptance of the order of nature.'[1] Pietism also tended
to reinforce the age-old tendency of the Germans to submit
themselves all too readily to what was deemed inevitable, in
situations where men of more active temper would have made
an effort of will, and even to luxuriate in the idea of a blind fate
working itself out, as the young Anton Reiser does in the novel
of K. P. Moritz, when he deals out death to flies, or with closed
eyes annihilates armies of cherry-stones with an iron hammer.

All these currents of opinion left their mark on Lessing. His
father, whose forebears for several generations back had been
protestant ministers, had already responded to the stimulus of
English rationalism by translating Tillotson's sermons, attracted
by their common-sense moral teaching. Pietism too had at first
appealed to him, in so far as it stressed conduct rather than doctrine, and he no doubt passed this view on to his son, who wrote
in his early essay on *Die Herrenhuter* (1750): 'What is the good of
having the right beliefs if we do not live rightly?' Like his father,
however, he was later repelled by the intellectual shortcomings
of the pietists, their contempt for culture. Lessing had the usual
education of a Saxon boy destined for the church, attending first
one of the Fürstenschulen and then the University of Leipzig.
To judge by some Latin sentences he added to a prose composition for the entrance examination at Meissen when he was twelve,
he already thought of Jews and Mohammedans as having as
good a claim as Christians to the possession of 'Humanität', the
criterion by which he judged the value of religions. In his youth,
as he reminds us, apologetics was a fashionable branch of literature, and he naturally read widely in it, seeking always, like
George Eliot, 'the truth that was in all religions from the beginning', for natural morality was for him the root of all religions,
and the measure of their worth. What most repelled him was

[1] Dilthey, *op. cit.*, III, p. 75.

the intolerance of the orthodox, not their dogmatic beliefs, for which he could nearly always find some reasonable explanation. His reverence for the faith of his fathers made him view the iconoclasm of the French Aufklärer with intense distaste, though he did not neglect their writings. 'Truth is always hidden', he wrote in an unfinished poem, 'from a mind which hates nothing but faith and loves nothing but argumentation.' He admired and was deeply influenced by English religious thought, from the seventeenth-century deists to Shaftesbury. Herbert of Cherbury seemed to him the first and the best of the systematic deists. He himself thought of primitive Christianity as essentially a 'natural religion', and all the better for that. He frequently quoted and discussed Shaftesbury and Bolingbroke, he translated Hutcheson's *Moral Philosophy*, and studied the work of Hutcheson's successor in Edinburgh, Ferguson, with profit. We see from the close examination he made with Mendelssohn of the ideas of Pope that he even knew the theodicy of William King, one of Pope's sources, with its doctrine of the 'great chain of being', that neo-platonic doctrine which we encounter everywhere in the eigh-teenth century.[1]

There is no doubt about Lessing's theological learning, but it is hard to be sure of his own personal views on religion, because he could seldom be quite frank about them in his published writings. Until late in life he considered himself a Christian, though sin and redemption, and the authority of the church, meant little to him, whereas humanity and charity, wherever he met with them, acquired for him religious value. A Leibnizian optimism is suggested by such remarks as that about the universe where 'everything turns out for the best' (*Hamburgische Drama-turgie*, 79). For him, God was to be approached above all through nature, and to be served not in ritual but in good deeds. The belief in immortality seemed to him an essential for any genuine religion, and the surest ground for an optimistic view of life.[2] It seems certain that in his last years Lessing went further, after the controversy with Goeze and renewed study of Spinoza. In

---

[1] See A. O. Lovejoy's book with that title.
[2] L. Zscharnack, introduction to vol. 20 of Lessing's Werke, Bong edition.

conversation with F. H. Jacobi in 1780 he revealed that in his personal views he found himself nearer to Spinoza than to any other thinker, and rejected the notion of final causes and Christian dualism.[1] In this respect too, as in his view of genius and other aesthetic questions, he outgrew the Enlightenment, and came to share some ideas of the Storm and Stress movement.

In the range of his interests Lessing came near to Voltaire, but a comparison between the two writers brings to light interesting differences between French and German rationalism, which are of some importance for our present study. Each of these lively authors criticised the orthodoxy of his country in the name of reason and toleration, but Voltaire's philosophy was essentially anti-religious, founded on an epicurean rejection of austerity in any form, while Lessing's was a philosophical religion, inspired by an unquenchable thirst for metaphysical truth. Voltaire's aim was eminently practical, to clear the ground of encumbrances, such as judicial and administrative abuses and the power of the Catholic church, and to eliminate a Christian view of history. These things he attacked with all the weapons of a journalist of genius, who adored the limelight. Lessing was well aware of political and social abuses, as we see from *Emilia Galotti*, but he avoided any open attack on them, as also on religion, partly out of reverence for beliefs and institutions which many still regarded as sacred, partly because his mind had a more theoretical than practical bent, and partly perhaps from the conservatism which Troeltsch, for instance, finds characteristic of Lutheranism, as opposed to Calvinism. Lutheranism, he says, makes for warmth and sincerity in personal relationships, and a strict view of the duties of one's calling. 'But it means at the same time a completely passive acceptance of existing circumstances. . . . At bottom it is indifferent to the world, resigned and passive, patiently and piously completing its earthly pilgrimage—rather than active, constructive and eager for social reform. It stands aside, and lets higher authority and fate have their way.'[2]

Other factors working in the same direction are of course to be found in the social and political condition of Germany, as

---

[1] H. Leisegang, *Lessings Weltanschauung.*   [2] *Ges. Schriften*, IV, p. 141.

Troeltsch clearly saw. The result was that over-emphasis on Bildung, on the things of the mind, to the virtual exclusion of political and social interests, which has only recently been generally recognised as a German weakness, though individual critics, like Heine, had long been aware of it. The practical reforms stimulated by the Aufklärung in Germany were therefore almost all due to the initiative of the absolute governments. The leading Germans of Goethe's day, says Troeltsch, 'were cosmopolitan on principle, indifferent to political and economic questions and intent only on thought and the inner life, aiming as they did at the purely individualistic culture of private citizens and intellectual aristocrats'.[1] This is a contributory cause of the ever-increasing attention paid to literary drama and the art of the theatre which we must not forget when we are considering the advances made in these fields by Lessing and his contemporaries.

LESSING THE CRITIC

When Lessing, in June 1748, was forced, owing to the debts that he, and some members of the Neuber company whom he had incautiously supported with guarantees, had made in Leipzig, to take to journalism in Berlin, he was still in close association with Mylius, who was for a time editor of what was later known as the *Vossische Zeitung*. Together they began to bring out in 1750 the first of the considerable number of periodicals devoted already in that century to theatrical matters. It was a modest beginning, still clearly in the Gottsched tradition even in its title, *Beiträge zur Historie und Aufnahme des Theaters*, the work of enthusiastic amateurs with big ideas. Lessing's preface promised the impossible in the way of theatrical history, as well as translations from the drama of the whole world, including, of course, that of England, but the jumble of English authors mentioned, and the omission of Calderon among the Spaniards, seem to indicate chiefly a certain skill in window-dressing. The actual contents of the periodical, of which only four parts appeared, are a disappointing medley. The theatrical news is about Paris

[1] *Ges. Schriften*, IV, p. 541.

and two or three German courts, especially Berlin, and none of it is concerned with German companies. The criticism of the French players in Berlin, where a theatre had been made for them in the Schloss, is written in such an offensive tone that it is difficult to believe that Lessing was the author of it, though on other grounds it seems probable. The young critic had evidently had difficulty in gaining admission, as this was strictly a court theatre. In December and January, we hear, there was also opera to be heard free by the privileged few (though others crowded in), performed by an Italian troupe in the newly built opera house. The king came to a comedy three or four times a year, but what he enjoyed most were the performances of his Italian intermezzo players at Potsdam in the summer months. The report does not criticise his neglect of the German theatre, but there is suppressed annoyance in the whole description, and the high cost of the court theatre and opera is emphasised.

Other items are a translation of the treatise on acting by Riccoboni the younger, of the *Théâtre des Italiens* in Paris, and an essay on Plautus, with a prose translation of the *Captivi,* by Lessing. A second translation from Plautus, *Der Schatz* (*Trinummus*), appeared in print and had some success on the stage after the periodical had come to an end. Plautus and Terence had been his 'world' at school, and in his essay Lessing expresses regret that Germany has lagged so far behind other countries in making use of Plautus. The preface had claimed that Germany could now boast of literary works which 'need not be afraid of the sharpest criticism from the least fair of foreigners'. There were not many of them, admittedly, but the readers were credited with enough taste to be aware of them themselves without prompting from the editors—an ingenious face-saving device, the need for which is obvious from the rest of the volume. It scarcely contains a reference to a German work, apart from a fierce review of a translation, by a magister from Kamenz, Lessing's home, of a Latin defence of school plays.

The *Beiträge* represent quite a small part of Lessing's output in his first years in Berlin. He was busily reviewing for two Berlin papers, and from 1751 was responsible for the literary side of the

Privilegierte Zeitung (later called the *Vossische*) and for bringing out its monthly literary supplement. He was reading voraciously, and trying his hand at every kind of writing, moved, as he says, by 'curiosity and ambition'. His most interesting personal contact was with Voltaire, for whom he interpreted in the unsavoury episode of the law-suit with the Jew Hirsch, and the contempt he felt in consequence for Voltaire as a man, combined with annoyance at Voltaire's suspicion of foul play in the matter of the borrowed proofs of *Le Siècle de Louis XIV*, goes far to explain the unmistakable prejudice against all Voltaire's work which mars many pages of the *Hamburgische Dramaturgie*. It was through Voltaire's complaints that Frederick the Great first heard of Lessing, and the unfavourable impression apparently persisted.

After taking a year off to become a Magister himself at Wittenberg in 1752, Lessing returned to Berlin and the *Vossische Zeitung*. His second theatrical periodical, the *Theatralische Bibliothek* (1754–58), had no connection with the contemporary stage and hardly any with the German drama, but the beginning of a rift between Lessing and Gottsched is indicated in the attention given in the first number to the *Comédie Larmoyante,* which had been found absurd in the *Beiträge*. Even now Lessing gives, with little comment of his own, a translation of Gellert's already mentioned Latin essay, and of a French one by an opponent of the genre, Chassiron. Lessing offers a sociological explanation of the fact that in France comedy has been in a sense raised in status, whereas in England it is tragedy that has been lowered. The French middle class, he says, did not like to see themselves always in ridiculous situations, and a secret ambition drove their authors to represent people like themselves in a dignified aspect. The ordinary Englishman hated to see crowned heads given any privileges in tragedy, and thought himself quite capable of high passion and sublime thought. This is in a way an anticipation of Brunetière's phrase about the middle class 'ordering its portrait'. A year later Lessing started off domestic drama in Germany with his own *Miss Sara Sampson*.

In the later parts of his second periodical we find little but translations or summaries, of the life of James Thomson (relevant because of his tragedies), of Dryden's *Essay on Dramatic Poetry*, of the life of Destouches, of St. Albine's *Le Comédien*, of Luigi Riccoboni's *Histoire du théâtre italien* (about the *commedia dell' arte*), and of French descriptions of unpublished scenarios and comedies of the Théâtre Italien. The last two show a revival of interest in improvised comedy, which was anathema of course to the Gott- sched school. There are summaries of Renaissance Italian plays, and of the *Virginia* of a contemporary Spaniard (Montiano), this latter a step towards *Emilia Galotti*. The 'only really original article' (J. G. Robertson) is one on Seneca. On the evidence of his first two journals, Lessing 'was mainly interested in the out- ward history of the drama', especially in Plautus and Terence. 'His critical interests, such as they were, were directed rather to the art of acting. Dramatic theory occupies a very subordinate place. His interest in the new form of tragedy which he himself with *Miss Sara Sampson* had established on the German stage is particularly meagre.'[1]

The *Theatralische Bibliothek* gives evidence of English studies, encouraged by Lessing's friendship in Berlin, in this second period of residence there, with Nicolai the publisher and with Moses Mendelssohn, the self-taught bookkeeper-philosopher, whose acquaintance Lessing had made through another highly cultivated Jewish friend, Dr. Gumpertz. Lessing found Mendels- sohn so understanding and stimulating in discussions that he was more than ever convinced that common ground could be found between men of goodwill, even if they were of different race, class and religion. Friedrich Nicolai, whose father was a bookseller before him, had had to pick up his higher education for himself. As a young man he gave promise as a critic with his *Briefe über den itzigen Zustand der schönen Wissenschaften in Deutschland*, published in 1754, when he was twenty-one. This work made Lessing seek his acquaintance, for he found in it a common-sense rejection of the various cliques which dominated German literature, a demand for free criticism, warm praise of the English theatre, with its talent for character-drawing, especially marked in Shakespeare, and condemnation of Gottsched's

[1] J. G. Robertson, *Lessing's dramatic theory*, p. 114.

methods of reform. Two years later Nicolai published the prospectus of a new periodical, his *Bibliothek der schönen Wissen-schaften und freien Künste*, which began to appear in 1757 and became the chief organ of German Aufklärung. At the same time he offered a prize of fifty taler for the best tragedy handed in by the end of the year. He wrote for the first number of his review an essay on tragedy which he summarised in a letter to Lessing at the end of August, 1756. This started a correspondence on tragedy between Nicolai, Lessing and Mendelssohn, which continued till the following May. One could indeed, reading these letters, written in the opening months of the Seven Years' War, believe that war 'in our civilised days is only a suit where the litigants are princes, where blood flows, indeed, but without disturbing any other classes of society', as Lessing was to write in the first *Literaturbrief*, for these long aesthetic arguments are never interrupted by references to mundane matters.

Lessing, restless as ever, had left Berlin at the end of 1755 for Leipzig, where he soon took a post as companion to a young patrician, whom he was to have accompanied on his travels, if the war had not broken out as they were on the point of leaving Amsterdam for England. Lessing answered Nicolai therefore after his return from Amsterdam to Leipzig. This first letter takes us to the heart of his view of tragedy. All art for him has an end in view, and the aim of tragedy is to enlarge our capacity for sympathy, and so to make us better men. 'The man with the greatest capacity for sympathy (der mitleidigste Mensch) is the best man, the man most disposed to all the social virtues, to every kind of magnanimity.' Nicolai had begun by contesting the truth of the view, which he described as that of Aristotle, that 'it is the aim of tragedy to purify the passions or improve morals'; in his opinion it had led to the writing of many bad German tragedies. Tragedy's aim was, he thought, to arouse strong emotion, not to improve morals, and he classified tragedies according to the kind of emotion aroused. Lessing countered with his interpretation of Aristotle, essentially the same one as we find still in the *Hamburgische Dramaturgie*. Tragedy, he agreed, had to awaken *certain* emotions, but its ultimate aim was to improve morals through the stimulation of these emotions. The emotions are Aristotle's pity and fear. Fear (still called 'Schrek͵ ken', 'terror', following Nicolai and M. C. Curtius, the German translator of Aristotle) is explained, however, as a variety of pity, a pity which takes us by surprise. Mendelssohn's contribution was the theory of mixed emotions, combining 'Lust' and 'Un͵ lust', the pleasing and the displeasing, which he had expounded in 1755 in his psychological essay *Briefe über die Empfindungen*. He considered admiration to be *the* tragic emotion, whereas Lessing, intent as usual on keeping every genre within well͵defined limits, wanted to reserve admiration for the epic. The whole discussion will seem to most modern readers academic and unfruitful, but it shows us Lessing's dramatic theory in the making, and helps us to interpret his own tragedies, with their pathetic effects, in the way which he intended.

It will be obvious that this view of tragedy is closely connected with the general philosophy of the period, outlined above. Walzel puts the matter clearly: 'Lessing's words remind us what the common attitude to life was in those days. British philosophers were looking for a bulwark against the claims of egoism, and welcomed any evidence of features in the human soul which indicated altruistic tendencies. Collectivistic theories of society were in the air at the time, the first attempts at a social theory in which the interests of the individual would combine harmoni͵ ously in a feeling of togetherness shared by the community as a whole. British philosophers were speaking about love as holding society together, just as the force of gravity keeps the universe from falling asunder. For Lessing, tragedy became a means of fostering such social virtues.'[1]

Between this correspondence and the *Hamburgische Drama͵ turgie* Lessing's principal utterances on the drama are to be found in the *Literaturbriefe* and in his writings about Diderot. The *Literaturbriefe*, a literary weekly in the form of letters, signed with pseudonyms, supposed to be addressed to a wounded officer, were begun in 1759 and written for two years almost entirely by

[1] 'Lessings Begriff des Tragischen', in *Vom Geistesleben alter und neuer Zeit*, 1922, p. 240.

Lessing, in an attempt to raise German literary standards by the unsparing criticism of weaknesses. They are very largely con-cerned with the innumerable translations being made at a time when Germany was borrowing freely from more advanced neighbours, but the seventeenth and eighty-first are of special interest here. The seventeenth letter is famous for Lessing's open repudiation of Gottsched's guidance, and his advocacy of Eng-lish rather than French models.

The opening is a good example of his trenchant style, and of his habit of introducing his views as a comment on those of another. He quotes from the *Bibliothek der schönen Wissenschaften* the sentence: 'Nobody will deny that the first improvements made in the German theatre were due in large measure to Professor Gottsched', and goes on: 'I am this nobody; I deny it absolutely. It would have been better if Herr Gottsched had never meddled with the theatre. His supposed improvements either concern trifling matters, or they are steps in the wrong direction.' Gott-sched had made the German theatre a frenchified affair, though he might have seen from the old plays which he drove from the stage that the natural German inclination was rather towards the English than towards the French taste, 'that in our tragedies we want to see and think more than the timid French type of tragedy gives us to see and to think about; that the great, the terrible, the melancholy have a greater effect on us than the charming, the tender, the love-sick; that excessive simplicity is for us more tire-some than excessive complexity, and so on. He only needed to follow up this line of thought to be led straight to the English theatre.' Lessing did not know, as we do, that the style of the old 'Haupt- und Staatsaktionen' to which he was referring was originally moulded by actual players from England.

It might be objected, says Lessing, that Gottsched had made use (even excessive use!) of an English play in his own *Cato*, but his choice of Addison as a model shows that he saw English litera-ture through French eyes, and did not know anything about Shakespeare, or Johnson, or Beaumont and Fletcher, and refused out of pride to read them later. 'If the masterpieces of Shakespeare, with some slight changes, had been translated for our Germans,

128

I am certain that the results would have been far better than they have been after their overdose of Corneille and Racine. In the first place the ordinary man (das Volk) would have found Shakespeare much more to his taste, and in the second place Shakespeare would have aroused much better talents here to emulation than those who have been stimulated by the French. For a genius can only be fired by a genius; and most easily by one who seems to owe everything to nature herself, and does not discourage emulation by the painful perfection of his artistry.'

In reading the paragraph which follows, we must remember what Lessing's correspondence with his two friends has taught us about his conception of the aim of tragedy, to enlarge the human sympathy of the audience. 'Even to decide the matter by the example of the Ancients, Shakespeare is a much greater tragic author than Corneille; although Corneille knew the Ancients very well, and Shakespeare hardly at all. Corneille comes nearer to them in the externals of technique, and Shakespeare in the essentials. The Englishman attains the aim of tragedy almost always, however strange and individual are the paths he chooses; and the Frenchman hardly ever attains it, though he follows the well-worn paths of the Ancients. Apart from the *Œdipus* of Sophocles, there can be no play in dramatic literature which has more power over our emotions than *Othello*, *King Lear* or *Hamlet,* and so on. Has Corneille a single tragedy which has moved you half as much as the *Zaïre* of Voltaire? And how far does Voltaire's *Zaïre* fall short of the *Moor of Venice*, of which it is a weak copy, and from which the whole character of Orosmane is borrowed?'

To clinch his argument, Lessing finally quotes from what purports to be a scene from the 'best-known' of the old German plays, *Dr. Faust*, which has a number of scenes, he says, such as only a Shakespearian genius could have invented. It is a scene in which Faust demands the swiftest spirit of hell to be his servant, and finally chooses the seventh to appear, who claims to be as swift as the transition from good to evil. The 'Shakespearian genius', it is generally held, was Lessing himself, for this is not a scene from any old play, though suggested by one, but the only surviving fragment from Lessing's own handling of the Faust saga, begun in 1755, soon after he had seen the old play presented by Schuch in Berlin, never completed, and finally lost twenty years later. It is a scene which leaves us quite unmoved, with its purely intellectual subtleties, and rather shocked at Lessing's disingenuousness and his use of the phrase 'Shakespearian genius', until we remember his impulsiveness and his delight in mystifying his public.

In the other *Literaturbrief* which concerns our theme, the eighty-first, practically his first explicit reference to the German stage of his own day, he has to admit, in February 1760, that nothing deserving the name yet exists. In the course of a not unkind review of Weisse's *Eduard der Dritte* he comments on the author's complaint about the lack of German tragedies and on his explanation, the early death of promising authors like Cronegk and Brawe, and the fact that through so few good plays being performed, potential writers are not stimulated into dramatic production. 'That', says Lessing, 'is without doubt of the first importance. We have no theatre. We have no actors.' Diderot complains, he goes on, about the low status of the theatre even in France, compared with ancient Greece and Rome, where the drama was performed before a whole nation on solemn festivals. 'So speaks a Frenchman! And what a fall from France to Germany! The French have at least a stage to play on, where the Germans can hardly find temporary booths. The theatre of the French is at least the amusement of the whole of a great capital, while in the German capitals the theatre booth is the butt of the mob. The French can at least boast of frequently entertaining their king, an entire splendid court, the most distinguished and respected in the land, the highest social circles; while the Germans must be well satisfied if a few dozen honest citizens, who have shyly slunk into their booth, will stay to listen to them.

'But let us be quite frank. That the German drama is still in such a poor way is perhaps not entirely the fault of the great, through their not giving it their protection and help. The great do not care to have to do with things which seem to them to have little or no future. And if they look at our actors, what promise do they offer? People without education, without breeding, without talent; a former tailor, a young woman who a few months ago was washing people's clothes, and so on. What can the great see in creatures like these which at all resembles themselves, and which might induce them to raise these, their counterfeits upon the stage, to a higher and more honoured status?'

It is not often that we find Lessing openly saying what he feels about the attitude of the ruling class to German literature and drama, and when he does, he shows himself well aware that their responsibility for Germany's slow progress was shared by many others. He also expresses a sturdy independence. Perhaps the most revealing passage is in the prose draft of an ode, *To Maecenas*. Has Maecenas left to us anything more than a name? he asks. 'Who is there in our age of iron, here in a land whose inhabitants, seen from within, are still barbarians as of old, who is there with a spark of your humane feeling, your virtuous ambition to protect the favourites of the Muses?' How often he has searched for such a patron in vain. 'There the ruler maintains a host of wits, and makes use of them in the evening, when he seeks relief in jesting from the cares of state, as his councillors of mirth! How far from a Maecenas is he!'—a thrust at Frederick, with his French entourage, combined perhaps with memories of his father's 'Tabakskollegium'. 'Never shall I be tempted to play such a sorry part, to gain mere honours and ribbons. A King may rule me, and I may admit his power, but let him not think himself a better man. No bounties in his gift are great enough to command of me what I hold base.'

The poem *Ich* strikes the same note, reminding us that Lessing did not have to go far for a model for his proudly self-reliant Tellheim and Nathan. Neither honours nor wealth have fallen to his lot, and soon he must go the way of all flesh. 'But what need is there for posterity to know whose ashes are beneath its feet, if *I* know who I am?'

> Wie lange währt's, so bin ich hin,
> Und einer Nachwelt untern Füssen?
> Was braucht sie wen sie tritt zu wissen?
> Weiss ich nur wer ich bin.

The passage from Diderot quoted in the eighty-first *Literatur-brief* is from the *Entretiens*, which form a frame for *Le Fils naturel*, and which Lessing translated in 1760, together with that play, as well as *Le Père de famille* and the essay *De la poésie dramatique*, under the title *Das Theater des Herrn Diderot*. His own preface expresses high admiration for Diderot, than whom no more philosophical mind, he thinks, has occupied itself with the theatre since the days of Aristotle. Diderot's importance for Lessing was, as is also clear from the preface, that he gave evidence of a revolt in France itself against the French classical drama extolled by Gottsched. Lessing expresses the hope that this critic of Corneille and Racine, who thinks that the theatre can stand far stronger meat than they have provided, will be listened to more readily in Germany than in his own country. 'At least this must happen, if we too wish to be counted one day among the civilised nations, by creating a theatre of our own.'

It was better tactics at this moment for Lessing, as a reformer of the German theatre, to tell the German public about the swing of opinion away from the French classics, and to introduce English ideas rather by way of France than directly. Otherwise one would have expected him, after the seventeenth *Literaturbrief*, to devote his energies to translating Shakespeare and other English dramatists rather than Diderot. But although he no doubt believed that it would have been better, ideally, to propose English models instead of French at the outset, he could not leave out of account the effect of a generation's propaganda by Gottsched and his followers. As we shall see, even in the 'seventies Shakespeare could only be introduced to German audiences in an adapted form, and in 1760 Lessing himself was not prepared, any more than Diderot, to lay aside all the French dramatic conventions to which he was accustomed in favour of English practices, for he probably felt vaguely what was clearly realised later by Herder, that the drama of any country is a product of its whole history, and this French phase was now a part of German intellectual and artistic history. Before anything resembling a Shakespearian play could even be acted with success, much less imitated, the way had to be prepared. One can imagine various approaches, but the one which was actually used was by way of the domestic drama. When the Hamburg public had grown accustomed to this, in the 'seventies, Shakespeare was presented to it by Schröder as a rather wilder kind of domestic dramatist.

Apart from the special usefulness of Diderot in Lessing's fight with the Gottsched tradition, this author, whom Goethe felt to be, in all respects for which the French reproved him, a true German, was likely in any case to make a strong appeal. It is no accident that the most outspoken admirer of *Le Fils naturel* on its appearance in 1757 was Melchior Grimm. Like the German Aufklärer, Diderot was an out-and-out *petit-bourgeois*, with many of their own characteristics, 'modest diligence and incorruptible honesty, a sound sense of the natural, a marked sentimental vein and an almost excessive moralism.'[1] He shared with them too their admiration for the natural morality of Shaftesbury, whom he had translated, and for the sentimental family novel of Richardson. He himself interpreted German literature to some extent in France, being kept in touch with it by his friend Grimm in particular. He expounded the philosophy of Leibniz, adapted an idyll of Gessner, and admired *Miss Sara Sampson* enough to translate it as a type of 'drame', though he was never in touch with Lessing himself.

Erich Schmidt has brought out the many striking parallels between the two men, in origins, strength of character and independence of spirit, fundamental benevolence and many-sided interest in the life of their fellows, in a certain restlessness too and delight in controversy.[2] Both were free-lance critics and lovers of the theatre, and open-minded seekers after truth in religion and philosophy, distrustful of systems. There were big differences in their immediate backgrounds, Diderot, as a Frenchman, even though a 'philosophe', having the support of a stronger literary tradition, and as the *habitué* of so many Parisian salons, and the guest of Catherine of Russia, more social opportunities than Lessing, but both were clearly children of the same age. What is perhaps most striking about them is the way in which they

---

[1] J. Petersen, introduction to Lessing's Werke, (Bong), Bd. 11.
[2] *Lessing*, I, pp. 304 ff.

both, Diderot more consciously than Lessing, helped to canalise the thought and feeling of the middle classes in their respective countries.

For what really made the success of the 'drame' in France, as its historian, M. Gaiffe, has proved, was what we should now call its ideological content. It was in all essentials created by Diderot the Encyclopedist, for whom the theatre was no longer an amusement for an idle public, but a powerful instrument of philosophical propaganda. French society was no longer what it had been under Louis XIV, a stable and relatively harmonious structure. The old hierarchy of ranks was breaking up, and the middle class, conscious of itself and its growing strength, aspired to political and social recognition. It was for this reason that it so eagerly welcomed English literature, where a similar move-ment in society had already had marked effects. It did not wish to be always amused, and it was out of sympathy with the aristocratic sentiments of seventeenth-century drama. M. Gaiffe defines the drame therefore by its content, not by its form, for not all plays which he calls 'drames' were in prose, like Diderot's, many, though not all, observed the rules strictly, some had a happy ending and some not, but all of them were bourgeois. A drame is accordingly 'un spectacle destiné à un auditoire bour-geois ou populaire et lui présentant un tableau attendrissant et moral de son propre milieu'. This is an exact description of the family pieces of Iffland and Kotzebue, which were to be the main-stay of German producers in the 'nineties, but these had developed gradually out of the bourgeois tragedy and comedy of Lessing, and although the German theatre did not, as in France, contri-bute in some measure to the preparation of a political revolution, it did become the mouthpiece of middle-class opinion, and much of its popularity must be attributed to its exercise of this function.

Diderot's own plays have little artistic merit, and it must be admitted that his influence on Lessing and the German theatre was, aesthetically speaking, deplorable. It encouraged the ten-dency, already so strong, towards sentimentality, moralising rhetoric and dull naturalism. 'Hinc illae lacrimae' is A. W. Schlegel's comment on his popularity in Germany, and it is the

German drama in his tradition which Schiller castigates in *Shakespeares Schatten*. Goethe and Schiller in their maturity wished to re/introduce in the name of art what Diderot had opposed in the name of nature, heroic subjects, verse in the grand style, and the aesthetically 'distancing' effect of scenes remote from the here and now. But even in Weimar their success was limited, we shall find, because even there the audiences wanted plays related to their own lives, and few among them had an imagination sufficiently cultivated for them to recognise the relevance of the new classicism to their purposes. The bourgeois drama had the one great merit, that for its age and audience it was alive, serving a purpose only in small part aesthetic, but drawing German audiences to the theatre as they had never been drawn before, and helping to give Germany what Lessing had desired, a theatre of its own. In the preface to the second edition of his translation of Diderot, written towards the end of his life, Lessing expressed his gratitude to one whose example and precept had given a new turn to his own development, and he rightly claimed that Diderot's influence on the German theatre had been greater than on the French.

Wisdom born of personal experience, Lessing thought, is infinitely more valuable than learning acquired from books, and certainly his own writings reflect the maturing of his wisdom as clearly as the growth of his learning. When he was persuaded, perhaps rather against his better judgment, to lend the somewhat dubious Hamburg Enterprise the support of his name, though as critic, not as theatre/poet, he had just spent five comparatively care/free years in Breslau, in easy war work which left him time to browse among books, as well as for a 'life not looking beyond the moment, in inns and pleasant company' (if that is what Goethe means by 'zerstreutes Wirtshaus/ und Weltleben'). He made many friends and acquaintances, some of them cultivated Prussian officers, as he had earlier in the war at Leipzig, where his friendship with the officer/poet Ewald von Kleist had already brought him into contact with men of action who combined a love of literature with an enlightened patriotism. Always a passionate book/collector, he built up again the nucleus of a valuable library, but like his earlier collections, this too had to be sold, when in Hamburg he put all his money into Bode's printing firm. Until he retired into his shell in Wolfenbüttel, Lessing was constantly extending his knowledge of men as well as of books, with the same eagerness as in his student days at Leipzig.

In Breslau Lessing had written his *Laokoon* and sketched out his *Minna von Barnhelm*, and he published both on his return to Berlin, but the King was not to be persuaded to take him, rather than a Frenchman, as librarian of the Berlin library. Lessing had continued to read widely in theology too. All these multi-farious interests can be traced in his *Hamburgische Dramaturgie*, the collection of essays in dramatic theory and criticism which he began, at the age of thirty-eight, with the confidence of a master. This great work seems to most readers now perhaps more of its time than for all time. To be fully understood it needs a commentary as bulky as itself. Even Lessing's criticism of individual plays and his dramatic theory have been shown by Professor J. G. Robertson to be less original than German scholars had considered them. But the *Dramaturgie* remains an invaluable and in many ways a fascinating work for the student of the eighteenth-century theatre. It has great merits of style. 'Others before him had attacked the rule-bound artificiality of the *tragédie classique*, but none was able to dethrone it so effectively as he, with his brilliant reduction of the plot of *Rodogune* to absurdity; the rules had been discredited, even in France, long before Lessing—but who has put the whole problem they involve more brilliantly and cogently than he?'[1] It has exerted a greater influence on the German drama than any other critical work. 'It sums up, draws together the threads, as it were, of all that the eighteenth century thought' on the subject of the drama. Every one of the classical dramas that followed showed signs of its author's acquaintance with it, says Petersen. Above all, for our present purpose, it shows us a leading German theatre in action at a critical period, informs us about its repertoire, and how it was received both by the public and by the ablest critic of the day, and it gives us vivid impressions of the acting.

[1] J. G. Robertson, *op. cit.*, p. 490.

In his preliminary announcement Lessing explains the aims of the new enterprise and of his critical notices. He dwells on the good results that should follow from the establishment of an endowed theatre, not run for the profit of a principal. The management, it is true, have a difficult task before them, because the German theatre, he suggests, has made a bad start, and much corrective work will be necessary. He warns the public not to expect wonders of the repertoire, because there is so little to choose from, but he does not intend to call a play good when it is not, though he realises that some plays, poor as literature, may offer certain actors good rôles. In general we have the impression that it is the acting in which he is chiefly interested, though his aim is to give both actor and dramatist their due. It was apparent from this first number that he was not attempting what we now usually mean by dramatic criticism, a verdict on yesterdays's play for us to read at breakfast. The first notice of the opening evening (22nd April, 1767) appeared a week later, and the next six numbers were all devoted to it as well, the last appearing a month after the performance. After a year, in No. 100, Lessing was dealing with the performance of 28th July of the preceding year. Four days later he held his post-mortem on the whole experiment in the final number, for after the first few weeks the theatre had had little success, and since December the company had been playing in Hanover. The theatre was wound up in November 1768.

As in the *Laokoon,* Lessing starts from particular examples, but always with a view to finding general principles. Criticism of the acting had to cease a month after the opening, though Lessing was extremely appreciative. But Mme Hensel did not like his suggestion that she was too big for a certain part. The German actor, as Lessing said in the last paper, was easily offended, and this was understandable, because all criticism so far had been purely subjective, a chaos of opinions. What he had hoped for was to reach the bed-rock of principles here too —we have already seen him translating foreign works on the subject, and he had begun a treatise of his own. Germany had actors, he said, but no art of acting, no tradition, and in the absence of objective standards, all actors were insatiable in their desire for applause and praise. He had regretfully confined himself to the criticism of the plays, but the German repertoire was so limited in extent, Lessing explains in summing up, that instead of discussing what had been accomplished, he had had to point out how the German drama could retrace its steps and start again, a procedure which had involved him in a close examination of French drama, the model so far followed. The great preponderance of French plays in what was actually presented almost forced him in any case to give them most of his attention.

The general line adopted by Lessing was to take every opportunity of weakening the prestige of French drama by contrasting it unfavourably with Greek and English achievements, and by proving that the authority of Aristotle had been wrongly claimed for its 'rules'. Against French theory and practice he appealed to the 'real' Aristotle, setting up new norms on the basis of a new interpretation of one whom he had come to regard, because of the sound reasoning behind his teaching, as just as infallible in his own sphere as Euclid in geometry. New canons of criticism were urgently needed, he felt, because of the havoc which was being wrought in German literary theory by the new conceptions of poetry, 'preromantic' notions, as we now call them, expressed most effectively by Young, in his *Conjectures on Original Composition* (1759). At the age of seventyeight the author of the *Night Thoughts* had repeated in more vigorous phrases the demand he had made thirty years before, as a disciple of Shaftesbury, for originality rather than culture in poetry. Not a knowledge of the rules and conventions of poetry, but selfknowledge and selfreverence, individual sincerity and the power of invention make the poet. Similar ideas had been much discussed in England for some time. Round about 1760 they spread to the Continent as well. In the same year as Young's *Conjectures* Hamann was writing in his *Sokratische Denkwürdigkeiten:* 'What makes up, in Homer, for his ignorance of those rules which Aristotle devised after his day, and in Shakespeare for the ignorance of, or noncompliance with, those rules? Genius is the only answer.'[1]

---

[1] *Schriften*, ed. F. Roth, II, p. 38.

All this was part of the theoretical preparation of Storm and Stress, and was carried farther, before Lessing wrote, by Gersten-berg and especially Herder. At the same time the example of Shakespeare and the English drama had convincingly proved that, without the rules, plays could be written which made a far greater imaginative appeal to many Germans than French work. 'What conclusion was drawn from that?' Lessing asks. 'This: that the aim of tragedy could be attained equally well without those rules, indeed, that it might be precisely because of them that we had often failed to attain it. And that might have passed! But they began to make no distinction between these rules and rules in general, and to declare it mere pedantry to try to prescribe to genius what it should do and not do. In short, we were on the point of wantonly casting to the winds all that the experience of the past had taught us, and asking of our poets instead that each should invent art anew for himself.'

Two things in particular strike the English reader about this last determined attempt at authoritarian criticism. The first is that Lessing is less than fair in the total impression which he leaves with us of French drama, especially tragedy, a point that has seldom been remarked by German scholars, because Lessing is regarded primarily as the liberator of the German theatre from French shackles. So he was, of course, but for understandable reasons he reacted too violently against Gottsched, so that his influence had to be corrected in its turn by Goethe and Schiller in their maturity. Although so many French works figure on the Hamburg repertoire, no play by Racine, and of Molière only *L'École des femmes* was acted in the period criticised by Lessing. The great majority of the French plays were character comedies by Regnard and sentimental comedies by Destouches, La Chaussée, Voltaire, etc., which had been favourites for many years. Of genuine tragedies there were three by Voltaire, one each by Pierre and Thomas Corneille and by De Belloy. Now Lessing conveys to us quite clearly his high admiration of Shakespeare, although not a single work of his was acted by the Hamburg National Theatre, and he could equally well have made a distinction, if he had chosen, between tragedy as represented by Voltaire, and tragedy as represented by Racine, and Corneille at his best. Instead of this, he turns all his guns on the plot of *Rodogune*, and of course has not a good word to say for Voltaire. It is strange that a critic so catholic in taste was not able to pierce through the conventions of French tragedy to its genuine greatness, especially as he had had opportunities of seeing it well acted in French, for instance in Berlin. Remarks such as the one about the sole merit of French verse being its technical difficulty, or about the vain, volatile, polite, amorous spirit which has prevented the French from writing moving tragedies are, however wittily phrased, only 'half-truths, and come badly from one who claims that Germany has never made herself ridiculous through a Bouhours (the seventeenth-century French Jesuit who denied all 'esprit' to the Germans). There is clearly personal animosity in much of his criticism of Voltaire, though he misses none of Voltaire's criticisms of the French, and in spite of the cosmopolitanism of the man who thought patriotism 'a heroic weakness', he often seems capable, concerning the French, of just such 'sweeping judgments about whole peoples' as he deprecated in the case of the Jews.

Yet for all his criticism of the French, Lessing could not reconcile himself to the irregularity and untidy complexity of English plays, whose plots, he said (piece 12) distract and weary the Germans. 'We like an uncomplicated plot, that can be seen at a glance.' This led to some contradictions in his ideas both about genius and about Shakespeare. He distinguishes more than once between a 'genius' and a 'wit' (witziger Kopf), as Warton had recently done in his essay on Pope, meaning by the former 'a genuine poet, of a lively plastic imagination, the true Maker or Creator', as opposed to a versifier of lively intelligence. Young had claimed freedom for genius, as a precondition of its arriving at 'unexampled excellence', and Lessing similarly often speaks contemptuously of the rules and mechanical laws which genius laughs to scorn. But as we have seen, he seems at other times alarmed at the deification of genius, at the kind of language used by Gerstenberg about Shakespeare, for instance. So in piece 96 he protests against 'the critics whose best efforts are directed towards making all criticism suspect. "Genius! genius!" they cry. "Genius scorns all rules! What genius makes is itself the rule!" So they flatter genius: I think, so that we shall take them for geniuses themselves.' For the logical consequence of this attitude would be to declare even self-criticism to be unnecessary to the poet, and to regard only his first stammerings as truly inspired.

Similarly with Shakespeare. In the 17th *Literaturbrief* Lessing had already made 'the most daring appreciation of Shakespeare to be found in any German writer before the Sturm und Drang',[1] yet what strikes us about his treatment of him in the *Dramaturgie* is 'how little he has to say, and how much he has left unsaid'. He uses him very effectively to depreciate Voltaire in No. 11, contrasting *Sémiramis* with *Hamlet* in the handling of the ghost, and No. 15, contrasting *Zaïre* with *Othello* as a picture of jealousy. But his language, at least, is very rationalistic in the latter passage, when he speaks of *Othello* as 'the most complete text-book' on jealousy. In piece 73, warning poets against trying to plunder Shakespeare, he says that 'even the least of Shakespeare's beauties bears a stamp which proclaims to the whole world: I am Shakespeare's!' yet, when objecting to Weisse's *Richard III*, the play under discussion, as the picture of a monster, he does not mention Shakespeare's Richard. Petersen is probably right in thinking that, for Lessing, such characters are unacceptable because of his Aristotelian notions about 'characters neither good nor bad'. He had claimed that Shakespeare observed Aristotle's rule in essentials, and he avoids discussing awkward examples. What he principally admired in Shakespeare was, no doubt, his realism and his power to move us, to arouse the one essential tragic emotion, pity. He could reconcile the first feature with what Diderot had taught him, and the second with Aristotle.

Some remarks made by Lessing in connection with Weisse's *Richard III* remind us that in his interpretation of Aristotle, though he thought he was getting back to a genuine truth, valid for all time, he was in reality subject, as we all are, to the influence of the mental climate of his age. This is the second point which

---

[1] Robertson, *op. cit.*, p. 247.

impresses itself strongly on the modern reader. In piece 74 he declares that Aristotle would certainly have rejected Weisse's Richard as a tragic character, because he is unrelievedly bad, the most abominable monster who ever trod the stage. 'I say the stage: that he ever trod the earth, I doubt.' The Greeks, he says, avoided the horror inspired by the sight of a man who takes a fiendish delight in working evil. 'They often preferred to ascribe the guilt to fate, they rather made the crime an action fore-ordained by an avenging divinity, they rather turned a free man into a machine than that they should leave us with the appalling idea, that man is by nature capable of such depravity.' In other words, man is good. And on the same topic, in piece 79, dis-cussing Richard's innocent victims, he says that whatever has really happened 'has its good ground in the eternal infinite nexus of all things. In this all is wisdom and goodness, which may appear to us in the few features selected by the poet as blind fate and cruelty.' The poet should however make a consistent and self-explanatory whole out of his selected theme. 'The whole of this mortal creator should be as the shadow thrown by the Whole of the eternal Creator: should accustom us to the thought, that as everything turns out for the best in the one, so it will also in the other.' He should not shock us by bringing the incompre-hensible ways of Providence into his small circle of light. For what good does it do? If we are to have confidence and courage in facing the ultimate mysteries as reasonable men, 'it is very necessary that we should be reminded as little as possible of the bewildering examples of such an undeserved and dreadful doom. Away with them from the stage! Away with them, if it were possible, from all books!' This brings tragedy very near to a theodicy, reminding us of Leibniz, of Shaftesbury, of the *Essay on Man:*

> All discord, harmony not understood
> All partial evil, universal good.

We have seen how similar ideas had influenced the develop-ment of European drama since early in the century. They are fundamental to the optimism of the Enlightenment. But our own age has found it increasingly difficult to believe in man's right to earthly happiness in the naive manner of the eighteenth century, and tragedy understood in Lessing's sense does not seem to it to be tragedy at all. 'If we are not bewildered by life', writes Professor McNeile Dixon,[1] 'we should be, and tragedy awakes in us this just bewilderment, arouses our pity not for merited but unmerited suffering, and gives us painful pause when we reflect that the ways of Heaven are not for our understanding.' Such a 'pessimistic' notion of tragedy was impossible for the Aufklä-rung. Clivio has clearly pointed out Lessing's limitations in this respect,[2] and J. Körner has shown that most German philosophers have wanted tragedy to be a theodicy.[3] A great exception was Nietzsche, for whom tragedy deals with the 'antagonism at the heart of the world', and the German reaction against the common view is mainly due to him, though the rediscovery of Kierkegaard and the influence of Karl Barth in theology, as of Jaspers and Heidegger in philosophy, have all contributed to that reversal of everything for which the Aufklärung stood, which marks the so-called 'existentialist' philosophies of to-day.

The details of Lessing's mature dramatic theory, his re-interpretation of Aristotle, do not concern us here so much as his practice, for this was much more important for the later develop-ment of the German drama. Apart from the central discussion as to the meaning of the definition of tragedy given in the *Poetics*, which Lessing read in what modern scholars hold to be a corrupt and misleading text, there are papers which, to throw light on particular dramas produced at Hamburg, deal with such general topics as the tragic character, the nature of comedy, the value of the new serious comedy and bourgeois drama, the treatment of history by the dramatist, the problem of 'imitation' and dramatic illusion, and many wider aesthetic questions. What Lessing said on all these matters, his indebtedness to earlier writers and the present value of his views have been made the subject of a search-ing study by Professor J. G. Robertson.

The *Dramaturgie* also contains some general remarks on the state of the German theatre, which take us beyond what we have

[1] *Tragedy*, Lon., 1924, p. 137.
[2] *L. und das Problem der Tragödie*, Zür., 1928.
[3] 'Tragik und Tragödie', *Preuss. Jahrbücher*, 1931.

143

found in the *Literaturbriefe*. Though he had been not without hope that the Hamburg National Theatre might lead to real advances, Lessing had to confess at the end that his hopes had been disappointed. From the beginning he encourages no illusions about the state of the German drama, and the attitude of the public towards its own literature. The first play performed had been *Olint und Sophronia*, the tragedy in alexandrines by J. F. von Cronegk, who had died at the age of twenty-six before completing this, his second play. The fifth act had been added, as Lessing tells us, by 'a pen in Vienna', a pen without very much of a mind behind it. Cronegk's first play, *Codrus*, had won Nicolai's prize, but Lessing clearly thinks little of either work. Summing up, in piece 96, he says that most of what has so far been produced in Germany consists of first attempts by young men, and that play-writing and so forth is felt to be something for the under twenty-fives. In this literature there is therefore little for thinking men. In the comedies which these young writers favour there is nothing beyond puns and everyday anecdotes, nor could much more be expected of authors with so little knowledge of the world. How great is the contrast between Germany and France, where poets are not regarded as useless members of society (piece 18). Hamburg is clearly in his mind when he goes on to speak of the poor support given to the theatre in prosperous towns, whose citizens have better, that is more profitable, things to do. In piece 80 again he complains how cold, how indifferent the German public is to its theatre, compared with the Greeks and Romans of antiquity. 'We go to the theatre, almost all of us, out of curiosity, to be in the fashion, from boredom, the desire for company, to stare and be stared at; and only a few, and these rarely, go there for any other reason.' In the last number comes the despairing cry: 'If the public asks what has been accomplished, and supplies the contemptuous answer "Nothing", I in my turn ask; What has the public done, so that something might be accomplished? The answer is again nothing, or worse than nothing. Not only did it fail to support this experiment; it did not even let it take its natural course.'

And he goes on: 'What a simple-minded notion that we could

give the Germans a National Theatre, when we Germans are not yet a nation! I do not speak of our political constitution, but merely of our manners and character. One is almost tempted to say that our character is not to wish for any character of our own. We are still the sworn imitators of everything foreign, and especially the humble admirers of the never sufficiently admired French. Everything which comes to us from beyond the Rhine is lovely, charming, adorable, divine.' Though Lessing had every reason to be indignant, he was wrong, as we shall see, in thinking that the Germans would never have a national theatre until they were a united nation. The next generation was to reveal an enthusiasm for the theatre which would have astonished him, and less than twenty years later we shall find the terms of his statement exactly reversed, and the theatre considered as a step towards national unity, when Schiller writes: 'If we could live to see a national theatre, then we should be a nation indeed.'[1]

[1] *Was kann eine gute stehende Schaubühne eigentlich wirken?* 1784.

THE PLAYS OF LESSING'S MATURITY

IN the *Dramaturgie* Lessing disclaimed the high title of poet, not feeling, as he said, the living spring within himself which leaps up of its own strength. All his critical study of dramatic literature had been necessary to enable him to compose, with much labour, his few essays in the art of the drama, though he flattered himself that the result was something at least approaching the products of genius. He had indeed an infinite capacity for taking pains, but none of the spontaneous ease and lyrical passion of a Goethe. Yet Goethe rated his work extremely high, and held its lasting effect on the production of others to be ample evidence of genuine poetic power. In Lessing's early comedies, as we have seen, there is little beyond a few hints of a deeper humanity which marks them off from the general run of Leipzig work for the theatre. They had however considerable success on the stage, as did also the Plautus adaptation, *Der Schatz*. But *Miss Sara Sampson* was the first of Lessing's plays which stood out from current production and altered its course.

It will be remembered that when Lessing wrote his play, in 1755, two English domestic tragedies, Lillo's *The London Merchant* (or *The History of George Barnwell*) and Moore's *Gamester*, which, though well received at first in England, had not founded a new genre there, had just been translated and the former, first acted in 1752 in Germany, was being played to admiring audiences by the three leading companies of the time, those of Schönemann, Koch and Ackermann. In the following year Lessing wrote, in the preface to a translation of James Thomson's tragedies, 'I would much rather be the author of *The London Merchant* than of *Der sterbende Cato*. . . . At a single performance of the former more tears have been shed, even by the most unfeeling, than can have flowed at all possible performances of the latter.' It was later in the same year that he was urging upon Nicolai and Mendelssohn his view that the only essential tragic emotion was pity. 'Tragedy may arouse as much pity as it possibly can; therefore all the characters on whom the author brings misfortune must have good qualities, therefore the best must also be the most unfortunate', the argument being that it is only the suffering of a good man which moves the spectator to tears.[1] He returns to the point on 29th November, giving a rather banal example of the kind of experience which in real life would move him deeply, the story of a beggar at his gate who lost his post through an excess of honesty. To move us to pity, a character must be neither too good nor too bad—the Aristotelian formula—and his suffering must be intimately bound up with his goodness. It is for instance very moving when Barnwell's uncle, stabbed by his nephew, begins to pray for him, 'because this magnanimous act proceeds from his misfortune, and has its ground in it'.[2] These theoretical reflections, of little interest now in themselves, throw light on Lessing's aims in *Miss Sara Sampson*, and on the popularity with contemporary audiences of a work which is now almost unreadable.

The first domestic tragedy in German proclaims the English origin of its inspiration in the names of its characters, taken from *Clarissa, The London Merchant* and some plays of Congreve. The theme has particularly obvious affinities with that of the first of these works. To draw from us tears of pity is Lessing's avowed aim, and if we do not weep, it is not for lack of example on the stage. Sir William Sampson arrives with his old retainer Waitwell at an inn to which his daughter has been persuaded to accompany Mellefont, a young man about town. Sir William is however not at all the indignant father we expect, for we see him in tears at the sight of this wretched inn where his daughter is staying, and eager to forgive her if she still loves him. In the second scene we learn that Sara still, after two months, spends half the night weeping in her room, watched by her devoted Betty, even her seducer, in his own room, calls himself a wretch not fit to walk

---

[1] To Nicolai, 13th Nov., 1756.   [2] To Mendelssohn, 18th Dec.

the earth, a sentiment applauded by his valet, and in the next scene, after Betty's tearful report, he wipes away the first tear he has shed since boyhood. And so the play goes on, as if the secret of stage success for every character were: weep, and the world weeps with you. The strange thing is that it did. At the first performance, so Ramler wrote to Gleim, the audience sat as still as statues for three and a half hours, and wept.

Lessing hated, he said, 'French tragedies, which only wrung a few tears from him at the end of the fifth act. The true poet distributes pity throughout the play. He introduces passages everywhere, in which the perfections and misfortunes of his hero appear in a moving combination, that is, call forth tears.' (To Mendelssohn, 18th December, 1756). The situation in which Miss Sara is shown to us, by the time we reach Scene 7, is a case in point. It is almost impossible however for us, who are familiar with the later developments of the Clarissa situation in literature, to share the emotions of the play's first audience. Since Richardson's day, it has been common practice to represent the woman in such a situation as more sinned against than sinning, but several stages of development can be distinguished, each reflecting to some extent the ethical and religious views of its time. There is a world of difference, for instance, between Lessing's Miss Sara and Goethe's Gretchen, whose conscience condemns her in the end, but who surrenders herself at first whole-heartedly to passion:

> Doch alles, was dazu mich trieb
> Gott! war so gut! ach, war so lieb!

and it is a still bigger step to the apathetic heroine who, after several Romantic generations of emancipated women, is parodied by Mr. Eliot:

> When lovely woman stoops to folly and
> Paces about her room again, alone,
> She smoothes her hair with automatic hand,
> And puts a record on the gramophone.

To the modern reader Sara Sampson seems lacking in vitality, but to contemporaries she was a touching figure, because her unhappiness was bound up with her goodness, and they saw in her no doubt a daring young woman, because she was prepared to flout public opinion with a good conscience, if only she herself knew that she was married in the sight of God. It was only right, they felt, that until the young man married her, however secretly, she should weep, for the consciousness of her wrongdoing would never leave her, and yet it was rather thrilling to see a good girl who sinned through excess of love. Lessing has taken the first timid step towards the virtuous prostitute of the Romantics. Sara in her small way is a parallel to the Lessing of the poem, *Ich*, quoted above, for both care nothing for reputation, if what they do satisfies their 'ideal self'. There is a 'subjectivist' element in Sara, as Brüggemann has pointed out, reflecting a conception of personality very different from that of medieval man, for instance, who was not important as an individual, but only as a member of some corporate body—family, guild, church or what, ever it might be. We can see how the new attitude fitted in with the philosophy of the Aufklärung, and also with the religious individualism of the Pietists.

The pathetic situations recur, according to plan, throughout the play. In Act III the sentimental highlight is reached in Scene 3, when Waitwell delivers to Sara her father's letter, and both father and daughter reveal a goodness and kindness which no suffering can shake. Waitwell's emotional trump-card is the appeal to Sara not to deny her father the delight of forgiving her. But in his effort towards psychological refinement Lessing makes Sara rather over-subtle, 'spitzfindig', and, like Waitwell, in-sufferably long-winded. His characters, here and in general, do not so much express their feelings as describe them, as one would those of another. Act II has administered to us a wholesome dose of fear, by the introduction of Lady Marwood, Mellefont's for-saken mistress. Lady Marwood is the most convincing character in the play, the prototype of Orsina (*Emilia Galotti*), Schiller's Lady Milford (*Kabale und Liebe*) and a score of similar figures in minor plays. She is an intense individualist of a more familiar type than her rival, one whose thoughts are not of virtue and the hereafter, but of the sensual here and now. For her the only sin is to be found out. Self-centred worldings like her are in the domestic drama invariably aristocrats, and though middle-class writers tended to exaggerate the idealism of their own class, there were good grounds for associating such figures with the traditions of a decadent nobility. Sara and her father, on the other hand, though they are county folk too, are presented in their purely human aspect, in a family context, and adorned with middle-class notions of virtue. Lessing did not go so far as to make them ordinary citizens, still less German citizens, or people might have laughed at them instead of weeping at their misfortunes, for that was the traditional attitude. Treated as they were here, vaguely conceived English gentry could fill the tragic rôles hitherto assigned to princes or mythical heroes in a distant age or clime, whereas Saxon merchants or tradesmen would have been felt to be lacking in dignity. Lillo, the London jeweller, could give expression to the same kind of pride in the merchant's calling which we find in the *Spectator*, but among the German middle class, independence was not common enough to be accepted as characteristic, and tragic status had to be acquired by it by slow degrees.

Throughout the rest of the play, the unscrupulous egoism of Lady Marwood is contrasted with the sentimental goodness and piety of Sara, her father and their servants. There is none of the class conflict beloved of the next generation, and none of the pert maids and wily valets of French comedy. A scene is expressly introduced in which Sir William promotes the faithful Waitwell from servant to friend, and promises him every comfort in his old age. The wicked Lady Marwood on the other hand does not shrink even from murder to win Mellefont back, or failing that to avenge her wrongs, but this eternal triangle, the favourite situation of the domestic drama, is made respectable, as it were, by the cautious and scholarly Lessing, by his suggestion of its good classical ancestry, in *Medea*. 'See in me another Medea', Lady Marwood cries, threatening the life of little Arabella, her child and Mellefont's, but the threat is not carried out. Instead, Lady Marwood persuades Mellefont (and here the motivation is weak) to introduce her as a relative to his Sara, 'that she may read her whole future fate in Sara's glance'. The confrontation of the rivals is excellent theatre, and the scene gives the proved controversialist Lessing good opportunities in the cut and thrust of its heated argument. In the eternally dramatic spectacle of a clash of wills expressed in dialogue we forget the dreariness of so much that has gone before. There are more tears before the close when Sara, ingeniously poisoned by Lady Marwood, and slowly dying through a whole act, at last sees her father, who has been waiting since Act I in the next room. She 'forgives the hand through which God punishes her', and Sir William, after the repentant Mellefont's suicide, adopts the very un-childlike love-child Arabella. 'Tout comprendre' could go no further.

Between the opposing ranks of the good and the bad stands Mellefont, stage ancestor of the Prince in *Emilia Galotti,* and of Goethe's Weislingen, Clavigo, Fernando; a very degenerate Jason, who neither throws over nor accepts the old morality, but stumbles on from one weak impulse to the next. He too rejects the claims of social institutions on the free individual, above all the institution of marriage. 'Sara Sampson, my beloved! What bliss lies in those words! Sara Sampson, my wife! Half of this bliss has vanished! and the other half—will vanish!—monster that I am!' Monologues such as the scene (IV, 2) where these words are spoken are freely introduced by Lessing. Every principal has his or her servant as confidant, the unities of action and time are strictly observed, and the unity of place only broken within limits which allow for easy stage presentation. The technique involves the use of the middle curtain to provide an alternation of 'long and short stage', common practice in Germany since the seventeenth century. In Scene 1 of the first act, for instance, the middle curtain, acting as backcloth, represents one side of the 'Saal' or broad first-floor landing of an inn, from which bedroom doors open off. In Scene 2 it is drawn up to reveal Mellefont's room, and Sara has to be brought to him (see the end of Scene 4) instead of his going to her for Scenes 7 and 8. After Acts I, III and IV the scenery was probably changed in dimmed lighting on the open stage, for the front curtain did not fall till the end of the play. At the end of each act the players have somehow to be provided with a motive for leaving the stage,

as when Mellefont says to his man: 'Come, show me the way.'
In Act III the same middle curtain is used as in Act I, being
raised for Scenes 2 to 6, and lowered again for Scene 7, but the
back stage is now Sara's room. In spite of his criticism of the
French rules Lessing found a reasonable observance of the unities
of time and place a practical convenience, because he was faithful
to the 'analytical' type of construction usual in French plays,
though after *Miss Sara Sampson* he made some slight use of
episodic scenes.

Minna von Barnhelm

Goethe, who was present as a student at the first performance
of *Minna von Barnhelm* in Leipzig in 1767, calls the play in
Dichtung und Wahrheit 'the first theatrical production the content
of which reflects important aspects of contemporary life'. 'It is
easy to see', he says, 'how this play was conceived between war
and peace, between hate and affection. From the literary and
middle-class world, in which poetry had hitherto moved, it
opened up vistas of a higher, more significant sphere.' The
greatest German comedy is indeed firmly rooted in its time, the
end of the Seven Years' War. It does not introduce leading
figures in the conflict, and the war and its consequences provide
only the background and the atmosphere, but we do see how
public events impinge upon the everyday life of ordinary people.
The essentially private theme of the piece thus acquires a deeper
significance, and its figures continued to recall a turning point
in German history when Lessing's immediate aim, the reconciliation of Prussian and Saxon after what had been in effect a civil
war, had long been forgotten.

As in *Miss Sara Sampson*, the principal characters are taken
from the upper ranks of society, but the emotions evoked are
simply human, not confined to any single class, while the
separateness of state from state and class from class are emphasised
as little as possible. The point of view is already the universal
tolerance of the author of *Ernst und Falk* and *Nathan der Weise*,
eager to reconcile states and classes, as well as religions, in the
name of their common humanity.

Major von Tellheim, the hero of the play, is a country gentleman from Kurland, evidently of considerable wealth. In winter quarters in Saxony he had with him a lackey, a keeper, a coachman and a running footman. He had become a soldier 'in support of he did not know what political principles'—a remark which surely does not imply much enthusiasm on his creator's part for Prussia's cause in the war—but principally to inure himself to danger, as a gentleman should, and he has no intention of making the army his career. He only approves of men becoming soldiers from love of their country, or to defend some good cause. Mercenaries he compares to butcher boys. When he has won his Minna, his only wish is that they should live for each other far from the madding crowd's ignoble strife, a good Augustan ideal.

After the defeat of Saxony, which had thrown in its lot with Austria in the war, Tellheim had been ordered to raise a war levy with the utmost severity in a certain part of Thuringia, in Saxony, and perceiving the difficulty which the 'estates', the responsible authority, found in collecting ready money quickly in a disorganised country, he had generously advanced a large sum for them himself. Touched by the Quixotic humanity of an enemy of her state, Minna von Barnhelm, a rich heiress in these parts, had made every effort to meet him, and they had quickly fallen in love.

But the course of true love does not run smooth for them, or we should have no play. Tension is provided, so abundantly that, as in *Le Misanthrope*, the comedy seems to be in danger of turning into a tragedy, by the unforeseen consequences, after the war, of Tellheim's magnanimous action, and by the deadly seriousness with which, made as he is, he faces an inherently absurd situation. The Prussian treasury, when he claims repayment of the sum advanced, from the Saxon indemnity now collected in full, is suspicious about his dealings with the Saxons. His claim is refused, and he is relieved of his command, until an official enquiry has been made into the affair.

Tellheim now feels that an officer under such a cloud, impoverished and disabled as he is, has no longer any right to claim

Minna. His fault is that, unlike Miss Sara Sampson, he pays too much attention to what the world says, and through wounded vanity gives himself up to a kind of proud self-pity. He calls himself dishonoured, though his conscience is clear, a beggar, though he despises money, and a cripple, because of an honourable wound. It is this exaggerated regard for 'honour' in the sense of reputation, a certain military rigidity natural to one who acts on abstract principles, which Minna, and the audience, find slightly ridiculous, though he never loses their liking and respect. In his admirable analysis of the play, Professor Staiger has pointed out that Lessing's remarks about Regnard's *Distrait* in piece 28 of the *Dramaturgie*, where he distinguishes between 'lachen' and 'verlachen', may well have been written with Tellheim also in view.[1] He amuses us, but he is not an object of derision, and the value of this kind of comedy 'lies in the laughter itself', that is, it makes us realise the value of what Tellheim so obviously lacks, a sense of humour.

Minna on the other hand, and Franziska too, have humour and common sense, and are guided by intuition rather than by principles. Tellheim would never have imagined or approved of a trick such as the one which Minna plays on him, to break down his inhibitions and make him see things from her angle, but we feel that her daring experiment is justified. Once more we see Lessing's conviction of the supreme moral value of pity when he makes Tellheim say that where even love could not clear up the confusion in his embittered heart, pity, the daughter of love, has succeeded, by showing him something more precious than himself to care for.

In the union of Tellheim and Minna common humanity triumphs over war and differences of 'national' character—for Saxony and Prussia were still separate 'fatherlands' for their inhabitants. It 'accomplishes symbolically', as Goethe says, 'that peace between the feelings of Saxon and Prussian which the political peace had not restored'. Minna and Tellheim, besides being individuals, are representatives of their respective states, and the contrast is further pointed by their supporters, Franziska on

[1] *German Life and Letters*, July 1948.

the one hand, and Werner and Just on the other. It is characteristic in the first place that the Prussians are men and the Saxons women—the relationship could not have been reversed—and these men, each in his own sphere, know their business, know their own worth, and know their place. Their seriousness and efficiency are accompanied by a certain humourlessness and angularity. They do not readily betray their personal feelings, which are deep and lasting. They care little for money, but loyalty and respect for their seniors are instinctive with them. They are all soldiers, and for Lessing's day their independence and self-respect were a part of their soldierliness, not qualities that would be expected of any good citizen, a sad comment on the times. There are of course differences between them, due in part to natural temperament and in part to nurture. Tellheim is gentle and melancholic, Werner restless and buoyant, Just sardonic and surly by nature, and they have the manners of their different social levels.

Minna and Franziska are decided personalities too, as loyal and affectionate as anyone could wish, and their spontaneity is in delightful contrast to the rigidity of the men. Having heard nothing of her Tellheim for some months after the peace, Minna had boldly set out to look for him, just as she had sought him out in the first instance. She is not a clinging, sentimental girl but, despite her twenty years, a woman with a will of her own, all the less likely to be deflected from her aim, which is Tellheim's happiness as well as her own, because, as a lady and an heiress, she has no doubt been accustomed to having her own way. Nor does she scruple to give money to a gambler to stake for her, when she is sorry for him and wishes to spare his feelings. She is in fact a natural, impulsive creature who reacts instinctively to the momentary situation. Franziska too, though she disapproves of her mistress's stratagem, is ready to take the initiative and propose to her Wachtmeister, and from the way these two ladies have with them one can well believe Werner's statement, that in winter quarters in Saxony a man might soon have a ring on every finger. The Saxon qualities then seem to be natural charm and sprightliness, and the easy manners that came of acquaintance with the polite society of Dresden and of 'Klein-Paris'.

The relations between social classes in both groups are tempered by humanity, as in *Miss Sara Sampson*, but more convincingly. Franziska is more of a companion and friend to Minna than a maid. Though a miller's daughter, she has lived with Minna since her childhood and shared her education. She teases and even reproves her with respectful familiarity. Tellheim has in Just a batman as devoted as the dog rescued by Just is to his master, and he has earned this devotion by many kindnesses. The only characters free from this touching sensibility are the big-town products, the grasping, inquisitive innkeeper and the caricature of a French adventurer, Riccaut. Lessing seems to suggest that Germans should overcome their provincial antipathies and reserve their ill-feeling for their true enemies, a view coloured not only by recent history but by his own experiences in Berlin, as well as by his growing distaste for French drama and strong desire for cultural independence.

Apart from this scene with Riccaud there is no patriotic note in the play, no jingoism or suggestion of triumph over former enemies, no glorification of war, but rather the opposite. The references to actual fighting are general and conventional, the readiness of officers and men to give their lives for each other, or share their precious flask of bad water, and so on—humanity on the battlefield. The king is praised for his justice, not for his military prowess. His officials are suspicious and dilatory in Tellheim's affair, but the king is just and generous, and intervenes personally to put everything right, as the general public would expect him to do. The atmosphere of Berlin is suggested by Franziska's mention of carriages, night-watchmen, drums, cats and corporals, with their various noises, making sleep impossible, and by the innkeeper's interrogation of his guests on behalf of the police, a scene which admirably serves to complete the exposition, and combines at the same time character-painting with a touch of local colour.

If all these features prove the truth of Goethe's remark that the play was the product of a particular time, there are others which remind us that it was written for the theatre of that time. Its conventions, like those of Miss Sara Sampson, are still in the main those of the French theatre. 'Act' and 'Scene' are used in the same sense as there, and the unities of time and place are again observed in essentials in this mainly 'analytic' play. The scenic arrange-ments are still simpler than in *Miss Sara Sampson*, and again the 'lieu théâtral' is the 'Saal' of an inn, with occasional scenes in a room opening off it, revealed by drawing up the middle curtain. Again Lessing always contrives to clear the stage at the end of the act, but here the last act ends with a tableau, on which the curtain would descend. Chodowiecki's illustrations make the stage practice of the day perfectly clear. Acts II and IV, in which the scene is the whole stage (for here alternate acts are played with the middle curtain first down, then up, and there are no changes within the act) open with two characters revealed in action, and in Act I Just is seen dozing in his chair when the front curtain rises, but in Acts III and V one or two characters have to walk on.

The action is all concentrated into a few hours in the morning and afternoon of the day following Minna's arrival in Berlin. Tellheim's situation and history are made known to us in natural dialogue in Act I, with unsurpassed skill, and we have already guessed that the new arrival for whom Tellheim has had to give up his room is Minna, when the first scene of Act II shows her in conversation with Franziska. This and the following scene with the innkeeper complete the exposition. We know the characters and their situation, and the 'ring' action has been well started. It is the method of the French classics, still the method of Ibsen in essentials, but though the confidant of the French tradition has not disappeared, the introduction of the innkeeper, and the neat inventions of the dispute about the room and the questioning of the new arrivals conceal the usual scaffolding, while strengthen-ing the structure. The exposition and the motivation in these two acts, the envy of all Lessing's successors, have the economy of great art. Lessing has allowed himself one episodic scene, between Tellheim and Marloff's widow, perhaps with the same idea of hiding the scaffolding while adding to our knowledge of

Tellheim, and there is another episodic scene later, between Minna and Riccaud, but apart from these, every scene carries the action a step further. The secondary action between Franziska and Werner is neatly bound up with the primary plot. This echo of the main theme is of course in the old tradition, and is a welcome addition to the comic element in a play which tends to be too serious for a comedy. It is with the same end in view that Lessing does not actually show us the scene which threatened to be the most tearful of all, when Minna is apparently deserted by Tellheim, but reports it through the innkeeper, who is 'outside the emotional interest of the play'.[1]

Emilia Galotti

In *Minna* Lessing had created a new type of German comedy, a character comedy, but not one in the old narrow sense of the *Deutsche Schaubühne*, where it would have centred round Tellheim conceived as an eccentric man of honour, but one whose 'characters' are complex individuals. They are not simply Saxons either, as in Gellert's plays, but 'Germans, whose fortune was closely bound up with the fate of the whole people . . . and who still speak to us to-day as human beings'. (Staiger.) Even before the existence of a German nation, this was a national comedy, and there has never been another in Germany to equal it. Here for the first time Lessing was, in spite of what he said later, a genuine 'Dichter', finding, with infinite pains, an adequate expression for what he felt about men and women in their ordinary relationships, in more than ordinary times. There is a grace and a naturalness in these scenes which are lacking in the model tragedy, *Emilia Galotti*, which Lessing was almost bound to attempt, after the *Dramaturgie*, where he had claimed that there was no play of Corneille's which he could not improve with the help of Aristotle's insight. As Erich Schmidt says, 'Every page (of the version he was making for the Hamburg Theatre before it failed) was an objective condemnation or acknowledgment of European achievements or tendencies in the drama.'

His new work was to prove very important in the history of

[1] C. E. Vaughan, *The Romantic Revolt*, Edinburgh and London, 1907, p. 175.

the drama, but it is hard to get away from Goethe's criticism of it, to Herder in 1772 (on other occasions he gave it high praise), as 'nur gedacht', an over-conscious product, where the why and wherefore of every detail could be seen. Friedrich Schlegel put the same judgment more strongly when he wrote of it as 'a good example of dramatic algebra', which leaves us unmoved in spite of our admiration. Its inspiration, in other words, is technical. There are things in it which are deeply felt, particularly man's inhumanity to man, but what strikes every reader is the caution with which any political, or even metaphysical, implications of the events presented are avoided.

Against this Lessing would have urged that he was concerned only with what was purely human in the theme, and the history of the composition of the play proves that he thought it possible to transfer to the contemporary world a tragic motif rooted in the peculiar conditions of ancient Rome, without the loss of any of its essential meaning. The story was, of course, that of Virginius, who killed his daughter to save her honour, threatened by Appius, the tyrannical decemvir. Its dramatic possibilities had been brought home to him, as we saw, by Montiano's play, and in the same year, 1754, by Crisp's verse tragedy, acted by Garrick with success at Drury Lane. A scene has survived of the prose translation which Lessing began to make of Crisp before he decided on a modernisation. In a reference to his plan in 1758 he says that he has freed the story of all political implications, 'thinking that the fate of a girl killed by her own father, because he values her virtue higher than her life, is tragic enough in itself'. It was to be in fact a domestic tragedy, leading to no political revolution as in the Roman story; but no tragedy on such a theme can be entirely domestic in its scope. Lessing worked at it on and off for years and finished it in Wolfenbüttel, where he had become librarian to the Duke of Brunswick. It was first produced on a court occasion, the birthday of the dowager duchess, in Brunswick in March 1772, on the initiative of Döbbelin, the director of the theatre there. Lessing, fearing that personal references would be seen where none were intended, sent the manuscript to the Duke beforehand, and obtained his express permission for the performance of his 'Virginia in modern dress', but Germans inevitably saw in the play an indictment of 'Kleinstaaterei'.

The decemvir of the old story naturally becomes the young ruler of a small state, nominally in Italy, but that is a transparent disguise. The picture drawn here reminds us that in his 'national' comedy Lessing had necessarily left unexpressed much of what was most important in the German life of his time. Staiger has said about *Minna:* 'Realism here does not come into conflict with the demands of beauty, because the kind of life that is imitated was still pure and harmonious, that is, "beautiful". The rococo is the last culture of which this may be said.' *Emilia Galotti,* showing as it does the other side of the picture, gives us a different impression of that age.

On the eve of his marriage, a political move, when he has been for years under the domination of a strong-minded mistress who apparently loves him, the prince has conceived a sudden passion for Emilia Galotti, the daughter of a gruff, independent old colonel, and the play turns on the danger which now threatens her honour. The middle-class element is represented by the retired colonel's family, with their incorruptible morality, which is brought into conflict with the hedonism of the prince and his entourage. There is here already a class conflict on the higher levels, but the point is not emphasised as it was to be later. In the first act, a miracle of ingenuity, we see the prince toying with state papers, hurriedly making a few decisions, and receiving his court painter and his all-powerful favourite. It is the most convincing presentation in German drama of the everyday life of a petty potentate, whose first thought is for pleasure, in spite of the responsibility which his position brings. By temperament he is no tyrant, but an amiable and cultivated young man, yet such is the corrupting influence of absolute power that, surrounded as he is by toadies, he is bound to misuse it in the end, like the dream Rustan in Grillparzer's *Der Traum, ein Leben.* In this masterly exposition we learn at the same time what we need to know about all the principal characters and their mutual relations, while the many coincidences on which the plot rests pass unnoticed. Marinelli, the unscrupulous adviser, is given full authority to deal with the complications produced by Emilia's marriage with the high-minded Count Appiani, arranged for that very day. It is again simply the crisis that we witness, and it is all over in a few hours. There is complete unity of place in the last three acts, after a first act in the palace and a second in the Galottis' town house, with no changes within the act.

Lessing's chief difficulty was of course the motivation of the father's tragic decision. The fixed point to which all the rest must lead is that he must kill his daughter, as this was from the outset a Virginia tragedy. Without greatly straining our power of belief Lessing contrives to bring Emilia to the prince's country palace, after the death of the count at the hand of 'bandits', in an attack engineered by Marinelli. Pending a legal enquiry she is to stay in the house of the chancellor, but Lessing does not go so far as to suggest that his prince would violently assault her. He makes her beg for death from her father, after he has prevented her from stabbing herself, not because she fears violence, but because she cannot trust herself to withstand the seductiveness of the prince, in the atmosphere of a pleasure-loving court. The never-ending dispute about Lessing's real intention proves in itself that he has not made it clear. Is Emilia a 'problematic' character, half in love with the prince? Goethe sometimes interpreted the play in this way, and Erich Schmidt and others point to hints Lessing took, they say, from Bandello and Richardson. Or is the cata-strophe the result of a mistake of judgment, on Emilia's part, in that she does not, out of deference to her mother, inform Odoardo while she can of the prince's advances to her in church, on the morning of her wedding day? In view of her phrase about her 'blood' and 'warm senses' we seem bound to accept the former view, but if so, the psychology of the heroine is baffling, as con-temporary critics like Engel and Claudius already thought. How can an innocent young girl on her wedding-day, immediately after the murder of the bridegroom, imagine herself abandoning all the principles she had learnt to respect, and after a few weeks in the murderer's company, yielding herself voluntarily up to him, against her conscience? The real trouble lies, as Engel said, in Lessing's over-boldness in uprooting the Virginia story, or rather in taking over the catastrophe without the circumstances in which it is rooted.[1]

But the chief defect of the play is that it is still concerned with the Richardsonian motif, a woman's defence of her honour against a high-born seducer, to the neglect of more promising aspects of the subject which would have taken it out of the purely family sphere. There is no intense feeling in its central scenes, but merely the working-up with admirable technique of a stock dramatic situation. This impression is intensified by the absence from Lessing's language of that 'element of obscurity' which, according to Goethe, every poem of genius must possess, those magical overtones which we should ascribe now to the working of the subconscious, not the conscious mind of the poet. Lessing's language is inimitably clear and witty, but passion and lyricism are not his strength, so we find something forced and slightly ridiculous even in phrases like Emilia's dying words: 'eine Rose gebrochen eh' der Sturm sie entblättert'. Lessing was not driven to express himself in tragedy because of his profoundest feelings about life. His personal philosophy, as we have seen, was the optimism of the Aufklärung, a philosophy for theodicies rather than for tragedies. Superficially at least a *tout comprendre* attitude is suggested even here, and the final responsibility seems to be removed from the prince to be placed on his evil counsellors, by his being given the final comment: 'O God, is it not enough that, to the detriment of so many, princes are men; must devils also disguise themselves as their friends?'

Yet if the fire has matter at the centre which does not produce its own heat, there are glowing coals all round. What really moved Lessing was indignation at the social and political abuses of his own day, and though he expressed this feeling only in-directly, it was strong enough to turn the play; for his younger contemporaries at least, into a social drama, and to inspire some of them to more outspoken utterances. 'The significance of the drama is not to be found', says Eloesser, 'in the individual catastrophe, but in the convictions here revealed, in that an opposition proceeding from the conditions of society, an enduring

---

[1] 'Der Philosoph für die Welt', in *Schriften*, 1801, I, p. 180.

protest, a state of war between irreconcilable enemies, is proclaimed.' The difference in this respect between *Emilia Galotti*
and *Miss Sara Sampson* is plain to all. There is no suggestion now
that the only thing necessary is a little more sweet reasonableness
all round, no more tearful forgiveness of the gravest wrongs, but
at least the beginnings of an understanding of the part played by
social institutions, by differences in legal rights and political
power, in making such evils possible as the murder of a count
and the threat to the honour of a respected middle-class family.
Among the episodes which remain longest in our memory are
the mention of a death sentence to be signed by the prince, and
his reply: 'With pleasure. Let me have it, quickly!' or his words
to Marinelli about the murder of Appiani: 'A count more in the
world, or fewer. Shake hands! I too am not afraid of a trifling
crime. But, my good friend, it must be a quiet little crime, a
wholesome little crime.'

Judging the play by Goethe's test, its effect on later writers, its
vitality is undeniable. For a generation or two its themes and
characters echoed through the serious drama, and the technique
of its construction was most attentively studied for longer still,
after a first reaction against its severity in the 'seventies. In one play
after another Lessing's idea of an Italian setting was imitated,
and subjects from the spectacular history of the small Italian
states were treated as a more colourful parallel to events nearer
home. The social criticism merely suggested in *Emilia Galotti*
was carried to extreme lengths under the influence of Rousseauistic
notions of freedom and a return to nature, and in particular,
tragedies of love and lust amidst a conflict of class loyalties were
worked out on various levels. Individual characters, the prince,
Orsina, the emancipated woman and intelligent, disillusioned
adventuress, and Marinelli, went through a series of re-incarna-
tions, we shall find, not only in the domestic drama, but in the
early works of Goethe and Schiller.

Nathan der Weise

Lessing's last play continues not so much his earlier work for
the theatre as the theological writings which took up most of his

attention in the last ten years of his life. His publication between 1774 and 1778 (as *Fragments,* ostensibly discovered in the Wolfen-büttel library) of parts of the *Apology for the Reasonable Wor-shippers of God* by the deist Reimarus (1694–1768), an orientalist whose family he had known well in Hamburg, led from 1777 to the lively 'Fragmentenstreit'. Though not in entire agreement with the author of the *Fragments,* Lessing defended their method and tried to obtain for them a fair hearing. His principal opponent was the Hamburg Hauptpastor Goeze, who declared the *Frag-ments* to be a danger to religion and the state, and heaped re-proaches and innuendos on their editor, whose devastating retort in a series of pamphlets was published in collected form as *Anti-Goeze* in 1778. This work expressed with all Lessing's old fire and wit the religious views of the later Aufklärung, bringing home to wider circles advanced ideas which, until now, had been more generally accepted in England and France than in Germany. In the last quarter of the century Germany made up for lost time, and Lessing's influence on this movement of ideas was extremely important. The best known of all his religious writings was the 'dramatic poem', *Nathan der Weise,* completed from an earlier plan in 1779, when exemption from censorship had been withdrawn from him in Brunswick, and he had decided to 'return to his old pulpit, the stage' though with no hope of having his play performed. It was published by subscription in 2000 copies, and a second and third edition were soon called for, a book-selling success comparable with that of Schiller's later plays. One of Lessing's aims, to earn some money by the publica-tion in case he should be dismissed, was thus attained.

As the first of the three greatest dramatic monuments of German Humanität, *Nathan der Weise* counts for much in the history of the eighteenth-century theatre, even though it was not con-sidered a possible play for the stage until after the century's close. It added greatly to the prestige of the literary drama by making it, for the first time in Germany, a vehicle for serious thought. In writing it, Lessing naturally made use of all his skill as a craftsman, but neither purely aesthetic nor entertainment values were his first consideration. It was frankly a work of propaganda, like Voltaire's religious plays *Mahomet* (1742) and *Les Guèbres, ou la Tolération* (1769). It was remarkable in its form, too, as the first notable German play in blank verse, another factor which made against a stage performance at the time. Verse was not employed by Lessing, as he admits, for its musical quality, but 'because it seemed to suit the oriental tone of the play', i.e. as an anti-naturalistic device. This verse is indeed anything but musical, and is more prosaic than most of his prose. In some other respects however Lessing still holds to the tradition of the domestic drama, perhaps even to excess.

In brief, *Nathan* is a dramatic allegory, based on Boccaccio's version of the old story of the three rings, which Lessing also knew from the *Gesta Romanorum*. In Boccaccio's novella, Saladin asks a rich Jew of Alexandria the embarrassing question which is the best religion in order to force a loan out of him, and the Jew tells the story of the three externally indistinguishable rings, one of which had been passed down for generations in a certain family, and made its possessor head of the family and heir to its possessions, until a man came to own it whose three sons were all equally dear to him. Unwilling to offend any of them, he promised each one the ring, and had two copies of it made, copies so exact that he could no longer distinguish the genuine ring himself. The dispute after his death as to which was the original was never settled. The three great religions, Christianity, Judaism and Mohammedanism are now equally indistinguishable in value.

In revising this rather sceptical story for this purpose, Lessing took a hint from the *Gesta Romanorum*, for in this version the genuine ring conferred magical healing powers on its wearer. So true religion, Nathan says, is known by its effects. The original ring had always been left not to the eldest, but to the dearest son, and had made its wearer pleasing to God and man if he had believed in its power himself. When the three sons brought the dispute before a wise judge, he pointed out that not one of the rings seemed to work in the old way, or one son would already have been acknowledged by the other two as the most beloved. Perhaps the genuine ring was lost, and all three were counterfeit? He advised them that each should try to prove his ring genuine by his conduct, to act as if it were so, and true faith would give the genuine ring its power. But it might be many thousand years before a wiser judge than he would be able to decide the matter on this evidence.

Leisegang argues convincingly that by his addition of the judge and his verdict to the story, Lessing has introduced an element of confusion. 'The inventor of the parable holds that one of the three religions is certainly genuine, though we shall only know which it is when its effects are seen. But Lessing's Nathan is aiming at the suggestion that all three religions are equally genuine and equally counterfeit, in accordance with Lessing's often ex/ pressed conviction that all positive religions are equally true and equally false, the conviction which he himself brought into relation with *Nathan* when he wrote (in an unpublished preface): "My attitude to all positive religions has always been the same as Nathan's." But as long as one of the three rings is undoubtedly genuine, the parable cannot be made to mean this. To make the rings equal in value, Lessing makes the judge play with the idea that the true ring was presumably lost, so that all three are value/ less. And here we have Lessing's true opinion, expressed through/ out *Nathan*. There are three positive religions, which are all both counterfeit and capable of good results, and there is a fourth, not on the same but a higher level and at the same time contained in them, the religion of reason, the only true and genuine one. The three counterfeit positive religions rest merely on subjective belief in truths incapable of proof, on a fiction, but one which produces results and *can* make men good. The religion of reason, however, rests not merely on a subjective belief, but on an objective content, the power of the ring, which unites with that of the wearer, as soon as he has placed his trust in it, when subjective and objective become identical.'[1]

It is not for nothing that Nathan is called the Wise. The personality of the exponent of these views contributes as much as his doctrine to the total impression left on us by the play. Nathan is not a contemplative, but a man of action, a wealthy

[1] *Lessings Weltanschauung*, 1931, pp. 156 f.

merchant who 'uses nobly the money which he is not ashamed to gain through his foresight and industry'. Here is a link with the family drama, with the *Merchant of London* itself, for instance, and a reflection of the middle-class point of view of that age. A century later a merchant-prophet would have been an impossibility. Nathan has not acquired his wisdom by abstract reasoning, but by living and suffering. The essence of it is very much the same as what Santayana sees as central in Spinoza's ethics, 'the perennial wisdom of the Jew, of the sorely-tried, plebeian, international positivist. God's thoughts, it said, are not our thoughts, nor His ways our ways; but the righteous prosper by His decree, and the way of the transgressor is hard. . . . If Job had said, "Though he slay me, yet will I trust in Him," Spinoza could express the same thought less ambiguously by saying, "He who truly loves God cannot wish that God should love him in return." '

There is an all-important pre-supposition in Nathan's view of life, as it is expressed, for instance, in his account of his reception of the infant Recha, after the pogrom in which his wife and seven sons had perished, when he finally submitted himself, and called to God, 'I will, if Thou willst that I will.' The presupposition is the same, Leisegang points out, as is expressed by Hegel in the first chapter of his *Philosophy of World History*, namely that reason rules the world. This basic pre-supposition is taken over by the whole idealistic movement, not always consciously, from the Christian philosophy of life which it had inherited. We may even see a hint in *Nathan*, Leisegang says, of the 'List der Vernunft' invoked by Hegel to explain the apparently irrational features in history, in the strange means employed by Providence in his story to reach Its goal—Orsina and Odoardo in *Emilia Galotti* had already made much play with similar ideas, in which we may perhaps see a relic particularly of pietism. *Nathan* abounds, in any case, in fantastic happenings mostly accomplished before the play begins and gradually revealed in their consequences—the familiar analytic technique—which bring together as one family Saladin, the Templar and Recha, and through her her adoptive father, Nathan, representing between them all three religions. This re-union is of course symbolic of the brother-hood of all races and creeds, the fundamental unity of mankind, the true ground of the toleration, or rather, universal love, which the play preaches. 'Little children, love one another', the Testa-ment of St. John, seemed to Lessing to sum up the moral teaching of Christianity, and of all religion. Without this symbolic inter-pretation the plot is trivial.

The characters too stand for something beyond themselves, some more and some less, though all are at the same time in-dividuals. They are clearly of the age of Humanität, the age of Herder, of Goethe's *Iphigenie*, Schiller's *Don Carlos*, all except the Patriarch, the Christian cleric, in whose features those of Goeze linger. It was decidedly provocative to make him the villain of the piece, so far as there is one, and a Jew its hero. Following Voltaire and the historian Marin, Lessing represents Saladin as an enlightened and generous ruler, so noble that it becomes difficult to show him laying a trap for a Jew. He is given a sister, Sittah, concerned for his finances and delighting in intrigues. Lessing invents too an impulsive young Templar, a Swabian, as he himself thinks, though he turns out to be Saladin's nephew. A love-interest is brought into the plot by his rescue from a fire of Nathan's adopted daughter, Recha, who is meant to be all innocence and natural piety, but becomes a mouth-piece for Lessing's ideas. Minor characters suggest other varieties of religious attitude, the eccentric Dervish, Al Hafi, Saladin's treasurer, an oriental Diogenes, and the simple kindly lay-brother, the proud patriarch's messenger. This motley crowd is handled with all Lessing's skill in the careful preparation of effective situations, and with more freedom than ever before regarding the place of action—there are three changes of scene in one act. But the unity of time is strictly observed. The whole construction is looser and the style much wordier than in *Emilia Galotti*, for this is at bottom not so much a drama as a series of arguments and addresses, almost an anticipation of Bernard Shaw.

Nathan was played for three nights in 1783, unsuccessfully, by Döbbelin, who had also been the first to stage *Minna* and

Emilia Galotti. He was now in Berlin, the focus of Aufklärung in religious matters, but outside the capital of the philosopher on the throne no one dared to act the play until orthodox Lutheranism had been weakened by twenty more years of philosophical speculation and vulgarisation, and a poetical drama which handled serious themes in verse was again acceptable on the stage, through the work of the Weimar classics. It was one of F. L. Schröder's ambitions to act Nathan, but it was easier to introduce Shakespeare to a German audience, in prose, than this outspoken and unorthodox native product, in verse. He gave much admired private readings of the play however, in Hamburg, and on a visit to Weimar in 1801. In July of that year F. L. Schmidt produced the play in Magdeburg, against the advice of his friends, and it was better received than *Wallenstein*. The whole cast were in an exalted mood, 'as if they were acting a play in higher regions'. A few months later it was at last acted in Weimar, in an adaptation by Schiller, though the Duke looked upon the performance as an 'alarming enterprise'. Berlin and all the larger theatres in protestant Germany followed, but it was 1814 when Munich and 1819 when Vienna attempted it. Once accepted it remained a favourite among classical plays everywhere.

THE THEATRE OF THE 'SEVENTIES

IN the German theatre of the 'seventies and 'eighties we find a further development of most of the tendencies which we have noticed in the companies immediately succeeding Frau Neuber. The aim of the better companies is to reduce touring to a minimum, by providing a varied programme, capable of appealing to an educated audience for a whole season at a time. Only a few theatres, with the help of subsidies from courts, become 'standing theatres', but their number steadily grows as the German theatre gradually raises its standards and builds up a better repertoire. From now on, stage and literature are in constant touch with each other, the number of dramatic authors, especially on the lower level, is constantly growing, and the interest of the public is reflected in its increasing support, as well as in the appearance of more and more dramatic criticism in newspapers and in special journals and pamphlets. The status of the actor continues to rise, as more genuine artists appear, and higher demands are made on their art, though the profession is still strongly opposed by most of the clergy, and the bohemian ways of a considerable number still give grounds for criticism.

The so-called National Theatre at Hamburg, as we have seen, was not established on a sound basis. Löwen had neither acting experience nor personality, and was never taken seriously as artistic director, even by the younger personnel of the theatre, and after a few rehearsals Ekhof, as senior member of the company, was left in charge of production. He had a difficult team to handle, was never a great organiser, and had a very poor repertoire at his disposal. The Hamburgers lost their enthusiasm after a few performances, the prominent citizens who had promised financial support drew back, and the original three, Seyler,

Tillemann and Bubbers, found that their extravagant promises, of a pension fund and so forth, could not be kept. The company was taken to Hanover early in December, 1767, after a seven months' season. They had had to resort to ballet from the third performance,[1] in spite of the contempt they had expressed for this kind of popular attraction, and later in the year, even acrobats could not draw a sufficient audience to make ends meet. When the company came back after five months in Hanover, where Schröder had joined them again, the management was continually being dunned by its creditors, and could not pay even leading actors regularly. In September Ackermann agreed to take over the theatre and company again from Easter 1769, on terms which seem to us very unfavourable to himself.

Ackermann remained the nominal head of the theatre for most of the remaining two years of his life, but Schröder had already most of the responsibility on the artistic side, and his mother continued to look after the finances for eleven years more, paying her son a fixed salary (of 16 taler a week). In a few months (August 1769) Abel Seyler persuaded Ekhof and several of the other leading actors (Boek, Brandes and Koch, with their wives) to join a new company which he was starting. Frau Hensel had left before Ackermann took over control again. This Seyler company, with its strong nucleus of players, became one of the best of its time, though for some years it suffered many hardships on tour. It was for two years in north-west Germany, playing in the winter in Hanover, where it had ousted Ackermann, obtaining a licence and some financial support from the court, and in the summer in Celle, Lüneburg, Stade, Hamburg and Lübeck, then in Osnabrück, Hildesheim, and finally for three months, under Ekhof's management, with more success, in Wetzlar. In 1772 Seyler succeeded Koch in Weimar, and continued to play there, subsidised by the court, until fire destroyed the Wilhelmsburg, with its small theatre, in 1774. Again Seyler had to take to the road, but in 1775 the Duke of Gotha established a court theatre, and took on the best of Seyler's actors, with some others,

---

[1] R. Thiele, *Die Theaterzettel der Hamburgischen Entreprise*, Erfurt, 1895, p. 11.

to staff it, while Seyler, with a new troupe, continued to tour in Saxony. The court librarian, H. A. O. Reichard, translator and theatre enthusiast, editor of the *Theaterkalender* (1775–1800) and the *Theaterjournal für Deutschland* (1777–84) became administrative director of the Gotha Court Theatre, under a court chamberlain, with Ekhof in charge of play production and Schweizer as head of the musical side. This was the first German court theatre in the fullest sense, a permanent theatre no longer run for private profit, in which some of the objects aimed at in Hamburg were for a short time attained, for everyone on the theatre staff was a state servant, with pension rights after a fixed term of service. Unfortunately the theatre only survived Ekhof's death (in 1778) for one year, under Boek.

But meanwhile other courts were beginning to imitate Gotha. Dresden was on the point of establishing a German theatre, based on Seyler's new troupe, when the War of the Austrian Succession made economy necessary, and a subsidy was granted instead, in 1777, to the former director of the opera, Bondini, who could speak only broken German. In 1776 the Emperor Joseph II founded the Teutsches Nationaltheater in Vienna, the capital of the Reich, where a national theatre had a better claim to the title than in Hamburg. By this reform he brought to an end the system of leasing out court entertainments to aristocratic managers, which had been in force since an empty tennis-court (*jeu de paume*, the old indoor tennis) adjoining the palace had been handed over in 1741 to Herr von Sellier, as the original Burgtheater. Here he had provided operatic and dramatic entertainment for the court at his own financial risk.

The farming-out system had continued unchecked until the death of Francis I in 1765. For eleven years before this the Burg had been occupied by a French company, and a gaming saloon had helped out the finances of the aristocratic *entrepreneur*, while the much older Kärntnertor Theatre had provided opera, ballet and German plays, for the most part improvised. Some regular German plays had however been acted here since the end of the 'forties, when a few remnants of the Neuber troupe, some of them, it will be remembered, in debt to Lessing, had been taken on to the theatre staff, but these plays were regular with a difference, for old traditions died hard. When *Miss Sara Sampson* was acted, for instance, the former Hanswurst Prehauser took the part of Sir William's sanctimonious man-servant, and the whole play assumed a comic aspect. In 1765 the Viennese Gottsched, Professor Sonnenfels, had begun a campaign for a regular theatre, in his periodical *Der Mann ohne Vorurteil* (The Unprejudiced Man, a typically rationalistic title), and in his *Briefe über die wienerische Schaubühne*, gradually interesting some of the nobility. In 1771 Maria Theresa, who looked upon the theatre as 'ce qu'il y a de plus vil dans la monarchie', was even prevailed upon to attend a German performance of Diderot's *Père de famille,* a sign that the German theatre was becoming respectable in Vienna. Several attempts were made about this time to persuade Lessing to go to the Burgtheater as manager, and he was particularly well received when passing through Vienna in 1775, but nothing came of it all.

It is strange that it was Joseph II, in catholic Vienna, and not Frederick the Great in protestant Berlin, who was the first among the heads of larger states to establish a German theatre, but it was not because he was more interested in art. On the contrary, he was moved by utilitarian considerations, thinking, like the good rationalist that he was, that the theatre could be made to serve moral ends. His interest in Lessing indicates too that he was impressed by literary developments in the protestant north, and did not want Austria to lag behind. Following the example of the *Comédie-Française*, the Emperor put the administration of his new theatre into the hands of the actors. At a weekly meeting, senior members of the company decided by vote about the choice of plays and the distribution of the rôles, and they were responsible for production generally. With some modifications this system of control, by a committee of 'régisseurs', lasted on into the twentieth century. It had many drawbacks, and the Burgtheater had a chequered history under it for a generation or two, but generous financial support was given to it, and the first-class talent it could command assured it of a certain distinction. The German theatre was now a cultural institution in Vienna, as in Gotha, with a salaried staff of civil servants, which gradually built up a tradition of its own and kept a number of playwrights busy with its demands, though none before Grillparzer can be said to have been in the front rank as poets.

A third 'Hof' und Nationaltheater' was founded in Mann-heim, largely as a consolation to the town when Karl Theodor of the Palatinate succeeded to the Electorate of Bavaria and trans-ferred his capital to Munich, in 1777. A beginning had already been made with a German court theatre in Mannheim, and Marchand's troupe from Mainz and Frankfort, which had been engaged for it, was now moved to Munich with the court, where it was mismanaged by a series of noblemen. But the new 'Court and National Theatre' established in Mannheim, under Baron H. von Dalberg, soon became one of the best in Germany. It opened in 1779, with a company drawn from the cream of the Gotha actors, whose Court Theatre had just closed down, and the best of Seyler's latest troupe, so that the north German theatrical tradition was now carried to the Rhineland. Before studying the development of this theatre in the 'eighties and 'nineties, it will be helpful to have a general impression of the German theatrical centres in the 'seventies, and of the repertoire offered by the best of them, especially by Schröder's theatre in Hamburg, in its relation to the literary drama and to social influences.

The first number of Reichard's *Theaterkalender* gave a list of fourteen German theatres, to which six more were added in the following year. The list grew in successive numbers, until in the 'nineties it included well over thirty. The principal names mentioned in 1774 are:

1. Ackermann's theatre, now managed by F. L. Schröder, in Hamburg.

2. Koch in Berlin, at the Theater in der Behrenstrasse, built in 1771. Koch died in 1775 and was succeeded by Döbbelin.

3. Seyler in Gotha. This became the Gotha Court Theatre next year.

4. Döbbelin in Dresden and Magdeburg. Bondini took over the theatre in Dresden in 1777.

5. Marchand in Mainz and Frankfort, moved to Munich in 1777.

6. Vienna. Here the Kärntnertor Theatre was the more active in 1774, but in 1776 the Teutsches Nationaltheater was established in the building later called the Burgtheater.

7. Schuch in Königsberg (run by Franz Schuch's widow).

8. Wäser in Silesia.

9. Wahr in Hungary (Esterhazy and Pressburg).

There were minor troupes in Münster, Prague, Innsbruck, Riga, Warsaw, Pommerania, the Palatinate, etc.

According to the same source there were foreign theatres in:

1. Berlin. Here there was the Italian Opera, in Knobelsdorf's Opera House, built in 1743, and usually a French company of actors, until 1778, in the French Comedy in the Gensdarmenplatz, built in 1774. This theatre became the home of the National Theatre when one was set up in 1786, under Döbbelin. Until the end of Frederick the Great's reign there was usually a small troupe of Italian intermezzo singers at Potsdam.

2. Mannheim still had one of the best Italian operas in Europe. This was moved to Munich in 1777.

3. Kassel had a French theatre and Italian opera.

4. Vienna had an Italian opera.

5. Prague had an Italian comic opera.

6. Dresden had an Italian comic opera from 1777.

7. Esterhazy had an Italian opera.

Travelling French comedian and Italian operetta singers were still often dangerous rivals for the German players in the 'seventies, as they had been in 1769 for the Hamburg theatre. Hamon's troupe, for instance, came to Hamburg nearly every season and was favourably contrasted by local critics with Schröder's company. It presented both plays and operettas in French. In 1776 there was a serious attempt made by Hamburg citizens to build a permanent home for it there. The same company was active in Vienna, Berlin and Brunswick. Noverre, who had raised ballet to a fine art in Vienna, also put in a season or two in Hamburg, and several less eminent foreign troupes visited the town from time to time.

One can perhaps best form an idea of the repertoire of the German theatre in the 'seventies by considering first the most progressive company, Schröder's in Hamburg, and comparing some of the others with it.

In the early years of the decade, the starting-point was the repertoire of the Hamburg National Theatre. Here verse tragedy was already slightly less to the fore than in Ackermann's repertoire of the preceding decade, but it was still important, as is obvious from the *Dramaturgie.* In the following analysis the number of performances is given in brackets after each title. Gottsched's *Cato* had disappeared, no Racine was played, and nothing by P. Corneille except *Rodogune* (8) or of Thomas Corneille except *Essex* (2). Voltaire however was well represented, with *Zaïre* (4), *Alzire* (3), *Mahomet* (4) in a blank verse translation by Löwen, *Mérope* (4) and *Sémiramis* (7). Three other contemporary French tragedians each supplied one work, Lemierre, De Belloy and Fontenelle, though the latter's *Ericie* (6) was really a 'drame', and in Paris it was prohibited by the censor until 1789 because of its anti-clerical content. Between them these French tragedies took up very nearly as many evenings as the German and English tragedies taken together. The English ones were the two domestic tragedies, *The London Merchant* (3) and *The Gamester* (4), with Thomson's *Edward and Eleonora* (5), which had all been on Ackermann's repertoire since 1756. The German tragedies were Schlegel's *Canut* (1), Lessing's *Miss Sara Sampson* (5), Cronegk's *Codrus* (1) and *Olint und Sophronia* (4), five by the prolific C. F. Weisse: *Eduard III* (2), *Richard III* (4), *Rosemunde* (3), *Crispus* (4), *Romeo und Julie* (9); the *Julie* (4), of H. P. Sturz and Ayrenhoff's *Hermann und Thusnelda* (1). The most popular, it will be seen, were the domestic tragedies, *Miss Sara*, *Romeo und Julie* and *Julie*.

Among the forty-three full-length French comedies acted, the great majority were of the serious kind, the old favourites of Destouches (5 plays), La Chaussée (3 plays), Marivaux (4 plays), and the contemporaries Voltaire (5 plays), Diderot, whose

Père de famille (12) went down much better than *Le Fils naturel* (1), de Falbaire with his sentimental *L'Honnête Criminel*, Beaumarchais with *Eugénie*, Mme de Graffigny with *Cénie* and Sedaine with *Le Philosophe sans le savoir*. Of true comedy, there were six plays of Molière, of which the most popular were *L'Avare* and *L'École des femmes*, and three of Regnard's character comedies, all in high favour.

The most popular German comedies were also of the newer serious type, *Minna von Barnhelm* (16), Weisse's *Amalia* and *List über List*, the Viennese Heufeld's version of La nouvelle Héloise, called *Julie*, two of the imitations of Lessing by the actor Brandes, *Der Schein betrügt* and *Der Graf von Olsbach*, and a play *Der Zweikampf* by a young Hamburg pastor, J. L. Schlosser, which gave rise to the heated controversy, stirred up by Lessing's later opponent, Hauptpastor Goeze, as to whether or not a clergyman might write for the stage. Of the older Saxon comedies, Schlegel's *Triumph der guten Frauen*, Krüger's *Kandidaten*, and two plays by K. F. Romanus still went down well.

Italian comedy, with its strong flavour of the *commedia dell' arte*, was represented by five plays by Goldoni, and was decidedly popular. Ackermann had staged his *Pamela* as early as 1756. The favourites in Hamburg were *Der Lügner* and *Die verstellte Kranke*. G. Colman the elder's *Jealous Wife* (from *Tom Jones*), well translated by Bode, was the only English comedy.

If we attempt to classify the Ackermann troupe's repertoire after the National Theatre's failure in 1769, we find that many of the stock works were carried forward, and that the experiments made, though fairly numerous, do not reveal any clear policy. Like the touring companies before them and their counterpart in England, whether in the provinces or at Drury Lane,[1] the National Theatre had gone in extensively for light afterpieces, for which the Italians had started the fashion early in the century. It had soon re-introduced ballet too, but not light opera. This genre had however meanwhile become very popular, as we have seen, in other parts of Germany, and it was now tried in

---

[1] See Sybil Rosenfeld, *Strolling players in the provinces*, 1660–1765, Camb., 1939, p. 75.

Hamburg. At the third attempt with *The Devil to Pay* Koch had made a great hit in Leipzig, and comic opera soon became all the rage there, then in Weimar, again through Koch, and in many small courts. Weisse, never at a loss, provided many adaptations of French operettas, to which Hiller and Neefe composed new music. Elsewhere local composers came forward, Wolf in Weimar, Schweizer and Benda in Gotha, André in Frankfort-on-Main. The first librettist to follow Weisse was D. Schiebeler, with *Lisuart und Dariolette* (1766), which goes back through Favart and Voltaire to Dryden, and ultimately to Chaucer's *Wife of Bath*. Seyler's theatre poet, J. B. Michaelis, wrote several one-act afterpieces of the same type, like *Der Einspruch*, J. J. Engel in Berlin provided *Die Apotheke* (1771), even Nicolai tried his hand at these trifles, and Eschenburg (besides revising Wieland's Shakespeare) translated and adapted a large number from French and Italian. In Weimar, Heermann, Musäus and Bertuch followed suit, and in Gotha F. W. Gotter, a rather superior Weisse, translated and adapted most diligently.

The sudden enthusiasm for this genre, the Singspiel, as it is fittingly called in German, because the dialogue was spoken and only the interspersed lyrics were sung, is difficult to explain, in view of the earlier failure of attempts to introduce ballad opera from England, where it had achieved spectacular successes as early as 1728 (Gay's *Beggar's Opera*), except in connection with its popularity in France, and for its success there, as M. Gaiffe has pointed out, one explanation is to be found in the social conditions of the time. Round about 1765, he tells us, the French public was crying out for 'drame' in one form or another. For various reasons, the *Comédie-Française* would not yet accept it, but it found its way on to the *Théâtre des Italiens* as 'opéra-comique larmoyant'. Even Favart, who had excelled in naughty songs, turned preacher in his old age, in *Les Moissoneurs*, 1768. For his *Der Teufel ist los*, Weisse had already used hints from Sedaine's version of *The Devil to Pay*, and we find that the whole development of the operetta in Germany after that was strongly influenced by French models, and that it was popular in both countries with the same middle-class public who admired serious comedy and the domestic drama. In both countries there was veiled social criticism of a Rousseauist type in the themes of the operetta.

There had been an element of social satire in *Der Teufel ist los* already, when the cobbler's wife, Lene, and the country squire's lady had by magic been 'metamorphosed', and Lene, as *grande dame*, had surprised all her servants by treating them like human beings. In *Lottchen am Hofe* (1767), from Favart's *Ninette à la cour*, there is a similar contrast between a naive innocent country maid and a prince's haughty mistress, the socially inferior again winning all our sympathy, and in *Die Liebe auf dem Lande* (1768), from Mme Favart's *Annette et Lubin* and Anseaume's *La Clochette*, there is again something similar, with an anticipation of the situation most familiar to us from the *Mariage de Figaro*. The count, moved by the sight of innocent love, does not claim his seignorial rights, and the piece ends with his words: 'Only in cottages is pure, unfeigned affection to be found, that genuine love which is the source of all happiness.' *Die Jagd* (1770), finally, is an adaptation of the play which was second in popularity only to the *Mariage de Figaro* at the *Comédie-Française* in the 'eighties, when the censor had at last allowed its public performance. This was Collé's prose comedy, *La Partie de chasse de Henri IV*, derived in its turn from Robert Dodsley's *The King and the Abbot of Mansfield* (1736). Sedaine had made a comic opera of it already in his *Le Roi et le Fermier*. The central scene shows the king sharing, unrecognised, the frugal repast of a peasant and his family, after an unsuccessful attempt on the daughter's virtue, and joining in toasts to himself, drunk by these so touchingly faithful, humble subjects, who express themselves freely about his court, his ministers, and the government of the country. Mme du Deffand wrote to Horace Walpole that even an aristocratic audience (in 1767) was moved to tears of pleasure at this scene. A similar attitude, critical of the ruler's servants but devoted to him personally, is repeatedly expressed in German domestic dramas down to the end of the century.[1] In the operettas sentimental passages and any implied social criticism are of

---

[1] See J. Minor, *C. F. Weisse*, Innsbruck, 1880, and F. Gaiffe, *Le drame au 18e siècle*, Paris, 1910.

course relieved by wit and humour, as in modern cabaret entertainments, with which interesting parallels might be drawn.

In Weisse's *Jagd* we have seen a subject for 'drame' becoming
one for comic opera, and vice-versa. The fact that subjects were
bandied from one genre to the other frequently in this way shows
how closely the two are connected, not in form but in content,
through the common social situation in which they arose. The
fate of *The London Merchant* on the French and German stage illustrates well the interplay of literary borrowings, dramatic conventions and social feeling. The first French stage version of
Lillo's play (a translation had been published for circulation as a
book in 1748) was a comedy with 'ariettes', a 'Singspiel' by
Anseaume, called *Le Barneveld français ou L'École de la jeunesse*
(performed 1765). Barnwell is made into a young man of
fashion, christened Cléon, who spends musical evenings with a
merry widow, to satisfy whose claims he forces open his uncle's
writing-desk in search of money. On finding there a will in
which he is made his uncle's sole heir, he is so much touched
that he turns over a new leaf, and in the end marries his virtuous
cousin. The same subject becomes in the hands of Mercier a
'drame', *Jenneval* (first performed 1776), again with a happy
ending. Barnwell does not murder his uncle, as in Lillo, but
saves him from an ambush arranged by an associate of the Mrs.
Milwood of the play. Only La Harpe kept the murder, in a
version (*Barneveldt*, 1778) not meant for the stage. Germany,
having fewer theatrical or social inhibitions, had, as we saw,
given an astonishing reception to a fairly direct translation, from
1754 on, 'in its commercial towns', as Sonnenfels was quick to
point out, but not in Vienna, where the audience included a
large aristocratic element, as it did in Paris. Both Anseaume's
and Mercier's versions were in their turn translated into German,
the latter by Schröder, who liked this form of *Barnwell* best.

On resuming control of his company, Ackermann began to
introduce Singspiele, and found that they were eagerly welcomed.
Weisse's were all performed as they came out, and new adaptations were constantly being made from the French, especially by
Eschenburg. The majority of plays of other types also came from

France in the first years. One or two old favourites were revived, character comedies, in which the troupe had always excelled, such as Regnard's *Le Distrait*, Destouches' *L'Ingrat*, Molière's *L'Avare*; sentimental comedies and 'drames' like Mme de Graffigny's *Cénie*, Diderot's *Père de famille*, and de Falbaire's *L'Honnête Criminel* (in German, *Der Galeerensklave*), a study of protestantism persecuted, which in France, until the Revolution, could only be acted privately, or in the provinces. All these, except the Destouches, had been given several times, as we have seen, by the National Theatre. New 'drames' in 1770 were Piron's *Les Fils ingrats* and Mercier's *Déserteur*, the first appearance on the German stage of a work by this prolific but uninspired author and theorist of the 'drame'. This play was not acted in France until the following year, in the provinces. An officer has to give the signal for the shooting of his own son as a deserter. Sedaine's one year older 'drame' with music under the same title was also produced in Hamburg in this year. Its popularity was not confined to one place. In Berlin, for instance, the operetta received twenty-three performances to *Emilia Galotti's* nine. Both the deserter plays are humanitarian and rather pacifistic in sentiment, going much farther than *Minna von Barnhelm* in their post-war feeling. They were followed, we shall find, by a host of German plays about soldiers. In 1772 Schröder produced Mercier's *Olinde et Sophronie*, no doubt because it was inspired by Cronegk's play with that title, though it was not acted in France. Mercier also copied Weisse's *Romeo und Julie*. More popular was Beaumarchais' *Eugénie*, a seduction story, humanitarian again, and prepared for by *Miss Sara Sampson* and, of course, Richardson's novels. Voltaire's toleration piece, *Les Guèbres*, was given in 1771, and even *Oreste* and *Tancrède* in new translations in 1772, but they were balanced by de Falvaire's 'drame', *Le Fabricant de Londres*. *Tancrède* was the last tragedy in alexandrines to be added to the repertoire. Next year, in inviting authors to submit plays, for performance at a stated, and quite generous, fee (it was not really a competition, though often referred to as one) the Hamburg management expressed its decided preference for prose rather than verse tragedies. The French 'comedies with songs' continued to include 'drames', such as Audinot's *Le Tonnelier* (1771), one of the occupational operettas which became so popular, and Monvol's *Julie* (1772), which advocated marriage for love.

From 1773 few new French 'drames' were given, though old favourites kept their place, and an exception was made for Mercier. Two plays of his appeared in 1773, *L'Indigent* and *Jean Hennuyer, évêque de Lisieux*. The latter was not acted in France, but this drama of a bishop who rejected his cruel orders on St. Bartholomew's day might have been written for a German audience. 'L'humanité a ses droits bien avant ceux de la royauté. Qui ne parle plus en homme, ne peut plus commander en roi.' Phrases such as these show that it was not only in Lessing that 'man' was a key word. Mercier's *La Brouette du vinaigrier* (also acted in Hamburg earlier than in France) gave Schröder one of his most popular rôles, as honest Dominique, the self-made man, who is as good as any rich merchant. Ekhof excelled in it too, when it was produced at Gotha, a week earlier than in Hamburg. The last in the series of these French 'drames' of the 'seventies, much beloved in their day, was *Gefahren der Verführung* (1778), Schröder's adaptation of Mercier's *Jenneval*, another form of the *London Merchant* which had started the whole genre. This sentimentalised version, with a happy ending, was even more popular than the original translation which had delighted German audiences a quarter of a century before.

The principal imports after 1773 came however from England, and by this time there was also a fairly steady flow of more or less original German plays. It was Bode, Lessing's publisher friend, who first drew Schröder's attention to English comedy, and translated two plays, Whitehead's *The School for Lovers* (itself from Fontenelle's *Le Testament*) in 1771, and Cumberland's *West Indian* in 1772. Cumberland's sentimental comedy, a most artificial affair containing good character rôles, continued to be a general favourite on the German stage until well into the nineteenth century. His *Fashionable Lover* followed (as *Miss Obre*, i.e. Aubrey) in 1774. Schröder's theatre poet, Bock, followed these up with a whole series, by Mrs. Lennox and Kenrick, Hugh Kelly (*False Delicacy*, and *A School for Wives*), Colman

(*The Clandestine Marriage* and *Bon ton*), and Burgoyne (*The Maid of the Oaks*). He went back to Beaumont and Fletcher for *Rule a Wife and have a Wife*, and to Vanbrugh for *The Provoked Wife*. The masterpieces of Goldsmith and Sheridan were of course quickly translated and acted in Hamburg, *She Stoops to Conquer* and *The Rivals* within a few months (in 1773 and 1775 respectively), and *The Good-natured Man* in 1777, nine years later than in England. *The Rivals* was translated by J. H. Engelbrecht, the Hamburg merchant in London who kept Schröder informed about the English theatre.

At the same time post-Shakespearian tragedy was not neglected. The first examples to be tried were Young's *Revenge* and *The Brothers*, in 1769. *The London Merchant* and *The Gamester* were revived in 1772, and a great hit was made next year with a combination of four English *Essex* tragedies (by Banks and three others), put together by C. H. Schmidt and given the title *Die Gunst der Fürsten*. W. Mason's pseudo-classic *Elfrida* was given in 1775 (translated by Bertuch) and Otway's *Venice Preserved* was revived in 1777. It is clear that English drama had been fairly thoroughly explored before Schröder ventured to present Shakespeare in 1776. The enterprise and industry revealed by the great range of Schröder's productions are most impressive, especially when we remember that he not only selected and produced, but also acted in most of the plays.

The way for Shakespeare was further prepared by the domestic dramas of Lessing and his imitators, and of the new 'Storm and Stress' school. Some half-dozen serious or at least sentimental German plays survived from the National Theatre into the repertoire of Ackermann's theatre, two each by Weisse and Lessing, *Richard III*, *Romeo und Julie*, *Miss Sara Sampson* and *Minna von Barnhelm*, and two by the actor-playwright, J. C. Brandes, who was an actor on the staff of the National Theatre in its last year. Brandes wrote several more plays in the next few years, which are particularly interesting as showing the way the wind was blowing, for they are almost entirely derivative, owing a great deal in particular to Lessing. In his work we see themes, ideas and forms taken over from Lessing, recombined and mingled with elements from elsewhere, and we can form some conception of how an original and powerful writer leaves his stamp on average minds coming after him.

J. C. Brandes (1735–99) had had a mediocre career as an actor, under Schönemann, Schuch, Döbbelin and others before going to Hamburg. His *Lebensgeschichte*[1] is the most informative theatrical autobiography of the century, as he accompanied Seyler later on his wanderings, and worked at Mannheim in its best days, and in Hamburg again under Schröder. His wife and daughter had real talent, but Brandes made his name not as actor but as author, though his plays naturally benefited particularly by his stage experience. His first success, *Der Schein betrügt*, acted seven times at the Hamburg National Theatre, though called a comedy, is entirely serious, except for a pert maid's sallies, and obviously indebted to Moore's *Gamester*. The gambler here is a woman, whose husband, a heart of gold, reforms his wife and unmasks her false friend and her sister by a due mixture of kind-ness and cunning. *Der Graf von Olsbach* or *The Reward of Virtue* is equally sentimental but more fanciful, reminding us sometimes of La Chaussée (*La Fausse Antipathie*) and sometimes of *Minna von Barnhelm*. It has a happy ending brought about, after much gloom, by a coup de théâtre, a recognition scene, but it has for its hero a sentimentalised Tellheim, with a faithful friend 'von Wernim' (Werner), and it deals with a tangle of events resulting from a war which is just over. Ackermann had a splendid part in the gruff but good-hearted old colonel von Stornfels, who was much imitated. In *Trau, schau wem!* or *The Inn* (1769), Lessing's innkeeper and Franziska appear in thin disguises, again in an inn. Brandes thought that the most successful of his plays was *Der geadelte Kaufmann* (1769), which was quite often played in Berlin down to 1812. It is full of good bourgeois feeling, for it satirises a merchant suffering from swelled head, who buys titles and squanders his money, and it contrasts with him the deserving bookkeeper Krims. Through a retired India merchant, Wöllner, a sort of *deus ex machina*, Krims is made a partner, marries the merchant's daughter and receives a wedding present of 50,000

---

[1] Re-published Munich, 1923.

talers, while Wöllner looks on, rubbing his hands and rejoicing in his own benevolence. Nothing could be better calculated to touch, and to raise the morale of, the faithful employee. Brandes cannot deny his audience a happy ending even when he sets out with strong characters in a so-called tragedy like *Olivie* (1774), where the villainess, a kind of Orsina, for *Emilia Galotti* had appeared by now, is poisoned by her own draught. Yet the play drew tears from Klopstock when he saw it acted, and regularly attracted bigger houses than Lessing's sterner work.

Among the later plays of Brandes one may be singled out for its interest as a picture of social conditions, *Der Landesvater* (1782, acted 1785 in Hamburg). It shows the influence of the realism and social and political criticism of the Storm and Stress drama-tists of the 'seventies, for Brandes was still keeping up with the times, and it forms an interesting parallel to *Kabale und Liebe*, which came two years later. It paints a small state, misgoverned by the corrupt and dissolute deputy left in control by a true 'father of his people' during his absence from the country. The king returns, unexpectedly, as in *Measure for Measure,* and justice is done, but the abuses typical of absolutism can thus be pilloried in perfect safety. From the governor down, most of the court class are represented as utterly selfish and disloyal. They take bribes, and sell offices and state lands, while the honest lower ranks bear the consequences. A good opening scene is provided by the governor's 'lever'. We see the crowd in his antechamber, his valet ordering 'suit No. 76' for him, a procuress offering her services in the replacement of a mistress, officials taking anything they are offered, from the gold snuff box of a business man in need of an import licence to the cheeses of a peasant seeking justice. Brandes lays the colours on too thickly, and the plot is weak, but the play is a reliable mirror of the average man's critical yet passive attitude to political questions. As already in *Minna von Barn-helm*, the remedy for misrule has to come from above, from a king who oozes humanitarian sentiment. To a peasant, in the last scene, he is made to say: 'I am just a man like you. My subjects are not slaves, but children entrusted to me by God. It is my duty to give them all the happiness in my power.'

The products of Bock and Brandes were supplemented from the pens of similar men of the theatre in other centres, such as Vienna and Gotha. In Vienna, Stephanie the younger (1741–1800), actor and author, provided the theatre with popular plays, especially about army life, which found a market also in Hamburg and elsewhere. The Seven Years' War had reminded the civilian, however retiring and reasonable he might be, of this strange anachronism in the age of reason, of the necessity for armies, and the human problems they raised. A spate of 'soldier pieces' followed *Minna*, and as we have seen, the human side of army life was attracting attention from playwrights in France as well, whose *Deserters* and so forth were eagerly welcomed in Germany. All these works owed much of their effect to a new realism. 'Army life is the first *milieu* presented by the serious drama with stark realism. The everyday life of a soldier in garrison and camp, equally capable of serious or humorous treatment, was eagerly seized upon as a rewarding subject with clear outlines. Where Lessing had been content with two officers and two privates, his imitators take us to the army itself in all its aspects. The peaceful citizen, who had only just recovered from the burden of indemnities and billeting, could here see and enjoy, at arm's length but in perfect safety, the colour and movement of a soldier's existence. . . . K. G. Lessing has described this new delight in military matters with some vigour in his life of his brother. "After *Minna*, every feature of army life was seen on the stage. Military justice, firing-squads, running the gauntlet, fife and drum, mutiny and desertion, camp-followers and spies. A theatrical wardrobe was like an army store, and in a town which had no garrison, many a troupe could not put on its most popular plays." [1] To illustrate this last remark: Schröder borrowed eighty soldiers from the local force for a performance in Hanover in 1771, and in 1777 he jokingly threatened Gotter with a visit from his stage army of two score if he would not come to see him.

Stephanie had seen service himself with both Prussian and Austrian regiments, and drew convincing army types and

[1] Eloesser, *Das bürgerliche Drama*, p. 98.

naturalistic scenes from life, loosely strung together. He borrowed freely from *Minna* in the plot of his first play, *Die abgedankten Offiziers*, making out of Tellheim two disgruntled Austrian officers, one of whom is run to earth in an inn by the young lady of good family who is in love with him. Even Just's scene with the innkeeper comes in again, and we hear remarks like Tell-heim's about mercenary soldiering. Instead of the king, a minis-ter this time makes everything right at the end, with wise obser-vations about justice, and if one officer marries his Fräulein, the other, with general approval, marries the innkeeper's daughter. Only the genre pictures are fresh and original. Stephanie's next play, *Die Werber*, transplanted Farquhar's *Recruiting Officer* to Austria, and the author drew again on his own experiences. Korporal Kauzer is an original creation, brilliantly acted by Ackermann on his last stage appearance. Then Stephanie made out of Mercier's *Déserteur* his *Deserteur aus kindlicher Liebe*, about a soldier who deserts in order to earn for his hard-pressed father the reward for capturing him. A harsh official is duly punished by the usual wise and just king. It will be seen that there is nothing militaristic about these soldier pieces. They express the humane point of view of the easy-going 'little man', about military discipline, so severe in that day, and about his superiors in general, and his touching confidence in the king as the instrument of Providence.

The most popular of all these soldier plays was *Der Graf von Walltron*, by H. F. Möller, a member of Seyler's troupe and an ex-soldier. Schröder produced half of it, as he wrote to Gotter, in 1777—the other half consisted of the cuts he had made. 'To the honour of Hamburg', he continued, 'it did not think much of the play, although my sister was applauded after every scene.' It is a crude melodrama full of thrills, leading up to the last-minute reprieve of an officer condemned by a court martial. In the same year Schröder produced Möller's second play, *Sophie, oder der gerechte Fürst*. 'A good ruler is the sun by which every-thing beneath it is warmed', the dedication to the Elector of Saxony declares. Joseph II himself is brought on to the stage in this dramatisation of an anecdote illustrating his love of justice, which took him, it tells us, into every corner of his kingdom and made him accessible to the meanest of his subjects. Visiting a prison, he sets free the innocent heroine, who has been languish-ing there for years. Möller's plays have no style and only the most stagey of characters, but he had an eye for a situation, and gave the public what it liked.

The best-written of the soldier plays are two short pieces by J. J. Engel, schoolmaster, philosopher, critic, and friend of Lessing in Berlin, *Der dankbare Sohn* (1771) and *Der Edelknabe* (1775). The former is a kind of martial idyll in a Prussian peasant's cottage, about the home-coming of the son, a young cavalry officer, advanced from the ranks during the war for con-spicuous gallantry, and personally honoured by the king. It breathes devotion to Frederick and invests military service with a democratic and patriotic glamour in a manner only possible then in Prussia, and sadly abused in many more recent works. In *Der Edelknabe* the king appears himself, in anecdotal scenes, as the ever just and kind father of his people. The attraction was the actual appearance of an actor made up to resemble as closely as possible the already legendary monarch, who had such a hold over the popular imagination of Europe that even in Paris, in 1789, a translation of this play had much success. To see wrong righted and the helpless succoured by a contemporary philosopher-king, even in a play, was a comforting experience for unsophisti-cated people everywhere. The sight of such interventions from on high suggested to them that their hopes and dreams might after all come true, in spite of all the injustice and inefficiency they saw around them. Those more clear-sighted could dismiss the happy ending as moonshine, and yet applaud the social criticism with which plays such as Brandes' *Landesvater* began. With the more literary dramatists of Storm and Stress, the grim realities came to take up more and more of the picture, and finally, in Schiller, no soothing close was provided.

Lessing's *Emilia Galotti* (1772) for all its restraint, made for a bolder treatment of political themes. It must not be assumed that because the dénouement of *Minna von Barnhelm* is brought about by a letter from the king, which evokes from a Saxon lady the admission that he must be good as well as great, Lessing approved of the use made by subsequent 'patriotic' dramatists of similar interventions by monarchs, and the complacent praise by such authors of the system by which happiness was in theory dispensed by decree from above, though from below the process felt like oppression. Lessing did not, like J. J. Engel, see 'in the darker, less accessible portions of the plan the same wisdom which shines out from the whole'.[1] His real opinion is to be found in a letter to Nicolai of 25th August 1769. 'Do not speak to me about your Berlin freedom to think and write. It comes to nothing more than the freedom to publish as many *sottises* against religion as you wish. And right-feeling men must soon be ashamed to make use of this freedom. But let anyone try to write as freely in Berlin about other matters as Sonnenfels has written in Vienna. Let him try to tell the well-born riff-raff at court the truth, as Sonnenfels has done. Let anyone come forward in Berlin to lift up his voice for the rights of the subject, and against exploitation and despotism, as is being done now in France and Denmark, and you will soon find out what country is to the present day the most slavish in Europe.'

Emilia Galotti revealed to all who had ears to hear what Lessing, and all thinking men, felt about political and social conditions in the innumerable small states whose rulers made no pretence of being the first servants of their people. Like Chekhov later, he felt it to be the artist's duty to state the problem, not to provide a solution, and that was one reason, no doubt, for not bringing in the Roman solution. But he made his commoners conscious of their human dignity, their personal and family honour, and that was the first stage in the struggle of the middle class for political rights. In seeing in the whole development of eighteenth-century drama a preparation for 1848, G. von Lukács is forcing into a formula something very complex,[2] but he is right in drawing attention to the didactic and tendentious nature of serious drama in that age. Looking back from our vantage point, we can see that, half-unconsciously, such works as *Emilia Galotti*,

---

[1] Quoted by Eloesser, *op. cit.*, p. 108.
[2] *Goethe und seine Zeit*, Bern, 1947.

and the imitations it evoked, did indeed contribute towards the political awakening of the German middle class. It is no accident that keen members of the 'democratic' party in Weimar Republic days, for instance, could quote their Schiller by the hour.

It is significant that although in most respects there was not a great deal of difference between the repertoire of Schröder in Hamburg and that of the Gotha Court Theatre, *Emilia Galotti* and the Storm and Stress plays which Schröder staged were not performed in Gotha, with the exception of *Julius von Tarent*, which has nothing revolutionary about it. In Weimar, with its accomplished and open-minded Duchess, and later on tour, Seyler, whose company provided the staff for Gotha, had frequently acted *Emilia Galotti*. It is true that Gotha was not fond of tragedies, and only did one play of Shakespeare while Schröder did seven, but the sudden dropping of *Emilia Galotti* was probably due to the Duke's disapproval of the work. We have seen that in Brunswick Lessing's apprehensions about the Duke's attitude did not prove to be justified, but the author prudently avoided attending any of the three performances. There was, naturally, some gossip about the resemblance between the Prince in the play and the heir to the Duchy, the future Duke of Brunswick of the Napoleonic wars, with his artistic interests and his beautiful imperious mistress, Frau von Branconi. Schiller could have taken Brunswick as a model for some of the features which he pilloried in *Kabale und Liebe*, for the state's finances were only restored by the subsidies received for troops furnished to England and Holland from 1776.

At Hamburg *Emilia Galotti* was first performed on the 14th May 1772 with a strong cast, including Brockmann as the Prince, Schröder as Marinelli, Borchers as Odoardo, and Dorothea and Charlotte Ackermann as Orsina and Emilia. It was felt to be necessary that Odoardo should explain his action in a rhymed epilogue, and the play was never really popular, though it kept its place on the repertoire. Koch staged it in April with fair success in Berlin, where no one objected to criticism of small courts, and Frau König, soon to be Lessing's wife, reported to him from Vienna in July that the Emperor had seen it twice and praised it highly to Gebler, though he confessed that he had never laughed so much at any tragedy. And she adds: 'And I can say too that I have never heard so much laughter during the performance of a tragedy, sometimes in passages where in my view tears would have been more in place.' No wonder, if Stephanie, as Prince, added such touches as to lick the blood from the dagger with which Emilia had been stabbed! Clearly audiences did not know how to take so unusual a play. They were much more at home with Brandes and his like.

In 1774 Schröder was able to offer two plays by Goethe to the Hamburg public, *Clavigo* and *Götz*. It is not surprising that he chose to give *Clavigo* first, because it offered no difficulties to the producer and was, in fact, simply a domestic tragedy on the model supplied by Lessing, closely imitating his technique. It was repeated six times in the remaining four months of the year, and remained on the repertoire, here and in most theatres. Koch did it in Berlin and it went down well in Gotha. The intellectuals in Hamburg said that Schröder should have played *Götz* first, which had had an enormous success as a book, but *Götz* was a very different matter from *Clavigo*. Koch had boldly tackled it the year before, in an adaptation which was, no doubt, all that Frederick had heard about when he wrote of the 'dégoûtantes platitudes' in the play, in *De la littérature allemande*. Schröder prepared his production very carefully. As a dramatised biography, not intended for the stage, and written by Goethe in the flush of his first enthusiasm for Shakespearian freedom, it presented, and still presents, very difficult problems to the producer. He adapted the text freely, concentrating the action, but even so, many actors had to play more than one part. Schröder himself, for instance, was Bruder Martin, Lerse and the President of the Vehmgericht. He had special scenery and costumes made for the production, rightly perceiving that much of its originality lay in its exploitation of historical atmosphere. The room in Götz's castle, the subterranean passage to the Vehmgericht, which, by the letting down of a single pillar in the middle could be turned into a prison, the 'historically correct' costumes, of knights in armour and retainers, a monk and a bishop, courtiers and citizens, are mentioned in a contemporary criticism, but it is hinted that the overstressing of externals had turned the play into a spectacle, and distracted attention from its poetic merits. Eventually it became much the most popular of Goethe's plays on the stage, when it had had time to establish itself. As a book it fired the imagination of large numbers and called forth numerous imitations. The attempt to produce these 'Ritterstücke' led to important changes in stage practice. Much more attention had to be paid now to 'correct' period costume, whereas hitherto the traditional French court dress had been used in heroic tragedy, with a mere suggestion of oriental or Greek or Roman costume where needed, and ordinary contemporary dress in domestic drama and comedy. Another consequence was that, with the frequent changes of scene, it became more and more common practice to lower the front curtain between the acts, though changes within the act were still carried out on the open stage, or contrived by using the middle curtain, as in Lessing's plays.

At the end of 1775 Schröder produced H. L. Wagner's *Die Reue nach der Tat*, the crude naturalism of this, the least gifted of the Storm and Stress writers associated with Goethe, being sure of its effect. Goethe's *Stella* came next on 8th February 1776, but after two evenings the Hamburg senate forbade further performances on moral grounds. Then on 23rd February it was the turn of Klinger's *Zwillinge*. This play had been selected from three on the same subject, of fratricide, sent in in response to the appeal for plays made by Schröder in the previous year. Four volumes of these so-called 'Preisstücke' were published between 1776 and 1781, as *Hamburgisches Theater*. It is a disappointing collection, consisting of several adaptations, mostly from the English, a comedy by Lessing's brother Karl, another by the actor Grossmann (*Henriette*), and tragedies by J. F. Schink (*Gianetta Montaldi*) and Klinger. The rival play by Leisewitz, *Julius von Tarent*, to which most modern critics would have given the preference, was published elsewhere. *Die Zwillinge* was strong meat for a Hamburg audience, and was not well received. In July Goethe's charming operetta *Erwin und Elmire*, with music by André, appeared in Hamburg. That it was popular is indicated by the fact that five other theatres staged it in the same year. But the great event of the year was the performance of *Hamlet* on 20th September, the first of a series of Shakespearian productions in Hamburg which established Shakespeare as one of the pillars of the German stage.

In the course of this summer (1776) Schröder had taken his first long holiday and spent six weeks visiting other German theatres, going as far south as Vienna, via Dresden and Prague, and returning by Gotha. In Prague he had seen a minor company perform a version of *Hamlet* adapted from Wieland's translation for Vienna by Heufeld, in 1773. Apart from Weisse's *Richard III* and *Romeo und Julie*, the one an alexandrine tragedy based on Colley Cibber, and the other a domestic tragedy in prose on a Shakespearian theme, both of which had been acted everywhere, a couple of Shakespearian comedies (*Merry Wives of Windsor* and *A Midsummer Night's Dream*) and this *Hamlet* had been attempted in Vienna in the early 'seventies, all in vulgarised prose versions, but it was reserved for Schröder to naturalise Shakespeare in Germany.

In judging his Shakespeare productions, we must remember at what point they came in the history of the German theatre, and what the current repertoire and its reception reveal about public taste. The Gottsched conception of tragedy was quite dead, as we have seen, but its place had been taken by prose domestic drama, which aimed not at the tragic, but the pathetic, not at heroic grandeur, but realistic intimacy, yet continued, with Lessing, to look upon a moral effect as selfevidently necessary. Hamburg had seen a succession of translations and adaptations, first from French, then from English sentimental comedy and domestic drama, a flood of operettas, and a number of German plays, written mainly by actors for actors, farces and unpretentious dramas of everyday life, which combined and recombined types and situations taken from a few literary models, such as *The London Merchant*, *The Gamester*, and Lessing's plays from *Miss Sara Sampson* on. There was a small reading public which had made the acquaintance of Wieland's prose translation of twentytwo plays of Shakespeare (1762–66), and had followed the growing enthusiasm of the leading critics for his work, J. E. Schlegel in 1742, Nicolai, Mendelssohn and Lessing in the 'fifties, Gerstenberg, Lessing and Herder in the 'sixties, and finally the positive worship of Shakespeare's genius in the early 'seventies, in the Shakespeare essays of Herder and Goethe, and the *Anmerkungen über das Theater* of Lenz. At the same time Goethe's *Götz* and other plays of Storm and Stress poets had been acclaimed as Shakespearian achievements.[1] One or two of these had already been presented in Hamburg, so that even the ordinary newspaper reader was beginning to have some notion of what was considered to be Shakespearian. But as Gundolf says: 'The public was intellectually still entirely under the sway of rationalism, and accordingly could not understand Shakes/ peare as art. The theatre could do no more than adapt itself to the level of the public, even where a bolder spirit like Schröder wanted to raise its taste, without being so very much above it himself.' In its emotional life, too, the public was weak, senti/ mental, incapable of taking Shakespeare undiluted.[2]

In the changes he made in the text of the plays, Schröder had in view therefore, in the main, practical, or sentimental or rational/ istic considerations, but he was also influenced by the dramatic theory and practice of Lessing's age, which had by no means given up the rules. In one or two plays he took hints from previous performances in Vienna. The basic text with which he began was a translation, at first Wieland's, then, as Eschenburg's revision appeared (1775–77), he made use of this too. In adapting *Hamlet*, for instance, he reduced the number of characters and scenes by cutting out the grave/diggers, Fortinbras, Rosencrantz, and at first even Laertes, though he appears again in the printed version.[3] He transferred the play/scene to the fourth act, to im/ prove the motivation, as he thought, and he followed Vienna in making the Queen confess her connivance in the murder of Hamlet's father. As she does so, dying, after Hamlet has killed

---

[1] See e.g. R. Pascal, *Shakespeare in Germany*, Cam., 1937, and G. Weydt, *Die Einwirkung Englands auf die deutsche Literatur des 18ten Jahrhunderts*, Minden, 1948.

[2] Gundolf, *Shakespeare und der deutsche Geist*, 2. A., p. 283.

[3] For a reprint of the 2nd ed. see D.L., *Aufklärung*, Bd. 11.

the King, there is a thunder-clap, and Hamlet cries, as she falls back, 'High Heaven confirms her words!' Worst of all, there is no duel with Laertes, the goblets, one of them poisoned, are put out that Laertes and Hamlet may drink a cup of reconciliation before Hamlet's departure for England, and Hamlet remains alive at the close. 'The real Hamlet of Shakespeare would not have pleased the audience half so much as this one, who triumphs over the malice and intrigues of his enemies, even if it was a victory due rather to chance than to wisdom and courage.'[1] They were sufficiently given to melancholy vacillation themselves, and preferred a triumphant hero, as an encouraging example. We should remember too, if Schröder's scant respect for Shakespeare's text offends our modern taste, that the same kind of thing was being done by Garrick and others in England, where the tragic close of *Lear*, for instance, was not restored until 1823, by Kean.[2]

This Hamlet, played by Brockmann, with Schröder as the Ghost and Dorothea Ackermann as Ophelia (her younger sister Charlotte had died in mysterious circumstances in the previous year), was immensely popular, a triumph sufficient in itself to draw attention to Shakespeare more effectively than any number of critical disquisitions, so that Gundolf can hardly be right in belittling, as he does, the importance of the theatre as an intermediary between 'Shakespeare und der deutsche Geist'. But as Geist means for him only the élite of the country, he can make the rather Stefan Georgian claim that 'one feeling of Goethe's is, even for the fate of the masses, more important than any mass epidemic'. That Goethe did not himself underrate Schröder is clear from the use which he made of him as a personality, an actor and producer in the Serlo chapters of *Wilhelm Meisters Lehrjahre*. Yet Gundolf's impatience with the eternal German philistine, with his unharmonised thought and feeling, is also understandable when we read of the behaviour of Schröder's audiences. *Hamlet* was excellent theatre, as it always has been, and Brockmann was a romantic figure, soon immortalised in engravings, medals and snuff-boxes. But when two months later

[1] Litzmann, *F. L. Schröder*, II, p. 207.
[2] D. Nichol Smith, *Shakespeare in England in the 18th century*, Oxford, 1928.

Schröder presented *Othello* to the same audience, without a happy ending (Brockmann was Othello, Schröder Iago, and Dorothea Ackermann Desdemona), he found that undiluted Shakespeare was too much for the nerves of Hamburg citizens. We must not forget that in the translations available, nearly all Shakespeare's poetry, which does so much to 'distance' and temper the horrors enacted, had evaporated. According to Schütze, 'One after another fainted away during the scenes of horror, at this first performance. The box doors were heard opening and shutting, people left or were carried out of the theatre, and according to well-authenticated reports, more than one Hamburgerin was so affected by seeing and hearing this over-tragic tragedy that premature labour was the result.'[1] This and a rather badly attended second performance caused the management to announce for the third performance, '*Othello*, with alterations', in the form of a happy ending, which left both Desdemona and Othello alive. Even so it was not very popular, being given only twice in 1777, whereas *Hamlet* had thirteen performances in 1776 and sixteen in the following year.

In spite of this disappointment Schröder went on to plan a production of *Macbeth*. Bürger, the author of *Lenore,* an excellent choice as a translator of the witch scenes, undertook to provide a new version of the whole play, but was so slow about it (his version eventually appeared in 1784) that Schröder contented himself with Eschenburg's translation, and produced the play in July 1779, improved by Bürger's witch scenes. The changes he made were again numerous, and still had some effect when Schiller came to adapt the play for Weimar.[2] Their general tendency was to make Macbeth himself a more pleasing character, but for the Hamburg audience, his character and that of his wife were still too repulsive. They had a strong preference for plays whose characters were unmistakably good. Meanwhile, Schröder had produced in 1777 *The Merchant of Venice,* where he was Shylock, the actor Grossmann's inept 'nationalised' version of *A Comedy of Errors, Measure for Measure* (very much 'after

[1] Schütze, *op. cit.*, p. 454.
[2] A. Köster, *Schiller als Dramaturg*, Ber., 1891.

Shakespeare'), and in 1778 *King Lear, Richard II* and *Henry IV*. All were in adapted prose versions. In *King Lear,* Cordelia came to life again in the last scene, in *Richard II* the first act and part of Act II were cut (many such expositions in action were replaced in Schröder's adaptations by narration), and *Henry IV* was boiled down from the two parts of Shakespeare's play. None approached *Hamlet* in popularity. *Richard II* was only given twice, and few of these plays achieved more than three or four performances in a year. It was after *Henry IV* that Schröder, disappointed at the unenthusiastic reception, came before the curtain at the close and said: 'In the hope that this masterpiece of Shakespeare, which presents different manners from our own, will be better understood on further acquaintance, it will be repeated to-morrow.' In this spirit he persisted with Shakespeare and with unpopular Storm and Stress plays for the cultured few, but he also offered a great variety of other entertainment, for it was a commercial theatre. 'Gradually, by mutual influence, stage and public can help to form each other's taste. That the public has a very decided will of its own Schröder learned—to the advantage of his box-office receipts. He wanted to raise the better regular play to the heights of perfection, to get rid of musical plays and give fewer spectacular, noisy pieces. But the public wanted these things, and he gave them what they wanted.'[1] So in 1776, besides *Hamlet* he gave the *Ariadne auf Naxos* of Brandes and Benda and the *Medea* of Gotter and Benda, the new type of musical play called a Duodrama, a fashion started by Rousseau's Monodrama *Pygmalion* in France. It was a lyrical drama spoken by an actor and actress to the accompaniment of instrumental music, another step towards serious German opera. Mme Brandes had introduced the use of more or less genuine Greek costume for her much applauded performances in Gotha of these two works. In the following year, in addition to the Shakespeare plays, Schröder staged Beaumarchais' *Barbier de Séville* and several other French and English plays. Of the German works, *Julius von Tarent* was the best from the literary point of view, but though Schröder admired it personally, his

---

[1] Schütze, *op. cit.*, p. 702.

judgment of the previous year as to its effectiveness on the stage proved sound, and it had no great success. Very popular items were Möller's *Graf von Walltron* and *Sophie*, mentioned above, and the 'comédie-ballet' of Grétry-Marmontel, *Zémire et Azor*, about Beauty and the Beast. As usual there were various revivals of old successes by Krüger, Weisse, Stephanie and Goldoni.

Undeterred by the poor reception of Storm and Stress literary plays, Schröder gave one of the most striking of them, the *Hof-meister* of Lenz, in 1778, but in spite of his drastic adaptation, which allowed Läufer to marry his Gustchen, it too aroused no enthusiasm. *Hamlet* continued to be called for, and Schröder now played the title rôle, Brockmann having left for Vienna. The mediocre success of the other experiments with Shakespeare was counter-balanced commercially by Schröder's *Jenneval* trans-lation, his naturalisation of Calderon's *El Alcalde de Zalamea* as *Amtmann Graumann*, Gozzi's *Juliane von Lindorak*, and a number of new and old operettas. It had been quite usual until now to make tragedy more palatable by following it up with a ballet, to give a 'ballet of sugar-dolls' for instance after *Emilia Galotti*, but from Easter of this year it was dropped, though light musical pieces continued to be played after serious dramas, *Lukas und Hanchen* for example after *Der Hofmeister*. The repertoire of 1779 was a very similar mixture, with only one new Shakespeare, the long-delayed *Macbeth*, many tried favourites like *L'Honnête Criminel* and even *The Gamester* and Holberg's *Politischer Kannegiesser*. A host of light German plays by minor writers like Brömel, Wezel, Engel, d'Arien and Sprinkmann were now available and went down well.

After Easter 1780 the Schröders, tired of the cares of manage-ment, took salaried posts under a new *Enterprise,* in which the ever-sanguine Bubbers was to the fore, and in 1781 Schröder accepted a very generous offer from Vienna, made to himself and his wife, and for the next four years became one of its stars. A little before this, in 1777, the custom of Gastspiele had been started by Boek of Gotha, which gave star actors a chance of emulating other virtuosos, and the audiences of the now fairly numerous standing theatres a welcome change from the old familiar faces of the home troupe. On a tour in 1780 Schröder had acted in this way in Berlin, in Vienna, where in spite of intrigues his first appearance, as Lear, had been greeted with tumultuous applause from all, from the Emperor downwards, and in Munich and Mannheim. He had visited Paris, with introductions from Fürst Kaunitz to the Austrian ambassador, and he had made Goethe's acquaintance in Weimar. This had all contributed towards making the 'Hamburg style' the model for all German theatres.

To indicate how similar the repertoires of most German theatres had by now become, since newspapers and special theatrical journals kept them all in touch with each other, we may quote from Reichard's *Theaterkalender* for the year 1777 a list of the most popular plays of 1776, performed at fourteen German theatres. In the table which follows, the plays are classified in the same way as in the preceding account of Hamburg, the names of authors are supplied, and the number of theatres where each play was produced is added, followed by the total number of performances in all theatres. The list was probably compiled early in December 1776, for Hamburg is credited with only one performance of *Othello* instead of three. It probably contains minor inaccuracies, but it gives a useful general picture of what was going on in the theatre at the height of the Storm and Stress period. The list was unfortunately not repeated in this form in later years.

The most popular plays of 1776 on the German stage

FROM THE FRENCH	Theatres	Performances in all
PLAYS		
Molière, *Tartuffe*	4	8
Voltaire, *Mérope*	2	3
Diderot, *Le Père de famille*	5	7
F. de Falbaire, *L'Honnête Criminel*	6	9
Beaumarchais, *Eugénie*	6	15
Mercier, *La Brouette du vinaigrier*	11	48
OPERETTAS		
Sedaine, *Le Déserteur*	11	50
Audinot, *Le Tonnelier*	5	18
Anseaume, *Les deux Chasseurs et la Laitière*	5	16

	Theatres	Performances in all
FROM THE ENGLISH		
Shakespeare, *Hamlet*	4	17
Shakespeare, *Othello*	3	5
Shakespeare (Stephanie), *Macbeth*	2	2
W. Mason, *Elfrida*	5	17
Lillo, *The London Merchant*	3	6
Cumberland, *The West Indian*	12	24
Cumberland, *The Fashionable Lover* ('*Miss Obre*')	7	12
FROM ITALIAN (THROUGH FRENCH?)		
Goldoni, *Le Bourru bienfaisant*	7	20
Goldoni, *Der Lügner*	7	28
Goldoni, *Die verstellte Kranke*	5	16
GERMAN PLAYS		
J. E. Schlegel, *Die stumme Schönheit*	3	5
Lessing, *Der Freigeist*	3	10
Lessing, *Miss Sara Sampson*	3	3
Lessing, *Minna von Barnhelm*	10	28
Lessing, *Emilia Galotti*	8	21
Weisse, *Richard III*	2	3
Weisse, *Romeo und Julie*	4	4
Leisewitz, *Julius von Tarent* (Döbbelin, Berlin)	1	6
Goethe, *Götz von Berlichingen* (Döbbelin, Berlin)	1	3
Goethe, *Clavigo*	7	13
Goethe, *Stella*	5	20
Goethe, *Werther*, dramatised	2	2
Brandes, *Der Schein betrügt*	4	7
Brandes, *Der Graf von Olsbach*	7	12
Brandes, *Der geadelte Kaufmann*	6	15
Brandes, *Der Gasthof*, or *Trau, schau wem!*	8	13
Brandes, *Olivie*	5	8
Brandes, *Die Mediceer*	7	20
Stephanie d.J., *Die abgedankten Offiziers*	4	6
Stephanie, d.J., *Der Deserteur aus Kindesliebe*	10	35
Stephanie, d.J., *Der Spleen*	5	16
Stephanie, d.J., *Die bestrafte Neugierde*	5	12
Grossmann, *Die Feuersbrunst*	5	8
Möller, *Der Graf von Walltron*	5	10
Plümicke, *Miss Jenny Warton*	5	15
Herr v. Jester, *Das Duell* (from Sedaine's *Philosophe sans le savoir*)	5	10
Ayrenhoff, *Der Postzug*	10	32
Hippel, *Der Mann nach der Uhr*	5	14
Engel, *Der dankbare Sohn*	12	21
Engel, *Der Edelknabe*	11	41

GERMAN OPERETTAS	Theatres	Performances in all
Mozart, *Bastien et Bastienne*	2	15
Weisse, *Der Teufel ist los*	4	11
Weisse, *Lottchen am Hofe*	5	7
Weisse, *Die Jagd*	9	27
Weisse, *Der Erntekranz*	6	19
Goethe, *Erwin und Elmire*	5	13
Schwan-Stegmann, *Der Kaufmann von Smyrna*	8	23
J. J. Eschenburg, *Robert und Calliste*	5	40

THE LITERARY DRAMA OF THE 'SEVENTIES. STORM AND STRESS, AND SOME SUCCESSORS

THE habits of thought and feeling of average theatre audiences, audiences not drawn from the least educated class—for we must remember that two-thirds of all Germans were illiterate peasants, are sufficiently evident from the last chapter to bring home to us the realisation that the literary drama was in no sense the expression of the people as a whole. The few Storm and Stress dramas acted at the most advanced theatre in Germany in the 'seventies had little success, and in a total view of the repertoire almost disappear in the mass of entertainment pieces offered. It was not that Schröder was ignorant of what was being written. He appreciated it fully and regularly discussed the latest literature and the use he could make of it with a circle of literary friends. But the Storm and Stress plays were almost all ill-adapted for stage production and in any case not numerous. The theatre advertised almost in vain for suitable German plays. The few which could be performed, after careful trimming, pleased only a small section of the public. There is nothing surprising or unusual in this fact. It has been the regular fate of original writers and artists to be in advance of the taste of their time, especially since the Renaissance, with the growth of individualism in art. In Germany, with its chequered history, its political and social divisions and the absence of a tradition, it was natural that writers should even more than elsewhere come to look upon it as their chief business to express *themselves*, not any body of accepted truth, and their particular interpretation of the gospel of Rousseau as an anarchic, irrational primitivism strongly reinforced this tendency.

The only German plays of some literary merit in the list quoted above for 1776 are those of J. E. Schlegel, Lessing, Goethe and Leisewitz. Schlegel had been dead for nearly thirty years, and Lessing was of the older generation. The only representatives of Storm and Stress here are Goethe and Leisewitz. The other dramatists generally regarded now as the leaders of the movement are Lenz, Klinger and Wagner, all of whom, as we have seen, had already had a work performed by Schröder. In the early 'eighties Schiller's first plays were to continue in much the same strain, and already at the end of the 'sixties there had been sufficient talk about the rights of genius to make Lessing nervous. The critic whom he had principally in mind, Gerstenberg (1737–1823), had produced an unactable play *Ugolino* (1768) which, though quite conventional in construction, exploited an atmosphere of horror and madness with complete absence of restraint and decorum, and showed what strange but powerful effects the enthusiasm for Shakespeare might have on a German imagination. From Gerstenberg to Schiller the 'Genie-Bewegung' covers a span of twenty years, but the term 'Sturm und Drang' is better reserved for the few years when the literary revolution was at its height in the 'seventies. Our remarks will be concerned only with the relations of this movement with the theatre, and with the social and political background of both drama and theatre, though it will be necessary to consider the more important writers individually, because they were genuinely individual talents.

The plays of these Pre-Romantics, as French and English critics tend to call them, possess together with obvious immaturities a freshness and spontaneity which are attractive even to-day, if we read the texts themselves, before losing ourselves in the web of theory which has been spun around them by generations of literary historians. They are clearly the work of young men, not unlike many young Germans we have known ourselves in those recurrent youth movements which are a German speciality. Like them, and like the Baccalaureus in *Faust II*, they were very conscious of the gulf which divided them from their fathers, full of the illusion of the superior insight of youth, and some, including

Goethe himself, were already great 'wanderers', with Rousseauistic ideas about the open-air life, as well as a passion for friendship and for abstract discussion. Looking back on this period of his life, Goethe speaks of the mists which veiled the world from his view, but also of the endless promise which the unfolding bud of life still held, of the 'reine Dumpfheit', the instinctive confidence in life, with which he was filled. His companions, less profound, told the world with assurance where it had gone wrong, though they found it as hard as anyone else to say what could put it right. Goethe himself, though he clearly belonged to the move-ment, and though Lenz and Klinger and Wagner were in many respects merely his shadows, has always something 'incommensur-able', was always his unique self, a lyrical genius with feelers out to life on every side. But in the others the link with the existing drama, for instance, was clear, and they may be said to have made of it very much what one would expect of enthusiasts for Shakespeare and Rousseau.

What Shakespeare influenced was above all the loose form of their plays, and their concentration on character-drawing at the expense of plot. This was a Shakespeare whose plays none of them had seen acted, and whom they had learnt to see, through Herder's eyes, as the author, above all, of 'histories', 'presentations of a world event, of a human fate', or as Goethe put it, of 'a raree show, in which the history of the world moves past our eyes on the invisible thread of time', a show 'not planned at all' in any ordinary sense. Accordingly Goethe dramatised in six weeks, 'without having made any previous sketch or plan', and with no thought of the possibility of a performance of his play, the autobiography of a south German knight of Luther's time which he had come across by chance. This novel in dialogue, slightly modified by Goethe before publication, after he had been told by Herder that 'Shakespeare had completely misled him', became the model for the other young writers. For all his admiration of Shakespeare and his rejection of French dramatic theory, Lessing had hardly departed at all from the strict form of the 'analytic play', in which the visible action is concerned only with the culmination of a series of events, the earlier part of which is brought to our knowledge by means of narration introduced into the dialogue of the opening scenes. We have seen how skilfully Lessing himself could contrive such an exposition. The Storm and Stress returned to the chronological snap-shot method, used already in the old 'Haupt- und Staatsaktionen', following the English tradition. With the more realistic staging to which the domestic drama was making audiences accustomed, the constant changes of scene required in these 'Shakespearian' plays caused great difficulties in production, as did also the large number of characters who appeared in their numerous episodes. For purely practical reasons Schröder had to use adapted versions of the Storm and Stress plays he produced, and often new scenery and costumes were necessary.

It has been shown from the figures for 1776 that *Clavigo,* the thoroughly stage-worthy play following Lessing's technique, which Goethe wrote soon after *Götz,* had at first a greater success in the theatre than *Götz,* because few managers were as enterpris- ing and energetic as Schröder. But the richness and vividness of *Götz* eventually won popularity for it in spite of the difficulties of production, to overcome which ever new ways were devised. In a hundred years from its opening in 1786, we find that in the Berlin State Theatre *Götz* was performed 123 times, and *Clavigo,* first staged there in 1787, twelve years before *Götz,* had in all only 48 performances. *Julius von Tarent* was given thirteen times (between 1793 and 1819), *Stella* seven times, and none of the other Storm and Stress plays of the 'seventies were acted there at all. The selection already made by 1776 held good, we are surprised to find, right through the nineteenth century, but only as regards the Storm and Stress plays of literary merit. Most of the remaining plays and operettes popular in 1776 did not keep their place in the repertoire for more than a decade or so.

The irregularities of the Storm and Stress drama went deeper, however, than the neglect of the unities of time and place. Many works have no discoverable unity of action or theme. *Götz* itself is usually defended by the critics as a tragedy of misplaced trust, centring round the hero himself, but it is doubtful whether its construction will really stand much scrutiny. There is no clear conflict in it, but a tangle of plots, with a pathetic close. Lewes said that it should never have been called a drama, but left in its original shape with its original title (*Geschichte Gott-friedens von Berlichingen mit der eisernen Hand, dramatisiert*). It is intended, he says rightly, to represent an epoch rather than a story, it lacks a central unity and it paints even the characters from outside, not making them transparent, like Shakespeare's. 'We stand before an enigma, as in real life; not before a character such as art enables us to see, and to see through.' In its use of language too it is unShakespearian. But as a historical novel in dialogue it is brilliantly successful, and it proved epoch-making, because it was the first German play to capture the romance of history. Though the reader felt that this past age had had its own unique form of life, he could understand it and feel with it. He was not tempted now simply to dismiss it as 'gothic', because *Götz* is inspired with the same spirit as the lyrical essay on the Strassburg Minster.

Moreover, the scene was Germany, and the age represented was not so remote as to appear entirely unfamiliar. It was not a time still remembered by living men, as in Scott's first novels, but there was a recognisable basis of specifically German experience which the audience shared with the people in the play, and to us now it is in fact just as interesting as a reflection of Goethe's age as of Luther's, for it was not the result of research, like Hauptmann's *Florian Geyer*, full of detail from the history books but stone-cold. Goethe did not pay 'kalt staunenden Besuch' to this Germany of the past, but felt himself into it by imagining it in the natural way, in terms of what he knew in the present. The contemporary audience saw in it a picture of their empire, still weak and divided, with its class conflicts and its chaotic administration, they saw the frenchified manners and personal intrigues at the court of a prince of the church contrasted with the plain living, right feeling and blunt homely speech of German country folk, whether peasants or petty knights, they saw Bruder Martin longing for the natural, active life of a family man, and little Karl, who has been taught words parrot-wise, contrasted with his father, who at his age had known only things, a reference to the kind of pedagogy that Basedow had learnt from Rousseau.

Rousseau! That is the name which is constantly coming to mind when we consider the ideas and values expressed in Storm and Stress writings. As in the French 'drame', the excellence of unspoilt nature and the corrupting influence of civilisation are continually being suggested to us. Uncivilised, primitive man, or the nearest approach to him, is contrasted with the product of modern civilisation. In *Götz* the gypsies are noble, hospitable and kindly savages, who behave to Götz with humanity when no one else will, and in the same way, here and repeatedly elsewhere, the country is opposed to the town, the working masses to the privileged few, and in historical plays like this, the good old times, of which Götz is a surviving representative, to the so-called 'enlightened' present. This note was already familiar in a number of foreign plays which were popular in Germany. There was G. Colman's *Inkle and Yarico*, for instance, repeatedly adapted from 1771 on, and a great favourite in Hamburg, there were many operettes from the French, much imitated, as we have seen, by authors like Weisse, where the nobility were outshone by village maidens, and 'drames' like *La Brouette du vinaigrier*, the deserter plays and presently the German soldier plays. A second strong impulse imparted by Rousseau led to the championing of passion against convention, feeling against abstract analysis, the individual against society. The attempt of the benevolent despots to order all things for their subjects' good, praised by the Aufklärung as the royal road to a rational social order, was seen by some, through the eyes of Rousseau, as an oppressive interference with human freedom. Yet the result in Germany was not a political revolution in the name of democracy, but a literary and philosophical movement, affecting ethical and educational theory. The path from Rousseau leads here not to Robespierre, but to Pestalozzi. The enthusiasm for everything natural and spontaneous combines with the new interest in historical and philological studies. Scholars work back to more primitive conditions, follow the streams of development to their sources, look for the expression of national ways of feeling in poetry and mythology, and see the past no longer as something dark and outworn, but in its own light, and with the links with the present restored. Instead of "toleration" and "reason" the new cry is for "nature" and "freedom". But freedom is not fought for in the present but sought out by yearning poetical hearts in simpler and more vigorous ages. Here the reactionary side of Rousseau's ideas is active, preparing the way for the legitimist notions of the German and French Romantics.'[1]

If we consider some of the principal dramas of the Storm and Stress from the point of view of content, we naturally find great differences in emphasis, and some purely private notions, for these young authors set out to be as individual as possible, following the new poetic theory, with its stress on natural genius and its personal perceptions, not on conformity with the rules and the pursuit of universal truth. But Goethe himself became increasingly aware as he grew older of his debt to others, and the lesser 'Originalgenies' were much more obviously affected by winds of doctrine blowing through their particular social and political landscape. Leisewitz, for example, the only dramatist of the group of mainly lyrical poets connected with the University of Göttingen, who formally organised themselves for a few years into the 'Hain' or 'Göttinger Dichterbund', a kind of literary society, with a Bardic ceremonial inspired by Klopstock (see his *Der Hügel und der Hain*), and an organ of their own in the *Göttinger Musenalmanach,* could be dated by us now after reading his *Julius von Tarent* (1776). The form is from Lessing, the language is free from idiosyncrasies, smooth and harmonious, but the hostile brothers are figures conceived by a naturally quiet man in the would-be tempestuous spirit of the Storm and Stress, and his theme, fratricide, haunts the whole period down to Schiller's *Räuber* and beyond. Rousseauistic thought is to be found in every scene, conveying a protest not so much against the existing form of society, as against society in any form. The two sons of the ruler of Tarent are of strongly contrasted natures. The elder, Julius, is a mixture of Hamlet and Werther, the younger, Guido, a cruder Hotspur. Julius has no wish to succeed his father, but

[1] Eloesser, *op. cit.*, p. 123.

his brother is eager for power and glory. As they have fallen in love with the same fair lady, not of their own rank, who has been put into a convent by their father, the end of the romantic story can be guessed. What is interesting is the kind of sentiments expressed, for both brothers are complete individualists, guided by feeling alone. Julius, though heir to the throne, has no sense of his duty to society, for he despairs of society, and longs to retire into private life with his Blanca. 'I have a heart and I am a prince—that is my misfortune. Only fools can dispute whether society poisons humanity—both sides admit that the state kills freedom.' 'Give me a field for my kingdom and a purling stream for my applauding people, a plough for myself and a ball for my children.' And his brother, equally sentimental, but in the heroic vein, cries: 'Lifeless nature bows before the hand of the hero and his plans can only come to grief through those of another hero.' Or: 'Beauty is the natural prize of the brave—and women have no voice in the matter.' The abbess too is up to date in her feelings, and reminds us of Bruder Martin when she exclaims: 'A saint is only a beautiful freak of nature.'

Leisewitz was a man of one book. After his student days he soon settled down, first as an advocate in Hanover, where he married the younger daughter of Abel Seyler, the merchant turned theatre-manager, then as an official in Brunswick, where he attained high rank, and wrote nothing more but fragments. Before *Julius* he had published (1775) two short dialogues expressing radical views on social and political matters. *Die Pfändung* is about a peasant about to be evicted, and *Der Besuch um Mitternacht* shows us a prince and his chamberlain, a pair like Lessing's prince and Marinelli, to whom the ghost of Arminius appears, to warn 'the tyrant of slaves and slave of a whore' that 'despotism is the father of freedom', i.e. of revolution. In the State of Hanover, because of the English connection, outspoken trifles like these could safely be published. Schlözer, the Göttingen publicist, kept up a running fire of comment which was to be taken far more seriously.

The other three dramatists of some importance were all to some extent friends of Goethe and very much under his influence.

They are often referred to as 'Die Goetheaner'. The most gifted of them, J. M. Lenz, was a far less harmonious personality than Leisewitz. He did not so easily distinguish the world of dream from the world of reality, for with the streak of genius which he undoubtedly possessed, his dreams were extraordinarily vivid. Professor Barker Fairley has emphasised, perhaps over-emphasised, in *A Study of Goethe*, the extreme volatility and irrationality of Goethe's temperament in youth, a feature which he shared with his Storm and Stress contemporaries. 'There seems no doubt,' he writes, 'that the emotional wave which swept over Europe at this time took a more irrational, a more violent form in Germany than elsewhere, and that it was too much for all but the wisest and most robust of natures. The violence is not surprising when we consider the poverty of cultural life that preceded it. . . . In Germany the lack of any broad and secure tradition, apparent at every turn in its political and cultural life, threw these young writers on themselves and gave them no clear sense of direction.'

There is, it is true, a general resemblance between all these writers, yet compared with Lenz, Goethe is a very tower of strength. In Goethe's early letters, for all his lability and impressionableness (he illustrates admirably the psychological theory that the precondition of genius is nimbleness of mind, a capacity for establishing connections between apparently disparate ideas and feelings), there is a fundamental sanity which is seldom in evidence in Lenz. There was no doubt a native instability in Lenz, but in addition he was a German from the Baltic provinces, at odds with his family, who was adapting himself in a hurry to the latest west German fashion of feeling, for he had no roots in his own native culture comparable with those of the patrician Goethe in Frankfort. Goethe uses the English word 'whimsical' of him, but from his recorded behaviour, 'irresponsible' would seem to be nearer the mark, though people for long treated him as they might a favourite puppy who tears the cushions. They liked him all the same. 'It is always himself he deceives first of all. He has no eye for facts. The veil only falls when someone laughs at him for his blindness. With no energy and stability of purpose, badly in need of guidance himself, he thinks he has a mission to lead others and re-fashion the world.'[1] The story of his astonishing escapades, culminating in some 'Eselei' for which at a day's notice he had to leave Weimar, whither he had followed Goethe and where he had been well received, is too long to be told here. But a knowledge of his character or lack of character explains a good deal in his strange chaotic plays, which combine a supposedly Shakespearian lack of plan with a depiction of whole classes and callings in the manner desired by Diderot, though he does not, like Diderot, press for moral and social reform by depicting models of virtue, but by displaying crass warning examples.

Here we may confine ourselves to two of his best plays, which were all written within the space of a few years, before the veil fell over his reason in 1777. The first is *Der Hofmeister,* published anonymously in 1774, and taken by many for a work of Goethe's, partly because Goethe had helped Lenz with suggestions and found a publisher for his earlier *Lustspiele nach dem Plautus.* Lenz had had unpleasant experiences himself as a tutor, but the point of *Der Hofmeister* is to suggest that the whole system of private education is wrong, and that children should rather be sent to school. Lenz consciously inverts the usual Clarissa situation, and shows us a young lady of birth led astray by a plebeian tutor. This originality would impress us more if we did not feel that Lenz turns everything upside down to see how it looks. But his sketches in dialogue of scenes from life in various spheres are astonishingly vivid and true to social character, and that seems to be what Lenz was chiefly aiming at. He was evidently well aware of the realities of social life, in spite of his inability to face facts in his own. He shows us the world of social relations, in which each character has been born and bred, but with much variety within the type. We see the aristocratic milieu which the tutor Läuffer enters, the student circle in which Gustchen's cousin moves, and the village schoolmaster, a delightful eccentric, with whom the tutor takes refuge. The only class shown in wholly favourable light is socially the lowest, this schoolmaster and a very well-drawn naive village girl. If the nobility are full of

---

[1] E. Schmidt, *Lenz und Wagner*, p. 9.

morgue, the middle class are servile and unheroic, as Lenz's mouthpiece, the Geheimer Rat, makes us observe. The school-master even stands his ground when the angry count bursts in on him, in search of Läuffer. 'In our village, sir,' he says to him, 'it is usual for people to take off their hats when they come into a room to speak to the master of the house,' and he threatens to call in the peasants to throw him out. This scene anticipates the famous one in Schiller's *Kabale und Liebe*, where the musician Miller, a more convincingly normal lower middle-class German, greets the all-powerful Präsident with 'Das ist meine Stube!—halten zu Gnaden'.

Lenz was a born sociologist, but his plots are fantastic to a degree. Läuffer, a second Abailard, punishes himself like his predecessor when he learns the fate of his Heloisa, Gustchen. But Gustchen is rescued in the nick of time, and her cousin marries her, in spite of the baby. Kissing it, he says to Gustchen, 'This child is now mine too, a sad reminder of the weakness of your sex and the follies of ours, but more than that, of the good that comes from the education of young women at home by private tutors.' The outrageous sentiment and stupid irony of passages like this and the chaotic construction of the whole work outweigh the play's other merits, and give us the impression that it was written in brief lucid intervals by a gifted but unbalanced mind. A surprising number of contemporaries however praised it to the skies. It is a striking tribute, for instance, to the genius of Lenz that we find in Melchior Grimm, editor of the famous *Correspondences littéraires* and one-time contributor to the *Deutsche Schaubühne* of his master Gottsched. In 1781, at the age of fifty-eight, he writes to the Empress Catherine of Russia that he has just read *Der Hofmeister* three times, and speaks with delight of its 'verve incroyable'. Flattering her country and his at the expense of France, he sees the day coming when Russian and German will be taught in the universities of America instead of Latin and Greek.[1]

Die Soldaten is also based on what Lenz had seen with his own eyes, as companion to two young noblemen, who were being

[1] Edm. Schérer, *Melchior Grimm*, Par. 1887, p. 303.

prepared to take service with the French in Strassburg. The fashionable soldier pieces, as we have seen, lent a certain glamour to army life, but at the same time aroused sympathy for the rank and file. Lenz shows us soldiery who are brutal and licentious in every rank. A domestic drama theme, about a Lille shopkeeper's pretty daughter who rejects her devoted bourgeois suitor in the hope of catching an officer of good family, and is betrayed by one after another, is smothered in episodic scenes of life in officer and middle-class circles. Again the author's interest seems to be in the class, not the individual, and in social evils arising from social conditions. The scene is constantly changing, sometimes after half a dozen words, but the scenario this time is bad, and the never-ending succession of brief glimpses of garrison life is tedious and disgusting. It was an impression of inanity and immorality that Lenz wished to leave with us, no doubt, but he seems unable to select and arrange. The shopkeeper and his two daughters are well drawn, again without any suggestion that the middle class have a monopoly of virtue, for Marie is an empty-headed coquette, and her father encourages her hopes of making a good match. The last scene, where the colonel's proposed remedy is that regiments of self-sacrificing 'amazons' should follow the army, to distract its attention from honest girls, shows us Lenz at his craziest. This is the kind of proposal which he tried to put in all seriousness before the Duke of Weimar.

Lenz's *Anmerkungen über das Theater* provide some sort of a dramatic theory for his new type of play. Lenz does not really go beyond the imitation theory, but what is to be reproduced is the poet's vision, from his unique standpoint, of the endless variety of real life, and this involves the total rejection of the rules already undermined by Lessing, and even the unity of action which he had advocated. A series of incidents, following each other like thunder-claps, are to be grouped round one central character. Aristotle is constantly being guyed and Shakespeare extolled in this half-incoherent introduction to Lenz's translation of *Love's Labour Lost*. Lessing, with some justice, called the introduction 'ein Gewäsche'. Consistent thought and self-criticism were impossible for Lenz, but at times he was capable of feeling his way into some phase of life which he had himself experienced, and capturing it in words with such skill that we can well understand how some of his lyrics and even plays could be ascribed to Goethe. For years he followed in Goethe's foot-steps with pathetic devotion, even to the point of making love to Friederike Brion. Perhaps the most moving lines he wrote are to be found in *Die Liebe auf dem Lande*, about the country minister's daughter, who in her mind's eye for ever saw the picture:

> Von einem Menschen, welcher kam,
> Und ihr als Kind das Herze nahm.

The passion for the theatre which was taking hold of the middle class may be illustrated both from Lenz's life and his works. The contemporary German theatre is a favourite subject of conversation with his characters, and in addition to the Plautus translations, four longer plays and several fragments he wrote a lively skit, *Pandaemonium Germanicum*, published long after his death, in which satire and parodies of contemporaries, containing some happy touches, alternate with self-glorification and homage to Goethe. 'Der brave Junge!' exclaim Klopstock, Herder and Lessing in chorus, about Lenz. 'Leistet er nichts, so hat er doch gross geahndet.' To which Goethe adds: 'Ich will's leisten.'

The *Zwillinge* of Friedrich Maximilian Klinger, 1752–1818, as we saw, was preferred by Schröder and his advisers to *Julius von Tarent*, and his *Sturm und Drang* gave its name to the move-ment, but he was on the whole less remarkable as a writer than as a personality. He was a handsome, self-confident Frankforter, the very incarnation of Storm and Stress for his contemporaries. Thanks to great strength of character and moderate talents he raised himself from proletarian origins to the rank of a Russian general, which carried with it personal nobility, and he married a natural daughter of Catherine II. It is surprising that no one has yet made a film, 'Sturm und Drang', around the career of Klinger. Some headings for the scenario might be, or might have been, for much of the background of Klinger's boyhood, old Frankfort, has gone for ever: Klinger, as a boy of six, doing the rounds of the Frankfort streets and alleys with his father, one of the city watch. They might sing their 'Hört, Ihr Herren, und lasset euch sagen, Unsre Glock hat elf geschlagen' outside the Goethehaus in the Hirschgraben, for the contrast with the boyhood of the young patrician in the same town would somehow have to be marked. We might be shown home scenes in the little house 'zum Palmbaum' in its dark, narrow alley, then little Friedrich, at ten, after his father's death, taking out to customers the washing done by his mother, or later, as 'armer Schüler' at the Gymnasium, lighting stoves, going to neighbouring families for 'Freitische'—here the novel *Anton Reiser* by his contemporary K. P. Moritz would afford useful hints, as well as Klinger's late dialogue, *Weltmann und Dichter*—and helping his mother in the little shop she now kept, consoling himself when he could with *Emile,* his book of books. At twenty we should see Klinger at the rowdy University of Giessen, holding his own at drinking or fencing, dancing in the villages and making conquests every-where, or welcoming a fellow 'genius' and 'brother' like Miller from Göttingen. His acquaintance with Goethe might be illus-trated by a shot of Goethe drawing his portrait at Frankfort (1774), or Klinger listening to Frau Rat's fairy tales, and accom-panying Goethe and the Stolbergs on a country excursion. We should see him in Werther costume, with a friend, riding beside Lenz's coach and escorting him into Frankfort, or following Goethe, close on the heels of Lenz, to Weimar, and behaving there like a bull in a china-shop. His wanderings with Seyler's troupe in 1777, as theatre-poet, his service with Austrian irregular troops in Bohemia in 1779, his taking leave of Schröder next year on his way to Russia, and writing in his album as his motto 'Marte Venereque' would show us a 'Kerl' in all his rude vigour. Finally we might see him making a career, 'by Mars and Venus' indeed, first in a Russian naval lieutenant's uniform, acting as orderly to the Grand Duke Paul in Rome, and seeing the sights with Heinse; then at the Russian court, amid scenes more lurid than his own works, culminating in the French invasion in 1812, and the death of his son as a Russian officer.

Extravert as Klinger would seem to have been, he did not, like

Goethe or Lenz, look to real life for the matter of his plays. He is more like a modern Expressionist than is any other writer of his day. In his plays, as Erich Schmidt says, 'one feels as if in a mad-house, surrounded by grotesques. Even his idealised figures have something contorted about them, and are usually so blown up with passion that we are afraid they will burst.' He began with the domestic drama *Das leidende Weib* (1774), for which the principal model was *Der Hofmeister,* though half a dozen other plays and literary echoes innumerable come in, with direct allusions to *Romeo and Juliet, Minna, Emilia Galotti, Laokoon,* and so on. Several love intrigues are loosely grouped round the story of an honest official at a corrupt court, whose beautiful wife deceives him, oh so tearfully, with the irresistible Brand. When the imbroglio leads to the shooting of another admirer, the prince's natural son, and the scandal comes out, the good husband behaves with great propriety, and at the end, when his wife and her lover are dead, we leave him, with his children, literally 'cultivating his garden'—a final literary reference. The inspiration is purely literary too in *Otto* (1775), the first of the Ritterdramen imitated from *Götz,* but one model is never enough for Klinger, so we have here too touches from *Lear, Hamlet* and *Ugolino.* His method is the exact opposite of Lessing's. Instead of admiring the skill with which one small seed of action is expanded to five acts, we are bewildered by four combined, or rather parallel, plots, and romantic incidents by the score. They range from the games of children to the tortures of the Inquisition, from battle and murder to tender love-making. We see poor mad Gorg, who has killed his brother, and a hermit digging his own grave. The castle and spectre tradition is well started which will produce romances for a generation, both dramas and novels.

Sturm und Drang (1776), like most of his later plays, has its scene in foreign parts, but the characters who, variously disguised, come together in an American inn, are two hostile Yorkshire baronets, Lord Berkeley and Lord Bushy, and their families, for this is a new *Romeo and Juliet.* Klinger has come round to the analytic technique, which makes the play actable, but the fact that they are narrated makes the wanderings of

Romeo-Wild, alias Carl Bushy, in Russia, Holland, Spain, Switzerland and the rest, scarcely more credible. The old trick of 'Agnition' is brought in to sort it all out, and after much wild talk the play ends happily. To cover up the deficiencies of the plot, Klinger adds a fringe of grotesques to the central characters, and brings them on in would-be witty conversation. The similarity between his next play, *Die Zwillinge,* and *Julius von Tarent,* is probably not accidental, for Miller of Göttingen may have brought him news of Leisewitz's plans. He then wrote his play in a spirit of rivalry on the same theme of fratricide. Leisewitz had 'poked a slow fire, but Klinger sets a great funeral pyre ablaze'. (E. Schmidt.) He takes over the idea of the hostile brothers, rivals in love, the fratricide and the father's act of justice, but this is less well motivated, as he is not himself the ruler and supreme judge. Klinger's two brothers are twins, and the wild Guelfo, who feels himself born to rule, cannot reconcile himself to the affront of fate which has made him slightly younger than his brother. Envy suggests the thought that he has been tricked out of his birthright. It was this motif which appealed to Schröder, as well as the undeniable vigour of many scenes. The action is still further concentrated than in *Sturm und Drang,* and better worked up to a climax, so that no subsidiary figures are necessary and the unities can be closely observed. This study in envy, hatred and self-pity is dominated by the one character, a good part for an actor 'in Ercles vein'. But many readers will share the feelings of Bürger, who was not afraid of strong effects, that the only thing to do with a beast like Guelfo is to shoot him like a mad dog.

Klinger had learnt something of the dramatist's art, but he really had nothing to say. The passion was all whipped up for stage effect, and its expression monotonously *fortissimo,* as in Gerstenberg's *Ugolino.* The one thing that the Kraftgenies could not learn was restraint. It was fortunate, as Erich Schmidt says, that their plays were unactable, or they would have been the death of German acting, which, thanks to the new claims made on it by Gottsched and Lessing, had been cured of the ranting that the Haupt- und Staatsaktionen had demanded. The word 'brüllen' is frequent in Klinger's dialogue, and the actor is always being tempted to roar like any lion. To see how far Klinger could go one must read his *Simsone Grisaldo* (1776), where he seems unconsciously to parody himself, in the picture of a Castilian king's incomparable general, a superman in war, in council, in potations and in love, who has 'conquered the lion and drunk his hot blood'. 'Löwenblutsäufer' was Klinger's nickname in Weimar. It says much for his fundamental sanity that in the skit written in collaboration in Switzerland, called *Plimplamplasko oder der hohe Geist (heut Genie)*, he could join in conscious parody of the Genies, and especially of himself, even before going to Russia, where his sterling qualities found scope in real life, though a boyish exuberance kept breaking through to the end in the ten novels which he wrote there.

With Heinrich Leopold Wagner, finally, we come back to earth. Wagner was born in Strassburg (1747) and as a student there and one of the Salzmann circle, he made the acquaintance of Goethe. He saw more of him in 1774, when for a time he held a post in Frankfort, and after taking his degree in 1776 he married a widow eighteen years older than himself and settled down in Frankfort as an advocate. He had tried his hand at many kinds of writing when he died at the age of thirty-two. It is characteristic that one of his many translations, which included *Macbeth*, was of Mercier's *Nouvel essai sur l'art dramatique*, for his work is wholly on the level of the 'drame' and has nothing 'irrational' about it. The vagueness of the conception 'Sturm und Drang' is brought home to us when we find that although Wagner is generally included among the typical Storm and Stress poets, he has hardly any of the characteristics of Goethe, Lenz or Klinger except those which they share with the domestic dramatists. He makes the impression of a shrewd, competent writer for the commercial theatre, a good observer of life on the everyday level, incapable of poetic flights.

His first full-length play, which had been preceded by a one-act sentimental sketch, *Die wohltätige Unbekannte*, was *Die Reue nach der Tat*, first played in Hamburg in December 1775. It fitted in well with the domestic dramas of Brandes and Stephanie and achieved quite a success, here and elsewhere. It gave Schröder another good character part in the worthy Walz, coachman to the Emperor. A young lawyer wishes to make what his mother, the narrow-minded widow of a high legal official, considers a misalliance with Walz's charming daughter. The aid of the Empress is invoked, first (by the mother) to have the girl put in a convent, and secondly (by a friend of the lawyer) to bring her out, but through misunderstandings it all ends like *Romeo and Juliet,* and a touch from *Hamlet* is added when the mother, after a sudden change of mind, treats us to a mad scene, mercifully brief. In this domestic tragedy everything is typical of the Enlightenment, the opposition to class prejudice, to the mis-use of parental authority, to mistaken ideas of education (in family scenes with children), and to anti-Semitism, and the expressions of admiration for the head of the State, in this case Maria Theresa and Joseph, whom Wagner goes out of his way to flatter. If these all-wise beings had only known the real truth earlier all would have been well!

In Wagner's second play, *Die Kindermörderin* (1776), the subject was borrowed from Goethe, as Goethe himself tells us in *Dich-tung und Wahrheit.* He had talked to Wagner and other friends about his *Faust,* of which nothing appeared in print until 1790, though we know from the copy of the manuscript made by Fräulein von Göchhausen in Weimar in the early Weimar days (*Urfaust*) what Goethe had written down by this time. The Gretchen tragedy made up the greater part of it. Seduction dramas were of course common enough at the time, but there are some details in Wagner's play which prove Goethe's assertion, the sleeping draught, the use of the phrase 'Du bist die erste nicht', Evchen's fainting-fit in church, and so on. Apart from this, however, the two versions are poles asunder. Wagner's is more completely naturalistic than even *Der Hofmeister,* and aims simply at stage effect. The characters and situations are very con-vincingly realised so long as they remain on an everyday level, when their 'photographic' technique reminds one of Hauptmann or Sudermann. But the more the tension rises, or should rise, the more inadequate the expression of character becomes. The plot turns on incidents obviously invented for the purpose, a stolen snuff-box, forged letters, an unfortunate illness. The tragedy does not arise inevitably from the characters or their social situation. As in the French 'drame' and Wagner's first play, a bad character may be miraculously converted overnight —it is enough if he is shown the evil of his ways. So the young officer who seduces Evchen, the butcher's daughter, after giving the impression, during the first act, of incurable levity and brutality, concealed under a charming easy manner, becomes as penitent as his victim, after his assault on her and some serious conversation next morning with Magister Humbrecht, a young candidate for the ministry, who has views on natural methods of education and the teaching of 'the facts of life'. But for an un-timely illness, and the gratuitous villainy of a brother officer, the officer would have been back to marry Evchen in good time. In the same way butcher Humbrecht, normally a very convincing 'strong father', another forerunner of musician Miller and a fine part for Schröder, after threatening blue murder at the very thought of being disgraced by his daughter, becomes all forgive-ness when the scandal is in everyone's mouth. This is all intended to make the final situation, Evchen's arrest for child-murder, more tragic, but it turns the play into one of those 'If only . . .' domestic tragedies condemned by Hebbel in the preface to *Maria Magdalena*. In the contriving of momentary effects, however, through misunderstandings which the audience sees through, Wagner is very ingenious, though the tone is often suggestive, and he seems to delight in the sordid for its own sake. 'The terrible appears in him as petty and depressing, because it is not linked up with anything great' (Eloesser), and he was quite ready to provide a stage version with a happy ending, and a few words from the Magister to point the moral.

Together with these plays of the 'Goetheaner', we may con-sider two domestic tragedies which appeared a year before Schiller's *Räuber* (1781), because their authors, like Wagner, take up the old tradition of the genre, little affected by anything 'Storm and Stress' in the sense of a revolt against Enlightenment.

It is obvious that the features to which attention has been drawn in Wagner, and there are many similar to them, are completely rationalistic and sentimental. There is no social criticism, no lyricism, no youthful 'afflatus' of any kind. His work is Storm and Stress only in its technique, in the 'English', though always easily stageable, construction, and the skilful use made of characteristic speech, freely interspersed with dialect and oaths.

Although the plays of the young Goethe and the Goetheaner had so little success on the stage, they were widely read, and they had left their mark in the work of the more popular dramatists even before Schiller, in the early 'eighties, gave Storm and Stress its most vigorous and effective dramatic expression. Two great stage successes of 1780, Freiherr von Gemmingen's *Der deutsche Hausvater* and Grossmann's *Nicht mehr als sechs Schüsseln*, show to what extent the ways of thinking of the mass of the people had been affected by the literary revolutionaries. They are both adaptations to German conditions of Diderot's *Père de famille*, which had been so influential in the early days of the domestic drama. Instead of giving extreme expression to a hot-headed younger generation, without regard to the judgment of their elders, they show us how a wise father could deal with such extravagances of feeling in his own children. Both are negligible as literature, but very interesting as social documents. *Der deutsche Hausvater* in particular presents the working compromise between old and new social ideals reached by a sensible, well-educated man, to the evident satisfaction of large audiences all over Germany.

Der deutsche Hausvater is a typical 'drame', where into everyday scenes from family life mild social criticism is introduced, but by a writer whose belief in the natural goodness of man and his fundamental reasonableness is quite unshaken. It deals with a 'family reunion', but its whole atmosphere is of course completely different from that of brooding guilt which we find in Mr. T. S. Eliot's play, for the basis of social and ethical convictions in author and public is still almost intact, and no attempt is made at metaphysical profundity. The point of view is on the whole that of the educated middle class of university-trained civil servants and professional men, though the author was a Reichs-freiherr, one of the comparatively small number of men of birth who attracted attention in the arts. His sympathies were those of a moderate conservative, firmly attached to the existing political system and not without aristocratic prejudices, but deeply influenced already by the humanitarian movement in literature and philosophy. In his plays and in the three short-lived periodicals which he edited later in Vienna he aimed at the spread of enlightenment and culture, and like Gottsched, and so many others since his day, he was active in the local literary and philosophical society, the 'Kurpfälzische deutsche Gesellschaft' of Mannheim, where he lived from 1777 to 1780. It was to the same group that Schiller, a few years later, read his paper on the *Theatre considered as a moral institution*. When the Mannheim National Theatre failed to obtain the services of Lessing, Herr von Gemmingen, at the age of twenty-three, was appointed as its 'Dramaturg' for a year, and his criticisms, which emphasised the moral utility of the theatre and praised Shakespeare and the English at the expense of French drama, were published, as *Mannheimer Dramaturgie für das Jahr 1779*. His dramatic work includes an adaptation and a translation of *Richard III*.

Gemmingen takes over from Diderot the figure of the model father, here too a widowed nobleman, but still more an *honnête homme*, as the descriptive list of characters (a feature imitated by Schiller in *Fiesko*) informs us. By his own wise guidance he solves all the problems of his grown-up family, one of the chief of which is again a threatened misalliance. But many new figures are introduced, a daughter and her husband, a second son and some subordinate figures. On his return from a long journey, apparently on state business, Graf Wodmar finds his daughter, who, like himself and all the 'good' characters, puts simple domestic joys above court frivolities, on bad terms with her empty-headed husband, who is attracted by a rich and fashionable widow, a 'philosophical' countess in the line of descent from Lessing's Orsina. His elder son Karl, a very weak version of Werther, with the same amateurish literary and artistic leanings and vague ambitions without a definite outlet, has become unduly intimate with the daughter of a completely unworldly painter, through taking drawing lessons from the father. But the Countess, a good match in the eyes of the world, has her eye on him, and he is tempted to abandon Lottchen, in order not to disappoint his father by marrying out of his class. Schiller's *Kabale und Liebe* clearly owes something to Gemmingen, both in its initial situation and in the characters of Ferdinand, Miller, Luise and Lady Milford. There is even a scene anticipating Luise's interview with Lady Milford, when Lottchen, in despair —she has already threatened to kill her still unborn child, like a Storm and Stress Gretchen or Evchen—appeals to the countess not to steal Karl from her. The Hausvater's younger son, a young officer, has meanwhile lost heavily at cards, and there are rumours of an affair of honour in which he has disgraced himself.

It seems quite a handful of trouble for any father to deal with in one day, but this one is a 'biederer, tätiger, deutscher Mann', who is soon on the best of terms with Lottchen's father, another 'deutscher Mann, ohne Falsch', who holds himself to be as good as any nobleman, for is he not an artist, 'a second minor creator'? The phrase recalls Shaftesbury's 'Prometheus under Jove', and the use by Goethe and others of the same symbol. Misalliances, both fathers agree, seldom turn out well, but an exception must be made in this instance, for as the count tells his son, 'Your rank does not absolve you from the obligations of an honest man.' He must marry Lottchen, but live in rural obscurity, managing the family estates, where the disparity of rank will cause less embarrassment. In Diderot, it will be remembered, the young woman was found to be of good family after all, and was only then approved, a solution which burks the issue. In Schiller alone we have uncompromising romantic love, but also tragedy. The count's remaining family problems are solved in sentimental fashion. His daughter is reconciled with her husband by their little son, whom neither will give up, and who demands them both to live with. The younger son, who had caused his father the severest shock of all, the fear that he had compromised the family honour by refusing to fight a duel, proves to be no coward, and his promise to reform is readily accepted. Here we see the noble/man's concern for the honour of a soldier, whereas the sentiment more usual in domestic dramas, that of the middle class, is entirely opposed to duelling. The author is completely conserva/tive too in his devotion to the throne, which he represents as well rewarded, for at the count's request, the ruler of the small state provides for both his sons. When his elder son is about to enter the prince's service, his father warns him against shaking the confidence of the public in the 'infallibility' of its government by too openly acknowledging its mistakes. In the early versions Gemmingen made propaganda for the reforms initiated by his Kurfürst in the treatment of the peasantry, in scenes which had to be modified in the third version because of aristocratic opposi/tion in Munich. His Hausvater is of course a good landlord to his devoted peasantry, their champion against a corrupt bailiff, much in the manner of the reforming landowners, the 'conscience/stricken gentry', in nineteenth/century Russian novels.

Attitudes originating in more than one class of society are reconciled by Gemmingen, it will be seen, in the optimistic spirit of humanitarian rationalism, and his play is full of literary echoes, of Diderot and Rousseau, Lessing and Goethe. There are allusions to *Werther* and to *Stella*, and when we first see the 'Naturkind' Lottchen she is singing at her spinning/wheel 'Ein Veilchen auf der Wiese stand'. But the Storm and Stress element is watered down or expressly rejected, as when Karl, a 'Genie' of sorts, is urged by his father to turn his vague activism into channels useful to his 'nation', that is, his small state. The one thing which is clearly Storm and Stress is the opposition here expressed to the ceremonious extravagance and insincerity of frenchified courts. The good characters are all 'bieder', which is taken as synonymous with 'deutsch'. The small boy, interro/gated like Karl in *Götz*, knows about Venus and Cupid, but not that he is a German. The count and the painter become firm friends as 'zween teutsche Männer', and the Hausvater ends the play with the wish that when he is dead, a German 'Bieder/mann' passing his grave will say: 'He was worthy of the name of German.' In the earlier editions, one for Mannheim and one for

Munich, the last word had been first 'father', as in the French, then 'Bavarian', a fact which seems to show that there was little genuine political feeling yet behind this 'Deutschtümelei'. We shall find a similar sentimental attachment to the good old German ways, very vaguely conceived, and above all, a distaste for everything frenchified, in the many imitations of *Götz*. Goethe gives his roystering students similar sentiments in *Urfaust*, though it is only in the *Fragment* (1790) that we find the line

Ein echter Deutscher Mann mag keinen Franzen leiden.

A technical point of interest in Gemmingen's play is the note preceding the descriptive list of characters, in which the author says: 'I have often been annoyed in the theatre when at moments of tense emotion a loud whistle announced a change of scenery. Then doors walked on with human feet, tables leaped out of the wings as if possessed of life and trees shuffled off again. I have therefore ventured to give some unusual scenic directions wherever I feared this kind of thing.' He asked, that is, for the front curtain to be lowered not only between acts, but between scenes within the act. No general change in stage practice in this respect took place however for another generation.

G. F. W. Grossmann (1743–96) was a Berliner of good education, acquainted with Lessing and his circle, who after a brief career as a diplomat took to the stage, very much as Wilhelm Meister does in the novel, after playing a missing actor's part in an emergency. He wrote a number of things for and about the theatre, but nothing so effective as the comedy *Nicht mehr als sechs Schüsseln*, first performed in 1779 in Bonn, where Grossmann was then manager of the Elector of Cologne's Court Theatre, which had in its orchestra no less a person than Beethoven. His 'père de famille' is a high legal official in a small state, a Hofrat but not a nobleman, who in a second marriage has allied himself with the nobility, only to find his wife's aristocratic relations a constant trial. When two of them, who practically live by his bounty, interfere persistently in his family affairs, he decides to have no more of it and, in spite of the unscrupulous intrigues against him at court of his wife's aunt, he contrives to turn the table on all his adversaries, though it is only possible because, like Gemmingen's hero, he has ample independent means at his disposal.

Grossmann sees things in black and white. His Hofrat has not the bland judicial calm of Gemmingen's Hausvater. He has a good heart, of course, and his daughter can twist him round her little finger, but he is irritable, self-righteous and obstinate. From Grossmann's life one can infer that his own character was some-what similar. He proved efficient but unpopular in one post after another and finally got himself into serious trouble for *lèse majesté* in Hanover, burst a blood vessel and died. Reading the play one soon perceives that he is outspokenly partisan. The types who represent the aristocracy are such obvious marionettes that his indictment fails to convince. But though Goethe in *Dichtung und Wahrheit* speaks of the 'schadenfroh' public to which Grossmann served up 'all the tit-bits of plebeian fare', the middle class thought differently, and though the play did not last as well as Gemmingen's, still less Schiller's *Kabale und Liebe*, it maintained its popularity for over a generation. It remained on the Berlin National Theatre repertory, for instance, until 1815 and was acted twenty times, while Gemmingen's play survived till 1827 (fifty performances) and Schiller's became a permanent feature, which had been acted nearly two hundred times in the first century. We can well understand, for instance, how contemporary audiences would appreciate the scene between an impecunious grand lady and a tradesman. The saddler tells her that the Jew Abraham has shown him the room where he keeps articles in pawn. 'There the Geheimrat and the Hofrat, the prince's mistress and the lady-in-waiting, the cobbler and the minister were all mixed up together' and her ladyship's silver-fringed Andrienne hung next to the plain dress of his neighbour, the shop-keeper's wife. It is indeed a 'family picture' that Grossmann gives us, as he says in the sub-title. In the background there is the usual little despot, as in *Emilia Galotti*, with his mistress, his unscrupulous favourite and his appetite for innocent girls (here for the Hofrat's daughter), but right in the centre of the picture we find the contrast between courtier and commoner in such every-day matters as the education of their sons and the openings in life available to them, or the different food and clothing and forms of address that mark social differences. While the Hofrat thinks 'six dishes' are enough for any dinner party, even if the guests include people of fashion, his in-laws demand their usual eigh- teen.[1] On more important topics Grossmann shows all the dis- cretion, not to say servility, of the older patriotic plays, and has no quarrel with enlightened despotism. The prince is capable of acts of injustice, but only when he is misled by flatterers and deprived of the advice of his faithful middle-class officials. On proper representations being made, he puts all things right by a personal letter, like the King in *Minna von Barnhelm*. Grossmann, no less than Gemmingen, was really comforting the bourgeoisie in serious political questions with wishful thinking. In other plays, like the *Bürgerglück* (1792) of J. M. Babo, another south- west German dramatist, active like Gemmingen in Mannheim and Munich, we find hard-working industrialists contrasted in the same way with idle courtiers, and here the king even visits their factory, dines at their table and assures them of his high regard.

Babo had made his name with 'plays of chivalry' (Ritter- schauspiele), another genre which became very popular in the late 'seventies. They were the direct descendants of *Götz* and of Klinger's *Otto*, the first imitation of Goethe's play, and most of them, like the family dramas, are a good index to popular senti- ment, especially in the south-west and south. The Goetheaner had imitated the freedom of form of *Götz* and made a watchword of the hero's cry for freedom. Other writers had been attracted by the romantic conception of German history which it suggested, especially if they had the strong regional and dynastic loyalties which underlay what was then called patriotism, for it must be remembered that 'Vaterland', in that divided country, still meant a man's native small state. Goethe himself had little of this feeling. Coming to the autobiography from Shakespeare's histories, his imagination had been fired by its picturesque possibilities and he saw in it something refreshingly different from the fashionable culture of his own day, so 'senile and genteel' (bejahrt und vornehm) to his youthful eyes. He liked to think of it at this time,

---

[1] See *Germany in the eighteenth century*, p. 92.

as he thought of Strassburg Cathedral and Erwin von Steinbach, as typically German, but he soon lost any narrow national pride he may have had, and regionalism had still less of an appeal for him.

After Klinger's *Otto*, which as we saw was a welter of themes, literary, not historical, in its inspiration, came *Der Sturm von Boxberg* (1778) by the Mannheim official Jakob Maier, which he followed up in 1782 with his *Fust von Stromberg*. Both were romantic spectacular dramas with a happy ending, the rescue by the hero of his lady-love as in a modern Wild West film. Apart from the romance of primitivity and the charm of medieval settings, these plays owed their effectiveness to their local appeal and to the contrast they drew between stalwart knights and pampered monks, a theme hinted at in *Götz* and sure of a response in the age of rationalism, especially in a protestant enclave. They are expressly called 'plays from the history of the Palatinate', and regionalism was similarly stressed in three other plays written in the same province about this time, one of which brought in songs and music, while another, not published till much later, was the *Golo und Genoveva* by Maler Müller, one of the Goetheaner, a lyrical piece founded on a local legend. From the Palatinate the fashion naturally spread to Bavaria, when the two states were united in 1777. We have seen that Gemmingen was active in both and appealed to local sentiment in each in turn. In the same year as the Munich version of his *Hausvater* there appeared a *Ludwig der Baier* by Längenfeld, and just before this J. A. von Törring had written a play about his ancestor *Kaspar der Torringer* (published 1785), which he followed up in 1780 with his famous *Agnes Bernauerin*. His two plays and J. M. Babo's *Otto von Wittelsbach* (1782) are considered the best of an unattractive bunch. Four more Bavarian plays of the kind appeared in the same year, 1882. Austria, especially under Rudolf von Habsburg, was celebrated in a group of plays in the 'eighties and 'nineties, several of them written by non-Austrians like Iffland because Austria had for so long played a dominant part in Imperial history. The separate provinces, especially Styria and Tirol, were also not forgotten. Other states, Prussia, Thuringia,

Hessen, Switzerland amongst them, produced their own historical dramatists, mostly in the 'nineties, but the largest group of all consisted of plays written for the open market, making a vague general appeal through their romantic medievalism. Kleist's *Käthchen von Heilbronn* (1810) is linked in this way by a living tradition with *Götz*. The historian of the Ritterdrama, Otto Brahm, lists nearly fifty titles.

The drama of chivalry appealed to the same public as the domestic drama and comes close to it in many of its sentimental features. It is in fact very often a family drama in an exotic setting. Two favourite situations in the invented pieces present the eternal triangle, for instance in the time of the crusades. In one variety the husband or lover 'to the wars has gone', and the wife or sweetheart left behind him, receiving false news of his death, marries or becomes engaged to another, who is then challenged by the warrior to mortal combat. In the other a stern old Castellan has a wondrous fair daughter, wooed by a young knight, brave and good, but poor. She returns his love, but is destined by her father for a rich but wicked and cowardly old neighbour. After many adventures and much suffering Jack, of course, wins Jill. The poverty of invention of these second-rate authors is seen too in the assiduity with which each copies his predecessors, especially Goethe, though here only in externals, for in its principal features *Götz* is not a Ritterstück. They all go farther back than the age of the Reformation, pictured in *Götz* as a period of transition from the good old days to the decadent present. The plays of chivalry prefer the heyday of the knights, the glorious days of the Medieval Empire, and give us in truth what Shaw finds in Schiller's *Jungfrau von Orleans*, 'a witch's kitchen of raging romance', as the mention of a few favourite motifs will indicate. Siege scenes come easily first—their masterly prototype is of course in *Götz*—then abductions, trial by ordeal, tournaments and the Vehmgericht. Favourite backgrounds are dungeons and subterranean passages or old hostelries, and picturesque incidental figures include, beside children, who come into family plays too, hermits, pilgrims, harpists, minnesingers, charcoal burners, gypsies, bandits and ancestral ghosts, imitated from

Hamlet. Even the same Christian names recur with fatal regularity, Adelheid, Mathilde, Bertha, Kunigunde or Adelbert, Fust, Gottfried, Otto. Among serving-men a Georg could never be wicked and a Franz never good.

The Ritterstücke, except for Maier's first one, which observes the unities, take advantage of all the Shakespearian freedom popularised by *Götz* and their authors revel in vivid spectacle, violent action, in sound and fury signifying nothing. As they were so popular, even the best managers were very glad to pro-duce them, for they at least helped to make up for the losses on better plays. So we find them acted in Hamburg and Mann-heim alongside the new Shakespearian productions and the few German plays of literary value which were attempted. Actors vied with each other in writing them, Ziegler of the Burgtheater wrote a dozen, Schikaneder and particularly Hensler, also in Vienna, turned out still more of the fairy-plays which grew out of the Ritterstück there, and half a dozen others, in different parts of the country, also attempted the genre. After a time Schröder and Iffland came to think that these noisy and spectacular pro-ductions tended to blunt the perceptions of the audience and coarsen the quality of acting. There can be no doubt about their effect on stage technique. They made a moderate use of changes of scene and of historical costume quite normal and with their tournaments, sieges and other crowd scenes they called for larger companies, more spacious stages and better stage machinery. As Wieland, one of the old school, admitted, there was something in these plays which, in spite of their crudities, fitted in with the temperament, the way of life and the political development of the Germans, and he hinted that this was perhaps Germany's most characteristic contribution to the art of the theatre. It was certainly widely accepted abroad as typically German, along with the novels in the same strain which grew up alongside the plays and were often written by the same authors, people like C. H. Spiess. The romantic and the spectacular were what chiefly appealed in Kotzebue when he became so popular in England in the 'nineties, in Sheridan's *Pizarro* for instance, from *Die Spanier in Peru*. There were two or three actual Ritterstücke in Benjamin

Thomson's collection of translations, *The German Theatre* (1800), while Monk Lewis's *The Castle Spectre* (1797), and the still earlier *Mysteries of the Castle* (1795) are direct imitations. They lead straight to nineteenth-century melodrama.[1]

In Germany this type of play was probably more important than is often realised as a basis for some of the best work of Schiller and his nineteenth-century successors, for from *Die Räuber* through *Wallenstein* to Kleist, Grillparzer, Hebbel, and above all Richard Wagner, we find much that strikes us as a sublimated form of Ritterdrama. 'If Klinger's "Kerle" tried to give vent to their "Kraft" in the tame present, they produced the effect of cannibals and blood-swillers; in the armour of a knight, in the framework of long ago they could be better understood, and audiences could more readily learn to accept a drama with figures larger than life.'[2] Some plays, moreover, notably Count Tör-ring's *Agnes Bernauerin* and Babo's *Otto von Wittelsbach*, were by no means bad plays in themselves. Törring had a genuine sense of tragedy, of the clash of equal rights, and even Hebbel's handling of this fine subject still owes much to him. Both Törring and Babo have finely conceived crowd scenes and Babo's study of a 'sublime criminal', the Wittelsbach who assassinated the Emperor Philip of Hohenstaufen in 1208, would be worthy of Schiller if the author had made more of the historical issues from which the clash of individuals arose. That was to be the great achievement of German historical drama, distinguishing it from even the best of the Ritterstücke, that it saw in historical individuals a symbolic quality, and in this way made drama again more philosophical than history.

Agnes Bernauerin was only acted eight times in Berlin, and was a back number by 1795, but *Otto von Wittelsbach* survived until 1829, receiving forty-six performances. All the Ritterstücke naturally had their greatest vogue in the south-west and south. In Vienna the genre was fused by K. F. Hensler (1761–1825) and others with the traditional 'Volksstück', which continued, as we have seen, the tradition of the old 'Haupt- und Staatsaktionen'

---

[1] See A. Nicoll, *18th-century drama, 1750–1800*, Camb., 1927, pp. 99 ff.
[2] A. Ludwig in *Das deutsche Drama*, ed. R. F. Arnold, Munich, 1925, p. 411.

even after Sonnenfels had had Hanswurst banished and extempore comedy had been replaced by regular plays. Philip
Hafner's *Megara, die förchterliche Hexe oder das bezauberte Schloss des
Herrn von Einhorn* illustrates the ease with which the romantic
element in the new plays could be assimilated, and it is interesting
that Schikaneder, librettist of *The Magic Flute*, wrote not only
serious Ritterstücke, but also burlesqued versions with a comic
part in dialect for Kasperl, the successor of Hanswurst. Hensler,
an amazingly productive writer for the theatre, author of over
eighty plays, introduced all the characteristic features of the
Ritterstück, often taking his plot from another play or novel of
this type, but he too combined them with humorous scenes in
Viennese dialect and also with songs and ballets, until the result
was something like an English Christmas pantomime. The most
popular of these 'Ritterpossen' was *Das Donauweibchen* (Part I,
1792, Part II, 1798), charming nonsense which was frequently
performed on all German stages until well into the nineteenth
century. Even in Berlin the two parts were given about fifty
times each in seven or eight years (till 1809). The charm of
Viennese music had of course a great deal to do with the success
of all these works.

The authors of these popular plays were all in touch with
musical circles and connected either as actors or managers with
one or other of the three oldest suburban theatres of Vienna, the
Theatre in the Leopoldstadt, the Theatre 'an der Wien' and the
Theatre in the Josefstadt, founded in 1781, 1786 and 1788
respectively. They had amazing facility, knew every trick of the
theatre and used any plots or gags that came to hand in their
'Ritterstücke' with variations, their mythological parodies, dramatic fairy-tales, and comic operas. In the nineteenth century
Vienna continued to delight in the same kind of fare, but it
became if anything more philistine in outlook and anxiously
loyal, owing to the strict censorship. The *Donauweibchen* type of
play became a 'Zauberposse', a farce with magic, in which fanciful and realistic elements were still combined, and the action
took place on two planes as in the oldest Haupt- und Staatsaktionen. A pair of lovers speaking High German, with servants,

the Hanswurst and so on speaking dialect around them, are united in the end after difficulties, everything being 'fated' to happen in accordance with a wager or some agreement or other among the fairies, magicians or gods and goddesses of the other, magic, half of the action, where the author gave free rein to his fancy, and transformations and so on provided a fine spectacle, again very much in the style of our pantomimes. Raimund's plays developed out of this type, while Nestroy cultivated the other, which was realistic farce with local colour, without the fantastic element. In both types Hanswurst was the main character, as of old, and the prevailing mood is joy in life and self-congratulation on living in the best of all monarchies.

THE YOUNG SCHILLER. THE GERMAN
THEATRE OF THE 'EIGHTIES

COMING to Schiller's *Räuber* after reading not only the literary drama of the 'seventies, but also the domestic dramas discussed above, one understands better the tone of the preface, in which Schiller is at pains to make his play more palatable to the ordinary reader. It is the content, not the form of his play, for which he asks indulgence. The freedom of its form was no longer anything extraordinary and he knows, he says, though we can hardly take this seriously, that the work is not suited for the stage. But he fears that a refined and virtuous reader may be offended by the realism of his picture of moral evil, for he claims to have drawn it not from 'compendia' but from life. The genuine moralist however must face the fact of evil in all its horror. His hostile brothers—for here we have the familiar Storm and Stress theme again—are both, he says, morally reprehensible. Franz is what we should now call a 'nihilist', whose intellect has been cultivated to the detriment of his heart. Abstract reasoning from false principles has robbed him of con- science and religion. Karl on the other hand has turned robber because of the strength this evil life calls for and the dangers that it brings. External circumstances have made him a Catilina rather than a Brutus, but as a 'remarkable man', a Don Quixote by nature, he was bound to become either the one or the other. His anarchic idealism drives him in this 'ink-splashing century' to a life of adventure in conflict with society.

Because characters such as these are open to misinterpretation by the vulgar it is not advisable, says Schiller, with his tongue in his cheek, that his play should be performed. But the enlightened reader will not fail to observe that whereas every *bel-esprit* nowadays is anti-religious, he has tried to vindicate religion and good morals by the fate he has dealt out to his two transgressors. He makes no apology for giving even bad characters the aesthetic attractions of intelligence and vitality, for Klopstock, Milton and Shakespeare have done the same and he could not otherwise have held the reader's attention. He concludes with the hope that whatever the reader may think of his art, he will not doubt that he is on the side of the angels ('den rechtschaffenen Mann in mir hochschätzen').

It is not easy for us now to take all this seriously. Schiller certainly wanted his play performed, but he knew what sort of sentiments had inspired it and felt sure of the inner opposition of many readers, so that an appeal to the universally accepted principle of a good moral effect was a wise precaution. Yet he was more than half in earnest all the same and the preface offers valuable clues to the understanding of his mind. The play was written, as his school-friend Scharffenstein tells us, 'not so much for the sake of literary fame as in order to give vent to his strong, free, unconventional feelings about life. In that mood he has often said to me: "We will make a book that will simply ask to be burnt by the knacker!" ' The ruling passion behind the work was moral indignation. We must remember that until Duke Karl Eugen of Württemberg had interfered with his father's plans Schiller had been destined for the Church, and that not merely because in his state theology offered to families with limited means the attraction of a free education for able boys, in the protestant 'monastery schools' set up at the Reformation and in the theological college, the 'Stift' at Tübingen University. Schiller was to have followed the same course of training which produced a Hölderlin, a Hegel and a Mörike. It would, moreover, have suited his temperament well enough, though he might later have kicked against the pricks like so many others. Christophine, his sister, tells us that his first compositions were sermons. At the age of six or seven he would throw a black apron round his shoulders, stand on a chair and compel the family to listen to his message. His father, the former barber-surgeon and recruiting-officer, was a man of principle and a stern disciplinarian, his mother had pietistic leanings and the boy was brought up in an atmosphere of simple and unquestioning faith. This explains his attitude to the amours of princes and other such abominations of 'God's giant dolls' in early poems like *Der Venuswagen, Der Eroberer* or *Die schlimmen Monarchen*. It was that of his family to the goings-on at Ludwigsburg, where he could not but see the shady side of Rococo culture while at the same time benefiting, as a future dramatist, from frequent visits to the Duke's magni-ficent theatre. At Karl Eugen's new military academy he had to simulate gratitude to his benefactor and his Mme de Maintenon, the well-meaning Franziska von Hohenheim, and he did it sometimes with almost unnecessary eloquence, but his feelings remained unchanged, though some of his religious convictions were shaken by the philosophy of the French *beaux esprits* and the individualistic exuberance of the German 'Genies'. What these literary influences brought home to him still more strongly, above all Rousseau and his idol Shakespeare, was the unnaturalness of all the petty restraints to which the pupils of the boarding-school, particularly the 'roturiers', were subjected. Storm and Stress in-dividualism was, no doubt, only a derivative experience for him, but he knew at first hand what it meant to have no freedom.

Yet the conviction which he was to express later as the first of his three *Words of faith*:

> Der Mensch ist frei geschaffen, ist frei
> Und würd' er in Ketten geboren

was a part of his Christian inheritance which he never lost sight of. The centrality for Schiller of this idea of man's inner freedom and moral responsibility comes out even in the anecdote told by another of Schiller's school-fellows about his behaviour in their secret society, whose members swore to stand by each other and to maintain the honour of the group. Any member who offended against the code was punished by the rest. Schiller did not much care for presiding over their courts of honour, but he would never be refused the office of executioner. It was pure moral indig-nation, this friend was sure, which lent Schiller's arm such unaccustomed strength in administering the corporal punishment prescribed by the court. 'Subjection to a moral tribunal', says F. H. Bradley in his *Ethical Studies*, 'lies at the bottom of our answering for our deeds.' Responsibility means for the common man liability to punishment by such a tribunal. Young Schiller believed firmly in man's moral responsibility in this sense, he believed in God as the supreme judge and therefore in immortality. 'The orphan and the widow hope for your immortality', he says of *The Conqueror* in one of his early poems, for they hope he will get his deserts. 'The thought of God awakens a terrible neighbour, his name is Judge', says Pastor Moser in *Die Räuber*, and it is largely from an outraged sense of justice that Karl becomes a robber, taking it upon himself, as a sort of Robin Hood, to avenge man's inhumanity to man and protect the weak. But though conscience is a reality for Schiller in spite of his inability to account for it—without this irrational datum one arrives at the position of Franz, the hedonistic materialist—its voice is not infallible. We do not discover all our true motives by introspection. So Karl is moved also, as the preface makes clear, by pride in the conviction that he is a 'remarkable man', whom nothing petty will ever satisfy. This is a Storm and Stress, pseudoShakespearian element. Franz is still more obviously conceived as a 'sublime criminal' who, when at the end he tries to pray, for he too has a conscience and knows there is an avenging God, reveals his private ethical code in the words: 'I have been no common murderer, O Lord—I have never stooped to trifles, O Lord.' It is the same attitude that is revealed when Fiesko says: 'It is shameful to empty a purse; it is impudent to embezzle a million; but it is unspeakably great to steal a throne. The disgrace grows less as the sin increases.' Love of freedom and contempt for the commonplace, partly moral and partly aesthetic in origin, distinguish Schiller's work from the beginning, but as he develops, his conceptions of freedom and 'das Gemeine' are gradually transformed.

This passionate awareness of the larger issues was part of Schiller's individual endowment, though it was fostered by the Christian tradition he inherited as well as by the literary atmosphere during his years of growth. It marked him off immediately from all the common run of domestic dramatists, and although his early plays might not make so great an immediate appeal as, let us say, Iffland's, it is this quality which has gained for them the admiration of each succeeding generation down to the present century. Their crudities lie on the surface, but that they have something great about them, too, is undeniable. Even Nietzsche, the relentless enemy of outworn values, though in one mood he might call Schiller the 'Moraltrompeter von Säckingen', spoke in another with biting scorn of the youthful conceit of those who learn at the Gymnasium 'to smile at the noblest and most German of Schiller's creations, at his Marquis Posa, at Max and Thekla —a smile which infuriates Germany's genius and will cause a better posterity to blush for shame'. We find indeed in Schiller some of the many anticipations of the Superman. Karl Moor, for instance, is represented as beyond ordinary good and evil, fated to be 'either a higher man or a devil' (III, 2).

This is not the place for a detailed analysis of *Die Räuber,* but before considering it as the product of a particular age and society, it seemed necessary to draw attention to the imprint of individual genius which it bears and which no sociological considerations can explain. The play was full of a genuinely revolutionary spirit, as Schiller's French contemporaries soon perceived, though the adaptation by the Alsacian Schwindenhammer, staged in Paris in 1792, breathed a 'social mysticism', as M. Eggli has pointed out, which was quite foreign to Schiller's intention, his robbers being turned into virtuous and idealistic Jacobins in search of a utopia. The real tragedy of Karl's position is however that for all his good intentions, he finds that he has unleashed forces which he soon sees to be preponderantly evil. In this respect too the individual conscience proves an insufficient guide. It was 'hybris' to think that one man could sit in judgment over the world and, seeing the wrongs which have inevitably resulted, he hands himself over to earthly justice which, though imperfect, represents on earth the moral order of the universe. 'Mercy, mercy', he cries, 'for the rash youth who thought to anti-cipate Thee—Vengeance is Thine alone!'

This point was no doubt missed by many Germans too, who

would take Karl simply as a Storm and Stress hero, like Goethe's bandit Crugantino in his colourful early operetta, *Claudine von Villa Bella*. But what none could fail to hear was the bold social criticism, which did not contrast the virtues of the common man with the vices of the aristocrat in the usual manner of the domestic drama, but measured both by an absolute standard. If Schiller pillories on the one hand the tyranny of Franz, a free Imperial Count, it must be remembered, a small-scale Nero, and that of the court where Kosinsky has lost his Amalia (III, 2)—a reminiscence of *Emilia Galotti* combined with *Measure for Measure* —he does not spare on the other the general run of middle-class philistines, petty, timid, self-seeking, irreligious or hyprocritical, degenerate in mind and body. In the scene (II, 3) with the catholic priest, the Church he represents is attacked as intolerant, covetous and hypocritical, though the protestant pastor, Moser, is taken seriously. Elsewhere lawyers are described as corrupt and doctors as contemptible money-grubbers. The tone was so unmistakable that before Dalberg produced the play in Mannheim he made Schiller revise it into a Ritterstück by putting the time of the action back to 1495. For unlike *Emilia Galotti,* this play dealt, as Schiller wrote it, with contemporary Germany and did not, like most of the social dramas so far considered, exonerate the rulers themselves from blame. Whatever else it might be, it was highly critical of all authority. In the first edition the motto on the title page was from Hippocrates: 'Quae medicamenta non sanant, *ferrum* sanat, quae ferrum non sanat, *ignis* sanat,' and in the second, more bluntly: 'In tyrannos'.

Technically *Die Räuber* was, of course, the work of a beginner, but of a beginner of genius, with a sure sense of theatrical values. The plot is a tissue of improbabilities, the language vigorous in the extreme, but often bookish and affected, the characters too obviously constructed round an idea, not natural growths. The old Count and above all the Klopstockian Amalia are conventional to a degree. But Schiller thought from the beginning in situations. The separate situations are dramatically effective and well varied, even the long monologues avoid monotony, and the action of the play is massed in groups of scenes so that it can be staged without an excessive number of changes, by the alternate use of 'long and short stage' in the manner familiar from Lessing. The play had a considerable but not an overwhelming success on the stage to begin with, for the public did not at first see or at any rate appreciate its revolutionary tendency. It was probably the Jena students at Weimar in the later 'eighties (Bellomo's performances) and 'nineties who received it with the greatest enthusiasm and started the tradition which made it such a favourite with German youth. At the first performance on 13th January, 1782, at Mannheim, it was the sentimental side of it, precisely what is now most distasteful, which pleased the audience, so that the fourth act, with the scene between Karl and Amalia, made the first deep impression, which the fifth act followed up with the pathos of Karl's conversation, unrecognised, with his father, the old man's death on learning who he is and Karl's final sacrifice of Amalia. The alterations made at Dalberg's request had of course obscured the contemporary references and little was left that could give any political offence. Out of respect for religious susceptibilities the priest had been turned into a 'Kommissar' and Pastor Moser had been omitted. The part of Franz was a great triumph for Iffland, new costumes and specially painted scenery added to the play's attraction and it was given a number of performances which compares very well with that of other successful works. Eight months later a bolder presentation was risked at Leipzig, in contemporary costume, but it was forbidden after the second performance. Hamburg, Frankfort-on-Main and Berlin soon followed and by 1784 even Stuttgart saw the play, but in Vienna it was not acted even on a private theatre during the poet's lifetime and not at the Burgtheater until after the 1848 revolution, in 1850.

If the revolutionary sentiment of *Die Räuber* made so little stir, it is not surprising that Schiller's next play, where an actual revolution was the theme, *Die Verschwörung des Fiesko zu Genua*, 'a republican tragedy', fell quite flat at Mannheim and had no success elsewhere. 'A conspiracy in those quiet times was too strange an idea', says Schiller's friend Streicher, his devoted companion on his flight from Stuttgart. Returning from the first performance of *Die Räuber* at Mannheim, Schiller, now a regimental surgeon, was sternly ordered by the Duke not to go again and not to publish in future anything but medical works. He went however in secret to later performances and when this was discovered and he was put under arrest, he decided to abandon the medical career for which he had been trained and stake all on his literary talent. Mannheim was naturally the first place he made for, but to his intense disappointment *Fiesko* made no impression on the actors when he read it to them and Dalberg would at first do nothing for him. A few months later when Schiller, in hiding at Bauerbach, had nearly finished a third play, Dalberg expressed interest in it and in September 1783 offered Schiller the post of theatre poet at Mannheim, which he accepted. *Fiesko* was the first new play he provided and was first acted in January 1784, in a version adapted to please Dalberg, and was only given three times. 'Republican freedom is a meaningless phrase in this state,' Schiller wrote, 'and no Roman blood flows in the veins of the people of the Palatinate.'

We have seen that the normal attitude of the German literary man to politics in the 'seventies had been that of the middle class in general, to whom the word suggested intrigues between self-seeking heartless people of the ruling class which were certainly none of their business. In *Emilia Galotti, Julius von Tarent, Das leidende Weib,* and so on, the virtuous characters want to have nothing to do with government and to live in country retirement. Schiller thought differently. It is clear from his plays that he understood how important for human happiness was the form taken by the government of a state and its consequent activities, and that he saw nothing immutable in existing political institutions. There was more political feeling in his native state, Württemberg, than in most small German states, and within living memory the Estates there had been a force to be reckoned with. From his reading of the Ancients as well as of Rousseau, Shakespeare's *Julius Caesar* and so on, he had some notion already of the liberal ideal which Marquis Posa was to expound so eloquently, and in the story of Fiesko he saw in the first place a struggle for democracy against tyranny, a combination of the

themes of *Julius Caesar* and *Emilia Galotti*. A further attraction in
Fiesko as a hero was that he was said to have been mentioned by
the great Rousseau as worthy of the pen of a Plutarch. It is
Plutarch whom Karl is discovered reading when we first see
him in *Die Räuber,* for he wrote of great men, 'men of great virtue
and sublime criminals' as the phrase goes in the same *Memoirs
of Rousseau* (by H. P. Sturz) where Fiesko is mentioned.

Fiesko was for Schiller therefore another sublime criminal, as
well as a heroic republican. In his first attempt at a historical
play he did not succeed in reconciling these two aspects of his
subject. With a political subject moreover he was not sure of his
ground nor of the interest of his public, so he tried to 'represent
the cold unfruitful web of political action as spun out from the
human heart', a phrase from the preface which anticipates the
Prologue to *Wallenstein* and reminds us why the sentimental
element remains so important in all Schiller's plays—because of
the political apathy of his audience. He foresaw quite rightly
that a struggle for democracy would leave them cold, so he
introduced a love interest which for an act and a half is very much
in the centre of the picture. Yet what probably interested him
most deeply was the idea of a great man tempted by power to
action which Schiller considered wrong, but sublime. He
bewilders us in the end with fragments of three different plays
rolled into one.

Genoa, happy under its old doge Andreas Doria, fears that
his nephew Gianettino will prove a tyrant. There is a conspiracy to set him aside and proclaim a republic. The only
strong and popular conspirator is Count Fiesko. Without him
the movement cannot succeed, yet at the beginning of the play
he seems to be completely taken up with Gianettino's sister
Julia, a proud coquette, neglecting his devoted young wife, who
would like him to retire to his estates. The other conspirators
are impelled by a variety of mainly personal motives. The most
striking is the fanatical old republican Verrina, a Brutus with
traits of Virginius, for his daughter falls a victim to Gianettino's
unbridled lust. Unlike Odoardo Galotti, this new Virginius
reacts to the situation in the old Roman way and vows to kill the

tyrant. Fiesko's levity, we presently learn, is a mask assumed to mislead Gianettino, and he is all the time actively directing operations for a coup. Schiller has still a rather schoolboyish idea of a 'Führer', as self-consciously handsome, witty, brave, and subtle, but it is a little surprising to find him so well aware of the fact that 'all power corrupts', for Fiesko turns overnight from a Brutus into a Caesar. The conspirators find themselves unable to attain freedom either with or without him, and in the moment of Fiesko's triumph the true republican, Verrina, must sacrifice him in the interests of the state. Gianettino being dead, power is restored to the old doge.

The volte-face in Fiesko which makes him see something sublime in stealing a crown is insufficiently prepared, though we have indeed seen that he believes the end to justify the means when he takes into his own service a grotesque black-skinned cut-throat sent to murder him, the best humorous creation of the young Schiller. One should probably not take all this as evidence of Schiller's rare insight into the nature of leadership, as some recent German commentators have been inclined to do, but rather as another instance of his love of the unexpected. He is continually springing surprises on us in *Fiesko*, as in the early plays generally, and he is particularly fond of showing us his favourites performing prodigies of moral strength. So the old doge Andreas, when the Moor betrays Fiesko's plot, sends him back to Fiesko under escort with the message that he will sleep without guards that night, while Fiesko, not to be outdone, gives him warning in person when the Putsch is about to begin. We even find Fiesko in his monologue at the end of Act II, though tempted to seize personal power, rejecting the thought with a proud gesture and the words: 'To win a diadem by struggle is great, to throw it away is divine.' In the Mannheim acting version this passage was transferred to the last act and the play ended on this note happily, with Fiesko as the noblest Roman of them all, but in the first and better version Fiesko appears corrupted already next morning by the mere anticipation of power.

It will be obvious that there is a hint of Wallenstein in this Fiesko. Schiller was obsessed with the notion of an abstract freedom even before reading Kant, and he remained so wedded to it that down to the end he was constantly drawing unaccount-able characters of this kind. F. H. Bradley, whom we have already quoted, might have asked whether these were really 'characters' in the ordinary sense at all, who could always 'do anything, or nothing, under any circumstances', for if the doctrine of free-will is pushed to the extreme of 'non-determinism', as he points out, 'freedom means *chance*; you are free, because there is no reason which will account for your particular acts, because no one in the world, not even yourself, can possibly say what you will, or will not, do next.'[1]

Kabale und Liebe is just as full of observed reality as *Fiesko* is devoid of it. There is probably nothing in German drama which conveys a more completely convincing picture of life than the first scene, or which more effectively and economically presents the dramatic theme and the relationship between the principal characters. The curtain goes up to reveal the musician Miller just rising from his chair and putting his 'cello on one side after practising. Mrs. Miller, who was down late for breakfast, is still at the table in her dressing-gown, drinking her coffee. 'Once and for all!' Miller begins, 'this thing's getting serious. My daughter and the baron are being talked about. My house is getting a bad name. The presiding minister will soon be on the scent and—well, I'm not going to have the young fellow in the house.' To which Mrs. Miller replies: 'You haven't talked him into coming here—you haven't thrown your daughter at his head'—and so on. We know at once that it is a play about the familiar Storm and Stress theme of class differences, with a young aristocrat paying his attentions to a girl not of his class, but be-longing to a respectable family rather above the ordinary crafts-man level—exactly as in Gemmingen's *Der deutsche Hausvater*. We have seen several of Miller's predecessors on the German stage, from Odoardo Galotti onwards, but Miller is more convincingly individual than any of them, yet typical of his class. He is a man of principle, he knows his place in society and he is not ashamed of it. A marriage of this kind is to him a social impossibility,

---

[1] *Ethical studies*, 2nd ed., Oxford, 1927, pp. 11 ff.

and any freer relationship is out of the question. In this household things could not easily go as far as in that of Gemmingen's
painter or Wagner's butcher, though the mother (who in
Gemmingen's play is dead) would not be the reason, for she is
an easy-going, rather silly woman, too fond of such luxuries as
snuff and coffee, and by no means averse to the idea of an aristocratic son-in-law—a Claudia Galotti on a lower plane. Both
husband and wife are cleverly characterised by their way of
speaking, their malapropisms (Makronenmagen), Miller's drastic
proverbs and sayings, and Mrs. Miller's mispronounced foreign
words (Bläsier, barrdu, disgushtüren). Miller calls himself a
'blunt, straightforward *teutscher Kerl*' and thinks the 'Bellatristen'
are a bad influence—an idea familiar from Lenz and Klinger—
but Mrs. Miller is greatly impressed by the lovely books brought
by the major, which Luise 'prays from'. It was literary culture
which was felt to be breaking down the traditional middle-class
ways of thinking and feeling, and their religious foundations,
putting ideas into young people's heads, for instance about romantic love without regard to rank. Miller is afraid the novels will
break up 'the handful of Christian notions in Luise which he
had so far managed to hold together' by his personal influence,
for she is very much her father's daughter, the apple of his eye.

In the second scene Luise's old admirer Wurm, secretary to
the Präsident, calls to see where he stands now that the major is
so frequent a visitor. Mrs. Miller, with her foolish talk of her
daughter's better chances, leaves him in no doubt, and Miller
himself, who would not object to Wurm if Luise liked him but
will not force him on her, cannot suppress his contempt for a
suitor who cannot do his own wooing. Wurm is a caricature of
middle-class obsequiousness and meanness of spirit, as his name
too obviously suggests, but he has an essential part in the plot.
When Luise returns from church we see the point of Miller's
talk about novel-reading. Every word she says makes the
influence of the 'Bellatristen' just as evident as that of French
materialism had been on Franz Moor or of Plutarch on Karl.
'Tell me where your thoughts lie and I will tell you what you
will do' is a psychological observation repeatedly illustrated by

9

Schiller. Unlike Goethe, he had never such a sure touch with his women as with his men, but Luise is the best so far and even her bookish talk is in character. Ferdinand in the next scene is just as clearly post-Werther, fresh from the university with his head full of sentimental and emancipated notions. In him, as the son of the unscrupulous Präsident, brought up among courtiers, one would not expect much firmness of principle. It is not surprising that he comes more completely than Luise under the sway of that 'mysticisme passionel' which French critics found so objectionable in *Kabale und Liebe* even in 1826, when it was acted in Paris. They called it 'amour allemand', M. Eggli tells us, though it was really 'amour rousseauiste'. It is the passion of St. Preux endowed with a metaphysical status, made into a kind of religion, by Storm and Stress writers, especially by Goethe in *Werther,* as Herbert Schöffler has shown us.[1] In Luise Schiller emphasises from the start the conflict between this kind of love and her religious and middle-class ideas. She cannot give her thoughts to prayer as before—'Heaven and Ferdinand are tearing my soul asunder', but at one moment she persuades herself that 'it must please God if she forgets Him in her joy over the masterpiece of His creation', a reflection which is very obviously 'the fruit of her Godless reading', as her father says, and at another, in a more Klopstockian strain, she renounces Ferdinand for this life, confident of their re-union in Heaven, where all ranks are equal. Ferdinand has no such scruples and surrenders himself entirely to feeling, which blots out all mundane considerations, but not his aristocratic possessiveness and wilfulness. 'Entrust yourself to me,' he tells her, 'you need no angels besides.'

Recent German criticism has rightly stressed the conflict which Schiller sees as given in the emotion of love itself, and not simply in love between noble and bourgeois. 'The freedom of love is not opposed to the limitations of rank, but love is brought up against the claims of circumstance and yet feels compelled to question those claims.'[2] What makes such a love as that of Ferdinand and

---

[1] *Die Leiden des jungen Werther, ihr geistesgeschichtlicher Hintergrund*, Frankfurt-am-M., 1938.
[2] P. Böckmann, *Die innere Form in Schillers Jugenddramen* in *Dichtung und Volkstum*, 1934.

Luise possible, or at least more probable, is the literary tradition of freer love by which they are affected, and this is itself a socio‑logical fact of importance. The play is no longer a crude seduction tragedy, Ferdinand's intentions are thoroughly honourable, yet even Luise's father is opposed to such a match, as Gemmingen's Hausvater had been, because class differences are still so great that they cannot be ignored by any prudent man. The 'Kabale', the trickery of the envious Wurm, backed up by Ferdinand's father, partly out of class feeling but principally because the marriage would cut across his own plans, would not have been effective but for the incompatibility felt by Luise to exist between romantic love and family and religious claims, and the blind abandonment to feeling of Ferdinand. In the last resort it only speeds up for dramatic purposes a conflict latent in their relationship from the beginning, given the conditions of that day. Seen in this light the play is a genuine tragedy proceed‑ing from a clash of loyalties, and not merely an 'Intrigenstück', but it must be admitted that Ferdinand is not entirely con‑vincing and these implications are not therefore as clear as they might be. It would not otherwise have taken critics so long to notice them.

What was however perfectly clear to contemporary audiences and what made the success of the play in middle‑class circles was the hatred and contempt for the court class in general which it so boldly expressed. Frau Miller's vanity was a peccadillo com‑pared with the monstrous self‑absorption and moral indifference of the Präsident. Let Ferdinand seduce Luise if he likes, he says to Wurm, it will be good practice for later conquests of ladies of rank, through whom he may make a career, but so that the father may retain his influence over the Duke, Ferdinand must go through the form of marriage with Lady Milford, the mistress whom the Duke must marry off for appearance's sake on account of his own approaching marriage. The laxity of court morals is constantly contrasted in this way with the strictness of the middle class. Even little Wurm 'prefers to be a Bürger' in this and have a wife 'fresh from the mint'. Everything the Präsident does is in keeping with this first impression we receive of him and the symbolic centre of the play is the scene (II, 6) in which plain Herr Miller, inwardly trembling, shows him the door on being insulted by him in his own house. 'Your Excellency is the master of the country, but this is my sitting-room . . . and if visitors can't behave themselves, it is my habit to throw them out—with all due respect.'

The Präsident's heartlessness is of a piece with the behaviour of his associates from the Duke downwards. It would require a chapter to appreciate Schiller's vivid presentation of the seamy side of court life—for it is of course only one side we see through Schiller's eyes. The same court of Ludwigsburg which he constantly has in view, down to details like the prime minister's removal of his predecessors by a criminal intrigue (Count Montmartin caused the fall of Colonel Rieger in this way) is presented in quite a rosy light by Justinus Kerner, for instance, in his charming *Bilderbuch aus meiner Kinderzeit,* though only perhaps because he confines himself to its colourful exterior features. The Duke is not exonerated in Schiller's play as in so many before and after it. The land is ground down as never before, the Duke's subjects are sold to foreign powers as cannon-fodder (we shall see that this scene, between Lady Milford and an old lackey, was omitted at Mannheim), the Duke lives for his pleasures, surrounded by marionettes like Hofmarschall Kalb—a caricature certainly, with his boast of twenty and a half minutes' conversation with His Highness at the lever. For his 'favourite', Lady Milford, the Duke can turn a desert into a paradise, he can give her fountains and fire-works and every luxury, but not a single generous feeling. We see him of course only indirectly through the eyes of his court, but as a type he is made convincing. Lady Milford, an invented figure remote from Schiller's experience, is frankly incredible. She serves as a foil to Luise and as our informant about the Duke, but her principal function is to enliven the fourth act by meeting her rival face to face, and finally making one of those magnanimous renunciations in which Schiller delighted, as we have seen in *Fiesko.* The confrontation of the two ladies brings out once more the contrast between the quietistic virtue of the middle class, not

free from priggishness in certain remarks of Luise, and the un⁄
principled hedonism of the fahionable world.

As H. A. Korff says: 'This drama pronounces judgment on
despotism in its fruits,' attacking not only the tyrant but the
system which results from his subjects' obsequiousness and lack
of inner freedom. 'If it is true that every nation gets the govern⁄
ment it deserves, it is no less true that every nation has as much
freedom as it inwardly possesses.' He sees in the christian resigna⁄
tion of such as Luise the underlying cause of the lack of political
freedom which arouses Schiller's indignation. To this Erich
Auerbach in *Mimesis*,[1] his illuminating comparative study of
realism in western European literature, adds that Schiller,
unfortunately, had a much clearer idea of what he was fighting
against than of what he was fighting for. He thought so much of
blackening his political opponents that his play seems to Auer⁄
bach a melodrama by a man of genius. He still cannot free him⁄
self from the tradition of the domestic drama and presents things
only from the personal, sentimental angle instead of tackling the
general social and political problems involved. The limitations
of the middle class in his play are only apparent to critical analysis
like Korff's, not to the audience in the theatre, who see Luise
only as persecuted, self⁄sacrificing innocence.

Even so, Auerbach continues, the play was unique in its time
and for long after. After this Schiller, and German literature
generally for nearly a century, turned away from the realistic
presentation of contemporary political and social problems. Their
realism is usually confined to historical or poetical and fantastic
subjects. When it deals with the present it confines itself to cir⁄
cumscribed subjects, unpolitical or merely regional, or it adopts
an ironical or idyllic tone, and shows us only individuals or
families, not social, economic and political complexes in their
tragic development. Society in Goethe and in German literature
down to the naturalists appears as something unchanging. In
later chapters Auerbach draws a contrast between German realism
and that of France and Russia, which is so much more dynamic.

Kabale und Liebe was first acted in April 1784 by Grossmann's

[1] Bern, 1946.

company in Frankfort-on-Main, and two days later in Mannheim. In both places it was well received, and other theatres quickly followed. It may well have been its sentimental features rather than its social criticism which made it popular on the stage, but no one can have mistaken its tone, and some court theatres, finding it too strong meat, either gave it few performances or revised it drastically. It was only given one performance in Stuttgart, for example, owing to the complaints of the nobility, and in Vienna it could not appear until 1808, and then in a much adapted form. Even in Mannheim Iffland's gentler pen was preferred. But what is most surprising is that it could be acted at all. The explanation is, no doubt, that in each little state the satire could be taken as referring to the others rather than to itself, and in any case the way had been prepared by Lessing, Grossmann and others, with whose work Schiller's play has this in common that it does not hint at the possibility of revolt. It is all the truer to reality for not representing its idealists as outwardly triumphant.

THE GERMAN THEATRE OF THE 'EIGHTIES

In the last twenty years of the eighteenth century, it became more and more usual for the larger centres of population in Germany, which were, of course, not yet very large, to have a repertory theatre with some artistic pretensions, which, following the example of Vienna (1776), they generally called a 'National Theatre'. The idea behind the use of the word 'national' in Hamburg and elsewhere had originally been, as we saw, to distinguish the new permanent theatres offering German plays from the touring companies on the one hand, and from the foreign theatres maintained by various courts on the other. The term very soon lost any definite connotation and came to be used of every standing theatre, unless it preferred to call itself a 'Court Theatre', or to combine the two titles, when it was under court patronage, as the majority of the earlier ones were. Even ecclesiastical princes like the Elector of Cologne established troupes 'to raise the art of the theatre to the level of a school of good morals', as Grossmann was told when he went to Bonn. The Elector of Mainz followed with a National Theatre, at first shared with Frankfort-on-Main, in 1787, and the Prince-Bishops of Salzburg and Passau set up permanent German theatres in 1793. Even quite small courts like Braunschweig-Oels maintained German troupes of their own for years at a time. All these semi-public foundations had similar aims to those of the short-lived Hamburg National Theatre, to raise the level of the art of the theatre and the status of the acting profession.

Patrons in other towns beside court towns followed suit from the early 'eighties. Linz, Innsbruck, Brünn, Frankfort-on-Main, Augsburg, Nürnberg, Altona, Breslau, Riga and others all had theatres before the end of the century, so that all the best actors came to be attached to some permanent theatre and the touring companies, still numerous if short-lived, were usually left with the dregs of the profession. There were German theatres in St. Petersburg and in the chief towns of Galicia and Hungary. The northern countries, especially Holland, were often visited by German troupes, so that, as Devrient says, even the French theatre could hardly claim to cast its net so wide. The Theatre Almanachs of the 'nineties mention at various times some seventy troupes, over half of which were permanent, or at least were settled in some centre for a number of months in the year.

Even when theatres received regular support from a court or from an organisation of patrons in a town, for the town councils did not take this burden on themselves yet, they had still to rely to a considerable extent on box-office receipts and therefore give the public what it wanted for the great majority of performances. We have seen how in the 'seventies already the various theatres quickly imitated each other's successes, with the result that much the same fare was offered everywhere. The levelling-out process continued in this period, and Schröder, closely followed in the 'eighties by Iffland in Mannheim, continued to set the pace, both in the style of acting and in the choice of plays. His appearances at many of the more important theatres as a 'Gast', his four years at the Burgtheater and the influential position attained in Berlin, Vienna, Dresden and so on by actors like Fleck, Brockmann,

Schütz, Reinecke who had worked for years under him in Hamburg all helped to spread the Hamburg school's ideal of acting, the convincingly natural representation of character, particularly on the ordinary human level. A great many of the plays first added to the repertoire by Schröder in the 'seventies were soon favourites on every stage, from his adaptation of English, French and Italian comedies and domestic dramas to his versions of Shakespeare. Their influence continued right through this period, and while Schröder was in Vienna he had time to make several new adaptations and write one or two original plays which had an excellent reception.

Schröder went back to Hamburg in 1785, gradually built up a new company and continued to run it till 1798. He spent the rest of his life in country retirement on a small estate he had bought, except for a short period from 1811 when he was unwisely persuaded to resume his management of the theatre, in which he had all along a financial interest. Even his second period of management brought him many disappointments, for he was now a man in his prime, with strong views of his own, both about plays and players. Unlike Goethe in Weimar, he was not subsidised at all. If the public refused to come he could not make them, however much he desired to be independent. He gave up the traditional 'theatre speeches' in which it had been usual to thank the audience and ask for their continued favour, but when he tried to force their taste, by giving no operas at all and specialising in spoken drama, he soon found himself compelled to give way. He could not even count on the co-operation of the Hamburg public in maintaining stage discipline and morality, in keeping his actresses' dressing-rooms free from male visitors, for instance, and punishing drunkenness and immorality in the company. The public looked upon him as too strait-laced and showed a decided weakness for actors and actresses whose names were not untouched by scandal, who were often more talented artists than those with better moral reputations. We find Goethe writing that Schröder could only afford to be so strict because he was content with plays which did not require actors of genius.

In *Dichtung und Wahrheit* (Book 13) Goethe has given us a good description of Schröder's adaptations of English plays. The Elizabethan and Restoration comedies which he favoured contained such surprising episodes that Schröder had to 'put more of his own into them than is generally known. He completely remade them, brought them closer to German ways of thinking and toned them down. But they always retain a bitter centre, because the comedy very often depends on the ill-treatment of certain characters, who may or may not deserve it.' Such plays did something to counteract the monotonous sentimentality of the family dramas. In his own plays, which always owe a good deal to foreign models, Schröder works on the same lines. In *Das Porträt der Mutter* (1786) for instance, where the basic idea was suggested by the episode of the portrait in *The School for Scandal*, the most fantastic things happen in a house in Hamburg when a son returns who has been unjustly disinherited and is thought by his father to be dead. Rekau, the son, is witty, ingenious and impudent. In no time Schröder has him escaping from the police, arranging marriages right and left and making himself indispensable to his eccentric old father, who does not recognise him. The father has been so much hurt by real life that he takes pleasure only in play-acting in his own home. The climax comes in a supposedly extempore comedy arranged by Rekau before the amateur performance begins. He thus contrives to unmask the villainous book-keeper who has maligned him, proves his innocence of the charges brought against him and recovers from the villain of the piece the 'portrait of his mother', the loss of which had brought about the final breach with his father. There is little character interest, but a series of ingeniously contrived situations give a good actor in the part of Rekau opportunities for continually springing surprises on the audience and provide an effective mixture of humour and sentiment.

Well-acted entertainments of this kind, together with the now popular Ritterstücke, made up an increasingly large part of the Hamburg repertoire during Schröder's second period of management. The productions which had been bold novelties in the

first phase, especially the adaptations of Shakespeare, were continued or revived, but few plays of outstanding merit were added
to them. There was one new Shakespearian production after
many years in 1792, *Much Ado About Nothing*. The high light of
these years for literary interest was Schiller's *Don Carlos*, given
its first German production with considerable success on 30th
August, 1787, in the original verse form but with cuts, made by
Schiller himself, to reduce it to a manageable length. Schröder
gave a fine study of King Philip. The verse was certainly a
difficulty by now, but Schröder even experimented with Racine's
Athalie, a new translation of Voltaire's *Alzire*, and two or three
French classical revivals two years later, all failures from the box-
office point of view. He could not close his eyes to the fact that
what the public liked best of all was good German opera or light
opera. Dittersdorf's *Doktor und Apotheker* (May 1787) and
Mozart's *Il Seraglio* (June 1787) and *Don Giovanni* (October
1789), together with *Adelheid von Veltheim*, a new forgotten
operetta by Grossmann and Neefe (December 1786) were
the great hits of the 'eighties. *Adelheid* could be sung to full
houses, Schütze tells us, as many as thirty times in a year. No
play approached these musical pieces in popularity until in July
1789 Kotzebue's *Menschenhass und Reue* reached Hamburg.
Here, as in Berlin, Mannheim and wherever else it was given,
this play earned golden opinions and restored to some extent the
prestige of the spoken drama. It was followed by *Die Indianer in
England* in the same year, and by three more from the same facile
pen in the next year (*Die Sonnenjungfrau, Das Kind der Liebe* and
Bruder Moritz), while Iffland's and Schröder's own family pieces
also continued to please. But though Schröder tried again in
1790 to dispense with opera, because of the never-ending difficulties he experienced with singers and orchestra, he was again
forced to restore it in a few months, and reaped a rich reward
from Mozart's *Figaro* (April 1791) and above all from *The Magic
Flute* (November 1793).

The finest German actor-manager of the century had in a
quarter of a century, as Devrient says, 'finally banished French
affectation and established Shakespeare as the supreme model

for the German stage. He had shown that without following the wild "geniuses" of Storm and Stress to extremes of crude naturalism a realistic school of acting could avoid the dull and common-place as well as the over-meticulous and the effeminately senti-mental. He had perfected what Lessing and Ekhof had begun, based German acting on the way of life of the German people and made it fully articulate in its own particular manner.'

Meanwhile Mannheim too was developing its own style of acting under the leadership of Dalberg and Iffland. The core of the troupe had worked with Ekhof in his last years, the greatest actor of the old school. Though reports about him are contra-dictory in details, as Uhde has shown, it is clear that he was a very serious, conscious artist and a man of character, who had begun as a master of declamation and adapted himself to the ever-growing but still moderate realism of the domestic drama. He excelled in rôles like Odoardo, fathers with good hearts and a gruff manner, and though much praised in certain comic rôles, he seems to have had little humour and to have tended to carica-ture less serious parts. Schröder went much further in the natural expression of individual character and of passion, as was realised in Mannheim when he gave nine performances there in 1781. Though the young Mannheim actors saw in Schröder their ideal, Iffland never allowed them to lose sight of the typical. It was a sentimentalised realism he aimed at, such as we find in his own writing. Dalberg, too, had a real influence in forming the Mannheim style, for he was not a mere figurehead like most of the aristocrats in nominal charge of court theatres. He had good sense and taste, and unobtrusively guided the discussion of policy at the meetings of the committee of actors which advised the pro-ducer and helped to maintain discipline. He never forgot that this was a court theatre which must keep within certain limits, for instance in giving expression to social criticism. So *Die Räuber* was turned into a historical play, while in *Kabale und Liebe* the scene with the lackey was omitted, where the sale of Germans as soldiers to foreign powers was pilloried, and at the end of Schiller's year as theatre-poet his contract was not renewed, no doubt because Dalberg found him too outspoken for such a theatre as his.

The following analysis of the repertoire of the Mannheim National Theatre during its first two years (October 1779 to October 1781), arranged here in the same way as Reichard's list of the most popular plays for 1776, quoted above (p. 199), shows how important Schröder's influence was here too, for the same tendencies are to be observed as in Hamburg earlier, and a high proportion of the plays, even the translated ones, from Shakes/ peare downwards, are the same, in the same adaptations. A noticeable feature among the original German plays is the popularity of domestic drama and of the first Ritterstücke.

FROM THE FRENCH	*Number of performances*
P. Corneille, *Rodogune*	2
Molière, *L'Avare*	5
Molière, *Tartuffe*	1
Voltaire, *Oreste* (adapted by Gotter as *Orest und Elektra*)	1
Destouches, *La Fausse Agnés*	1
Marivaux, *Le Jeu de l'amour et du hasard*	5
Voltaire, *Nanine* (adapted by Gotter as *Jeanette*)	3
Beaumarchais, *Eugénie*	3
Beaumarchais, *Le Barbier de Séville*	5
Falbaire, *L'Honnête Criminel*	2
Mercier, *Le Déserteur*	1
Mercier, *Jenneval* (adapted by Schröder as *Die Gefahren der Verführung* or *Jugend hat selten Tugend*)	6
Ten minor comedies (afterpieces by Dorat, Montfleury, Chamfort, Saint/Foix, Collé, Boissy, Marin, Le Grand)	30
Ten operettas (including Sedaine's *Déserteur*, Grétry's *Zemire et Azor*, Audinot's *Tonnelier*, Anseaume's *Les deux chasseurs et la Laitière*, etc.)	5

making in all 75 evenings with programmes from the French (neglecting afterpieces). Forty of these were operettas

FROM THE ENGLISH	
Hamlet (Schröder's adaptation)	4
King Lear (Schröder's adaptation)	3
The Taming of the Shrew (*Die gezähmte Widerbellerin*)	4
Banks, *The unhappy favourite* (translated by Dyck as *Essex*)	1
Dr. John Brown, *Athelstan* (translated Leonhardi)	2
Moore, *The Gamester* (from Saurin's *Beverley*)	2
Kelly, *School for Wives* (adapted by Koch as *Der flatterhafte Ehemann*)	5

Sheridan, *The Rivals*	8
Sheridan, *The School for Scandal*	3
Goldsmith, *She Stoops to Conquer*	3
Cumberland, *The West Indian*	3
Colmann-Garrick, *The Clandestine Marriage*	6
Colmann-Garrick, *Bon Ton*	2
making 46 evenings with English programmes	

FROM THE ITALIAN

Goldoni, Eight plays (mostly from Hamburg)	31
Gozzi, Three Plays	8

FROM THE SPANISH

Calderon, *El Alcalde de Zalamea* (Schröder's *Amtmann Graumann*)	5

GERMAN PLAYS

Cronegk, *Olint und Sophronia*	2
Lessing, *Minna von Barnhelm*	2
Lessing, *Emilia Galotti*	3
Lessing, *Der Freigeist*	2
Goethe, *Clavigo*	3
Lenz, *Der Hofmeister* (Schröder's adaptation)	4
Wagner, *Der Familienstolz* (*Reue nach der Tat*)	2
Brandes, *Der Schiffbruch* (*Miss Fanny*)	2
Brandes, *Die Schwiegermutter*	4
Brandes, *Der geadelte Kaufmann*	2
Brandes, *Die Mediceer*	2
Stephanie, *Die Schule der Damen*	5
Stephanie, *Der Deserteur aus Kindesliebe*	3
Stephanie, *Die Werber*	4
Stephanie, *Die abgedankten Offiziers*	3
Stephanie, *Der Spleen*	3
Stephanie, *Das Loch in der Türe*	1
Stephanie, *Die Wirtschafterin*	6
Brömel, *Der Adjutant*	5
Plümicke, *Der Husarenraub*	3
Müller, *Präsentiert das Gewehr*	4
Engel, *Der Edelknabe*	6
Engel, *Der dankbare Sohn*	1
Gotter, *Marianne*	3
Gotter, *Der argwöhnische Ehemann*	4
Gemmingen, *Der deutsche Hausvater*	3
Grossmann, *Henriette* (after *La nouvelle Héloise*)	3
Grossmann, *Nicht mehr als sechs Schüsseln*	3
Wezel, *Rache für Rache*	3

Iffland had made his début as a dramatist even before Schiller's arrival. His first great success, *Das Verbrechen aus Ehrsucht,* was acted in 1784, just after *Kabale und Liebe,* and pleased Mannheim better. No less than thirty-seven plays of his were produced in all at Mannheim between 1781 and 1808, and given an average of over a dozen performances each. In the same period *Kabale und Liebe* was acted only seven times, and *Die Räuber* only fifteen, while *Fiesko* and *Don Carlos* were given only three times each. It is evident that Iffland was able to give his audiences what they wanted, yet at the same time he was convinced, as can be seen from his letters, that the stage was 'a school of wisdom, of beautiful feelings'. He was a product of the sentimental age, brought up on Richardson as a boy and sent at the age of eight by his father, an official of some standing in Hanover, to see *Miss Sara Sampson* acted, because 'it taught a good lesson'. He had been destined for the Church, like Schiller, but after successes in school performances felt an irresistible call towards the stage, and ran away from home to join the Gotha company, persuading himself that this was his best pulpit. His school-fellow, K. P. Moritz, was full of the same ideas, but proved to have no talent for the stage and took to writing. Iffland satisfied Ekhof that he could act and soon distinguished himself. After *Das Verbrechen aus*

Ehrsucht he realised that by his writing too he could, as he had hoped, 'draw tears of sympathy for a good cause' and vowed, he tells us, 'never to use his power of influencing a multitude other' wise than to direct their feelings towards the good'.

Iffland's secret was his understanding of the ordinary man and woman of his day, and no one has drawn them better, at least as they liked to think they were. It was ten years after *Werther*, when to act as a man of feeling was no longer the privilege of a few, but the claim of almost all who had the least pretension to culture, all who had seen a few plays and read a few novels. Iffland counts for his effects in comedies and serious plays alike on an appeal to sentiment. His works are accordingly a perfect museum of touching motifs, amongst which we recognise all the old favourites from literature and the drama since Rousseau and Richardson.[1] Nearly all his plays deal with middle-class family life and the father of the family, conceived in the tradition descended from Diderot through Gemmingen, is always suffi' ciently well educated to be as sentimental as the mass of the audience. He is an official, professional man, manufacturer or officer, devoted to his children, though he may not wear his heart on his sleeve, and he is matched by a busy Hausfrau of a wife, a heart of gold who has usually not received much formal education. Iffland does not delight in romantic love in its early stages, unless it is unhappy, but rather in everyday scenes between man and wife, with surface disagreements perhaps but deep affection beneath them, or in Darby and Joan with their touching reminiscences, and touching relationships between children and their parents or grandparents. Imaginative sympathy being the very root of goodness for this age, we are also shown touching relations between master and servant, as in Gellert and Lessing earlier, and between the ruler and his subjects, as in the patriotic dramas. A nation is thought of as just one great family, who love their Landesvater. Iffland tells us with relish in his memoirs how he wrote his one-act play *Liebe um Liebe* in a few days as a prologue for a gala performance in Mannheim which was to be attended by the newly married Count Palatine, the heir to the throne

[1]See A. Stiehler, *Das Ifflandsche Rührstück*, 1898.

(later Maximilian I of Bavaria) and a distinguished company. They were all so moved by the sight of a loyal countryman plant/ ing a tree whenever a prince was born that 'the princes embraced their wives heartily in public' and the whole theatre rose to cheer the new Pfalzgräfin. Next day Iffland received two hundred Louis d'or, various gold watches and so on in recognition of his expression of Mannheim's feelings. He followed up this triumph with a series of similar official pieces for the Emperor and lesser rulers, including an anti/revolutionary play, *Die Kokarden* (1791), written at the special request of the Emperor Leopold II. His autobiography and letters make clear how well he deserved the Order of the Red Eagle bestowed on him in Berlin by Frederick William III.

Another fruitful source of sentiment is nature and country life. Pets are much in evidence; even the sight of sleeping flies moves a character to say: 'O do not touch them! They are asleep. When the winds of life become too harsh, they go to sleep. They are not dead. With the spring wind of hope they will wake up again. A comforting thought for us!' It is the pathetic fallacy all the time, about virgin nature or fading flowers or memorial trees; or the pathos of parting and the passage of time, regretful memories of the old home, the old arm/chair, or happy childhood and student days.

Country and town are contrasted in Rousseauistic fashion. The peasant is poor but virtuous, and exploited by a master in the town and his minions. Iffland's naive village girl, Margrete, in *Die Hagestolzen*, is one of the best drawn of her class, which we have come across already in Storm and Stress plays. Goethe said to Eckermann that this was the only play where Iffland had risen to poetry. Margrete artlessly captivates a confirmed bachelor in a few hours when he has fled from his avaricious sister and rascally man/servant, and the conversation is so well imagined that the touching conversion is almost credible. In Iffland's best 'drame' too, *Die Jäger*, the good people rooted in the soil are con/ trasted with the scheming heartless creatures from the town. How deep an impression was made by this play, which was chosen for the opening performance of the Weimar Theatre, is shown by its survival on the repertoire of many theatres down to this century—it had had 160 performances in Berlin by 1885—and by the extensive use that was made of its themes by later play-wrights, notably by Otto Ludwig in *Der Erbförster*. It is the Rousseauistic idea of the corrupting effects of civilisation that underlies Iffland's situations and most of his little homilies here, as it does those of the French 'drame', and 'nature', that ambiguous norm, means what the respectable middle-class family man feels to be right. With his strong sense of honour and duty this forester is devoted to his work, to the King and to the com-munity, not forgetting that 'those who come after us will need wood too', but he has no respect or liking for self-seeking auto-cratic officials. He likes to live according to the best traditions of his class, but not to ape the aristocracy. He is God-fearing but tolerant, agreeing with the pastor, who has no objection to the marriage of young people of different religions and, like Nathan the Wise, values religions according to their fruits in conduct. It is his duty, the minister says, to increase happiness and encourage toleration, while the forester goes so far as to say that toleration *is* religion. There is the same norm in everyday manners. Iffland effectively contrasts the forester and his superior, the Amtmann, at table. The Amtmann, who holds that luxuries are for those who can appreciate them, turns up his nose when he discovers that what he had taken for ice-cream is merely cheese, while his hostess, unused to such luxuries as ices or their French names, misunderstands 'glace' as 'glass'. A wealth of such details make the picture of manners convincing and produce an atmo-sphere of reality, amidst which we readily accept the coincidences and accidents necessary for the working-out of the plot through moments of suspense to a happy ending. It is only when we see how selective the picture is, and how all the deeper problems are carefully excluded, that we understand how sentimental such a work is at bottom.

For all his faults Iffland is however a much more sincere writer than Kotzebue, the very type of a rootless intellectual. Both Goethe and Schiller respected and liked Iffland as a man, admired his management of the Mannheim and Berlin theatres, and saw much merit in some of his plays, but Kotzebue (1761–1819) antagonised almost all his fellow-writers by his vanity and spitefulness. He was a native of Weimar, where as a boy he saw Koch's and Seyler's troupes and was stimulated by early contacts with the Weimar writers to try his hand at poems and plays. At twenty he took a post as private secretary in St. Petersburg and quickly attained high official rank. While serving in Reval he made his name with a novel in 1785, and two years later his play *Menschenhass und Reue* began its triumphal progress in Berlin. It had a success comparable with that of *Werther*, not only in Germany but in England and several other countries. Everything he produced was now eagerly awaited by managers. F. L. W. Meyer, Schröder's biographer, is eloquent in praise of *Menschenhass und Reue* and its author, for at a critical period he did more than any other writer to build up a repertoire which would draw and hold large audiences.

Kotzebue's first success is certainly very good theatre, and probably as good as anything he ever did, for there is no develop-ment in his work. The piquant subject offered the same sort of attraction in its time as things like *The Second Mrs. Tanqueray* in Victorian days. Though Kotzebue undoubtedly laid a trap for the easy-going sentimentality of his contemporaries, the principal artistic defect of the play lies in its exploitation of situations which do not form a consistent unity and in its crude black and white character drawing. If on reflection we could believe that a young wife who had left a devoted husband and their two infant children for the sake of luxuries promised to her by a lover could, when disappointed in him too, suddenly become a saint, or that this one blow would turn her husband overnight into an eccentric misanthropist, we might find the much-debated re-union of husband and wife a live issue. Otherwise we must consider this simply a melodrama, depending for its effect on legerdemain, on the clever substitution of one conception of a character at the suitable moment for a totally different one. Kotzebue was an extraordinarily good conjuror,. but fundamentally insincere. That explains his phenomenal stage success and the failure of his work to satisfy genuine poets in his own day, or any literary historian after his death. As Devrient said: 'Perhaps no other author will ever be so clever at finding the sensitive spot in the body of his time.' There is no character in *Menschenhass und Reue* which is not purely stagey, no sentiment expressed which is not put in to please the average audience. It is full of touching benevolence and touching gratitude and it culminates in a magnanimous act of forgiveness. The plot is a tissue of improbabilities, but it is all subtly contrived to bring together the misanthropic stranger and the charming woman with a mysterious past when the audience, but none of the people in contact with them, know who they both are and what their relationship has been. The tension is skilfully worked up to this meeting at the end of the fourth act, in a scene without words, when one swoons and the other rushes away. The fifth act brings in the inevitable children to ensure a happy ending. Behind the play one can see a whole vista of successful 'drames' going back at least as far as La Chaussée's *La Fausse Antipathie*.

Kotzebue's innumerable farces are usually much more attractive for a modern reader than his serious plays and offer good, clearcut rôles for amateur actors. He had a genuine comic vein, inexhaustible fertility and no scruples about adopting good situations and characters from any predecessor. He rewrote in this way many plays of Iffland, Schröder and the older domestic dramatists, and even tried to rival Schiller in verse plays. One of the best of his lighter pieces is a satire on the German mania for titles, *Die deutschen Kleinstädter*. It is a caricature of the selfsatisfied provincial philistine which reminds us a little of Gogol's *Revisor* but lacks its character interest. Kotzebue knew his subject, of course, and the play is still readable for its faithful picture of externals. It has become a period piece. *Die Indianer in England*, another great favourite with contemporaries, is on the other hand too obvious an exploitation of Rousseauism to please any longer with the wouldbe naive charm and candour of Gurli, the child of nature, and her adventures in London.

What is most impressive after all about Kotzebue is the record of his quite phenomenal productivity and popularity. Iffland's production figures in his own theatre, Mannheim, for instance, are quite eclipsed by Kotzebue's, of whom three plays were acted to one of his, for a higher average number of evenings (15), and it was the same in every German theatre, including Weimar, as we shall find. In Dresden one evening in three was given up to Kotzebue between 1789 and 1813, while Lessing, Goethe and Schiller only had one evening in twenty-five between them, and Shakespeare was scarcely acted at all. At the Burgtheater in Vienna his share worked out at an average of over forty-five performances a year over the eighty years to 1867, so it was by no means a flash in the pan. It is not surprising if in England, down to the death of Goethe, Kotzebue was considered *the* literary representative of Germany, for Chamisso, on the voyage of exploration that took him round the world in a ship commanded by the dramatist's son, found the father's fame so universal that he called him the 'de facto' poet of the world.

THE EARLY BLANK-VERSE DRAMAS OF
SCHILLER AND GOETHE. 'HUMANITÄT'

Schiller's *Don Karlos*

THE first three plays of Schiller are full of protest against his age, and of the bitterness of a disappointed optimist. His favourite Shakespearian play at this time was *Timon of Athens*. In *Don Karlos* we see what he holds to be good and worth striving for, his fine humanity as well as his desire to be free from the shackles of the past. Yet there is an intimate connection between *Don Karlos* too and the thought and ideals of Schiller's own time, as is made clear to us by Schiller himself in the *Letters on Don Karlos*, which he wrote on finding his play so frequently misunderstood. It deals with 'a favourite topic of our century, the spread of a purer and gentler humanity of feeling, the desire for the maximum of freedom for the individual combined with the highest advantage to the community as a whole'. It was hoped by many that ideas such as these might some time inspire a young prince to reform society from above, and in his play Don Karlos was imagined as such a prince, not the Don Karlos of history, the sickly son of Philip II of Spain, but the hero of St. Réal's romance and of Otway's play *Don Carlos*, based on this story. He was trying to present vividly in a work of art, he says, ideas hitherto found only in scholarly writings like those of Montesquieu, truths most sacred to all friends of mankind.

The tone of the play itself leaves us in no doubt about Schiller's passionate agreement with the aspirations voiced by Posa. He is protesting here too against the German life of his day, not against class differences and social abuses this time, but against the unworthy acceptance by his countrymen of the system of absolutism. The figure of Marquis Posa has of course haunted the imagination of liberal-minded Germans ever since. We think of him above all, as Hettner says, when we call Schiller the poet of freedom. 'What young German does not go through a phase when Marquis Posa is his highest ideal?' he asks, but that was in mid-nineteenth century. Yet there is an episode in recent German history which again reminds us strongly of *Don Karlos*. When Dr. Goerdeler, after careful preparation of the revolt of the generals, declared himself ready in 1943 to say to Hitler personally what it was necessary to say in the name of common sense and humanity, he wrote to General Olbricht: 'It is not certain that such an interview, if it can be arranged, will necessarily end badly; surprises are possible, though im-probable, and the risk must be taken.' (17.5.43.) It is more than likely that he was thinking of Posa before Philip. Some of the German criticisms of *Don Karlos* published in the nineteen-thirties, however, seem to play down Posa by stressing the un-realistic, fantastic aspects of this figure. They credit Schiller with insight into 'Realpolitik', making Philip into the hero of the play and equating this particular system of absolute government with government in general.

It was principally through a philosophical study of history that Schiller arrived at his mature interpretation of life. In *Don Karlos* he created a new type of historical drama, a type which seems to C. E. Vaughan specifically German.[1] The historical plays of Shakespeare, he thinks, offer no fair analogy to it, retain-ing still too much of the mere chronicle or of the purely personal approach to historical themes. The German historical drama, which came into existence in the same age as modern historio-graphy, 'brings the corporate, as distinct from the individual, life of man upon the stage' and 'embodies, more or less completely, some aspect of the national, political and social conflicts of humanity'—a formidable task for any dramatist. In such dramas 'the character which moves before our eyes is a symbol of some-thing wider and greater that looms behind'. Dilthey, in his

[1] *Types of tragic drama*, London, 1908.

Deutsche Dichtung und Musik, makes Schiller's dramas symbolic of still more general truths. They do not aim at reproducing history but at interpreting for us the meaning of life. 'They create a new world in the imagination, in which the meaning of the real world is made apparent.' The two descriptions are complementary. Schiller's historical dramas are a step towards a 'Study of History', such as Arnold Toynbee is attempting in our day. What interested Schiller in history was its philosophy, the light it threw on human destiny, and that was why, after this first attempt at a historical drama, he felt it necessary to devote himself for years to the systematic study of history and philosophy before returning to the theatre.

Don Karlos then is a work of the widest scope, concerned with 'der Menschheit grosse Gegenstände', but aesthetically it has the obvious defect that it is not all of a piece. The composition of it lasted from 1783 to 1787, Schiller's conception of his theme developed during this time and he unfortunately published the first two acts serially in his periodicals, *Rheinische Thalia* and *Thalia*. His first plan was for a 'domestic tragedy in a royal household', keeping fairly close to St. Réal, as Otway had done and, just before Schiller, Alfieri in his *Filippo*. Next the interest shifted for Schiller from the love of Karlos for his step-mother, Elizabeth of Valois, formerly his affianced bride, and the resulting conflict between father and son, to the passionate friendship between Karlos and Marquis Posa. Out of this grew the final main theme, the struggle between the forces of freedom represented by Posa, and those of tyranny represented by Philip. An unmanageably elaborate plot resulted which Schiller felt it necessary to explain in the *Letters on Don Karlos*. Hettner's judgment seems incontrovertible: 'The violent and psychologically impossible way in which Marquis Posa plays his break-neck game with the fate of his friend Karlos, and at last courts his own death like a bankrupt gambler . . . is only a confession of incapacity on the part of a poet who does not know how to get his characters off the stage, because there is something radically wrong with the structure of the play.'

For a modern reader the sentiments in certain parts of the play, though often eloquently expressed, are decidedly 'dated', the 'German love' protestations of the Prince, for example, or even the friendship passages, though these were inspired by Schiller's own experience, the same passionate friendship with the devoted Körner which gave rise to the 'Hymn to Joy'. But the contrast between those who think highly of man and those who do not, essentially the same as that drawn in *Kabale und Liebe* between the middle class, with their inward values, and the heartless ruling class, is symbolised for all time in Posa and Philip. Speaking to Alba, the King's confessor, Domingo says of Karlos (II, 10):

> Sein Herz entglüht für eine neue Tugend,
> Die, stolz und sicher und sich selbst genug,
> Von keinem Glauben betteln will.— Er denkt!
> Sein Kopf entbrennt von einer seltsamen
> Schimäre — er verehrt den Menschen — Herzog,
> Ob er zu unserm König taugt?

This is the liberal, humanistic philosophy of life which Posa and Karlos have shared at Alcala. They do not believe that all the problems of life have been solved once and for all by super-natural help. They hold that man can solve his own problems by thought. Domingo has tried in vain to 'break the Prince's fiery spirit through the sensual pleasures of this age', like the Jesuits who 'condition' the mind of the young Prince in Schiller's fragment of a novel, *Der Geisterseher,* into which he seems to have directed much of the anti-clericalism originally intended for *Don Karlos.* The Church—of course the Catholic Church, but Schiller was no admirer of the Protestant Church either, for to judge by the poems his religious views were now decidedly Spinozistic—is an organisation still more heartless than Philip. The Grand Inquisitor (V, 10) has to remind Philip, in whom a spark of humanity has been fanned to life by Posa, that: 'Men are for you merely cyphers. Must I go through the elements of the art of government with my grey-haired pupil? Let the God of the earth learn to do without what can be refused to him (by his subjects).' The King, that is, must dispense with sympathy, or he makes the world his equal. The catholic system of thought and the hierarchy of church and state in which it is embodied are as near to perfection as man can come, and not even the King may safely interfere with them at some prompting of an individual mind or heart. It is a grandiose conception, which Dostoievsky raises to still more paradoxical heights when he makes *his* Grand Inquisitor, in the famous passage in *The Brothers Karamazov*, say to the returning Christ himself that He has no right to add a single word to what He has said already. It is in accordance with these notions of a sacrosanct order handed down from generation to generation that everything at the Spanish court is governed by fixed rules, every movement allowed to the Queen, even the hour at which she may see her own child.

Philip is a potentially great man, reduced to the position of an engineer of political power in the grip of this mechanical system. It is his personal tragedy that though he can never quite suppress his human feelings, his office calls for inhumanity. Schiller has finely realised this conflict, one familiar to him early in *Julius von Tarent* for instance ('What king ever had a friend?'), and has made of Philip one of the best studies of incarnate power in dramatic literature. There are not only ideas of Montesquieu and Rousseau in his drama, but also Voltaire's 'Écrasez l'infâme!' Posa is the rebel and idealist, the rejector of systems and believer in man's goodness and creativeness. The phrase with which he immediately explains to Philip his absence from court: 'Ich kann nicht Fürstendiener sein!' the supreme expression of 'Männerstolz vor Königsthronen', must have had an electrifying effect on contemporary audiences, and the whole scene (III, 10) is dramatic rhetoric of the highest order, another monument of Humanität like *Nathan der Weise*, for we are at once reminded of Nathan before Saladin. What is common to both authors is the same liberal conviction that truth has not been finally revealed and embodied in some system, religious in the one case, political and religious in the other. Man must still constantly search for new truth, for it can still be found, and the effort to find it is his noblest function. In order to be thus creative, he must be free. Freedom will always be abused and seems to those in authority not only dangerous but wasteful of effort, yet it is the necessary condition of the world's self-renewal. A world without it will run down like an unwound clock and its peace will be 'Die Ruhe eines Kirchhofs'. Like Philip, Posa too has his personal tragedy, the tragedy of the idealist, for there is no cheap optimism in this play. Not only do the forces of reaction prevail, for the idealist must not expect results in a hurry, his love being for

Die Welt mit allen kommenden Geschlechtern,

but idealists too are men, in their limitations as well as in their greatness, and the best of them have a streak of the tyrant in them. So Posa uses even Karlos for his 'higher purpose' and deprives him of his freedom, when he unexpectedly obtains the confidence of the King, and when his plan fails and he decides to give his life for Karlos, he has no answer to the Queen's charge that in his self-sacrifice he has courted admiration.

Don Karlos was to achieve great popularity after the turn of the century. In Berlin only *Die Jungfrau von Orleans* and *Maria Stuart* were performed more frequently (336 and 268 times respectively by 1886, compared with 246 for *Don Karlos*). But at first its verse form was a hindrance and Schiller even had to prepare a prose version for performance in most theatres. He had deliberately chosen verse, following Lessing's example in *Nathan*, to lend increased dignity and ideality to the work. He was feeling his way back gradually to the grand style of heroic drama. In the preface to *Die Braut von Messina* he was to claim that the artist cannot use any element of reality just as he finds it, and to possess unity his work must be 'ideal' in all its parts. Everything on the stage is only a symbol of real life. By the use of metrical language that 'vulgar idea of the natural' is counteracted which is so destructive of art. With the introduction of verse the diction was correspondingly raised and dignified and the Great of a bygone age and distant country were again chosen as protagonists. Humour was totally banned and the analytic rather than the chronological type of construction was followed, though the variety of sub-plots and the frequent changes of scene would have scandalised Gottsched. In form the play is nearer to the French classics than to any of the popular types of German drama. In

content, as we have seen, it is full of the liberal idea of the per-
fectibility of man and society through the exercise of his own
powers. In both respects it represents an intermediate stage
between Storm and Stress and the classicism of Weimar.

GOETHE'S DRAMAS AFTER GÖTZ

In the same year as *Don Karlos*, 1787, there appeared also,
in verse, Goethe's *Iphigenie auf Tauris*, which had been completed
in prose and acted in 1779. It was followed next year by *Egmont*,
the conception of which went back to 1775, and in 1790 by
Tasso and *Faust, ein Fragment*. The immediate occasion of the
publication of these plays in rapid succession was that Göschen
was bringing out the first collected edition of Goethe's works
and most of the necessary revision of older unpublished writings
had been done by Goethe during the later part of his stay in Italy.
Since *Götz* he had not published any drama as considerable as
these. *Clavigo* (1774) was simply a well-made prose domestic
drama, such as others could turn out too, as Merck had quite
rightly said, a dramatisation of part of an autobiography again,
this time of an episode in the life of Beaumarchais. The play was
written in a week at the request of a Frankfort lady, but it was not
merely a *tour de force* without deeper interest, for as already in the
Weislingen-Marie sub-plot in *Götz*, Goethe drew partly on his own
experience and made out of this anecdote a symbolic 'confession'
of his feeling of guilt in relation to Friederike Brion. Apart from
this the play is chiefly remarkable for its skilful construction,
which ensured its immediate success on the stage, as we have
seen. Goethe had made a careful study of Lessing's technique
in *Emilia Galotti* and proved that he was quite able to write plays
capable of stage performance if he wished. *Stella* (1776) was
equally stageworthy, and as it called itself a 'a play for lovers', no
one could be surprised to find it full of Wertherism. It contains
some charmingly natural scenes and well-drawn women characters, but the erotic individualism of the age of *Werther*, as we see
it here in the weak hero Ferdinand, seems a fitter subject for
artificial comedy or satire than for a domestic drama. The total

effect is sentimental, because Goethe does not really face the moral issues involved in the situation of a young man who, in a mono-gamous society, marries one woman, then lives with another and is brought face to face with them both. In the first version he adopted the same solution as some of the writers of Ritterstücke, who make their returning crusaders found a *ménage à trois* with ladies from the east and west, and Fernando's wife appeals in fact to the medieval example of the Graf von Gleichen. It is no wonder that in England the play furnished important ingredients for the amusing parody of German drama which Canning and some fellow M.P.s wrote for the *Anti-Jacobin* in 1798, when England was threatened with invasion from France. Other plays which gave them hints were *Die Räuber, Kabale und Liebe* and *Menschenhass und Reue*, all revolutionary and disruptive influences in the view of these supporters of Pitt, because the German stage 'with its aspiration after shapeless somethings' seemed to them to be undermining morality and making for the 'dissolution of the frame of every existing community'. The moral of their skit was 'the reciprocal duties of one or more husbands to one or more wives, and to the children who may happen to arise out of this complicated and endearing connexion', a not unfair reference to *Stella* and Kotzebue's problem-play, performed that year at Drury Lane.

Goethe showed technical facility and lyrical genius in two operettas after the French model, *Erwin und Elmire* and *Claudine von Villa Bella*, during these Frankfort years, and constantly used dramatic form for the high-spirited satirical improvisations, mainly directed against literary men of the time, in which he was so productive. The best known are *Satyros, Götter, Helden und Wieland* and *Pater Brey*. We have seen that Lenz and Klinger tried this kind of thing too, for the Storm and Stress poets were very conscious of their uniqueness, but Goethe's satires are in a class by themselves in the verve, spontaneity and fundamental sanity of their humour. In Weimar some of these lighter works were acted by Goethe and the amateur actors and actresses of the court circle, and many new ones were thrown off by him for immediate representation with the utmost facility and unfailing charm—*Lila, Jery und Bätely, Die Fischerin, Proserpina, Der Triumph der Empfindsamkeit, Die Vögel,* and the stage version of *Das Neueste von Plundersweilern.*

The four major dramas first published at the end of the 'eighties give evidence again of supreme lyrical powers but also of great breadth of vision and profound understanding of life. Goethe was not a born reformer, endowed like Schiller with passionate moral convictions. He did not feel indignant, even as a young man, as Schiller did, about whole classes of his fellow-men and their behaviour, indeed his Leipzig comedy, *Die Mitschuldigen,* comes very near to modern nihilism, and *Stella,* as we have just seen, is, ethically considered, a very dubious product. His deepest urge was perhaps to be as fully conscious of life as possible, to define in words, in the first place for his own satisfaction, what he thought and felt about an ever increasing range of experiences. From the early Faust's

> Und was der ganzen Menschheit zugeteilt ist
> Will ich in meinem innern Selbst geniessen,
> Mit meinem Geist das Höchst' und Tiefste greifen

through the monologue in the scene 'Wald und Höhle', with

> Gabst mir die herrliche Natur zum Königreich,
> Kraft sie zu fühlen, zu geniessen,

to the song of Lynceus the Watchman, at the end of *Faust* II, 'Zum Sehen geboren', through the whole vast extent of his writing this is his characteristic attitude to life, the attitude of a lyrical poet and 'grand contemplatif'. With it went an incomparable intelligence, which would not rest content with discrete experiences but was eternally seeking to bring them into relation with each other. No one since Leonardo da Vinci, it has often been said, has been appreciatively aware of so much in the world around him and within, and in the experience of 'der Vorwelt silberne Gestalten', the poets, the saints and the sages of old. Inclusiveness, catholicity of culture was his aim from early manhood, 'to raise the pyramid of his existence to a point as high as possible in the air'. His creativeness was a constant readiness to respond and a constant search for wholeness. In people, what interested him above all was to understand by sympathy what made the deepest appeal to them in life and what they felt about it all. 'It would be a glorious sight to see how the world is re-flected in this mind' is for instance the characteristic comment he wrote under the silhouette of Frau von Stein given to him by Zimmermann in 1775, before Goethe knew her, and in his letters to her later during his travels with the Duke of Weimar he is constantly drawing portraits and collecting items, as he says, 'for his political moral dramatic file'.

What Goethe gives us in the first place then in his dramatic pieces of all kinds, even the slighter satires and so on, is his con-ception of various attitudes to life in relation to some imagined situation. Lowes Dickinson, that great admirer of Goethe, gives us the same kind of thing more explicitly and prosaically in *A Modern Symposium* and of course the great model is Plato him-self. There is very often an autobiographical reference, because the attitudes which Goethe most fully appreciates are naturally those for which he finds the germ in himself, though he has an amazing capacity too for interpreting the minds of women. It is a mistake in any case to read Goethe, as so many of the Goethe-philologen have done, as if our purpose were merely 'to observe how rich and varied an inner life he had, and how skilfully he disembarrassed himself of his sufferings at every stage'.[1] Various possibilities of experience, generalised from hints found in his own life or that of others, form the ground work of his main characters. The 'caractères' of the French and English moralists and the comedy developed from them pointed the way towards this kind of dramatic character, but they are much more abstract, being organised principally round certain recognised and named complexes of feeling and habit like avarice, jealousy, irresolution. Goethe generalises too, because of his need to clarify his experience intellectually, but his unconscious classification of his observa-tions, like Shakespeare's, takes place according to categories of his own, never consciously analysed in his greater creations, but so vividly are his characters imagined that Faust and Mephisto-pheles and Gretchen become types by reference to which we seem

[1] R. Peacock, *Goethe's version of poetic drama*, P.E.G.S., 1947.

to have a better understanding of living people whom we know. In some later works Goethe seems to have become too conscious of the process of creation of character, and the result is the excessive abstraction of the figures in *Die natürliche Tochter*, or the later chapters of *Wilhelm Meisters Lehrjahre*.

These figures are obviously symbolic, but so are Faust and Tasso, and even Egmont and Götz. Like Schiller's historical characters, they stand for something beyond themselves, but whereas Schiller is interested in history, man and fate, Goethe is interested in the 'Naturformen des Daseins', the functional relationships of men in the ever-recurring situations of life, and the natural laws which they illustrate. The differences between them can be well seen by comparing *Don Karlos* with *Egmont*. *Don Karlos* is concerned with events at the Spanish court just before the despatch of Alba to the Netherlands, and *Egmont* with what he did there. Both involve a discussion of Philip's totalitarianism, which neither poet likes. But Schiller ranges all his figures on one side or the other in this question and takes sides passionately, from the point of view of his own time and situation, against 'cold statecraft' though, as we have seen, he is aware of the human limitations of idealists as well as of the merits of his tyrant. He makes of a historical romance a representation of the clash of Catholicism and Protestantism, absolutism and the incipient movement towards democracy. Goethe, in the discussion between Egmont and Alba, is more objective, making Egmont appeal to the old and, as he claims, harmonious order of the estates of the realm, with rights and duties adjusted by a gradual process of give and take, an order which the Spaniards are sweeping away in favour of a 'rational' system imposed on *a priori* principles from above. Egmont is nearer to Burke and Posa to Robespierre. There is the same reverence for the free products of natural growth as in *Götz*.

In construction, Schiller's play is more traditional, working with characters and plot on lines suggested by Shakespeare and Lessing and the French, while Goethe, though following the same traditions in some respects himself, and using characters and plot in what looks like a free Shakespearian manner, is chiefly concerned with conveying an impression of an attitude to life, that of a man like the sailor in the poem *Seefahrt*, composed about the same time, who in spite of the warnings of his anxious friends puts out to sea in his frail bark, 'trusting in his Gods, whether he be wrecked or saved'. He saw in Egmont someone like him-self when he embarked on the Weimar adventure, one who has no great belief yet in his power to shape his life according to a preconceived purpose and surrenders himself to the moment, confident that life is good. Egmont likens himself to a charioteer whose steeds, racing almost out of control, can only be guided here from a boulder, there from an abyss, and Goethe used these lines himself to calm the misgivings of Fräulein Delph at Heidel-berg, when the Duke of Weimar's carriage at last arrived for him. He interprets the historical fact that Egmont remained in the Netherlands, and was executed by Alba, as the result of such an 'amor fati'. Everything else has to fit in with this conception, so his Egmont is brave, handsome, successful, a popular favourite, of buoyant temperament, who lives in the moment with all the insouciance of a young bachelor. He is opposed to Alba and potentially dangerous, but his death is not the result of a deter-mined stand for freedom but rather of his temperament. He stumbles into martyrdom, and in the final vision of freedom persuades himself that this is all for the good of his country. The other figures are either part of the picture of the times, full of colour and atmosphere as in *Götz*, or they are subordinated to the study of a temperament. There is a general contrast between the free play of individuality among the Flemings, shown in crowd scenes like genre pictures, and the dour fanaticism of the Spaniards, so that the one nation seems to be, as it were, summed up in Egmont and the other in Alba.

In his review of the play Schiller expressed high admiration for the crowd scenes and the character drawing, but he quite naturally did not see the point of this presentation of Egmont's character and found the play lacking in unity. The historical Egmont, with his large family dependent on him, had a better reason for his action, he thought, and though Klärchen was altogether charming, he evidently did not think that a popular hero should flout ordinary morality, whereas Goethe characteristically felt that an Egmont, as he had imagined him, would not be a family man and would no doubt have a devoted mistress. Schiller's adaptation of the play for Weimar in 1796, when Iffland was to appear in the title rôle, was 'cruel, but consistent', as it seemed to Goethe later. Margareta von Parma was cut out altogether, a change which heightened the contrast between Flemings and Spaniards and contributed, together with some transpositions and combinations of scenes, towards making the staging more manageable, while a few slight touches gave Egmont a more commanding air. A number of minor additions such as warnings to Egmont and the appearance of Spanish patrols in the streets made the danger which threatened him more obvious, increased the tension and reduced the lyrical element. A comparison of Schiller's version with the original brings out the difference between the experienced man of the theatre and the lyrical poet expressing himself in dramatic form. Even the language in the additions is in a different key, somewhat over-emphatic language that would not be lost on a large audience, not the quieter language of ordinary life, rising at moments of crisis to great intensity and towards the end of the play often falling into an iambic rhythm.[1]

Egmont is in form and content still close to *Götz* but it shows a tendency towards a more openly lyrical kind of drama. In the closing scene, Egmont's dream in prison, the poetic presentation of a subjective experience is supported by instrumental music, and the introduction of the vision of liberty with the features of Klärchen in itself reminds us of operatic practice. Goethe was already drawing away from the Shakespearian 'history' towards a poetic drama which would be in some ways nearer to Gluck's operas and even to Racine, a drama with the utmost simplicity and concentration of plot, with little outward action but no lack of psychological interest and emotional appeal for an educated and refined audience, able to follow with sympathetic attention the subtle movements of the mind and heart at moments of crisis, without needing the stimulus of the more obviously dramatic

---

[1] See A. Köster, *Schiller als Dramaturg*, Berlin, 1891, pp. 2 ff.

and spectacular. The touching figures and the historical colour of *Egmont* were a greater attraction for the mass of play-goers, and combined with the strong appeal of Beethoven's incidental music (from 1810) they ensured for it greater popularity in the nineteenth century than *Iphigenie* and *Tasso* enjoyed.

Iphigenie is pure poetry, a drama on a higher imaginative and spiritual level than anything preceding it in Germany. Again, as in the two great monuments of 'Humanität' already discussed, *Nathan der Weise* and *Don Karlos*, a figure voicing the highest intuitions of human values stands before the embodiment of power and at great risk appeals to the man in the king. In *Nathan* what was at stake was religious toleration, in *Don Karlos* political and intellectual freedom. In *Iphigenie* new ethical conceptions applicable to all mankind, the respect for human life, truthfulness and trust in one's fellow-men are successfully asserted against the narrower loyalties of the family and the clan and older religious notions of jealous and vengeful deities. Underlying all three works is the Christian conception of human personality which is also at the root of Kantian ethics, for Kant formulated, as Korff says, what the finer minds of the age already felt about the principles of conduct. It is true that Kant renewed the old conflict between body and soul in his pessimistic dualism, leaving man 'only the anxious choice between sensual happiness and peace of soul', as Schiller's early poem *Resignation* puts it, and this led to important differences between his views and those in the optimistic tradition of the Enlightenment, but he too in the last resort 'thought nobly of man'. Man was 'an end in himself', not the instrument to another's end, and the idea of human dignity, an appeal to a kind of pride, was for Kant as for the rest a sufficient support for idealism even when all else failed.

There is a symbolic quality in Goethe's *Iphigenie* as in Schiller's historical plays. In and through his figures the poet conveys to the reflective mind a conception of the ethical development of mankind, just as in *Faust* he suggests symbolically the spiritual history of Europe since the Renaissance, but it is truly a symbol and not an allegory that he gives us. Goethe 'generalises without losing concreteness', to use A. N. Whitehead's phrase. His figures remain completely satisfying in themselves, but they suggest, though not as unambiguously as allegory, general ideas.

Goethe's starting-point was the *Iphigenia in Tauris* of Euripides, into which his imagination read a meaning equally compatible, as it seemed to him, with the Greek or a modern view of life, for the best in both is for him, as for Winckelmann, 'purely human'. There is however a vast difference between his handling of the theme and that of Euripides, for 'the humane values embodied in Iphigenie, her dignity, nobility, faith, are unthinkable without the continued effort of European thought'.[1] The modern poet cannot be content with presenting the outward incidents. 'What in Euripides is of little or no moment—the inward conflict, the strife of motive and emotion, the struggle in the heart of the heroine between desire and duty—to Goethe becomes the dominant theme of the whole drama; that on which the imagination is centred from beginning to end. And the conflict on which our attention is thus fastened is among the deepest, the most inward, which it is possible to conceive. The last word, throughout the whole play, is said not by passion, nor by desire, nor by reason, but by instinct. Instinct, the dim instinct of a woman's heart—that is the true hero of the piece. Nothing could well be more opposed to the spirit of the ancients; nothing could be more essentially modern—in the widest sense, more romantic—than this. Yet it is precisely this which Goethe has chosen to embody in a purely classical form.'[2]

In thus turning the play of Euripides inside out, Goethe was not doing anything unprecedented in his age. Professor Barker Fairley sees this work as one of those so completely dominated by Frau von Stein's ethical purism and 'inwardness' that he calls them 'Charlotte poetry'. But would there have been anything so very surprising in Goethe's *Iphigenie* even if we had never heard of Charlotte von Stein? Since the revival of Greek studies in the German universities and especially since Winckelmann's *Über die Nachahmung griechischer Kunstwerke,* the preliminary study for his *Kunst des Altertums,* it had been usual to see a moral

---

[1] W. Rehm, *Griechentum und Goethezeit*, Leipzig, 1936, p. 137.
[2] C. E. Vaughan, *op. cit.*, p. 224.

significance in much that for the Greeks had probably had a purely aesthetic or even sensuous appeal, to see everywhere in Greek art a 'noble simplicity and serene greatness'. Lessing had rightly criticised this very subjective view of Greek art in some respects in his *Laokoon* and Nietzsche was to insist on quite other aspects of Greece, but this was the view for which the peculiar conditions and experience of Germany in Goethe's age made it sensitive. Greece inspired reverence, sadness at the thought of the passing of greatness and the contrast with the present, com-bined with pride in the living connection between old and new, in the unity of western civilisation. What Goethe and his con-temporaries looked for in Greece was human life at its finest, the same 'humanity' which, as Lessing's generation had urged, was to be found in the natural religion underlying Christianity, so that a fusion of both strains was no impossibility. In his Storm and Stress writings we already find Goethe transferring to 'the Gods' emotions derived from the Christian tradition, speak-ing of 'der heilige Homer' and using 'God' and 'the Gods' as synonyms. He believed with Herder that 'Humanität' was something which had indeed a history but which had also a natural basis, so that the best minds of all civilised peoples had been in fundamental agreement about it.

That Goethe should have made the representative of 'schöne Menschlichkeit' a woman does indeed strike us as something characteristic of him personally and not so much of his age. The relationship of Orestes and Iphigenie does remind us of that between Goethe in the restless early Weimar years and the 'angel' who 'infused moderation into his hot blood', and his perception of this similarity may have been the starting-point of his play, as Gundolf suggests, for that was Goethe's way of creating. But this completely unGreek view of woman has more than a personal history behind it. Even in Euripides, the rationalist among the Greek tragedians, Iphigenie cannot believe that the Gods require human sacrifice. It was still more natural to think of a priest-like purity and moral sensitiveness as essentially feminine however after the growth of the cult of the Madonna and of the conception of courtly love, the platonising of the Renaissance poets and the glorification of woman in the sentimental age. We know from the *Italian Journey* that Goethe consciously derived inspiration from this long tradition, built up step by step by successive generations like the pyramid with which he compares Raphael's art. At Bologna he saw that artist's St. Agatha and admired so much her 'healthy confident maidenly bearing, without any hint of coldness or insensitiveness', that he resolved to put no words into the mouth of his Iphigenie which this saint could not have spoken.

The nobility and beauty of Goethe's conception of his heroine has seldom if ever been questioned and the poetic texture of the play is equally irreproachable. Every scene brings fresh and memorable lyrical and reflective passages which give classical expression to the eternal themes, the longing for home, the heroic aspirations of youth, the mysterious ways of the Gods to men and above all, the lot of woman in a society in which she has few rights and many duties. There is no chorus, but the lyrical monologues of the heroine partly perform its function. The real triumph however is the presentation of the interplay of minds in the almost entirely inward action of the drama, for though the characters are known only from within and seem to be simply there in the field of attention with little or no background, resembling statues in this rather than figures in a picture, they are no mere abstractions but living presences. Iphigenie has the changing moods, the hesitations, joys and sorrows of a natural woman, and the other four figures, though like her they have in the first place the character typical of their station and history, arouse our full sympathy too as human beings. The drama does not lie so much in the clash of will with will, but in the conflict they occasion in Iphigenie's mind through their various claims on her. At the crisis in Act IV, she is torn between the desire to return with her brother to Greece, which it seems she can only do by deceiving the King, and the desire to avoid soiling her conscience with a lie and acting disrespectfully and insincerely towards one who deserves her gratitude. Pylades, with his common-sense morality, almost persuades her that in the world of action no one can remain free from conflicts of conscience, 'rein und unverworren', and that our first duty is to act as the social situation demands, to comply with 'die Forderung des Tages'. Any ordinary woman would have accepted his argument, but Iphigenie is not an ordinary woman, but as it were a growing-point of 'Humanität', one of the 'grandes figures morales' by whose intuitions of a morality with a wider sphere of application than the clan, the closed society, the advance has by steps been made, according to Bergson,[1] to the highest ethical and religious conceptions. They have all had something irrational and heroic about them and have made their appeal by the force of their example. 'Leur exemple a fini par entraîner les autres, au moins en imagination. La volonté a son génie, comme la pensée, et le génie défie toute prévision.'

In discussing *Antigone* with Eckermann (1st April, 1827), Goethe explained the origin of morality (without distinguishing, as Bergson does, between two kinds of morality, that of a closed and that of an open society) in much the same way. Morality came into the world, he thought, 'through God himself, like every good thing. It is not a product of human reflection, but an inborn beauty implanted by nature. It is native to a greater or less extent in men generally, but in a high degree in exceptionally gifted individual souls. In great deeds or doctrines they have revealed the divine depths of their nature, which so compelled the love of men through its own beauty that they felt a strong attraction to honour and imitate them.' So it is with Iphigenie in the drama. Her heart tells her that the old conception of the Gods as cruel and capricious, the idea behind the myth of the race of Tantalus, is false, but if she must do evil that good may follow, her faith in a moral universe will be shaken. She resolves on an act of moral heroism, an 'unerhörte Tat', for women too are capable of heroism, she claims. She decides to tell the truth to the King though the heavens fall, staking everything on an appeal to his humanity. Goethe has carefully prepared us both for her need for absolute sincerity and for the possibility of a generous response from Thoas, for he is not the barbarian of Euripides, but a fellow-man and one already changed in nature

[1] *Les deux sources de la morale et de la religion*, 1932.

by the radiation of her finer humanity over many years. Even so, the happy issue seems to many readers over-optimistic, inconsistent with Goethe's often expressed disbelief in petitionary prayer and the special interventions of Providence which his Pietist friends confidently claimed. Perhaps that is why Goethe himself later referred to the work as 'verflucht human'. But if we think of this conclusion as symbolic of the reality of the world's moral advance, through the infectious faith in human brotherhood of a moral genius, it loses its unconvincingness. It is only by such acts of faith that 'Humanität' has spread at all. In the history of mankind there have been saints and on occasions they have worked apparent miracles. For dramatic purposes the history of the human race is telescoped to a single symbolic episode.

One might perhaps go further and suggest that like so many German poets, including Nietzsche in his *Zarathustra*, Goethe was consciously or unconsciously drawing for us here his version of the Saviour of mankind, the particular mythical form in which his imagination at that time, under the influence of Frau von Stein, liked to picture to itself the sum of 'all wisdom revealed through men and to man', which he and Humanists like him 'accept and revere, as sons of God worshipping Him in themselves and all His children', as he says in the letter to Lavater of 22nd June, 1781, in which, while acknowledging that 'the Saviour was indeed a crystal clear vessel and as such deserved to be revered by all', he rejected the exclusive claims of Christianity put forward by Lavater. For the eight years in which Lavater had repeatedly tried to convert him Goethe had said, in letter after letter, that he looked for God in his own heart ('Gefühl ist alles') and was convinced that throughout history God had only revealed Himself through the hearts of men. Since the publication of his letters to Frau von Stein it has been clear that she was his immediate inspiration when he gave his vision of goodness this particular shape. In expressing his worship of her he goes to extravagant lengths, as when he compares a ribbon of hers to a phylactery which he winds round his arm as he addresses his prayer to her and desires for himself a share of her goodness, wisdom, self-control and patience (12.3.1781). But there is point too in Gundolf's remark that in Goethe 'love was always there before the beloved', that in every phase he was always unconsciously seeking just the type of muse whom he found, and it is there that the importance of the western tradition to which we have drawn attention lies.

Torquato Tasso

For Schiller the distinction and uniqueness of *Iphigenie* lay 'in what one could call "Seele"; what was brought before the eye was the play of moral feeling in the heart.' In this more than anything else it was the fine flower of the age which supervened upon the ages of faith, an age when the deep concern about salvation, as understood particularly by Protestantism, had been gradually secularised. What was still felt to be of supreme importance for man was to save his soul alive, but the super-natural now played no part in this process. Man's real end was to cultivate his mind and heart, in that capacity lay his claim to uniqueness. In some (like Lessing and Kant) the stress was on ethical values, freedom and independence of outlook, the power to think for oneself, in others (like Goethe) the sense of beauty and 'pure humanity' were equally important. The idea of culture was in this way taking the place of faith in God. The work in which the culture of past ages had found its embodiment, the 'creations' of that 'just Prometheus under Jove', 'in apprehen-sion so like an angel', the 'Ebenbild der Gottheit', became the most precious things on earth. This process of the divinisation of man can be traced from the Renaissance through Shakespeare, Shaftesbury, and so on (to name only those most celebrated in Germany) to the 'natural geniuses' of the Storm and Stress period. In protestant Germany more than anywhere else, largely because the outlets for the energy of the middle class there, which might have led to wealth, power, or technical triumphs, were so narrow, it resulted in a point of view which placed the inner, personal values far higher than happiness and worldly success. Behind it all and constantly feeding it, through such movements as Pietism and through the influence of the numerous sons of the clergy who took to literature, was the consciousness, ultimately Christian in origin, of a last inner stronghold which man possessed within the mind, in conscience, faith, the feeling of one's own worth as a conscious self. So Wilhelm Meister, for instance, can find no satisfaction, as his friend Werner can, in the handling and accumulation of mere merchandise. 'To cultivate myself, just as nature has made me, that was the desire and aim of which I was dimly conscious from my youth on.' We have the same idea in Goethe's own letter, quoted above, about the 'pyramid of his existence'. The Romantics finally adopted the frank attitude of worship towards the things of art which is to be found in Wacken-roder's *Herzensergiessungen eines kunstliebenden Klosterbruders*, or in such sayings of Friedrich Schlegel as: 'Do not squander your faith and love on the world of politics, but offer up what is best in you to the sacred fiery stream of everlasting culture in the divine world of scholarship and art.'[1]

These considerations help us to bring *Iphigenie* more clearly into relation with other sides of Goethe's work and to understand his final version of *Tasso*. It is disconcerting to most students of Goethe to find him writing the *Roman Elegies* immediately after *Iphigenie* and while still engaged on *Tasso*. He seems to us a 'chameleon' indeed and we are reminded of what some of his friends have told us about his quick changes of mood. But our principal difficulty results from confusing his literary with his everyday personality. He could imagine an Iphigenie who was as sensitive to ethical values as he was himself to aesthetic, but it does not follow that as a man he was like her. He was, as he said, 'ein Mensch mit seinem Widerspruch'. The *Elegies* probably bring us nearer to his ordinary personality, though we must remember that here, as he said himself, he was writing in the vein of Propertius, and also not lose sight of the effect of his years in Italy and of the study of natural science, which all through the 'eighties had been fostering the growth of that soul, of the two which Faust-Goethe finds within him, that 'clings to the world as in a lover's fierce embrace'. He came to look upon his earlier relationship with Frau von Stein as unnaturally 'inhibited', as the

[1] See e.g. E. Franz, *Deutsche Klassik und Reformation*, and E. Troeltsch, *Werke*, IV.

modern phrase goes. In a letter to the Duke for instance (1st October, 1788), we find these lines, which clearly refer to Christiane Vulpius, with whom his liaison had just begun: 'May Heaven give us the sense to keep to what is nearest to hand; bad habits grow on us apace, till the natural seems unnatural. I have no longer to struggle with myself about this, but I have always to remember it.' The 'bad habit' was his soul-friendship with Frau von Stein.

Torquato Tasso is obviously closely linked with *Iphigenie* both in form and content but, though it is much concerned with the world within the mind, as a study of a poet's inner life was bound to be, it reminds us that practical activity with one's fellow-men and the qualities of character it demands had by now their own importance for Goethe too. Because so many, both in his own time and since, above all the Romantics, put 'inwardness' above everything, they could not understand Goethe's treatment of his hero, for they took it for granted that the author was on his side rather than Antonio's. But the point of the play seems to be to indicate the dangers that lie for the poet in his exclusive cultiva-tion of the 'inward', the threat to his sanity and the conflicts which will arise between him and those around him. The theme is the 'malheur d'être poète'. Tasso lives wholly for his art, he is all im-agination and sensitive perception, but the pre-occupation with his own and imagined emotions, one of the conditions of his greatness as a poet, has left him no opportunity to mature as a man among men. He lives in the most sheltered environment imaginable at the court of his patron, the Duke of Ferrara, in the very conditions desired by the poet of the Vorspiel auf dem Theater in *Faust*, who cries:

> Nein, führe mich zur stillen Himmelsenge,
> Wo nur dem Dichter reine Freude blüht,
> Wo Lieb' und Freundschaft unsres Herzens Segen
> Mit Götterhand erschaffen und erpflegen.

Goethe has of course combined with thoughts of Renaissance courts his own experiences at Weimar but he has again, as in *Iphigenie*, kept his picture quite general, almost timeless, for what concerns him is the problem of the artist as it must arise at any time. The artist is also a man and a member of some kind of society. Even in the most sympathetic of circles, such as that in which Tasso moves in the play, he will grow to fear and mistrust men if he avoids their company and rejects all claims made on him as a social being. That way madness lies.

The conflict between Tasso and Antonio, the man of affairs, also highly esteemed by the Duke because of his practical achievements, for even a state most devoted to the arts must maintain itself by the activities of such servants in a largely hostile world, is a particular instance of Tasso's maladjustment to life, much as in *Werther* the unhappy tragic love for Lotte is the final revelation of an instability of long standing, again in one who has given himself up wholly to the inner life, 'sich durch Spekulation untergraben'. Goethe approved of the description of *Tasso* as '*Werther* in an intensified form'. The contrasted figures Tasso and Antonio recall too Wilhelm Meister and Werner, but the social justification of the merchant in the novel is less stressed than that of the statesman in the play. 'Politics' is not counted as nothing beside culture, as by Friedrich Schlegel and by the educated classes generally in the Germany of Goethe's day. It is given its relative justification as a social necessity. Similarly 'Sitte', what Tasso feels as the tyranny of convention and the Princess defends as the essence of a necessary social discipline, towards which the instinctive feelings of cultivated women are the surest guide, is justified as the 'polar' or correlative opposite of spontaneous impulse, which is the basis of individual freedom and happiness. Again the characters are convincing individuals but at the same time symbols. 'The dramatic propriety that normally rests in the relation of character and action is less important than the sense of contrasting ideals; it is a drama that goes on behind the drama of persons. Everywhere the poetic voice transcends the limits of a scene in a plot, creating a new dramatic order.'[1]

[1] Peacock, *op. cit.*, p. 42.

IX

THE WEIMAR COURT THEATRE

THERE was no doubt some connection between the craze for amateur acting which took hold of cultivated circles in Germany from the 1770's and the similar movement in France from the 'sixties, for social fashions of all kinds were imitated by the aristocracy from France. Where a taste for the theatre had once been excited among people with leisure it was a natural development, which worked in with the general literary awakening taking place in Germany in those years. Like all passions, it grew with what it fed upon and was by no means confined to towns without professional theatres. In Vienna, for instance, when Schröder was there (1781–85), it reached such absurd proportions that we are told it had a bad moral effect on wide circles. In all the larger towns and many small ones informal societies came into existence for this purpose and in his *Guide des voyageurs en Europe* (1793) Reichard lists these 'théâtres de société' along with the picture collections, manufactures, and so forth, of the German towns he describes, as evidence of their claim to culture. Weimar was naturally no exception in this respect, for Anna Amalia came from the gay court of Brunswick, and since her earliest days in Weimar had had German companies there whenever she could, beginning with Döbbelin's in 1756. For about six years before the fire which destroyed the Wilhelmsburg with its theatre in 1774, a professional troupe had been playing there regularly, as we have seen, first that of Koch and then that of Seyler. Two groups of amateur actors kept a taste for the theatre alive after this unfortunate event, one of ladies and gentlemen of the court under Graf von Putbus, who acted almost exclusively plays and operettas in French, and a middle-class dramatic society under the enterprising Bertuch, a business man with literary interests, which produced German plays. After Goethe's advent, and favoured by him, a mixed group came into existence, which drew on both of the older ones and performed hardly anything but German or translated pieces. There was also an amateur theatre of officials in Eisenach and of students in Jena. In Weimar everyone in the court circle was interested and a large number took an occasional part, from the Dowager Duchess Anna Amalia and her two sons Karl August, the young Duke who had invited Goethe to visit him in 1775, and his younger brother Prince Konstantin, with the military tutor Knebel, gentlemen-in-waiting of literary tastes like Einsiedel and Seckendorff, ladies-in-waiting young and old, even funny little Fräulein von Göchhausen, to whom we owe our knowledge of the *Urfaust*, down to the numerous middle-class intellectuals in the Duke's service, the pages' tutor Musäus, the musician Wolf, the artist Kraus, Bertuch and Bode, business-men with literary interests, and several higher officials. The Hofkapelle of three or four singers and Wolf's seven or eight instrumentalists could always be counted upon and from the end of 1776 Corona Schröter, whose acting and singing Goethe had admired in Leipzig and whose personal distinction made her an excellent choice was brought in to support the amateurs. The court carpenter Mieding had had experience with the professionals and was able to give skilled help with scenery and stage management, while Kraus, the artist, often designed scenery and costumes (he edited the *Modejournal*, published by Bertuch) and has left us records in his drawings of many performances. The life and soul of it all was of course the young universal genius, invited in the hope that the author of a *Götz* would bring a little life into the stuffy court atmosphere, and destined to spend in Weimar the rest of his life. The poem written *On Mieding's Death* (1782) brings back very vividly the early days when he was often author, producer and actor, and in a crisis might have to snuff the candles which were the only stage lighting,

> Wo selbst der Dichter, heimlich voll Verdruss,
> Im Fall der Not die Lichter putzen muss.

As in all the courts, the same people were leading spirits in theatricals and in the elaborate fancy dress balls or 'redouts' which were a favourite entertainment in the winter. A year after the fire Hof-Jäger Hauptmann, an innkeeper, carrier and contractor, built a Redoutenhaus for these balls which could serve also as a theatre, and it was here that Goethe organised his first entertainment in February 1776 as part of a fancy dress ball. It was a kind of pantomime of the Temptations of St. Antony, with a procession of devils, like Satan's following in the *Faery Queen*, each representing a different vice, gluttony, drunkenness, and so on. Goethe, mounted on stilts and wearing wings of peacock-tails, was Pride. This interlude was found a little too much in the Storm and Stress taste by the older people. It was the first of a long series of mascarades devised by Goethe, who did not lose his taste for this kind of thing even when he had given up the theatre. Several scenes in the Second Part of *Faust* remind us of it still. By the early summer *Erwin und Elmire* was being performed, with new music by Anna Amelia and Schweizer, then Die *Mitschuldigen*, and a week later Bode's translation of *The West Indian*, a favourite in Hamburg and elsewhere, as we saw. Goethe was the unconventional hero and Frau von Stein the young Miss Russport who wins his heart, while the Duke and his brother were also in the cast. Corona Schröter made her début as Sophie in a repetition of *Die Mitschuldigen* in January 1777, Goethe playing Alcest. On January 30th, when there was always some performance, to mark the Duchess Luise's birthday, a second operetta of Goethe's, *Lila*, was given, with music by Sekkendorff. Both operettas were repeated and various popular comedies of the day were attempted, by Colman, Brandes, Goldoni, Gozzi, also Lessing's *Minna*. In January 1778 Ekhof came over from Gotha for a few days and played the father of the *West Indian*, who was again Goethe, a visit from which the *Theatralische Sendung* no doubt benefited. For the Duchess's birthday this time the play was *Der Triumph der Empfindsamkeit*, a delightful skit on the sentimental age, in which his own *Werther,* together with *La Nouvelle Héloïse*, is one of the dangerous books with which the effigy of the bride is found to be stuffed.

It was a little earlier in the same month that a young lady-in-waiting, Fräulein von Lassberg, crossed in love, had been found drowned in the Ilm with Goethe's novel in her pocket.

Most of the works of Goethe performed so far were not new, though sometimes revised. It was in the midst of many distractions that a few new ones were written and that all were produced. In December 1777, for instance, he had made his journey to the Harz, in May of the next year, after the productions just spoken of, he is in Berlin with the Duke and receiving very unfavourable impressions of 'the great world', then in October he plays no fewer than three parts in the dramatic version of his *Jahrmarktsfest zu Plundersweilern* at Ettersburg. The play was followed by a banquet and a dance which lasted till morning. Shorter visits to neighbouring courts and above all the many journeys connected with his growing official duties came in between. He had been given the impulse to his scientific studies by his attempts to start the mines again at Ilmenau. In 1779 he took charge of recruiting and road-making and in March he writes from a Weimar village where he is trying to finish *Iphigenie* while recruits are being measured. The prose *Iphigenie* was first performed on April 6th at the Redoutenhaus, and repeated in July at Ettersburg. At performances in town it was possible to invite a number of guests from outside the court circle, but at the country palace there was usually only a very small and select audience, and it was then, if at all, that Anna Amalia herself took a part. Heinz Kindermann thinks that we should perhaps date from this performance of *Iphigenie* the first beginnings of the Weimar style which Goethe as manager tried later to introduce into the Court Theatre, for he finds in the well-known drawing by Kraus of the recognition scene evidence of a dignified manner of presentation influenced by Winckelmann as well as by court ideas of reticence and decorum. The combination of play and cast certainly makes this a quite outstanding event in German theatrical history. Beside Goethe and Corona Schröter as Orestes and Iphigenia, the players were the Duke as Pylades, Knebel as Thoas and Seidler as Archas. The need was now felt for a better theatre building and Hauptmann was allowed next winter to build with state assistance an improved Redoutenhaus theatre opposite the Wittumspalais, which was finished when Goethe and the Duke returned in January 1780, after being away since September on their Swiss journey. Amateur performances went on for a year or two after this. The year 1780 brought three light productions by Seckendorff and Einsiedel and Goethe's *Die Vögel* and *Jery und Bätely*, and 1782 *Das Neueste von Plundersweilern* and *Die Fischerin*, the latter remarkable for being an open-air performance by the banks of the Ilm at Tiefurt. A warm clear night, Corona's enchanting voice singing *Der Erlkönig* to an accompaniment of nightingales, and remarkable effects from torches and alarm-fires reflected in the river were the things that one spectator remembered most vividly. An earlier performance under the night sky had been that of a gypsy play by Einsiedel two years before; others had taken place by day in the Ettersburg park. As Goethe writes in his poem on Mieding; they had played

In engen Hütten und im reichen Saal,
Auf Höhen Ettersburgs, in Tiefurts Tal,
Im leichten Zelt, auf Teppichen der Pracht
Und unter dem Gewölb' der hohen Nacht.

But by 1783 Goethe's enthusiasm had cooled off with his in-creasing responsibilities and there was a general lack of interest, so professionals were again called in. In the autumn an Italian company was allowed to give half a dozen performances of comic opera, and later in the year it was arranged with Bellomo's company of Dresden that they should come to Weimar and play three times a week in Hauptmann's new building. The Duke provided this theatre with its modest stock of scenery and costumes, his small court orchestra, now about a dozen strong, and a subsidy of 300 taler a month for the six winter months. The court was to be admitted free but others to pay the usual prices. A court official, at first Seckendorff, exercised general supervision, but otherwise Bellomo remained responsible for the financial and artistic management himself.

Except for one or two good singers, Bellomo's was a second-rate company and even with his subsidy he could not afford to take many risks, so he offered the kind of repertoire that was safe anywhere, operettas, domestic dramas, Ritterstücke and very occasionally a classical play, two plays of Lessing, three each of the younger Goethe and Schiller, and several of Shakespeare, following the Hamburg productions closely. Most of the titles are familiar to us from the repertoires of the 'seventies, but Schröder was now writing and adapting family dramas, Iffland was extremely productive and Kotzebue even more so from 1787. There were more distinguished newcomers in opera, Mozart of course above all with his early work, but also the very popular Dittersdorf and some others. The standard of performance could not be very high when the same company had to undertake spoken drama, light opera and even ballet of a kind. Of the more literary plays the great favourite was Schiller's *Räuber*, to see which crowds of Jena students would flock into Weimar on a Saturday in high spirits and make their presence felt in the pit. In the summer months the company kept itself in being by per‐ forming in neighbouring holiday resorts, particularly at Lauch‐ städt, then a popular spa, where Bellomo built himself a modest wooden theatre.

By 1790 there was general dissatisfaction with Bellomo's theatre, especially after the Dowager Duchess's visit to Italy, and she and Karl August took the initiative in setting up a regular Court Theatre in place of Bellomo's semi‐private undertaking. Advice was sought from Reichardt in Berlin and Schröder in Hamburg. We can see from Goethe's letter to Reichardt (of 28th February 1790) that Schröder's reply had not been very encouraging and that Goethe himself was not at all enthusiastic now about what he had called, in a letter to the Duke a few weeks before this, 'the most mechanical of all branches of knowledge, the German theatre'. 'Our public', Goethe writes to Reichardt, 'has no conception of art.' Then comes the sentence already quoted about Schröder's preference for actors who are respectable citizens rather than men of talent, with all their inevitable failings —an interesting comment on the problem of the artist, after *Tasso*. He evidently thinks that in the theatre first‐rate talent and respectability do not go well together. Schröder's public being satisfied with mediocre pieces, he is right to take the moral line. 'The Germans', he continues, 'are good honest people, but they have not the slightest idea what originality, imaginative appeal, distinctive character, unity and finish mean in a work of art. In a word, they have no taste. I mean of course on the average. You can take in the uneducated by variety and exaggeration and the more cultivated by what appears to be morally improving. Medieval knights, robbers, benevolent and grateful characters, a true-hearted *tiers état*, an infamous nobility etc., and in general a competent mediocrity, from which you only move at most a few steps down into vulgarity or a few steps up into nonsense, these have been for ten years now the ingredients of our novels and plays. When things are like this you can imagine what hopes I have of your theatre, whoever is in charge.'

This was written when changes were imminent in Berlin, but Goethe's views were the same about Weimar. However, he consented unwillingly in January 1791 to exercise a general supervision over the theatre, as he had to do something for the salary which he still received from the Duke, and had asked on his return from Italy if he might be left in charge of cultural matters only. The main field of his interests in the early 'nineties was neither literature nor the drama but science, especially the theory of colours, and when once a new company had been established he did not at first give much time to the theatre. Routine duties and financial matters were looked after by Franz Kirms, a treasury official who had had some experience in such things in Bellomo's time. Goethe told Jacobi in a letter in March that he was setting to work very 'piano', but that he would at least make a closer study of the theatre and write a couple of actable plays a year. He appointed a Prague actor (F. J. Fischer) as producer, and Kirms wrote round to Schröder and other leading managers to find out what talent was available at the modest salaries which Weimar could offer. Goethe had an opportunity of discussing his problems with Schröder in person in Weimar in April and had asked him earlier for the standing rules of his theatre. Meanwhile, until 5th April 1791, Bellomo was still performing. When he left half a dozen of his troupe were kept on and, to begin with, about a dozen newcomers were engaged. They came from small companies all over Germany and, as Goethe said in the prologue he wrote for the opening of the theatre, their first task was to learn to act as a team. His ideal clearly was what he had put into the mouth of Wilhelm in the *Theatralische Sendung,* a company in which all the players would aim at a harmonious total effect, like musicians in an orchestra, an ideal nowhere yet attained on the German stage, not even in Hamburg or Mannheim.

The theatre opened on 7th May 1791 with Iffland's *Die Jäger,* and the choice of plays for the remaining month of the winter season was equally 'safe', as it almost had to be while the company was settling down. Eleven popular modern comedies and domestic dramas by the usual tried favourites were presented, nearly all familiar from Bellomo's repertoire, together with three operettas. A 'ballet' devised by one of the company followed each performance as an afterpiece, a light-hearted, semi-improvised affair like most of the Hamburg ones mentioned above. For financial reasons the Court Theatre had to continue Bellomo's practice of playing in Lauchstädt for the holiday season, from mid-June to mid-August, and often in one of the neighbouring towns such as Erfurt or Rudolstadt for a month in the late summer, returning to Weimar in October. Neither Goethe nor Kirms went with them. The troupe travelled, like any of the old touring companies, in seven open waggonettes followed by three farm carts containing the most important scenery and properties. For many years after this the country still looked on them with suspicion, as we see from the story told by Genast about an inn-keeper's wife who, seeing this caravan approaching, said to her maid that it would be safer to take in the washing: 'Marie, duck de Wäsche wäck, de Bande kummt!' With their petty jealousies and intrigues they were certainly a handful for the producer, who on tour was virtually the principal, but he somehow managed to add eighteen new pieces to the repertoire in the two months at Lauchstädt and three more at Erfurt, in preparation for the winter season. Bellomo's barn-like booth at Lauchstädt was purchased from him and remained in use until 1802.

In Erfurt *Don Karlos* was attempted, but only in a prose version specially revised by Schiller. Back in Weimar, more experiments were made during the season than ever again for the next few years. There was not much of interest before Christmas except Mozart's *Il Seraglio*, Shakespeare's *King John* in Eschenburg's prose version and Goethe's *Der Grosskophta*, the first of the 'act-able' plays which he had planned to write. It is a comedy about Cagliostro and the Diamond Necklace affair, disappointing and lacking in unity, though it has some well-realised scenes. It had only a *succès d'estime*. After Christmas the outstanding events were *Clavigo*, Mozart's *Don Giovanni*, Schiller's *Don Karlos* in verse, with which the older actors had much difficulty, in spite of Goethe's many 'reading rehearsals', and a version of *Henry IV*, combining Parts I and II. Goethe had taken over from Schröder the idea of 'Leseproben', stressing at first above all the proper speaking of the lines. At a preliminary reading of *Henry IV* he read Falstaff's part so well himself that the actors could hardly read for laughing, but when produced the play did not go down very well. Operettas and family pieces were much more popular than Shakespeare or the German classics. The Weimar public proved to be no exception to what Goethe had said about German taste, and for several years, after this first season, the management seemed reconciled to this fact.

Until Schiller's later plays came along, beginning in 1798, the Weimar repertoire was almost indistinguishable from that of the general run of smaller theatres. After the first year, when the new company had to make a special effort to build up a basic reper-toire, one or two new plays of real merit and as many operas were added each season. Together with the popular successes of Iffland, Kotzebue, Schröder, Jünger and the rest these novelties kept the Weimar programme well up to the average level. For the first few years the event of the season was the production, usually several years after the earliest performances elsewhere, of a new opera of Mozart, *Il Seraglio* (1791), *Don Giovanni* (1792), *Figaro* (1793), *The Magic Flute* (1794), and finally *Cosi fan tutte* (1797), all great favourites, especially *The Magic Flute*. The great composer did not live to see his triumphs all over Germany. He had died at the end of 1791, soon after the first performance of his most popular work.

There is no getting away from the fact that *the* German art is music. The love of it was so widespread that no German theatre, however literary the leanings of its manager might be, could dispense with opera and operetta. We have seen this in Hamburg, and it was just the same in Weimar. Nearly a third of the total performances during Goethe's twenty-six years as manager were given up to musical plays and ballet, usually one of the three evenings on which the theatre was open each week. Grand opera such as could be seen in Paris, Vienna and Berlin, presented by highly trained singers in special opera houses, was of course out of the question in Weimar. It was a great feat to perform Mozart's Italian operas, *Don Giovanni* and *Figaro*, with so small an orchestra and so few trained singers. Even *The Magic Flute* and *Il Seraglio*, glorified 'Singspiele' such as these small theatres had long delighted in, were done in a way which would strike a modern audience as decidedly homely and was adversely criticised when the company visited Leipzig, much as its acting was admired there. The part of Sarastro was sung for several years by Herr Malcolmi, the actor from whom Goethe drew the widower with two daughters in *Wilhelm Meister*, whom he calls 'Der Polterer' because he usually acted heavy fathers, comic old men and peasants. He could not read a note of music and had to learn his rôle by ear. Caroline Jagemann, for long the company's leading singer and actress, tells us of the unconsciously comical effect sometimes produced, by the three Genies, for instance, awkward country boys in ill-fitting brick-red tights, wearing clumsy rose wreaths on their unruly hair, but the ill-natured criticisms of a spoilt favourite should not blind us to the good use that was made of rather indifferent material. Anyhow, all classes in Weimar took great delight in them, and to satisfy them, Italian and French light opera were brought in as well as Mozart and Dittersdorf. Some pieces were newly translated by Vulpius and Einsiedel and later performed on many other theatres.

If the Court Theatre in these early years was not on the whole startlingly different from Bellomo's, that was principally because the governing conditions had changed little. One of the chief difficulties was that here, as in Hamburg, one theatre had to attempt to do what was divided between three in big centres like Paris, the *Opéra,* the *Comédie-Française* and the *Théâtre des Italiens.* It produced opera and light opera, plays for entertainment and classics of the drama. To begin with, the first two categories were about equally represented and the third lagged well behind, but it was Goethe's policy of course to encourage serious drama and he gradually succeeded in doing so. In the best period of the theatre, for ten years or so from 1798, there was a fairly regular sequence of opera or operetta on Tuesday, classics and experi-ments on Thursday and light fare on Saturday, when Goethe and the notabilities were seldom present, and the Jena students could, within reason, let themselves go. If Goethe did happen to be there, he might ask them to remember where they were, for whatever the programme might be, it was the ducal theatre and decorum had to be observed. No strong expression of disapproval like hissing was allowed; when the students could not contain their enthusiasm at the first performance of *Die Braut von Messina* and honoured Schiller with a *vivat,* they were reproved for it through the university authorities next day. If the Duke was in his box, it was not considered correct to applaud until he did so, and on one famous occasion, when the audience found Friedrich Schlegel's stilted *Alarcos* more ridiculous than sublime, Goethe silenced them in a moment by standing up in his box and calling out in a voice of thunder: 'You must not laugh!' Hostile news-paper critics too were liable to be deported, but such extreme measures were seldom needed and, though it was clear enough even in the theatre that they were living under the *ancien régime,* the people of Weimar were in general very pleased with their theatre and very proud of it. Through catering for all tastes it came to be visited frequently by all and to acquire a civilising influence. In the new century, we are told, it was not uncommon for illiterate Weimar craftsmen to know whole speeches from Schiller's plays by heart through hearing them in the theatre and there was certainly nothing to which Weimar more gladly saw state money devoted than to its theatre.

If we are a little surprised to find the management comparatively unenterprising for the first seven years or so, in spite of
Goethe's high ideals and the authority he enjoyed in this small
state with its highly centralised system of absolute government,
we must remember the composition and the tastes of the audience,
which was quite an ordinary assemblage of small-town citizens
together with an upper class of court aristocracy and government
officials and a handful of literary men. As only about one-third
of the expense of the theatre was covered by the Duke's grant
(the military operations in which Weimar was involved as an
ally of Prussia made state economies necessary from 1792), it was
essential to attract the general public. Goethe did not approve
of running into debt. He kept strictly to his budget for the further
reason that, according to his own statements to Eckermann
later, he believed in the spur which is given to all concerned by
the knowledge that they must make a theatre pay its way.
'Nothing is more dangerous for the good of a theatre than if those
who manage it are in such a position that box-office receipts are a
matter of indifference to them personally.' Moreover, Goethe
had many other interests. Science took up much of his time, and
in 1792 and 1793 he paid the long visits to the Duke's headquarters which he recorded in his *Campagne in Frankreich* and
Belagerung von Mainz. It is true that the times were no more
propitious after 1798 and the audience had not changed. What
made it possible for the Weimar Theatre nevertheless to attain
real distinction was a change in Goethe's attitude and the stimulus
of Schiller's co-operation.

Goethe had undertaken the supervision of the theatre as a duty,
at a time when he was conscious more of the difference between
his own artistic aims and view of life and those of the German
public, even the enlightened element in Weimar, than of any
common ground. To deepen his own understanding of the world,
for the present mainly through his scientific studies, had seemed
to him more worth while than to try to raise the level of public
taste, in the theatre, for instance. He continued to write poetry,
as always, when the spirit moved him, but he did not greatly
care whether the result was to please or to shock his readers. There

was no time in his life when he was more proudly conscious of his uniqueness. This 'Selbstgefühl' is illustrated by his flouting of public opinion by taking Christiane Vulpius into his house. Even after 1794, when his relations with Schiller began to ripen into friendship, though he was encouraged by Schiller's under/ standing sympathy to give more and more of his energies to literature and went through one of the most creative periods of his life, it was not for the contemporary German public in the first place, but for an ideal public of the future that he wrote, in the spirit of the poet in the *Faust* Vorspiel (written in 1797):

> Was glänzt ist für den Augenblick geboren,
> Das Echte bleibt der Nachwelt unverloren.

This mood found a ready response in Schiller, for he too hated mediocrity, and the first result of their association was the collec/ tion of 'parting gifts' or *Xenien* for the personalities they despised in current literature. If, again encouraged by Schiller, he now devoted much time and thought to the improvement of the theatre, his opinion of public taste had not changed. 'No one can serve two masters,' he wrote to Schiller, 'and of all masters, the public that sits in the German theatre is the last I should choose.' While continuing to give the mass of the public what it liked for quite two/thirds of the performances and thus ensuring the finances of the undertaking, he used the theatre freely on the remaining evenings for experiments with poetic drama and even for attempts to revive Greek and Roman practices like the use of masks, whether the public liked them or not, telling them (in the essay *Weimar Court Theatre*, 1802) that it was a compliment to them if they were shown things they did not easily understand and praising university people from Jena, in particular, for their ready response. We must remember that Goethe, being a kind of minister of culture in the state, looked upon the theatre as a court and university theatre, half a place of entertainment and half, like the university, a cultural institution.

The improvements made in the Weimar Theatre from about 1798 may be considered from two closely related aspects, that of acting and that of the repertoire. As to acting, Goethe had interfered very little in production in the early years, though under his management various attempts had been made to improve the discipline of the troupe and to make it into a team. Several of the more troublesome members were dismissed after two years (at Easter, 1793) and others were engaged in their place. As the producer Fischer left at the same time, problems of day-to-day management were entrusted to two joint 'Regisseurs', Vohs looking after production and Willms the business side, but after a year Willms left too and his work was further subdivided. At the same time rules of conduct were drawn up for the company, but their easy-going Bohemian ways were not easily reformed and continued to cause Goethe so much annoyance that he tried to resign at the end of 1795, and was only with difficulty persuaded by the Duke himself to stay on. A month or two later he had an actor arrested and lodged in the Hauptwache for slapping the face of a woman colleague in a quarrel. Goethe's contacts with the theatre helped him with the transformation of *Wilhelm Meisters Theatralische Sendung* into the *Lehrjahre*, which he had begun to effect early in 1794, but otherwise they were rather distasteful. His ebbing interest in the art of acting was greatly stimulated however by a visit paid to Weimar by Iffland in 1796. Schiller and his wife were invited over from Jena for the month of Iffland's stay, he appeared in a dozen different rôles and greatly impressed everyone by his finished art. About half the plays in which he appeared were his own and the rest, except for Schiller's *Räuber* and his adaptation of *Egmont*, were by Gemmingen, Babo, Schröder and Kotzebue, but even with this material Iffland proved what a wide range of characters he could convincingly present in his elaborately studied but never offensive realistic manner. After seeing Iffland Goethe was more than ever convinced that, as he had already said in *Wilhelm Meister*, no one is really an actor who can only play *himself*, and this was the principle he now tried to bring home to the Weimar company. He wanted them to realise that acting is an imaginative re-creation of character and to free themselves as far as they could from the tyranny of the 'Fach', the special line of characters (jeune premier, chevalier, soubrette, etc.) for which, by old tradition, actors and actresses were engaged in their contract with the management. Even within the sphere of realism a creative art of acting was possible, as Iffland's example proved. He was a model too for clear enunciation and for the high ideal he entertained of his art. As Mannheim was in the war zone Iffland would have been glad to give up his post there and thought of accepting the post of manager of the Weimar Theatre which was offered to him, but Berlin was also anxious to secure him. After months of negotia, tions he decided in favour of the National Theatre there. Goethe had to continue in office but a system of 'Wöchner', imitated from Vienna, was instituted, under which the routine duties of pro, duction were entrusted to three members' of the company, each of whom was on duty for a week at a time.

Schiller liked Iffland's acting, but not his plays. He was planning his *Wallenstein* before the Iffland visit, and a month or two after it he wrote the Xenien making up the poem *Shakes, peares Schatten*, as it was later called, in which he speaks his mind about the kind of play which the German public liked. Goethe had complained at the end of the preceding year that although everybody seemed to be writing, they were in urgent need of plays in the theatre. The lack of a suitable German repertoire was still a great stumbling block. Goethe and Schiller were agreed that though the domestic drama was good enough entertainment, it was not a high form of art, perhaps not art at all. In Schiller's provocative poem, a dialogue with Shakespeare in the Shades, he explains to his great predecessor that tragedy is now out of fashion, for coarse humour and sentimental pathos, 'nasser Jammer', and anything that is thoroughly domestic and pedestrian, with a good Christian moral, are the order of the day. 'What!' exclaims Shakespeare, 'may not Caesar show himself now on your stage, nor Achilles, Orestes, Andromache?' 'None of them!' he is told. 'You will see nothing but parsons, leaders of commerce, ensigns (a reference to Schröder's best, known play), secretaries or majors of hussars.' 'But I ask you, my friend, what great things can happen to such folk, what great things can be accomplished by them?' 'Oh, they weave petty schemes, they lend money on pawn, they pocket silver spoons, risking the pillory and worse.' 'But where do you go then for the majesty of inevitable doom, which exalts man's soul even while it crushes him?' 'Those are old-fashioned notions! What we look for is ourselves and our good acquaintances, our troubles and our wants, and that is what we find.'

The incomparable correspondence of Goethe and Schiller, in which, when the one was in Weimar and the other still in Jena, every few days they exchanged news of their activities, and we seem to see *Wilhelm Meister,* the *Xenien, Wallenstein, Faust, Maria Stuart,* and many minor works growing before our eyes, contains in 1797 a long discussion on the poetic drama and the epic, leading up to the joint essay on epic and dramatic poetry at the end of the year. We find the two poets reading Aristotle's *Poetics* (Schiller for the first time) and expressing high appreciation of it. They realise that he was generalising without preconceived theories from the plays he knew. Schiller reads Greek tragedies and Shakespeare again, and both agree that all good drama should be in verse. What they particularly dislike is the naturalism of the contemporary theatre, which leaves nothing to the imagination, and they discuss various ways of fighting it, Schiller suggesting for instance the introduction of symbolic devices and an approach to opera, in which 'the servile imitation of nature' has never been demanded. This is all part of the theoretical background to Schiller's classical dramas and also to the reforms carried out at the Weimar Theatre in connection with the performance of these and of other far less stageworthy dramas.

The nature of this reform can be learnt in detail from the *Rules for Actors,* edited later by Eckermann from Goethe's notes of the lectures he began to give in 1803, particularly to promising young beginners like P. A. Wolff. These 'Rules' deal with the grammar of the actor's art with regard to speech and movement. Goethe taught his actors how to enunciate clearly, to avoid gross dialectal pronunciations, to control tone and speed according to the context and finally to recite verse and to declaim it in character. By dint of constant practice, even in everyday life, they had to learn how to stand and move and group themselves on the stage with ease, dignity and grace. It was a kind of spoken opera

Goethe had in mind, as we see from what Wolff tells us about his rehearsals of a poetic play, when his manner was exactly that of a conductor; according to a Weimar tradition he often made use of a baton. 'He was constantly appealing to the analogy of music in his instruction,' Wolff says. 'The cast were trained to speak their lines in just the same way as an opera is rehearsed: the speed, the fortes and pianos, crescendos and diminuendos were determined by him and most carefully watched. Yet it would be a mistake to think that this procedure made the acting any less natural and convincing.'[1] Movements were just as carefully rehearsed. 'On the stage marked out in squares every single position and movement was determined beforehand with the aim of producing a harmonious and pleasing spectacle. "The stage is to be considered as a picture", the pupils were told, "in which the actors are the decorative figures (Staffage)." That was the principle governing the composition of the settings. The actor was never allowed to forget that it was the impression made on the audience which mattered; it was considered a mistaken piece of naturalism to act as if there were no spectators present; to turn one's back on the audience or to speak up stage was condemned as an offence against theatrical decorum.'[2]

Anyone who has seen Racine acted by the *Comédie-Française* will easily realise what kind of performance Goethe was aiming at. English play-goers have seen what fine results can be achieved in the way of a spoken opera from the production of Mr. Eliot's *Murder in the Cathedral*. It is interesting to note that the French classical tradition exercised a renewed influence on Weimar through Wilhelm von Humboldt's enthusiastic descriptions of the acting of Talma. A long letter from him in September 1799, published in the *Propyläen*, praised the rhythm of Talma's move-ments, in perfect harmony with the words, and pointed out that on the French stage the music of spoken verse, together with beauty of grouping and movement, counted for more than expressiveness of gesture and depth of feeling. Humboldt con-cluded that in aiming at the natural expression of character the

---

[1] Quoted by Wahle, *Das Weimarer Hoftheater unter Goethes Leitung*, p. 166.
[2] J. Petersen, *Das deutsche Nationaltheater*, p. 69.

Germans had neglected the aesthetic appeal to the eye and ear of the audience.

It was after this reminder that Goethe and Schiller took the the step which must have made Lessing turn in his grave, of translating French classical tragedies into German verse just as Gottsched had done, except that they used blank verse instead of alexandrines. The Duke and many at court had never lost their admiration for the French classics, but Goethe's principal aim, no doubt, in re-introducing them into the repertoire was to train the actors in a supremely difficult task. If they could do justice to Racine they could act German dramas in the grand style too. Goethe translated Voltaire's *Mahomet* and *Tancrède*, and Schiller Racine's *Phèdre*. The conflicting emotions with which Schiller viewed these experiments, which attracted only small audiences, are expressed in the poem he wrote *To Goethe, when Mahomet was performed in Weimar*. It opens with the rhetorical question whether Goethe, who first freed them from French bonds, is now burning incense to the 'false muse' of the *ancien régime*. The Germans have now a worthy drama of their own, and can never return to the bondage of their infancy. The anxious compliance with the unities, the rhetorical 'tirades' and unnatural 'convenances' of the French stage have given way to the free expression of true human feeling. Yet the chariot of Thespis is lightly built; like Charon's ferryboat it can bear only shades and phantoms and may easily overturn if life thrusts rudely in. 'Der Schein soll nie die Wirklichkeit erreichen, Und siegt Natur, so muss die Kunst entweichen.' Naturalism, that is, is the death of art. Truth in the veil of fiction is presented on the stage, a world of the imagination. In this respect Germany can still learn from the French theatre what art is, even if it is not the highest art. A paraphrase of Humboldt's letter follows and Schiller concludes with the grudging admission that French art can be for the Germans a guide to better things, though they should not forget that no living spirit speaks out of it and must still prize truth above false delicacy.

The tone of Schiller's poem, it will be seen, is anything but enthusiastic and leaves us in no doubt as to who had taken the initiative in this experiment. Goethe is much more urbane in the essay of 1802, already mentioned, *The Weimar Court Theatre*, a review after eleven years of the various phases through which the theatre had passed and a plea for open-mindedness on the part of the public. A little later in the same year he wrote in a few days a dramatic prelude, *Was wir bringen*, for the opening of the new theatre put up to replace Bellomo's booth at Lauchstädt. Unlike the old Weimar Theatre, which was destroyed by fire in 1825, this building still exists. *Was wir bringen* is a short allegorical play illustrating the range of their productions, into which Goethe has introduced the fine sonnet which indicates how deeply rooted in his whole philosophy of life at this time these at first sight rather arbitrary theatre reforms were. Law and freedom, nature and art, are for him now correlative conceptions in every sphere of life. A sonnet can be just as natural as a 'Lied', a classical tragedy as a domestic drama, for ease in all things comes through mastery and an artist's freedom of expression comes through long and intelligent practice in strict forms:

> Natur und Kunst, sie scheinen sich zu fliehen
> Und haben sich, eh' man es denkt, gefunden.
> Der Widerwille ist auch mir verschwunden,
> Und beide scheinen gleich mich anzuziehen.
>
> Es gilt wohl nur ein redliches Bemühen,
> Und wenn wir erst, in abgemess'nen Stunden,
> Mit Geist und Fleiss uns an die Kunst gebunden
> Mag frei Natur im Herzen wieder glühen.
>
> So ist's mit aller Bildung auch beschaffen.
> Vergebens werden ungebundne Geister
> Nach der Vollendung reiner Höhe streben.
>
> Wer Grosses will, muss sich zusammenraffen.
> In der Beschränkung zeigt sich erst der Meister,
> Und das Gesetz nur kann uns Freiheit geben.

To carry through such a transformation in the whole style of acting and production called for very determined effort on the part of the management. The new ideas were readily accepted by young idealists of good education like P. A. Wolff, the best of Goethe's products, but the older actors were another matter.

Goethe's reforms were anyhow very little concerned with the
everyday dramatic fare and the musical pieces which made up
two-thirds of the repertoire and earned the loudest applause, for
the theatre continued to be three-in-one and this fact was still a
problem for everybody. It was difficult to persuade actors who
had settled down to a comfortable routine to make so much
effort for a few performances which they would look upon as
'highbrow' luxuries. But Goethe was a very determined man, he
had very high prestige and a position of power in the little despotic
state which he did not hesitate to use. Even Wolff, his blue-
eyed boy, found him before long overbearing and tyrannical.
His manner was kindly, and with older actors usually tactful, but
he knew exactly what he wanted and would not tolerate any
slackness or breach of discipline. He was capable of giving an
eighteen-year-old actress a week's 'house arrest', with a sentry in
front of her door for whom she had to pay, because she absented
herself without leave to play in Berlin. No wonder that when the
company heard him arriving for a rehearsal, a hush fell on them
all. They found Schiller, who also helped in rehearsals for the
first year after his removal to Weimar, much more homely and
likeable, but he always backed up Goethe. Genast tells a story
illustrating the very different attitude of the two poets towards
the actors. At the dress rehearsal for the first performance of
Schiller's translation of *Macbeth*, Vohs, in the title rôle, though
he had an excellent conception of the part, did not know his
lines, so that Goethe was only with difficulty dissuaded by
Schiller and Genast from cancelling the performance. Next day
Vohs had a great success with the large audience and after the
second act Schiller went behind the scene asking in his Swabian
dialect: 'Wo ischt der Vohs?' When Vohs, somewhat shame-
faced, came before him, Schiller threw both arms round him and
congratulated him on his performance, which he called 'Meischterhaft, meischterhaft!' Vohs had expected a different reception
and thanked Schiller profusely, but when he had gone Schiller
turned to Genast and said: 'Sehe Sie, Genascht, wir habe recht
gehabt! Er hat zwar andere Vers gesproche, als ich geschriebe
habe, aber er ischt trefflich!' (We were right, you see. He didn't

speak my verses, but he was first-rate.) 'He was a man', adds Genast, 'whose gentleness and kindliness irresistibly attracted all who were fortunate enough to come near him.'

It is difficult now to express a positive opinion about the artistic level attained by the company at its best, because contemporary accounts differ so widely. Some performances are very highly praised by exacting critics like A. W. and Caroline Schlegel. Caroline's letter about the performance of her husband's *Ion* (4th January 1802, to Sophie Bernhardi) is a charmingly vivid impression of a gala day at Weimar, when there were nineteen carriages outside the two inns in the market square. Before the curtain rose she heard Herder, on one side of her, talking to the attentive Dr. Hufeland, evidently rather disparagingly, about Greek plays (perhaps such pseudo-Greek modern imitations as they were about to see), and in the interval Böttiger, headmaster of the Gymnasium, on the other side, was to be heard pointing out to Schütz, the artist, Schlegel's errors in Greek mythology. The pit was full of Jena students. The play was well acted and tastefully produced but Caroline says later that if the actors are left to themselves, they act 'comme des cochons'. Friedrich Rochlitz, a Leipzig literary man who was made a Weimar 'Hofrat' for his comedies, was in Weimar for the first performance of *Wallensteins Tod*, and gives us a similar impression of a 'Festspiel' atmosphere, the solemn silence in the theatre, the hundreds of Jena students in the pit, who had entered Weimar in procession, decked with green branches and singing well-chosen songs, the harmony, dignity and force of the performance, which, though very simply presented, was more impressive than any of the much more elaborate performances he saw later in Berlin. The play was the subject of eager discussion everywhere and next day his barber declaimed passages to him.[1] On the other hand F. L. W. Meyer, Schröder's biographer and therefore a witness with leanings towards naturalism, finds the company 'statuesque' in *Tell* in 1810, and says that they form an ensemble only in the sense that it would make no difference if they all exchanged rôles with each other, so little feeling do they

---

[1] Quoted by Kindermann, *op. cit.*, pp. 640f.

put into any part. The truth seems to be that there were few actors of real distinction in the company—how uncultivated some must have been is indicated by Goethe's mentioning in his 'Rules' that they must not spit on the stage, and he said himself that 'a stalwart grenadier' was good enough for him—and their lack of talent had to be disguised by careful drilling. 'The artist's individuality', says Wahle, 'was suspended by a fiat of Goethe.'[1] He could never let himself go, and this tended to reduce acting to declamation. What is certain is that actors who had spent some years in Weimar seldom fitted in well if they left it for some other theatre.

The decided improvement in the repertoire began in 1798, when *Wallensteins Lager* was first produced at the opening of the Weimar season. In the course of the summer structural altera-tions had been carried out in the theatre itself and it had been redecorated. With the advice of the architect who was to build the new palace, the interior of the theatre had been transformed, and made at once more convenient and more dignified. It had been a plain hall with benches and a simple gallery, for it had been intended as much for dances as for theatrical use. Now a proper balcony and gallery were constructed, the one supported by columns and the other by pillars, in classical orders, and painted to resemble granite and marble respectively. Greek masks in low relief surmounted the columns under the balcony. As Schiller's Prologue puts it, the theatre had been turned into a cheerful temple, full of harmony and dignity. The various social classes of the little town could now be fittingly divided. The court, its guests and people of rank and standing occupied the balcony, the nobility sitting on the right, officials and so forth on the left of the ducal box in the centre. Goethe had his own box under the Duke's, at the back of the pit, which was occupied by respectable citizens and students. The gallery accommodated the 'Volk', the working class. This is the theatre described with such enthusiasm by Crabb Robinson in 1802 as a charmingly intimate little theatre, 'free and easy in its aspect', but elegant and convenient, provided with numbered seats with arms. The informality of it pleased him. He saw Schiller, who had a small

[1] Wahle, *op. cit.*, p. 167.

box next to the Duke's, leaning over and talking to the occupants of the ducal box. Others tell us that children sometimes sat on the low balustrade of Goethe's box and were regaled with cream tarts by him in the interval. The theatre held about five hundred people comfortably, but eight hundred could be squeezed in for a special attraction like *The Magic Flute*. It was now lit not by tallow candles, as before 1798, but by oil lamps. A cluster over the auditorium could be dimmed during the performance by being raised into a recess and the stage lighting from the wings could also be more or less controlled. There was still only candle-light in the dressing-rooms. The stage was small, about forty feet square, with a proscenium opening thirty-six feet wide, and the stage machinery and scenery were very simple, with the usual system of five sliding wings on each side and a back cloth which had to be rolled up to be changed, as there was no rigging-loft above the stage.

The patriarchal simplicity of many of these external features and, as we shall see, of the costumes and scenery in the best period should not blind us to the ambitious nature of Goethe's aims. They have never been more clearly stated than by Eduard Devrient in his great history of the German theatre: 'The school of Weimar, although the first demand it made on its actors was to produce "something similar to nature", applied new standards of dignity and beauty to every feature of the art of the theatre. The previously prevailing tendency in acting had by no means neglected beauty, but it had aimed simply at beautiful reality. Now a subtle distinction was made between reality and truth, and beautiful truth was demanded. Up till now everything had been judged according to its correspondence with living nature, but now all had to satisfy a cultivated taste. The actors had to lay aside their specifically German manner and find a freer, more universal conception, they had to rise from a faithful but limited expression of individual character to imagining generalised types, from the real to the ideal. These were unexpected and exacting demands.' There was no time to educate them up to the required pitch of taste, refinement and even scholarship, and Goethe had to be content with surface polish attained by constant drill. He and Schiller felt it to be their primary mission to raise the level of poetry, of literature, and the theatre was only a secondary consideration, in fact a means to this end. They were not in the position of a Shakespeare or even a Lessing, their connection with the theatre was far less intimate, and the result was a renewal of the old conflict between entertainment for the people and poetic drama. They came down on the side of book-drama and were in his opinion rather casual in their methods of staging it.[1]

Let us examine finally how far these ideals became reality in the repertoire, especially in the years 1800–1805, when Goethe and Schiller, working in close partnership, were giving their best energies to the theatre. The first of the many outstanding stage successes achieved by the plays of Schiller's last period was the performance of *Wallensteins Lager* for the opening of the winter season of 1798. The rehearsals were all conducted with the greatest care by Goethe, as Schiller was busy on the text till the last moment. Great attention was paid to the speaking of the verse, the grouping of the numerous figures on the stage, on which point Goethe consulted his Swiss artist friend, Meyer, and the costumes and setting, a measure of historical accuracy being aimed at, with the help of seventeenth-century woodcuts and so forth. On the whole the demands made on the audience in this dramatic prelude were not high. It was full of colour and spectacle, unusually concrete for Schiller, it had many of the attractions of the popular military plays and 'Ritterstücke', and its central feature was the Capucin monk's sermon with its homely humour. Schiller's prologue drew attention to the new theatre, referred to the stirring times they lived in and their challenge to the dramatist, half suggesting a parallel between Wallenstein and Napoleon, and insisted finally on the detachment and serenity of art, to maintain which he claimed that the use of verse was a powerful aid, for

> Ernst ist das Leben, heiter ist die Kunst.

To make a full evening's programme a play of Kotzebue was acted before the *Lager* on this first evening, and comedies by

[1] Devrient-Stuhlfeld, *op. cit.*, p. 281.

Jünger or Beck at the three repetitions which were given before Christmas. After this, cheerful military music was heard, then the first stanza of a 'wild soldier's song' before the curtain went up for the first scene, with all on the stage and some behind singing several more stanzas. The song is not in the printed play and several stanzas were added by Goethe. With the right 'Stimmung' thus ensured it all went exceedingly well and made everyone eager for the continuations, so much so that higher prices were charged for the whole series.

Apart from the repetitions of the *Lager* the usual mixture of opera and entertainment pieces was given till January, when on one evening *Emilia Galotti* was revived. Then on 30th January (1799), still always a gala day, as the Duchess's birthday, and marked by the performance of one of the chief attractions of the season, *Die Piccolomini* was presented, in a version which for the first year included two acts of what was printed as *Wallensteins Tod*. The rest of *Wallensteins Tod* followed on 20th April. There were no further novelties of literary interest until 30th January of the next year, 1800, when the translation of *Mahomet* by Goethe, discussed above, was given its first performance. It was only repeated at the request of the Duke. Schiller had adapted it for the stage, but as his own contribution towards the raising of the repertoire, while *Maria Stuart* was ripening, he rapidly made a stage version, not of a French classic, but of *Macbeth*, first acted on 14th May. It was an old favourite of his among Shakespeare's plays, its influence is clear in *Die Räuber* and in *Wallenstein*, but in his very free translation he makes Shakespeare too conform to the Weimar notions of classicism. The hero is made to appear as a consistently 'noble' character, brought 'humanly nearer' to the German audience, like Wallenstein, by having most of his guilt unloaded on to Fate, in the shape of the three weird sisters, who here become solemn figures not of this earth, more like Greek Furies than witches. Unfortunately the music used was Reichardt's, made for Bürger's translation, where the witches were very much witches. On the principle of the purity of the genre, the porter's bawdy humour was replaced by a pious song.[1] It was

---

[1] For a detailed comparison see Köster, *op. cit.*

the best verse translation up to date and was well received, but there was no great enthusiasm for Shakespeare among the Weimar public, any more than in Berlin. They were not ready for the real Shakespeare of Schlegel's translation yet. As in Hamburg, where the idea of the 'noble' Macbeth had its origin, they liked their heroes good.

A month after the *Macbeth* a crowded theatre greeted *Maria Stuart* with the greatest enthusiasm, on 14th June. The actors were by now accustomed to Schiller's blank verse and spoke it with ease and confidence. Some of them amused themselves by addressing each other in verse in private life, and thanks to this facility the men playing Mortimer and Leicester were able to improvise verse dialogue, Genast tells us, for a few minutes when Caroline Jagemann, as Elizabeth, forgot one of her entries and had to be fetched. This young actress, who had earned golden opinions as Thekla in *Wallenstein*, was by all accounts magnificent, so imperious in the famous scene between the two queens that she quite outshone Mary, who had good looks but less temperament. Herder and some others objected to the communion scene, which in many theatres was omitted to avoid offence.

There was little else of note in 1800. The repertoire, in spite of all Schiller's efforts, was still thin, it will be seen, in German plays of high merit. The offer of a prize that year for good comedies brought in nothing of any account. 1801 was a still leaner year because for various reasons it was found impracticable to give *Die Jungfrau von Orleans*, which was now ready, its première in Weimar, and it was done first by Leipzig instead, where they murdered its verses. The ostensible reason was that it required too big a cast, but the real reason was that Caroline Jagemann, the only possible choice then for the heroine's part, was known by all to be the Duke's mistress, a situation which reminded readers of French of Voltaire's *La Pucelle*. This burlesque epic made it difficult in any case for those of the older school to believe that Joan could be made the heroine of a 'romantic play', as Schiller called his work. The 30th January performance was of Goethe's second translation, *Tankred*, which

fell completely flat not only because few wanted to see another
Voltaire play, but also because some leading parts were given
by Goethe to inexperienced people who bungled them. The
next 'event' was not till 24th October, Anna Amalia's birthday,
when Terence's *Adelphi* was given in Einsiedel's translation.
Here Goethe went a step further in his stylisation, because the
comedy was acted in masks, or half-masks, and rather surprisingly
was well received and several times repeated. Goethe had experimented with the use of masks first in an occasional piece of his
own modelled on the Ancients, *Paläophron und Neoterpe*, acted
privately at Ettersburg a year before this. The only other interesting performance was that of *Nathan der Weise*, now done for the
first time in Weimar, after Magdeburg had shown the way. The
text was re-arranged, simplified and cut by Schiller. We have
seen that until now hardly any theatre had been bold enough
to make the stage a pulpit for Lessing's advanced ideas. The
difficulty in Weimar was not so much with the ideas as with the
unmusical, jerky verse, but after a few performances Graff, as
Nathan, made a success of it and the play gradually came to be
one of the classics of the German theatre.

Extreme stylisation also marked the novelties of the year 1802.
The first was A. W. Schlegel's uninspired re-handling of the *Ion*
of Euripides, which provided another occasion for the use of
masks. It was an interesting occasion for the élite of Weimar, as
we saw from Caroline Schlegel's letter, but it could only be
performed twice. The gala performance on 30th January was
much more entertaining and maintained its popularity in Weimar
for some time. It was Schiller's *Turandot*, an adaptation in verse
of one of Gozzi's plays based on fairy-tales, which had all been
translated in the late 'seventies by Werthes and proved very
popular in Hamburg and on the German stage generally. Quite
recently they had influenced Tieck in his romantic 'Märchen-
dramen'. It was a strange choice for Schiller and only went
down well in Weimar, where what interested Goethe was Gozzi's
use of 'masks' like Pantalone and Tartaglia from the *commedia
dell' arte*. He told the actors how much he had enjoyed such plays
in Italy and initiated them into the spirit of them successfully.

There was an element of pure fantasy in *Turandot* which may have recommended it, coming as it did between *Ion* and the May performances of *Iphigenie* and Friedrich Schlegel's *Alarcos*, all severely classical. The fate of *Alarcos* has already been mentioned.[1] *Iphigenie* on 15th May was naturally a different story, but it was not a good performance for lack of adequate principals, though Schiller had tried to bring more dramatic movement into this 'Seelendrama' by a few discreet touches. He had wished to go further, to introduce the Furies for instance as visible figures, but Goethe had not agreed to this. The first performance that won general approval was in 1807, after *Tasso*, with Frau Wolff as Iphigenie and Oels as Orest. The verse *Iphigenie* had first been put on the stage, over twenty years after its publication, at the Burgtheater in 1800, oddly enough through Kotzebue's initiative. It was soon after the first Weimar *Iphigenie* that Goethe proclaimed in *Was wir bringen* that nature and art were beginning to be recon-ciled in their theatre.

The repertoire of the next year, 1803, certainly went far towards justifying this claim. It was an *annus miravilis* during which Schiller alone contributed two major and two minor works, and Goethe also produced a considerable new play. None of these were ready for the 30th January however, and the entertaining tried favourite *Soliman der Zweite*, a French operetta, was given. Schiller's most ambitious attempt to rival the Greeks, *Die Braut von Messina*, with its chorus, its varied metres and long speeches was particularly difficult to produce. It was prepared in six reading rehearsals spread over four weeks, following by eight rehearsals on the stage. These figures indicate the amount of labour with which Goethe's company earned their big successes, for *Die Braut* certainly was one. Schiller aimed at and obtained an overwhelming effect in the theatre from situations which, as our analysis will suggest, are not without a large element of artifice, but he had certainly achieved his ambition of making the maximum use of the dramatic form. The first performance was on 19th March. On 2nd April came Goethe's *Die natürliche*

[1] Genast has caused some confusion by associating Goethe's famous: 'Do not laugh!' with *Ion* instead of *Alarcos*. See e.g. Biedermann, *Goethes Gespräche*, I, p. 319.

Tochter, revealing him too at the height of a classicism dominated by a one-sided theory. This was to have been the first part of a trilogy dealing with the French Revolution, or rather presenting symbols in eternal human situations suggested by the Revolution. The pure humanity of a woman was to be seen again as in *Iphigenie* bringing harmony into the lives of those around her, but this time in a political and social conflict. The princess was well acted by Caroline Jagemann, but the audience found the play cold and abstract. Discouraged by its reception, Goethe wrote nothing more for the theatre but the command work, *Des Epimenides Erwachen*, at the end of the wars. Schiller however never lost touch with the public. *Die Jungfrau von Orleans*, though highly theoretical in its underlying conception, offered sentiment, romance and spectacle in almost excessive profusion, and when staged at last in Weimar on 23rd April was hailed with acclamation. It strained the resources of this small theatre both through the size of the cast required—parts had to be doubled and trebled—and through the suggestion of splendour that was necessary for the coronation procession and the court scenes. But cardboard and tinfoil did good service and when Goethe and Schiller both protested against the use of a blue silk curtain for the coronation robe, the economical Kirms had to sanction the purchase of one in imitation velvet, the only valuable article, according to Genast, in the Weimar Theatre wardrobe. It was used after that by one stage royalty after another. In addition to these original works Schiller provided this year two translations from comedies of a popular French contemporary, Picard, to please Karl August, slight entertainment pieces called in German *Der Neffe als Onkel* and *Der Parasit*. Einsiedel translated the *Andria* of Terence as *Die Fremde aus Andros*, and *Eunuchus*, as *Die Mohrin*. The best translation of the year, Schlegel's *Julius Caesar*, though it made an enormous impression on Schiller when given at the beginning of the winter season, did not go down too well with the public and was only given a few times. The repertoire must be unique in German annals for its combination of German works of high merit with a most cosmopolitan range of translations. At the same time, as will be seen from the full list printed in the Appendix, opera and everyday 'good theatre' were being provided as usual.

1804 was not quite up to this level. For the Duchess in January the play was Bode's translation of Racine's *Mithridate*, the third French tragedy to be done for such an occasion. The event of the year was *Wilhelm Tell* on 17th March, again a difficult enterprise for the small company, but one which called out all their best qualities. The enthusiasm of the audience was 'un, exampled'. Some of them had been there by three o'clock for a performance which began at half-past five and went on till eleven! Schiller took the manuscript back with him to cut it down to reasonable proportions. It is easy to imagine that a drama celebrating so eloquently a people's fight for indepen, dence would have a very special appeal at a moment when Napoleon was preparing to crush his German opponents. It was natural that Goethe should think this a favourable moment to revive his own drama of freedom, *Götz*, though he was at heart so entirely out of sympathy with it that he found the adapta, tion difficult. With Schiller's help he reduced the number of scene-changes by one-half, but that still left two dozen, so that on the opening night this play too lasted six hours, though it was enthusiastically received. After this it was played for a time in two halves, and various attempts were made by Goethe to produce a satisfactory stage version, but without real success. In the process Götz lost much of his fire, Weislingen his subtlety and Adelheid her seductiveness.

In 1805 the first interesting novelty was Schiller's translation of *Phèdre*, which was naturally performed on 30th January, the last new work of Schiller that the world was to see. His death on 9th May was an irreparable loss for the German theatre and of course for Weimar in particular. Goethe's *Epilog zu Schillers Glocke*, perhaps the finest memorial poem in German, was spoken by Amalia Wolff, after a dramatised version of Schiller's *Lied von der Glocke* which was produced at a memorial performance at Lauchstädt on 10th August. The words 'Denn er war unser!' had a particular poignancy there, for he had been the Shakespeare of this 'Globe' and the German dramas that he had created with these particular actors in view had come as near to being the German national type of drama as anything we know. After his death Goethe's interest in the theatre again became more and more perfunctory, and though the company, with P. A. Wolff and his wife, Oels and a few other young actors who had assimilated Goethe's teaching, were perhaps at their best for the next few years, the historic days of Weimar were over.

In the year of the battle of Jena (1806) the company was kept together and played even on the eve of the battle (13th October), when the guns could be heard in Weimar, but next day they were given six weeks' pay and the theatre was closed until Christmas. Soon afterwards, Goethe heard to his surprise that the Wolffs, Oels, Becker and Fräulein 'Silie' (her real name had 'Peter' in front but Goethe did not like the German for 'parsley' as an actress's name and himself suggested the truncation) had begun to rehearse his *Tasso* on their own initiative, thinking they were now capable of overcoming the great difficulties it offered, and it received its première in this way on 16th February, in an entirely worthy performance, nearly twenty years after its publication in book form. Goethe had been reviving *Die Laune des Verliebten* and *Stella*, but did not himself try to stage either *Tasso* or the first part of *Faust*, which was published in 1808. It had to wait until 1829, when Weimar performed it to celebrate Goethe's eightieth birthday, but in his own absence. No professional theatre had attempted it until earlier in that same year, when Brunswick did so. In the summer and autumn of 1807 came the two series, each of twenty-five performances, given by the Weimar company by invitation in Leipzig, where the perfection of their ensemble in spoken drama was greatly admired.

The ten years from now until Goethe's resignation was finally accepted in 1817, owing chiefly to the intrigues of the all-powerful Caroline Jagemann, were marked by a number of experiments with Romantic dramas, some of them surprising enough, the Fate Tragedies of Zacharias Werner and Müllner, for example. Kleist's *Der zerbrochene Krug* received a single performance in 1808, partly owing to bad acting and partly to Goethe's complete lack of sympathy with Kleist. It was on this occasion that an official who dared to hiss was immediately arrested on the Duke's orders. Goethe's comment was that he should have waited until he was outside. Shakespeare was still comparatively neglected and certainly not markedly popular, in spite of Schlegel's fine translation. Perhaps the least creditable of all Goethe's productions was his amazing travesty of *Romeo and Juliet*, using Schlegel's translation, in 1812. His essay *Shakespeare und kein Ende* (1813) explains his new point of view. There are things in Shakespeare, he says, which when he reads the plays, or better still, hears them well read (he would have been delighted with some modern broadcasts!), appeal strongly to his imagination, but if he sees them acted he finds them annoying. He mentions *Hamlet*'s ghost, the witches in *Macbeth* and certain 'cruelties', and means apparently whatever offends a refined and humane modern taste. The words and the inner world they call up are what is important in Shakespeare, not the external action. 'Shakespeare's works are not for the eyes of the body.' No praise is high enough for Shakespeare's power of conjuring up a world of living men, reflecting all the varied life of his own great age and country (one reads a certain envy here between the lines!) but it is a picture for the eyes of the mind. In short, Shakespeare's plays are book-dramas for Goethe now, like his own, and he adapted *Romeo and Juliet* even more arbitrarily, from a narrowly 'classical ' point of view, than Schiller had adapted *Macbeth*.

X

SCHILLERS' CLASSICAL PLAYS AND GOETHE'S FAUST, IN THEIR RELA´ TION TO THE THEATRE AND THE PUBLIC

WE have followed the growth of the theatre in Weimar under the influence first of Goethe, then of Goethe and Schiller, from the amusement of a small circle to an institution of great importance in the history of German culture. The Court Theatre under Goethe, while continuing to provide for the amusement of a public which now included all classes in the small state and frequent visitors attracted by its fame, carried to new heights the aims of the 'Bildungstheater' of the age of Lessing and helped to mould the nineteenth´century German theatre everywhere. These influences will be dealt with in the final chapter. What we are now concerned with is the permanent literary result of these efforts, the classical German dramas *par excellence*. They are the plays of Schiller's last period and Goethe's *Faust*, which, though it played no part in the theatrical history of Weimar during Goethe's management and was composed only in part during those years, symbolises more completely than any other single work this whole age and con´ stituted such a challenge to producers that its later influence on stage history has been by no means negligible.

Wallenstein

The Weimar Theatre was seen at its best in the first and perhaps greatest of Schiller's later plays, *Wallenstein*. The web of relations linking this work with contemporary life and thought as well as with the dramatic tradition of Europe is so complex

and has been so thoroughly studied that only a few of its interest
ing features can be discussed in the following pages with our own
particular aim in view, to see drama, theatre and public in their
mutual interactions.

Schiller's letters, especially those to Körner and Goethe, show
how deeply he pondered over this play and how often he changed
his plans during the three years from 1796 when he was engaged
on its composition. His interest in the subject was aroused when
he was writing his *History of the Thirty Years' War*, before 1790,
but as we have seen, after *Don Karlos* he decided to write no more
plays until he had prepared himself for the task by the study of
history and philosophy, for it was a superhuman task that his
conception of classical drama prescribed, nothing less than the
interpretation of history and a metaphysical interpretation of life
itself through historical symbols. As in most of his later plays,
he is concerned with the general problem of man's fate in the
world as revealed in significant moments of history, but here alone
it is a turning-point in German history with which he deals.
How deeply he was interested in this question of Germany's
place in world history, here approached from the angle of
political history, is shown for instance by the fragment *Deutsche
Grösse*, written about this time, where he encourages his fellow-
countrymen to find in Germany's achievements in the intellectual
sphere ground for the hope that her final cultural contribution
will be at least as great as that of any of the neighbours who are
so far ahead of her in political and economic power.

After writing the history of the war by which the fate of
Germany for more than a century and the ultimate collapse of
the Empire had been virtually determined, Schiller had tried to
select some figure from that age round which he could best con-
struct a tragedy of the 'clash of historical forces' such as it was
now his ambition to write. Wallenstein was his second choice,
after he had rejected Gustavus Adolphus. It was not the personality of Wallenstein therefore which first attracted him, but
the crucial period in which he lived. He seems to have regarded
Wallenstein himself for long however in much the same way as
his earliest tragic heroes, namely as a 'sublime criminal'. It was

only gradually, as his notion of the sublime itself developed under the influence of his philosophical reading and wider experience of life, that he began to see a deeper meaning in Wallenstein's fall, and greater aesthetic possibilities in the subject. In his history he found words of praise for him as a leader of genius, but not as a man, and even in 1796 he told Körner that among the many difficulties of this subject, a struggle for political power manifesting itself in rather petty episodes at many scattered points, the greatest of all was the 'coldness' of Wallenstein's motives—ambition and the desire for revenge. 'His character is never noble and cannot be allowed to appear so. All through he can only inspire fear and never display real greatness. In a word, I am cut off from every approach to this subject to which I have been accustomed. I have nothing to expect from the content, the effect can only be produced by the form which I give to it.'

According to this quotation, Schiller's inspiration in writing *Wallenstein* was in the first place aesthetic in origin, the desire to make the best possible use of the dramatic form with a difficult, and therefore for him as artist all the more interesting, subject. But like all his later plays it became at the same time a vehicle for philosophical and ethical ideas, and the danger arose that the reader might take as an expression of the author's convictions what was only introduced for aesthetic effect. The aesthetic and the ethical are not perfectly fused into one consistent whole. It is mainly for that reason that the hero makes the impression which Korff, after the first World War, described, in spite of his admiration for the work, as 'misleadingly ambiguous' (bedenk-lich schillernd and compared with that made on the outside world by Bethmann Hollweg and his diplomacy. Germany, he said, was not a Hamlet, as Freiligrath had asserted, but a Wallenstein. After the second World War the catholic poet and historian Reinhold Schneider has gone further and con-demned Wallenstein as an immoralist, whose fascinating figure has long misled German youth. M. Andler already saw in him one of the forerunners of Nietzsche's superman, and Otto Ludwig in mid-century had criticised the ever-shifting moral values in the play. As there has never been any doubt about Schiller's own high moral ideals—it is well known that Goethe found in him a Christ-like quality—it is important to try to discover how this unresolved contradiction which so many find in *Wallenstein* comes to be there, and what the audiences of his own day found in it.

Though Schiller's later dramas are not simply the practical application of the theories he puts forward about tragedy in his aesthetic essays, of which all the most important were written before *Wallenstein*, these certainly throw much light on his intentions. He is a very literary philosopher, not nearly as precise as we should wish in his use of words, so that it is very difficult to state his theories satisfactorily, especially as they develop from essay to essay. He begins with ideas of Lessing and Mendelssohn and ends up with a theory of tragedy of his own, based on Kant's notion of the sublime. But what is always clear is the value which Schiller attaches to the idea of human freedom. 'The will', he says in the last of these essays, *Über das Erhabene* (1801), 'is the distinguishing characteristic of the human race. . . . All other things *must;* man is the creature that *wills.*' He quotes with approval Nathan's phrase: 'Kein Mensch muss müssen.' The sublime, for him the tragic emotion, makes us conscious of man's freedom by showing it to us in conflict with suffering, with the worst that fate can do. Sometimes Schiller represents this conflict as taking place in the tragic hero on the stage, sometimes in the mind of the spectator. The attitude of mind behind it all is not unlike that in Bertrand Russell's *A free man's worship*. The important point for light on the Wallenstein problem is Schiller's insistence (e.g. in *Über das Pathetische*) that it is not the use made by the hero of his freedom that matters aesthetically, but his freedom itself. 'For the poet it does not matter whether his heroes are to be classed as good men or bad, since the same measure of energy which is necessary for the good may very often be needed for consistency in evil.' Hence it is still possible for him to approve of 'sublime criminals'. What is behind this is a perfectly sound distinction between the ethical and the aesthetic attitude, but it easily leads to works of art which present characters who are aesthetically satisfying, to those capable of the aesthetic attitude, but may well be taken by others as ethical models and prove socially disastrous. Problems of this kind have been much discussed with regard to the influence of the cinema on young minds.

Wallenstein, whom Schiller did not admire as a man, made a satisfactory tragic hero for him then if he displayed great powers of will, of 'freedom' as such, but the spectator might easily believe that moral approval was implied where that was not Schiller's intention. Another feature connected with Schiller's love of freedom is his weakness for tragic heroes shown in the act of arriving at decisions. Influenced by Kant's conception of freedom as 'indeterminacy', he liked incalculable characters, of whom no one could say what on earth they would or would not do. Such characters tend to strike us as bundles of contradictions, 'bedenk-lich schillernd', not characters in the ordinary sense at all. (See above, p. 244).

There is another approach which throws much light on Schiller's intentions in *Wallenstein*, as also in the plays which followed, the study of the poet's technique on the lines suggested by W. Spengler in one of the most illuminating books on Schiller of recent years.[1] Spengler's analysis of the genesis of Schiller's plays is based on the full notes left by Schiller of his work on the unfinished play, *Perkin Warbeck*. For other plays, only his letters throw some light on the process of composition, but here we can see every step he took and in Spengler's view, we can to some extent reconstruct, by analogy with *Warbeck*, his plan of work for each of the later plays.

By the time he came to write *Warbeck* Schiller had come to attach great weight to the tradition of the principal poetic genres. He was influenced in this by his discussions with Goethe on the epic and dramatic, and by his renewed study of the Greeks and Shakespeare. Each genre, tragedy or comedy, for instance, had acquired characteristics of its own in the course of time, an essential nature to which the poet attempting it might not with impunity do too much violence. This nature prescribed certain features in the form of any new work. If a play was to be called

[1] *Das Drama Schillers, seine Genesis*, Leipzig, 1932.

a tragedy, for instance, the author was not free to introduce any kind of hero or plot he pleased. Schiller's first step in considering any possible dramatic theme was to decide what genre it was best suited for and, having decided this, to adapt it further to the needs of that genre. So in *Warbeck*, if it was to be a comedy, the line to take would be to develop the contrast between the pretender and the great rôle he was playing, but if it was to be a tragedy, one would have to show him as born for just this rôle. To comply with the demands of the genre, the hero of a historical tragedy must have tragic dignity, whether he has a corresponding character in the history books or not. The unlikable character of Wallenstein is accordingly raised, he is brought 'humanly nearer 'to us, by being given a speculative subtlety which reminds us of *Hamlet*, combined with an infectious belief in himself and his star, symbolised in the astrological scenes. This appeal is reinforced by the apparent devotion of all ranks, in the intro⁄ductory *Lager*, to his person, and the suggestion that the position of supreme power which he has attained is itself an irresistible temptation to him to make his power absolute—'Only his camp explains his crime', i.e. all power corrupts. At the same time it is suggested to us by Max, who has readily accepted the idea from Wallenstein, that his only motive in opposing the Emperor is his concern for the Whole, his desire to give the world peace. The hero⁄worship of this one pure idealist among the men around Wallenstein tends in itself to make us think better of Wallenstein, and, moreover, his opponents of the imperial party are represented as false, petty and self⁄seeking.

But another requirement of the genre as Schiller now sees it, after his study of the Greeks and particularly of *Œdipus Rex*, is tragic inevitability. At one point he wrote to Goethe that fate was playing too small a part and Wallenstein's own guilt too great a part in bringing about the catastrophe. What he parti⁄cularly admired was a plot in which, given a particular initial situation, everything seemed to unfold itself like an opening bud. He tried to produce this effect above all by choosing the most favourable view⁄point in time and place, presenting a situation which the hero has reached by his own conscious action, but where it *seems* as if he were in the grip of circumstance. This is what Schiller calls the 'pregnant moment' in the action. In Wallenstein it is when the generalissimo, having summoned all his commanders with their forces to Pilsen, is in active negotiation with the Swedes, the enemy, and the Emperor, informed of this, is seriously considering his dismissal. A final fillip is given to the action by what Schiller called the 'punctum saliens', an incident, often invented by him for the purpose, which sets the ball rolling. Here it is the capture of Sesina, the go-between, by the imperial party, after which Wallenstein, still on the razor-edge of delibera-tion, must make his final decision. It is at this point, in the first act of *Wallensteins Tod*, that Schiller's hero most resembles Hamlet, especially in the monologue in I, 4:

> Wär's möglich? Könnt' ich nicht mehr, wie ich wollte?
> Nicht mehr zurück, wie mir's beliebt? Ich müsste
> Die Tat vollbringen, weil ich sie gedacht?

A few scenes later, when Countess Terzky is urging him to act, it is Macbeth we seem to see before us. But Schiller makes it quite clear that his Wallenstein could not seriously consider making his peace with the Emperor at the cost of sacrificing his ambitions. He is represented as playing so long with the mere thought of treachery in order that we may fully realise his potential freedom, whatever use he may make of it. Schiller, in fact, is trying to have it both ways. At one moment we are told that Wallenstein's demonic love of power is the explanation of his action, at another that at any time he is free to act in any way he likes.

The introduction of this essential element of Schiller's own philosophy of life at this point in the play is a feature which, as Spengler shows, is common to most of his later dramas. It is his way of combining a fate tragedy with a character tragedy, the best feature of Greek practice, as he thought, following the one-sided view of Greek tragedy which had become current, and the best feature of Shakespeare's. He wanted to show Nemesis work-ing itself out, and at the same time his hero maintaining his freedom of will in the struggle with fate. Objectively considered his hero's fall is therefore represented as just, poetic justice is done, but we are made to identify ourselves to such an extent with the hero, he is brought so humanly near to us, that we feel his fate as nevertheless tragic because his punishment seems disproportionate.

For all his insistence on freedom Wallenstein is an anticipation of a realist in politics, who reckons with the ugly realities and uses men as his pawns. As a foil to him and his self-seeking generals Schiller introduces two pure idealists in the lovers Max and Thekla, 'glad hearts without reproach or blot', or what Schiller's time called 'beautiful souls', who for most of us now seem rather too good to be true in such a milieu. Following in everything the voice of the heart, shrinking from the sordid world around them, they serve to remind us of the values of inwardness, of unselfish love. Schiller confronts the realist with the idealist, as he had brought Luise before Lady Milford or Posa before Philip, in order to bring out the moral implications of Wallenstein's action and at the same time the Utopian character of Max's ideals. Only the man who goes through life without desire, Wallenstein is made to say, can keep himself unspotted. Those who live for the power and glory of this world are necessarily committed to evil, and true virtue is for hermits. Later, torn by conflicting loyalties, Max finds his heart no longer a sure guide but, allowing Thekla's still purer nature to decide for him, he finds a way out in a suicidal charge—with all his men. These scenes on the human and even sentimental level came from Schiller's own heart, as he said, but he knew too how dear they would be to his German public, whose probable reactions to each scene we find him carefully noting in the *Warbeck* fragment.

Critically examined then this ambitious drama of ambition is German and of its time in its inchoate vastness, its historical learning, its awareness of innumerable models, its philosophical suggestiveness, its unashamed sentimentality. For the ordinary play-goer there was spectacle reminiscent of opera, the Ritterstücke and Shakespearian histories as well as homely humour and pathetic love-scenes. For the more sophisticated there was something of Greek, something of French and something of

Shakespearian tragedy, and there was an idealistic philosophy which reminded them of human freedom and the values of the heart. And all this was in a form which took account of the actual theatre and lent itself admirably—except in its excessive length, which none of the divisions attempted entirely overcame —to performance on the stage.

Maria Stuart

None of the plays following *Wallenstein* cost Schiller so much trouble as it had done. He had found his mature style and knew his aim, though he still experimented freely in the means he adopted to attain his end. He had thought of Maria Stuart as a subject soon after writing *Kabale und Liebe* but his actual work on it lasted little over a year. He takes a historical subject again that opens up wide perspectives of world history, for in this conflict the English throne is at stake and Catholic and Protestant in their fight for supremacy in Europe are vitally involved. The inter-play of outstanding characters and events of great moment, which appear to unfold themselves with the inevitability of fate, is again in the centre of interest. Intense concentration on the main conflict of personalities does not allow of the introduction this time of any scenes to convey atmosphere or local colour or of any comic relief. The construction is analytic. Through events in the last three days of Mary's life the meaning of it all is conveyed. Schiller never came so near to French tragedy as in this play. We are reminded of it even in details of technique like the perhaps rather too obvious use of Hanna, the nurse, as confidante in the exposition, the much reduced total number of principals (compared with Wallenstein), the small number of changes of scene, none occurring within the act except in Act V, the reporting of the behaviour of the London crowd in IV, 7 and 11, instead of showing it in a Shakespearian crowd-scene, the invented love intrigue motivating political actions, and so on. The grand style is maintained throughout with little variation of tone for individual characterisation. How different for instance is the nurse, who speaks in Act I like a father-confessor, from the nurse in *Romeo and Juliet* who herself, in Goethe's Weimar adaptation, was characteristically given so much dignity as to be unrecognisable.

As in *Wallenstein*, the main action can be considered from several points of view, and it is the skilful interweaving of various chains of cause and effect which gives to the play its convincing fullness of meaning, as an interpretation of history and of life in general. There is the rivalry between Elizabeth and Mary as women, on the personal plane, and as queens and representatives of competing religions, on the political plane. The outcome of these two rivalries is the sentence of death pronounced on Mary before the play opens, which produces a tension subtly varied from scene to scene, until Elizabeth finally signs it. Finally there are the moral and metaphysical questions raised by Mary's execution.

Like so many of Schiller's heroes, Mary has a crime on her conscience, the murder of Darnley, and it is her guilt in this which she holds herself to be expiating by her death. But Schiller has given her tragic dignity and sublimity by throwing all the light on her noble bearing in captivity and when face to face with death. He naturally therefore assumes the Casket Letters to have been forgeries and makes her innocent of the charge, of complicity in the plots against Elizabeth's life, on which she had been condemned by her English judges. She has no part either in Mortimer's plot, the immediate occasion which leads Elizabeth to sign the death sentence. Her innocence makes her death a tragedy, her noble bearing is for Schiller an example of sublime composure and at the same time her earlier guilt provides an inner justification for her suffering and vindicates the moral order of the universe.

To show us Mary in this perspective Schiller takes various liberties with history. He brings together in time events widely separated, the discussion of a French marriage for Elizabeth and the execution of Mary, so that both queens may still be young and attractive. Bolder inventions are the mutual love of Mary and Leicester, the fanatical Mortimer's part and the personal meeting of the queens. The first two, very reminiscent of French practice, serve to intensify for dramatic purposes the personal conflict and to raise the audience's hopes of Mary's escape from an otherwise certain doom. The third was too good a situation to be missed and it provides a splendid centre to the action where its many strands join, the wider significance of the conflict is revealed and a tragic reversal is made possible, for Mary's doom is sealed when our hopes for her are highest, though she triumphs morally over her physically irresistible rival. Here once more we have the symbolic clash of great historical forces, a scene that sums up an epoch. 'The incomparable excellence of this scene lies in the combination of the purely human and personal question of guilt, freedom and justice with the political necessities, so that we see not just one woman facing another, but an English protestant queen and a Scottish catholic one, and the human and moral conflicts of the two women and queens become symbols of historical issues which eclipse the two protagonists.'[1]

Die Jungfrau von Orleans

Die Jungfrau von Orleans was written still more quickly and easily than *Maria Stuart*. The phrase used by Schiller of his Johanna, 'Dich schuf mein Herz' and the sub-title, 'a romantic tragedy' prepare us for the 'raging romance' which Bernard Shaw, approaching the subject in a totally different spirit, finds in his predecessor. The play achieved lasting popularity with the public, the mass of whom no doubt accepted it naively as a kind of dramatic fairy-tale, satisfying the heart, especially the patriotic heart, and delighting the eye with its 'Shakespearian' abundance of movement and spectacle, its rhetoric and lyricism. Here, with a medieval subject, Schiller abandons the severe analytic construction in favour of the chronicle form, throwing the unities to the winds and bringing battles on to the stage in the Shakespearian manner. To the reflective mind this work is far less satisfying than its two predecessors unless one reads into it Schiller's own aesthetic theories, as his modern interpreters usually do. Here there are no symbolic interpretations of great historical forces. Schiller knew little about the history of the period, though he dutifully read collections of documents and the early connected accounts of the Maid's life, with their legendary accretions. As

[1] B. von Wiese, *Die Dramen Schillers*, Leipzig, 1938, p. 99.

Schiller draws them, English and French make exactly the same impression on us, for there is no hint of their different back grounds. The English are simply invaders and might have come from the moon. It is in fact not a historical drama at all but a rather superior 'Ritterschauspiel' with a patriotic purpose.

To understand what it meant for Schiller and his time we must remember the international situation in 1800. Germany was in serious danger through the disunity of the Empire, with its countless jealous dynasties and the political indifference of their subjects, and though Schiller had said hard things about patriotism, at least in private, it is impossible not to see in this play a plea for a more normal and vigorous attitude towards an invader and a higher regard for the value of national culture than he saw about him. His sympathies are clearly with Joan when she cries:

> Der fremde König, der von aussen kommt,
> Dem keines Ahnherrn heilige Gebeine
> In diesem Lande ruhn, kann er es lieben?

for he did not at all share Goethe's admiration for the demonic Napoleon, who for him was wholly evil. He draws Joan's father and chief critic on the other hand as a philistine without vision, who says to his children:

> Kommt an die Arbeit! Kommt! und denke jeder
> Nur an das Nächste! Lassen wir die Grossen,
> Der Erde Fürsten um die Erde losen.

Behind the unreal wish-fulfilment of the action is the conviction of the power of ideas and faith to influence events, the power of patriotism in particular as an inspiring moral force, which could turn a woman into a heroine and the saviour of her country. This play and *Wilhelm Tell* were an important factor therefore in the national recovery after Jena and in the preparation of the War of Liberation. That they were recognised as such by the French is proved by their being banned in the theatre under the French occupation.

It is not only in this respect that Schiller's *Jungfrau* shows signs of having grown in the same psychological atmosphere as the works of the German Romantic School, in spite of the strained personal relations between Schiller and the older Romantics. It has affinities with Tieck's *Genoveva* and it anticipates in some respects Kleist's *Penthesilea* and *Die Hermannsschlacht*. It uses a profusion of verse-forms, celebrates the catholic middle ages and makes great play with irrational features. Nothing could be further removed in spirit from Voltaire's *La Pucelle*, the only handling of the legend known to most contemporaries. It is odd that it should have been a German and a by no means orthodox Christian who contributed so much to the mystical cult of St. Joan, with an idea taken from a doubtful play of Shakespeare's, *Henry VI*, Part I. In the first act of that play, where Joan is taken more seriously than in the closing scenes, she tells of her transformation after the appearance of the Virgin to her in a vision, and when the Dauphin, immediately after she has proved herself superior to him in swordplay, declares himself madly in love with her, she rejects him with the words:

> I must not yield to any rites of love,
> For my profession's sacred from above.
> When I have chased all thy foes from hence,
> Then will I think upon a recompense.

In Schiller the peasant girl is similarly transformed and retains supernatural powers which manifest themselves in second sight, the gift of prophecy, superhuman insight, courage, generalship, powers of persuasion and actual miracles such as the bursting of heavy fetters, and these powers are confirmed by thunder from on high and a rainbow in the sky at her death. But it is only so long as she remains the completely self-forgetful instrument of God that Joan possesses these powers. When she allows human feeling to sway her and spares the English leader Lionel through love at first sight, they are taken from her. Realising her 'guilt' she allows herself to be regarded as a witch when denounced by her own father at the moment of her greatest triumph, the coronation of Charles at Rouen, and thunder from on high is made to seem like the voice of a *deus ex machina* that condemns her. She too now is guilty and guiltless at once, like Wallenstein and Maria Stuart. She looks upon this false charge and its consequences as Heaven's punishment for another real fault, her momentary relapse into merely human feeling, but having suffered this disgrace, been captured by the English and overcome her love for Lionel she is re-instated in divine favour. Her miraculous intervention brings about the final defeat of the English and she dies in glory on the field. It is so free a version of the tale of

> Jehanne, la bonne Lorraine
> Qu'Anglois bruslerent à Rouen

that Mr. Shaw's outburst is quite understandable. Shakespeare (if it was Shakespeare) burns her of course and is very insular about it, but Schiller took over from him not only the hint of the mystical powers of a pure maid, an idea common enough in German literature, but also the telescoping of widely separated historical events and the representation of Joan as an active combatant, instead of as the 'mascot', to use Anatole France's apt word, which she seems to have been in actuality.

It is surprising to find Goethe referring to this work as 'artistically the most perfect of Schiller's dramas'. Perhaps at the height of his passion for the Ancients he saw in it Schiller's most consistent attempt at a drama of fate, for we can see here a third variant of a modern substitute for the fate of the Greeks, after the rather fumbling attempt in *Wallenstein* and the death-sentence hanging over Maria Stuart. Joan's fate is predetermined by Providence itself, intervening in human affairs as directly as Bossuet believed but Schiller certainly did not, and announcing the future in visions instead of oracles. Yet how different were the moral implications here from those of *Iphigenie*. Instead of pure humanity, what is glorified in the name of piety and patriotism is a fanaticism which forbids the sparing of an opponent's life. Schiller's principal aim no doubt was 'Die Darstellung des Übersinnlichen', the representation of that in man which is master of the physical, his unconquerable mind, but that innate tendency of the absolute idealist to exceed all human measure which we found in Posa takes a form here from which it is only a step to the ferocity on principle of *Die Hermannsschlacht* and *Germania an ihre Kinder*, Kleist's 'Hymn of Hate'. It is still very theoretical in Schiller, but we can easily see the reason for the unmistakable Schiller-revival in National-Socialist times, to the detriment of Goethe. His political insight was suddenly re-discovered, we heard admiring references to his 'Diktatorengesicht' and his characters were praised as 'inspired grey soldiers of the Weltgeist'. 'Schiller's tragedy', we were told, 'made out of the *petit bourgeois* who formed round about 1800 the marrow of the German nation men fit to wield world-power.'[1]

Die Braut von Messina

The historical element in Schiller's subjects had been decreasing steadily since *Wallenstein*, where he had been almost overwhelmed by the sheer mass of material to be digested and in spite of all his efforts had been compelled to leave his play inconveniently long. In *Die Jungfrau* he had played fast and loose with history and invented freely. Now in the *Braut von Messina*, abandoning history, 'das obligate Historische', he tried to invent a perfect plot out of his own head, a plot to convey the very essence of the tragic as he had found it in the incomparable *Œdipus Rex*.

The two features which immediately remind us of *Œdipus* in his new play are first, that in the imaginary situation which, with its maximum of horror, is to evoke the maximum reaction of human freedom and thus, according to Schiller's theory, present the sublime, the tragic emotion, at its purest, Schiller shows us the utmost perversion of a natural family relationship, not a son who kills his father and marries his mother but hostile brothers, one of whom kills the other after both have fallen in love with one who proves to be their sister—Schiller at least spares us incest. Secondly, this family catastrophe has been foretold and in their attempts to avoid it the parents, who alone know of the prophecy, help to bring it about. The plot turns as in *Œdipus* on an 'anagnorisis', the revelation of an unsuspected and disastrous relationship, namely that Beatrice, whom Manuel and Cesar have both separately determined to make their own, is their sister.

In the first particular Schiller's invention is as we have seen on familiar lines, for the motif of the hostile brothers was just as much

[1] See H. Smith, *Present-day tendencies in the German interpretation of Schiller*, P.E.G.S., 1935, and H. G. Atkins, *German Literature through Nazi Eyes*, London, 1941.

a favourite with Storm and Stress, from *Julius von Tarent* to *Die Räuber*, as the father-complex was thirty years ago with the Expressionists. In *Die Braut von Messina* there is no father, as in *Julius von Tarent*, to exact the supreme penalty from Don Cesar. In addition to turning the lady for whom the brothers are rivals in love into their sister, Schiller improves on *Julius* by making Don Cesar freely do justice on himself, asserting the freedom of conscience in the face of destiny. Schiller's tragedy is in fact, as Bellermann points out, not strictly a Fate Tragedy of the *Œdipus* type, where it is of the essence that the hero, on reflection, feels himself to be without personal guilt, as it made clear in *Œdipus on Colonos*. The Fate Tragedy brings home to us how little our will counts and teaches submission, but Schiller says 'The greatest of evils is guilt', though he explains Cesar's guilt as the last in a long chain of evils resulting from a curse that lies on this family, as in the *Orestria*.

To produce such an imbroglio with plausibility was no easy matter. It is, in fact, only by assuming some extraordinary coincidences and by arbitrarily withholding from one character information known to another that Schiller can give his plot even the appearance of coherence. The last scene of the second act in particular contains many such flaws, the most obvious being when Don Cesar is removed from the stage just long enough for the old servant Diego to make a communication to his mistress (about the presence of Beatrice at the Prince's funeral) which puts her son Manuel, whose forebodings have been aroused, off the scent and would have put Cesar, if he had been present, on to it. In either case the tragic catastrophe would have been impossible.

The second feature from *Œdipus* which we have noted can only be imitated by the introduction of prophetic dreams, the interpretations of which are accepted equally readily by the parents whether they are made by an Arab or by a monk. Their nondescript religion, to suit which Sicily is chosen as a background, an island influenced in turn by Greek, Mohammedan and Christian civilisation, has funeral rites which sound Christian (with an anticipation in one respect of crematorium ceremonies) but has in general so little content that Korff says not unjustly that there are no Gods behind Schiller's fate. Isabella's faith stands or falls according to whether the future has been correctly fore-told or not, whether by the Arab, the monk or a hermit gifted with second sight. It is clearly the aesthetic effect of tragic irony which is all important for Schiller, Isabella being given lines exactly echoing Jocasta's rejection of divination, and being com-pelled before long to eat her words in the same way. The doom which works itself out in this royal house can also be in large measure rationalised, as it can in the Greek play, in terms of hereditary influences, the curse being a fiery temper and over-hastiness. There is a third feature in *Œdipus* which Karl Rein-hard, for instance, stresses more than the other two, the restless and entirely admirable activity displayed by the hero in pursuit of what he holds to be the good and the pious course. This is in the centre of interest in Sophocles, but there is little to correspond to it in Schiller. Only Cesar's rise to moral insight and resolute action at the close shows anything which is comparable with the Greek hero's determined probing for the fatal truth.

By these various devices Schiller bodies forth a theme, a possible human experience of the utmost horror, a 'sight of what is to be borne', together with accompanying features which help the spectator to hold the imagined experience at an aesthetic 'distance' by investing it with a solemn dignity and beauty. As in Greek and indeed in all successful tragic drama the spectacle of suffering is only one element in an artistic whole which includes 'language made beautiful in different ways' and the appeal of characters which, however mistaken in their actions, are shaped in the heroic mould. Arrayed in flowing robes, they move with numerous attendants, often to the strains of music, against a back-ground of royal splendour. In Act IV, the final act of the tragedy, when into the pillared hall of Isabella's palace at night are borne first Beatrice, overcome by the murder she has witnessed, to awaken to the greater horror of learning who she is, then, as the choir chants a solemn dirge, the body of Don Manuel, greeted by Isabella, when told who is under the pall, with the fierce repudia-tion of oracles, beginning

So haltet ihr mir Wort, ihr Himmelsmächte?

Schiller has contrived one of the most impressive tragic crescendos in dramatic literature and risen to the occasion with splendid poetry. Everything here is according to the best Greek models, the tragic reversal of fortune, tragic irony, wise words of warning and comfort from the chorus, all superbly timed and put into well-chosen language. Finally, followed, in the vision of the chorus, by the Furies, Don Cesar enters and is greeted by his mother as her only son. When he learns from her that Beatrice, in whose arms he killed Manuel, is their sister, he reveals to Isabella the final horror of his crime, curses the secrecy which has borne this fruit and, in spite of the pleading of mother and sister, expiates his guilt in death.

Our one criticism of this magnificent tragic finale is that it does not follow with the remorselessness of a natural law from what has gone before, or impress itself upon us as a true interpretation of life. It is a stage effect, a 'schöner Schein' produced by artifice, which may move us deeply for the moment but does not leave us with deepened insight into the nature of existence. In other words, it is feeling for feeling's sake. This is partly because of the defects in the plot already mentioned, and partly because of the synthetic nature of the cultural and religious background. There are indeed no Gods behind it and no men known to history. Schiller has intentionally left out of account the inherited religious attitude of his German audience as well as their normal ways of thinking about such things, let us say, as the interpretation of dreams. But on the other hand he could not accept the Sophoclean view of fate presented in Œdipus, in which is involved the removal of responsibility from the individual. For Schiller the hero has a moral guilt, and this notion is reconciled with the idea of fate by assuming a chain of guilt, linking one generation of this accursed family with another. The combination of the two ideas produces however an unfortunate confusion. We feel neither the full tragic inevitability of Œdipus nor the full sense of the hero's responsibility, for a crime which has, after all, been foretold and therefore presumably forms part of a deterministic series of events.[1] Like the popular Fate Tragedies which followed

[1] See Bellermann, op. cit., II, pp. 329–337.

it, the play seems to appeal in one respect to popular superstition, which accepts fortune-telling and the like, whereas in others it is aimed at the educated, who do not really believe that the future can be exactly foretold.

Like Wieland before him Schiller had principally had in mind 'the thinking man with a taste for the Classics', who could take pleasure in imagining himself, for the moment, an ancient Greek and could appreciate the learned allusions and imitated tricks of style. One can imagine Böttiger ticking them off, as Caroline Schlegel heard him doing at the performance of *Ion*. We have seen that the play went down almost scandalously well with the Jena students, but it was amongst the least successful of Schiller's plays with average audiences. For the initiated, including Goethe, Schiller had touched the high level of classicism, but with the ordinary citizen, whose culture was no less genuine for being purely German, he had overreached himself. If we ask what is the connection between *Die Braut von Messina* and the society of the day, the short answer is that there is none, and that that is precisely the point of it. Schiller asked Wilhelm von Humboldt, rather naively, it may seem, whether he, who had elsewhere shown himself so well aware of his modernity, might have gained the prize for tragedy as a contemporary of Sophocles —which means that this play is very superior pastiche. Yet after the philistine excesses of the domestic drama, only too well rooted in German life, his experiment with 'das grosse gigantische Schicksal' is completely understandable. The spirit in which he wrote is clear from his introduction, one of his best aesthetic essays, in which he makes an eloquent plea for the use of the chorus in tragedy. To judge by his later plans he cannot however have regarded it as essential to the grand style in drama, nor was it accepted as essential by his successors. His handling of this difficult problem in his own play is by common consent quite masterly.

Die Braut von Messina has generally been regarded as 'Die *Ahnfrau der Schuld*', the first of the series of Fate Tragedies which had such a vogue in the Romantic period and included Werner's *Der vierundzwanzigste Februar*, produced by Goethe on 24th February,

1810, Müllner's *Die Schuld*, also produced by him in 1814 and, though here reservations must be made, Grillparzer's *Die Ahnfrau*. L. Bellermann's analysis makes clear what they all have in common with Schiller's play, the oracle-substitute and the confused combination of the notions of fate and moral guilt through a family curse working from generation to generation, but the Romantic Fate Tragedies bring in 'fatal stage-properties', accursed daggers and the like, and a number of motifs in the worst taste which go back rather to the 'castle-spectre' Ritter-dramen and the domestic dramas. They reduce the idea of a 'high nemesis' to crude sensationalism. But as we have seen, Schiller's play cannot be quite absolved from the charge of working on the superstitions of a time when the decay of genuine religion had opened the way to substitute religions of the crudest kind.

Wilhelm Tell

If *Die Braut von Messina* is almost without roots in the culture of Schiller's time and country, *Wilhelm Tell* is a 'Volksstück', a play which immediately made and has continued to make a profound appeal to the mass of the people, and expressed perhaps better than any other German play except *Faust* the native culture of a German-speaking country. Like *Die Jungfrau von Orleans*, it could easily become a symbol, serving to rally national feeling in defence of the Fatherland, and that too has been one source of its lasting popularity. For the same reason it has repeatedly been banned by occupying powers, in Hamburg, for instance, in 1811, or in Koblenz in 1923. Having satisfied his desire for an entirely invented plot, Schiller turned once more to history and legend. Tschudi's sixteenth-century chronicle, his principal source, was supplemented by Johannes von Müller's history, Fäsi's geography of Switzerland and a number of other works, Schiller's own extracts from which show how carefully each telling detail was selected. Schiller drew too on Goethe's memories of Switzerland and was influenced in his conception of the Tell story by Goethe's plans for an epic on the same subject. His play has an epic breadth and atmosphere, and a correspondingly looser dramatic structure than most of its predecessors. It captures the spirit of Switzerland better perhaps than any drama by a Swiss author, or at least it presents it in a form more easily assimilable by a large German audience. A curious feature about the play is that Schiller, whose inspiration was history, seems here to have Goethe's sensitiveness to natural influences, for the actual appearance of the Swiss landscape, of mountains and lakes in sunshine and in storm, with all its living creatures and its peasants, herds, huntsmen and fishermen, who seem to live here closer to nature than their like elsewhere, are an important element in the poetic effect of the play from the first scene. Goethe's *Götz*, we saw, presented the atmosphere of history in a way that seemed magically new. Much the same could be said of the atmosphere of a natural landscape in *Tell*, and nature more than once takes a hand in the action with her sudden storms. It is nature, of course, viewed by Schiller, a 'sentimentalischer Dichter' who, in contemplating nature, never forgets God and man, and it is consciously opposed to the wicked world of man. 'Nature takes a part in the political drama and mysteriously accomplishes the Divine will. The storm forces the tyrant to seek Tell's help and thus to put him on the way to the liberation of his country.'[1]

There is no attempt here to find an equivalent for the destiny of the Greeks. The action of the characters in the play is consciously planned by themselves, though they remember the limitations of humanity and are not easily stirred to revolt even against the intolerable. It is a conservative revolution that is depicted, inspired by the kind of view put forward by Egmont to Alba, the determination of the Swiss to defend their chartered liberties granted by the Emperor. It is contrasted with the French Revolution, for instance, in the verses sent by Schiller with the play to Karl Theodor von Dalberg, in that the Swiss desired no foreign lands and even in anger did not forget their humanity. There is nothing in his play which is inconsistent with *Das Lied von der Glocke*, where violent revolution is deprecated. As an idealised picture of common life it constantly reminds us in its tone of such works as this and Goethe's *Hermann und Dorothea*,

---

[1] B. von Wiese, *op. cit.*, p. 133.

but it drives home the lesson that though there is no freedom without order, the price of freedom is vigilance and readiness if necessary to fight.

As the theme is the throwing off of the Austrian yoke by the three original cantons of the Swiss Confederation the hero is not any individual, but the Swiss people. Following Tschudi, Schiller represents the revolution as due in large measure to the conspiracy of the representatives of the three cantons meeting on the Rütli, as a consequence of intolerable oppression of which Schiller shows us examples in all three. According to the chronicle Tell was one of the conspirators, but Schiller accepts Goethe's suggestion and makes him a rugged individualist of enormous strength, who is not present on the Rütli, though in sympathy with the conspirators. It was not known till later that the Tell story is not history but legend, exactly the same story being told in Denmark for instance in the late twelfth century by Saxo Grammaticus, about a bowman who is said to have lived two centuries earlier. It is also told elsewhere, in Scotland for example about McLeod of Braemar. Accordingly even in Tschudi his part of the story is episodic. The rebellion is not hastened by his assassination of Gessler but is carried out as planned before this. Schiller devotes most of Acts III and IV to the Tell story, after two acts in which Tell appears as a fearless helper of the victims of the Austrian overlords, but which are mainly taken up with a general picture of the plight of the Swiss people and with the Rütli conspiracy. A third element is the action of the Swiss aristocracy, old Attinghausen, the patriarchal baron, who longs to see his countrymen as free as they were before the Austrians came, his nephew and heir Rudenz, who has been won over, rather like Weislingen, by the superior surface culture of the Austrian aristocracy, compared with which Swiss life is provincial, but changes his views with unbelievable haste when he learns that the lady he loves, Bertha von Bruneck, is on the other side. Attinghausen is admirably drawn, but the Bertha-Rudenz episode is generally admitted to be a weak invention, to provide a love interest in the French tradition and to serve to motivate the rapid progress of the general uprising.

In *Tell*, Schiller makes use of well-tried features which he knows to be theatrically effective, he deals discreetly with themes and sentiments which appealed to the middle class and at the same time expresses his own idealism, but this time without excessive demands on the attention or the culture of his audience. The spectacular element is more a matter of scenery and accessories, like the cow-bells which are heard before the curtain rises, than of elaborate costumes, the love-interest is more conventional than ever, but there is an opportunity for idyllic family scenes with children, as in the domestic drama, and picturesque crowd-scenes bringing in all classes of society, as in the histories and plays of chivalry. These serve a clear dramatic purpose however in presenting the main features of the legend, the apple-shooting and the assassination of Gessler. The latter much criticised episode was one which had to come in if Schiller meant to keep to the legend, and anyhow was just what the crowd would want to happen to such an obvious villain as Gessler, an excellent bit of theatre. The strong, silent Tell explains himself perhaps at excessive length, and there are other purple patches, like Melchthal's speech about blindness, which a modern reader would like to tone down, but Schiller never lost his admiration for the 'tirade' and wanted to make his motivation plain to all. Besides political freedom on a basis of inherited rights the play celebrates social unity, proceeding not from equality, but from the due observance of degree in patriarchal conditions, where all can see that they are members one of another and human sympathy binds them together. In extolling the simple life of a peasant people[1] it implies some criticism of aristocratic ways at court, of the jealously guarded game rights and the exploitation of serf labour, for instance, with which the German audience was familiar. The play ends with the proclamation by Rudenz, on gaining Bertha, of the freedom of his serfs. This mild Rousseauism was a common feature of the family plays, e.g. of Iffland's, as we have seen from *Die Hagestolzen* and *Die Jäger*, and clearly reflects the point of view of the solid middle class.

[1] E.g. Tell to Walther in III, 3.

Faust

Goethe's *Faust*, the unique dramatic poem which came to be looked upon in the nineteenth century as the *Divina Commedia* of the modern age, is not nearly so closely associated in our minds either with Weimar classicism or with the public of a particular epoch as the dramas of Schiller discussed above. Its composition extended of course over the greater part of Goethe's life and the range of experience it reflects seems wider than that of any individual. Goethe's thoughts were occupied with the subject, he tells us, in his Strassburg student days, the so-called *Urfaust* was written down before he went to Weimar in 1775, and the final touches were given to the Second Part just two months before his death in 1832. Even the First Part was not written with a stage performance in view. After toying with the thought of one in 1810 Goethe lost interest and it was on the initiative of others that the First Part was at last performed in Weimar in 1829. Though Goethe did not attend the performance he helped in the rehearsals, coaching the Mephistopheles, Laroche, with particular care. His conception of the part was evidently as that of a 'humourously negative, wittily mocking, comically doubting, cunningly watchful spirit'. (Holtei.) Several other theatres attempted *Faust* at about the same time and since then it has been the ambition of almost every producer to put *Faust* worthily on the stage, while the rôles of Mephistopheles and Gretchen have been as great a magnet for actors and actresses as those of Hamlet and Ophelia.

Although *Faust* ranges so widely over the whole range of possible human experience and suggests something fresh to every age and every reader, by revealing new meanings in experiences which are in some measure known to all, there is nevertheless much in it which reminds us of a Germany that has passed away, something that is neither purely subjective nor common to the human experience of all times, but directly representative of the public world of Goethe's own day. It is these features, fitting as they do into the framework of this book, to which our brief discussion will draw attention, together with some of the symbolism which makes this work too, like so many of the dramas already discussed, into an interpretation of world history.

In the completed First Part (1808), there is first of all the 'Prelude on the stage', written in 1797 or soon after, when the Weimar Theatre was in the forefront of Goethe's thoughts. This masterly dialogue between a theatre manager, a theatre poet and the Merry Andrew of the troupe presents the respective points of view of audience, dramatist and actor with a depth of under-standing and a vigour of phrase which to any student of the theatre are an endless delight. For simplicity's sake the troupe is imagined as one of the better touring companies of the second half of the eighteenth century, preparing to play on a stage hastily set up for them in a wooden booth. The audience, which is no longer quite unsophisticated, belongs rather to the end of the century, but the problems discussed are those of the theatre of all time.

The manager's one aim is to fill his theatre by accommodating his entertainment to his public's taste, and the actor's to move a full house to applaud his art, but the poet's ambition is to write a play of lasting value, which will express his individual vision of man and human destiny. The thought of his motley audience puts his inspiration to flight, for like the Goethe of the 'Dedica-tion' to *Faust*, he cannot trust them to applaud the good and he is afraid of being infected by mass emotions. But his colleagues will not listen to him and overwhelm him with advice. The player wants fancy, feeling, sense and humour in his lines, the manager insists on visible action and spectacle. To aim at artistic unity is a waste of time, for no one will perceive it. The audience come with their private interests and passions, desiring nothing but an evening's entertainment. No one will give his whole mind to the play—some will have dined too well, others will be distracted by thoughts of pleasures to follow, and the ladies are there that they may themselves be admired. As these various tastes have no common measure, the audience must be bewildered into acquiescence. The poet's reply is a plea for the humanising, idealising art of the German literary drama, an art in which a sensitive mind integrates experience for others and colours it with the values of the human heart. But the actor sees in this merely an argument for Ifflandian realism and senti-ment and the manager, cutting the discussion short, reminds his colleagues of their immediate task, to entertain the assembled multitude, for the commercial theatre must always live more or less from hand to mouth. The Goethe who despised the public and thought Shakespeare too good a poet to have written for the theatre has virtually explained why the play which follows is not one which will be seen on the stage.

The 'Prologue in Heaven', for all the apparent naïveté of a setting resembling that of a miracle-play, where the Lord holds audience and receives reports from every corner of the universe, is full of that confidence of man in his ability to save himself by his own efforts which we have found to be characteristic of post-Renaissance times and of the eighteenth century in particular. Goethe does not hesitate to make the Lord himself express his confidence that man will make good use of his 'freedom', for in Goethe's view the Divine enters into all creation and even evil ultimately serves God's purposes. The problem of the Book of Job is re-stated in terms which make God seem to justify the ways of man to shame the Devil. But this official philosophy, of the 'good man who in his vague striving is always conscious of the right way' is a late addition to a work which Goethe had begun without much reflection, by feeling himself into the position of a mythical scholar who had revolted impatiently against traditional forms of learning and 'believes, or is willing to believe', as Mr. Santayana puts it,[1] 'that apart from any settled conditions laid down by nature or God, personal will can evoke the experience it covets by its sheer force and assurance', can be its own Provi-dence. It was the inexplicable spontaneity of his own imagination, creating, Prometheus-like, men after his own image (*Prometheus*) which provided the analogy for Goethe between himself and Faust in the old story, and with Thomas Mann we can regard the alliance with the Devil as the poet's self-surrender to the 'genius' within him, the incalculable, morally neutral 'demonic' element of which Goethe was so fully aware. All this is good

---

[1] *Three philosophical poets*, Harvard, 1910, p. 167.

eighteenth-century doctrine, such as we have found more crudely expressed in other Storm and Stress poets. The nature worship of Rousseau and Ossian also comes into Faust's first monologue, as he turns his eyes to the melancholy moon. The longing for a full, adventurous life of the senses is a mood which, as a reaction against a dry intellectualism, would seem natural in any age or place, but it made a peculiarly strong appeal to Germans in the stuffy atmosphere of their little towns where, as it seemed to Mme de Stael, 'time fell drop by drop', and it made of *Faust* the supreme expression of the second Renaissance which, as Mr. Santayana says, was taking place in Goethe's time in the souls of men.

But the 'little world' of the First Part is still more obviously observed reality. We see the townspeople in holiday mood on Easter Day, pouring out of the narrow alleys of an old town like Frankfort through one of the gates in its wall into the sunlit country beyond, climbing the hills, rowing on the river or walk-ing out in twos and threes to the villages near by. Through Faust's eyes we see the spring landscape and the joyful response of young and old to the season when nature seems reborn. From the empty-headed young apprentices and servant girls to the philis-tines who so love to talk of the wars away in Turkey, while they sip their wine in safety and watch the gay barges gliding down the stream, even the minor characters are distinctively German and of the pre-industrial age, just as the students in Auerbach's Cellar, with their song about the dear old Holy Roman Empire that can hardly hold together, are of the First Reich which came to an end in 1806. The whole Gretchen tragedy, finally, is so German that the heroine herself has become the accepted type of the German maiden. While avoiding the naturalistic parti-cularity of the *Kindermörderin* Goethe has unobtrusively introduced concrete contemporary detail in abundance and immortalised a particular phase of middle-class German life in the small towns of the catholic west and south. Most of it would apply equally well to the slow-moving centuries from the days of the historical Faust or earlier, but in less than a century after the play's appear-ance it was a picture of a vanished time, with its peaceful walled towns, its spinning wheels and its naive piety. Mr. Santayana has suggested that without the poetry of Christianity which surrounds her, Gretchen would be frankly vulgar. Perhaps it would be truer to say that Goethe has conveyed the impression of a community with a genuine popular culture rooted in religion, 'an organised way of life, based on a common tradition, and conditioned by a common environment' (Christopher Dawson) which he did not invent but found before his eyes, and that this feeling of a solid world beneath and behind the figures gives some of their Shakespearian quality to these magni/ ficent scenes. But what is still more important is of course the convincing presentation of varied individual characters in their complex relations, the range of emotions expressed in the love/ scenes, the lyrical monologues of Gretchen, the satirical comedy round Martha and Mephistopheles and the tragic closing scene in the prison.

In the Gretchen tragedy Faust himself plays a far from admirable part, and it is important to remember that it was written by the Storm and Stress author of *Werther*, who freed himself from obsessions by confessing them in poetry, at a time when he felt himself to be something of a Faust, but published as a fragment only after a long interval (in 1790) when, as Burdach says, he had ceased to be Faust and was anxious to put these juvenilia behind him. 'He rounded it off, under pressure from Schiller, to a First Part, at a time when he saw in the "barbarous" work of his youth only "wavering figures", the product of a "clouded mind", even of "illusion", and he completed it in a Second Part only by throwing a veil of symbolism round the individual experience contained in it.'[1] It is not therefore the picture of an ideal man, but 'the tragic story of an erring life, which he carried on from Storm and Stress enslavement to passion to a stage of clearer vision and saner aims, and finally to a change of heart'. The artistic unity of the completed drama has to be sought for, it does not leap to the eye. The disillusionment with book/learning and the self/abandonment to sexual passion (an episode dispropor/ tionately swollen out) of the First Part are followed by miscel/ laneous experiences at the Emperor's Court, in which Goethe's

[1] 'Das religiöse Problem in Goethes *Faust*', *Euphorion*, Goethefestheft I, 1932.

intimate knowledge of the ruling class at work and play finds veiled expression. These scenes lead up, by way of the oppressively learned Classical Walpurgis Night, to the third act, depicting the union of Faust and Helen, of northern vitality with Greek ideals of beauty. The broad lines of the symbolism here are unmistakable when we remember how much Goethe and his contemporaries, not to speak of Europe generally since the Renaissance, had owed to the culture of Greece. That those born of this revived European culture remained wilful and 'demonic', unmindful of human limitations, is symbolised by the fall to death of Euphorion, a second Icarus bearing the features of Byron, 'the greatest genius of the century'. The pursuit of beauty was also just an episode. Faust had to return to the world of action, inspired and refreshed by his vision, just as in Schiller's *Das Ideal und das Leben* man is reminded that imagined harmonies, though an indispensable solace, cannot save him from the struggle of existence. The garments of Helen bear Faust through the sky above the common world to the last temptation put in his way by Mephistopheles, for all this time the spirit of evil has been trying to content him, or at least to tire him out, with a kaleidoscopic whirl of experiences.

After further satire directed against the Emperor, representing the great and lesser rulers of the West, their folly in war and peace, their attempts to enjoy and to rule at the same time, instead of 'finding their happiness in commanding' like Frederick the Great and Napoleon, we see Faust engaged, in the last act, as a typical Westerner of modern times, in establishing control over nature, symbolised by the reclamation of land from the sea. Still the magic of Mephistopheles is his tool, and the Three Mighty Men bring in for him rich prizes from foreign trade, war and piracy, which they speak of as an indissoluble trinity—a thrust at Europe's economic development by ruthless state-aided capitalistic methods, just as the magic enrichment of the Emperor in Act I by the issue of paper money had satirised the recent rapid expansion of credit. Faust realises at last the suffering which his lust for power may bring to others when he sees its results close at hand, in the treatment of Philemon and Baucis, who stand for an older equivalent of 'displaced persons'. Now comes the 'change of heart', the rejection of magic when all the experiences it has brought him in life at its intensest pitch, in physical love, in aestheticism and in the pursuit of power, are seen by Faust, but only when death is in sight, to have led him nowhere, and he wishes to be merely a man again. He is not spared by Care now, who leaves him blind, but he foresees the possibility of contentment for himself and for man, not in any form of excitement or enjoyment, but in work in a free community for the common good, winning his life and freedom every day anew. Finally, lest we should take him for an advocate of a kind of socialism for which a particular earthly community is a satisfying object of devotion, Goethe, a mystic now in some degree, like all old men, introduces a 'Dantesque' close, in a scene in Heaven forming a pendant to the initial Prologue. Using Christian symbolism freely adapted to his purpose he hints darkly at the possibility of a life beyond this, at the necessity, for man's salvation, of grace from above, and at the insufficiency of humanism as an ideal, except in so far as it realises eternal values.

THEATRE, DRAMA AND PUBLIC AT THE DEATH OF SCHILLER

IN the development which we have been tracing the death of Schiller makes a good halting-place, for both drama and the art of the theatre had, in Weimar during his last years, reached the highest level yet attained in Germany, a level deemed so high by succeeding generations that the eleven years of close friendship and co-operation between Goethe and Schiller have come to be considered the heart of the classical period of German literature and of the drama in particular. They are classical in the sense that in many respects an accepted model had been established which became of particular importance in the great development of education which was to follow. If we ask ourselves now what the outstanding achievements of the eighteenth century had been in the whole field of culture which we have been studying, and what features were to prove relatively permanent, it is less easy to answer the question with regard to the drama than with regard to the theatre, as an institution with a material embodiment and a form of organisation which can be described without great difficulty.

A fact beyond dispute is that in the course of the century a German theatre worthy of the name had at last been established. At the beginning of the century special buildings had existed in the larger court towns where Italian opera in particular was performed at certain seasons by Italian companies engaged for the purpose, but German plays, or at least, plays in German, were only acted by a few touring companies in halls, barns or wooden booths temporarily adapted to their ends. The repertoire and performances of these troupes were on a low level of taste and culture, though they might afford excellent entertainment, and the actors themselves were looked upon as vagrants beyond the pale. Their managers borrowed freely from any higher forms of drama and theatre known to them, and there was not such a gulf between them and the worthy citizens and courtiers who despised them socially, that they could not, on occasion, give pleasure to audiences of some standing and education, but ordinarily they played to the common people. It was only when respected writers like König and Gottsched persuaded some companies to try their luck with plays of literary merit that the theatre came to be looked upon by the average citizen as something better than a circus. As Germany had as yet hardly any actable plays which were also literature and no native dramatic tradition had been able to establish itself, a beginning had to be made with translated plays. We have seen how the alliance between literature and the theatre gradually became closer, in spite of the risks which any troupe had to run which offered its audience something too literary to be enter-taining to the majority. Managers were not always well advised by their educated patrons and the supply of good yet stageworthy plays was for long very scanty. The repertoires of even the best companies remained very mixed, for they were constantly in financial difficulties.

Prospects only began to improve for them and for the literary drama with the establishment of the first 'national' theatres, repertory theatres freed to some extent from the tyranny of the box-office by the generosity of a group of patrons or a ruling prince, after the manner of the French state theatre. We have seen how from the 'seventies a series of such theatres came into being, for the most part in the capitals of Germany's innumerable states, where there was a well-established tradition of state patronage for the arts. The main motive behind the movement was the desire for at least cultural unity in the much-divided German Reich, through a theatre reflecting middle-class manners and speaking to the whole people in the German literary language which had gradually been built up since Luther's time. In both respects the National Theatre was the antithesis of the Court Theatre of the old stamp, though the courts, especially the smaller ones, played such a big part in its establishment. It is significant, as we have noticed, that the nearest German equivalent to 'the King's English' is now 'the language of the stage'. The unity achieved culturally was to pave the way for political unity in the following century.

It was natural in Germany's little absolute states that control should be exercised from above, especially when the power of the stage over public opinion came to be rated so high as it was by the Enlightenment. By the end of the century theatres were coming to be looked upon as cultural institutions comparable with picture galleries, conservatoires of music and academies of science. The great development of state and municipal theatres all over German-speaking lands in the nineteenth century was merely an extension of this movement. The theatres were numerous because in the old days the political and, therefore, the cultural centres had been so numerous, and there was much rivalry between them all. German political disunity had in this way the beneficial effect of producing a more widely diffused appreciation of the more expensive forms of art, like grand opera, than was possible in England, and that in itself tended to give music, for instance, a far more prominent place in the life of the people. State theatres encouraged non-commercial forms of dramatic art and experiments in production, for theatres continued to be as individual in character as their producers, but Schröder had proved, as we have seen, that given favourable conditions a commercial theatre under a talented manager could do at least as much to raise artistic standards as a small state theatre under a Goethe. State theatres, moreover, inevitably reflected to some extent the policy of the state. In France before the Revolution and in Germany after it they tended towards an anxious conservatism in anything which might affect the loyalty of the subject. We have found evidence of a strict censorship even in Weimar. It was far stricter in Vienna, where nothing that might seem in the least prejudicial to the state, the nobility, the army or the church was passed for performance.[1] One effect was the very late appearance of most of the German classical

[1] See H. H. Houben, *Hier Zensur, wer dort*, 2nd ed., Leipzig, 1918.

dramas at the Burgtheater, or their serious mutilation. Grill-parzer's struggle with the censorship, it is well known, produced in him a feeling of frustration fatal to his work. In the present century we have seen the whole character of the German theatre changed under successive forms of government. There is a continuity in all this which reminds us that all the forms of a nation's life are interconnected, and that a theatre supported by the state is not in every respect superior to one dependent on a fickle public.

From the actor's point of view the new system had of course many advantages. He was more secure, he was relieved from the discomforts of a wandering life and the status of his profession was raised in society, the more it came to cater for an educated public and was recognised by the government. The actor became in many places a civil servant with pension rights, so that Ekhof's dreams became a reality. Long before this German actors had come to be invested with a certain glamour for many among their audiences through the dignity of the parts they now acted on the stage, and when the domestic drama became the vogue, with heroes who oozed unction, enthusiastic young play-goers came to think in all seriousness that 'a comedian could give lessons to a parson'. But old prejudices died hard among their seniors, while many actors and actresses, the more talented, in Goethe's view, were still not models of respectability in their private lives in spite of the Ekhofs, the Schröders and the Ifflands. Even in Weimar, though Goethe asked members of the troupe to his house and some of his friends imitated him, actors and actresses, apart from a few stars, were merely tolerated in educated society and not looked upon by worthy citizens as their equals. Their social position was lower than this in most German towns, and only higher in two or three capitals like Vienna and Berlin, where many were lionised. Those at the top of the profession, like Schröder and Iffland, had their villas like any rich merchant and enjoyed the same sort of consideration as Garrick in London. Sons of professional men quite often made the stage their career and the general level of education and culture was much higher than in the days of Frau Neuber, though her company had already included several men who had been at a university.

Whether standing theatres had produced better actors than the touring companies is at least an open question. We have seen that Goethe considered too much security a bad thing for a manager. A. W. Schlegel, in Romantic times, says much the same about the rank and file. He calls the national theatres refuges for soured personalities and people who had neglected their talents through idleness. 'An actor needs a certain light-hearted enthusiasm for art and grows rusty in settled conditions. As soon as it becomes his first thought how to secure for himself and his wife and children a decent living it is all over with his progress.'[1] It seems, to judge by the ease with which untrained young people still obtained posts, that the supply of good actors was hardly equal to the increased demand, and according to Martersteig there was a considerable tail to most companies, as was very obvious in historical plays and Shakespeare.

The higher esteem enjoyed by the theatre and those who served it depended too on a more general factor, a change in the ways of thinking and feeling habitual first among the educated, and then among the bulk of the middle class. At the bottom of it is the weakening in the hold of dogmatic religion over men's minds and the secularisation of much of its content. More and more, as the century advanced, came to see in scholarship and art a substitute for religion. From the time of Gottsched the educated began to look to an improved theatre for assistance in the task which the 'moral weeklies' were performing, of carrying enlighten-ment and 'humanity' to wider and wider circles. They countered in this way the opposition of the orthodox to the theatre, and succeeded so well that family drama and sentimental comedies came to be regarded as the equivalent of sermons, and the stage as a secular temple. A parallel movement had much to do with the spread of the 'drame' in France, but though the same belief in the innate goodness of man and confidence in his creative powers were behind both, German Rationalism was here, as usual, ethical and philosophical where French was political and social. Theorists like Sulzer (1771) and the young Schiller

---

[1] E. Gross, *Die ältere Romantik und das Theater*, Hamburg and Leipzig, 1910, p. 109.

accordingly praised the theatre as the best means of raising public standards of morality, and even the drama of the German classics is a philosophical drama concerned with man's chiefest end.

Men of the theatre like Iffland and Kotzebue contrived to combine uplift, or what sounded like it to a sentimental age, with theatrical entertainment, but serious writers tended to neglect the requirements of the stage. Critics as different as Lukács and Gundolf agree that there was a conflict between the desire for ideas and the tradition that the theatre should merely entertain. According to Lukács bourgeois drama, *the* modern drama, gradually adapted an existing theatre to the requirements of a rising social class. It was didactic and tendentious, consciously preparing the way for a middle-class, democratic revolution. If so, it is surprising how few plays were considered dangerous by the courts who were the chief patrons of the new standing theatres. It seems nearer the truth to regard this drama, and literature generally at that time, as a safety-valve for unpractical dreamers. But Gundolf agrees as to the clash between the two elements. 'The alliance of theatre and literature has always had something forced and artificial about it, and the dramas we rate highest are good not because they were written for the theatre, but in spite of that fact. None of the plays of our greatest writers fit the frame provided by the stage. They either project beyond it or do not fill it completely. Our drama did not create its theatre, nor our stage its drama, but the two reached a compromise, defended on all kinds of non-dramatic and non-literary grounds, a compromise which goes back in the last resort to Gottsched, who forced stage and literature together again with the typical rationalist's lust for domination.'[1]

Gundolf however seems to speak as one who is out of sympathy with the whole attempt to close the gap between the stage and literature. In itself the attempt at a synthesis was surely justified, and Lessing and Schiller at least attained a large measure of success. Having no native tradition behind them, but being acquainted with an ever increasing number of foreign models,

[1] *Shakespeare und der deutsche Geist*, 2nd ed., Berlin, 1914, p. 156.

German dramatists encountered the greatest difficulties in their search for a style which should make a distinctive German contribution comparable in value with Greek, French or English drama. A period of frenchified plays was followed by one under English influence, and many writers had always one eye on the Greeks, especially in the last twenty years of the century. Here again, purely aesthetic motives were hardly ever decisive in the establishment of types of play which could pass the test of public performance. The audience had always to be taken into account. Even Gottschedian tragedy, though it proved in general a failure because of the difference between the Parisian audience for which its models were written and the German audiences which yawned at the imitation, expressed some of the ideals and emotions of the thoughtful middle class, their stoic self-sufficiency for instance, and their belief in reason and culture as moral forces, while attracting still more through its social prestige.

With the emergence of sentimental comedy, and still more when Lessing had introduced domestic tragedy, the influence of the audience was clear for all to see, and both content and form of the drama ran parallel in their development to the values and intellectual assumptions of the group or groups for whom the author was primarily writing. While pure theatre survived in the catholic south, untouched by the general spread of intellectual culture characteristic of the north, the plays of the Leipzig school of Lessing and his imitators, those of Storm and Stress, the popular drama of the 'eighties and 'nineties and finally the work of Goethe and Schiller, especially the latter, all reflect, of course in varying degrees in different authors and works, the mind and heart of various sections of the middle class. Outstanding literary dramas like *Nathan der Weise, Iphigenie* or *Faust*, being aimed at an ideal audience, could be appreciated at first only by a small minority and did not find their way on to the stage. Even in plays of high literary merit like those of Schiller, if they were popular, there was always a non-literary source of appeal. The truth of this is particularly obvious from the reactions of early nineteenth-century audiences to Iffland's efforts to introduce the Weimar repertoire when he became manager of the Berlin

National Theatre, reactions which show a marked continuity with those we have traced above and at the same time point to the future.

According to Rudolf Weil's analysis of the taste of the Berlin public,[1] German opera was very popular, as in Weimar and elsewhere, not so much for musical reasons as because of its fantastic, burlesque or spectacular elements. *The Magic Flute* and its descendents had this in common with grand opera at court a hundred years earlier. Sentimental comedy was losing its appeal for the educated before the end of the eighteenth century, and for the mass of the public from the early years of the nineteenth, when it was outstripped by Schiller's mature plays. But what the average play-goer appreciated in Schiller was anything sentimental or spectacular, not the heroic and tragic features. Iffland produced Schiller with a lavishness hitherto reserved for grand opera. The coronation procession in *Die Jungfrau von Orleans*, for instance, was the talk of the town, but the verse was seldom well spoken by his actors. His leading lady, Friederike Unzelmann, had her part as Maria Stuart written out in prose in order to get the hang of it, and Iffland himself destroyed the rhythm by interjections and repeated words. *Iphigenie* and *Tasso* naturally made little appeal in Berlin in spite of all Iffland's efforts, for they could not be turned into a riot of sentiment and spectacle. Even *Hamlet* and *King Lear* in Schlegel's new translation were not popular when they first appeared, and the management had to return to Schröder's old adapted versions.

Iffland soon discovered too that he had to satisfy not one public but several in the same theatre, and he tried to please them all in turn. He gave the masses primitive fare, served up everyday realism and homely sentiment to the clerks and tradesmen, and appealed to the aristocracy's love of elegance and refined sensuality. For a time a revival of French tragedy in new translations had considerable success, partly because the court liked them, as it did in Weimar, and partly perhaps because Schiller had given the public a taste for rhetoric. His audience was of one mind only when the performance made a patriotic appeal,

[1] *Das Berliner Theaterpublikum unter A. W. Ifflands Direktion*, Berlin, 1932.

like that of *Die Jungfrau* in 1806, the year of Jena, or of *Wallen-steins Lager* in 1805 or 1813, when all had friends and relatives in the field. Exactly the same happened in Weimar, but there the nucleus of a public with artistic taste did exist, whereas in Berlin there were such differences between the various sections in social background and education that as an English traveller wrote even in 1842: 'You see the travelling strangers and the young people of the middle class when any celebrated actor or play appears, and on opera nights the upper classes, but the real people . . . you never see.'[1] Similarly Eichendorff asserted that the gap between the educated and the masses was still too great for Germany to possess a national drama.

We must allow for some Romantic prejudice in Eichendorff, but on the whole his statement is true. Nevertheless, considering the social and political as well as the purely aesthetic difficulties in his way, it must be admitted that Schiller came very near to the desired goal. John Russell tells us that in the early 'twenties when a tragedy of Schiller was to be performed, he never found an empty theatre in any corner of Germany. On such occasions, moreover, the theatre was not crowded with the usual regular play-going loungers. The audience consisted chiefly of respect-able citizens, who felt much more truly what nature and passion were than the ribboned aristocracy of Berlin or Vienna.[2] Grill-parzer sums up Schiller's claims to greatness well in these words: 'Goethe may be a greater poet, and probably is. But Schiller is a greater possession of the nation, which needs strong, inspiring impressions, something to move the heart in a time that suffers from a misuse of brain. He did not come down to the level of the people. He placed himself on a level where it is possible for the people to come up to him, and the amplitude of expression which some criticise in him is in fact the bridge by which travellers from all grades of culture can reach his heights.'[3] Schiller held his public partly by spectacle and sentiment, but he put before them in an assimilable form the best thought of his age and brought them under its spell.

[1] S. Laing, *Notes of a traveller*, London, 1842, p. 270.
[2] *A tour in Germany*, Edinburgh, 1828, I, p. 55.
[3] Entwurf eines Briefes an den Schillerverein in Leipzig, 1855.

As to Schiller's influence on later German drama, it was simply overwhelming. Grillparzer says that if he did not think Schiller a great poet, he would have to consider himself no poet at all, for he has always followed in his footsteps. Grillparzer of course was an Austrian. The German Romantics were no friends of Schiller and tried to play off Goethe against him. As the stage found their extravagances unusable, they poured scorn on those who dreamt of a union between the theatre and literature and repre/ sented the theatre public in Berlin, for instance, as composed entirely of philistines. Until Zacharias Werner made his great hit with *Der vierundzwanzigste Februar* and started the vogue of the 'fate drama', almost all their many plays were book/dramas and gloried in being so. Goethe took the work of the one dramatic genius among them, Kleist, for the same kind of thing. But within a few years of his death Schiller was being quite obviously imitated by a series of verse dramatists, much of whose work found its way on to the stage, except during the years before 1848, when 'Young Germany' was everywhere to the fore. After the year of revolutions the conservative strain was heard again until naturalism began to prevail in the late 'eighties.

The usual recipe in the earlier period was Schiller with a dash of Romanticism. The type is described as follows by Robert F. Arnold. 'Subject—historical, with a marked preference for Germany in the Middle Ages, usually the Hohenstaufen period. Hero—very heroic, and in tragedy, unmistakably guilty, his fate being determined by his character and not by destiny alone. His character is usually free from complications, transparent, with no hidden depths. The noble and the belle passion both in evidence, often after the unfortunate Bertha/Rudenz model. Stirring and sententious blank verse. Monologues, declamatory narration, *vaticinationes ex eventu*, crowd scenes. Analytic, stageworthy construction. Few come anywhere near the master in their grasp of historical movements, their philosophy of life or distinction of personality. The less there is in them, the more slavishly they follow in his footsteps, and certain combinations occur time and again, such as Karlos and Philip, Mary and Elizabeth, character/groups like that in the *Jungfrau,* the reports of the Swedish captain and Raoul, the exposition of Tell, the death of Attinghausen.'[1]

The dramatists with genuine talent, like Kleist, Grillparzer, Hebbel, could neither wholly accept the Schiller model nor wholly escape its influence. They found themselves still in the same difficulty as Schiller himself. 'The Germans think,' wrote Grillparzer, 'that knowing (Wissen) is all that is necessary. But art is a matter of knowing how (Können).'[2] German writers do not dare to be themselves. They all think they should aim higher than that.[3] They overload their works with philosophy therefore, and their critics, who know all the models, are always demanding that they should excel Sophocles and Shakespeare and Calderon.[4] The Germans in general have more thoughts than will and are always longing for something, they know not what. Every ten years they apply a new irritant plaster and they will go on doing so until they have acquired some external practi/ cal interest, like the English, who have remained freest from that romantic longing, just because they have practical interests.[5]

There is a note of embitterment in many of Grillparzer's criticisms which warns us to treat them with caution, but they are often extremely acute. The last passage quoted raises the question of the relation between the pursuit of intellectual culture and political and social action, a question on which Thomas Mann, for instance, has seen reason to change the views he expressed in 1918 in the *Betrachtungen eines Unpolitischen*, where he proclaimed himself completely unpolitical, content to leave all decisions to the authorities, the experts, in the traditional manner of the German Bürger, if he could be left in peace to cultivate his own soul. In *Culture and Politics* (1939), he wrote: 'The absence of political experience on the part of the cultivated German Bürger and his contemptuous attitude towards democracy, his scorn of freedom—which to him was nothing but libertarian cant—all this resulted in nothing less than the enslave/ ment of the citizen to the state and to power/politics.[6]

[1] *Das deutsche Drama*, p. 562.
[2] *Sämtliche Werke*, ed. Sauer, 5th ed., XVI, p. 73.   [3] *Ibid.*
[4] *Op. cit.*, XV, pp. 79 ff.   [5] *Op. cit.*, XVI, p. 36.
[6] See my article 'British and German ideas of freedom', *German Life and Letters*, No. 2, 1948.

The emphasis laid in Goethe's day on the pursuit of the things of the mind, it will be seen, brought with it the danger of escapism. The more active natures, the leading liberals of 1848, for example, would have agreed with Ranke in seeing in German literature 'one of the most essential factors making for German unity; through it we became conscious again of belonging together. . . . No single German would be what he is without it.' But it had done little or nothing to reduce the distance between social classes, and it had led the more passive members of the community to live, as Laing puts it, in two worlds, a world of idea and a world of reality. After the passage already quoted, about 'the real people' in the theatre, we read: 'If this lower class ever come to the theatre at all, they sit as quiet as mice in the little hole allotted to them. A German theatre is a true picture of the social state of Germany—princes and functionaries occupying the front boxes—the educated and middle classes looking up to them from the pit below, in breathless awe and admiration, and the people out of sight and hearing of these two masses of the audience.'

Germany in 1842, Laing tells us, was reckoned to have 65 theatres, employing a staff of some 5000 actors, singers and musicians. As 'in all countries which have no civil liberty, no freedom of action independent of government, and no free discussion of public affairs' it was counted 'a great educational and social influence, a power not to be entrusted out of the hands of the state'. The result was that 'the fictitious incidents of the drama superseded the real incidents and interests of life'. In the cult of the theatre Laing saw one more instance of the division of life into two distinct existences. 'All evaporates in speculation. Books, theories and principles are published and read, and there the matter rests. A new set of books, theories and principles are published, and overwhelm the first, but all this never goes beyond the world of ideas. . . . Energy of mind and vigour of action in the real affairs of ordinary life are diluted and weakened by this life of dreamy speculation. . . . The literature, scholarship, and wide diffusion of the imaginative faculty in Germany are in this view actually detrimental to the social development of the German people, to their industry, material interests, and activity in ordinary affairs of a mechanical kind, and to their energy and interest in claiming and exercising civil liberty or free-agency in real life.'[1]

But the words of this hard-headed Scot hardly strike the right note for the conclusion of this history. There was in truth a dangerous dichotomy in the life of the German people, the consequences of which were to reveal themselves more and more clearly as the century wore on. The attitude of the Germans towards culture, Troeltsch points out, was the necessary complement to their attitude to the state, just as the rich development of personal religion had earlier made tolerable the subordination of the individual to a highly organised church. Conditions in the little despotic states had turned men in upon themselves. They sought in what Schiller called 'das Ideal', the realm of thought and imagination, a compensation for the shortcomings of 'das Leben', the real life about them. The inner freedom thus acquired was the only kind they valued. With this opportunity for a personal life they could accept Hegelian ideas about merging their identity in the State as their real self, glorifying in its freedom, that is, its power, and considering their own, in this sphere, to consist of duties rather than of rights.[2]

It is obvious how easily such notions, themselves ultimately religious in origin, could degenerate into the quietistic repudiation of any responsibility for political decisions, especially in a middle class which had for centuries seldom been granted or even desired such responsibilities. These considerations are of the greatest importance for the understanding of the German conception of politics, both then and now. It was as clearly marked in Goethe, for whom politics and 'Geist' were mutually exclusive, and 'public affairs had no interest', as in the Thomas Mann of the *Betrachtungen eines Unpolitischen*.[3] But we should also remember the other side of the picture, the neglect of 'Geist', according to Matthew Arnold's writings in mid-century, in this country. It seemed to him that his countrymen, for the most part, were only too much concerned with the practical, with money-making and

---

[1] *Notes to a Traveller*, p. 266.   [2] *Deutsche Zukunft*, 1916.
[3] See W. Mommsen, *Die politischen Anschauungen Goethes*, Stuttgart, 1949.

politics. He saw them as either aristocratic 'Barbarians' or middle-class 'Philistines', hardly aware of the things of the mind. Arnold borrowed the term 'philistine' from the German Romantics, and the idea of culture chiefly from Goethe, pointing back to the same supreme models of true humanity, the Greeks. But it takes all kinds of men to make a balanced world, and from the present distance in time we can begin to see the Germans and the English of that time as complementary to each other in their one-sidedness. The 'dreamy speculation' of the former made for the enrichment of the spiritual life, not only of Germany but of the world, as the great influence of German literature, philosophy and scholarship on Victorian England itself indicates,[1] music and the drama gained treasures for all time and the art of the theatre was stimulated by new ideas of organisation and production. Viewed from this angle, Germany is not *Hamlet* or *Wallenstein*, but *Tasso*. Her one-sidedness and its later tragic 'Selbstkorrektur' is the price she had to pay for her fertility in works of genius, the character of which, as Schopenhauer says, is to be useless—or, in less romantic language, exempt, as the product of free creative minds, from any necessity of serving immediate practical purposes or being relevant to social or political needs. 'That is their patent of nobility. All other works of man are there for the maintenance or easing of our existence, but these are there for their own sake, and seem to us, in this sense, to be the fine flower, the ultimate yield of human life.'

[1] See W. F. Schirmer, *Der Einfluss der deutschen Literatur auf die englische im 19. Jahrhundert*, 1947.

APPENDIX

The Weimar repertoire in the opening months of 1803, from C. A. H. Burkhardt, *Das Repertoire des Weimarischen Theaters unter Goethes Leitung.*

(The titles of plays of literary interest are printed in SMALL CAPITALS, those of musical plays in *italics* and those of light entertainments in roman type. When a play is repeated, the author's name is not given.)

January 1   WALLENSTEINS LAGER (Schiller), followed by music, and PALÄOPHRON UND NEOTERPE (Goethe).

       3   *Die Müllerin* (Paisiello).

       5   IPHIGENIE AUF TAURIS (Goethe).

       8   Die zwei Figaro (Jünger).

     10   Die Versöhnung (Kotzebue).

     12   Der argwöhnische Liebhaber (Bretzner).

     15   *Don Giovanni* (Mozart).

     17   Die Aussteuer (Iffland).

     19   Die zwei Figaro.

     22   CLAVIGO (Goethe).

     24   Herr von Hopfenkeim (v. Reinbeck after Molière).

     26   *Soliman der Zweite* (Favart).

February 1   *Soliman der Zweite.*

       2   Die Hagestolzen (Iffland).

       5   Der Hausverkauf (Herzfeld).

          Die Zaubertrompete (ballet, by Morelli).

       7   WALLENSTEINS LAGER.

          Die Zaubertrompete.

       9   Der Hausfriede (Iffland).

     12   NATHAN DER WEISE (Lessing).

     14   Armut und Edelsinn (Kotzebue).

     16   Die Verwandtschaften (Kotzebue).

     19   DIE MOHRIN (Terence-Einsiedel).

          Die Zaubertrompete.

     21   Der Wirrwarr (Kotzebue).

     23   Der Jurist und der Bauer (Rautenstrauch).

          Die Zaubertrompete.

     26   *Das unterbrochene Opferfest* (Winter).

     28   Der Taubstumme (Kotzebue, from the French).

March 2   Das Vaterhaus (Iffland).

       5   *Die Saalnixe* ('Volksmärchen' with songs, by Kauer).

       7   DIE MOHRIN.

          Adolph und Clara (d'Allayrac).

       9   TURANDOT (Schiller after Gozzi).

     12   *Das Kästchen mit der Chiffre* (Salieri).

     14   Offene Fehde (Huber).

March	16	Die beiden Billets (Wall).
		Der Dorfbarbier (Weidmann and Schenk).
	19	DIE.BRAUT VON MESSINA (Schiller).
	21	DIE MOHRIN.
		Die glückliche Zurückkunft (ballet, by Morelli).
	23	Der schwarze Mann (Gotter).
		Die glückliche Zurückkunft.
	26	DIE BRAUT VON MESSINA.
	28	Die Versuchung (Meyer, from the French).
		Es ist die Rechte nicht (Rochlitz).
	30	Die Schachmaschine (Beck).
April	2	DIE NATÜRLICHE TOCHTER (Goethe).
	11	*Das unterbrochene Opferfest.*
	12	Alte und neue Zeit (Iffland).
	16	DIE NATÜRLICHE TOCHTER.
	18	Das Mädchen von Marienburg (Kratter).
	20	*Cosa Rara* (Martini).
	23	DIE JUNGFRAU VON ORLEANS (Schiller).
	25	CLAVIGO.
	27	*Die Müllerin.*
	30	DIE JUNGFRAU VON ORLEANS.
May	2	Die Jäger (Iffland).
	4	Cervantes' Porträt (F. L. Schmidt, after Picard).
	7	DIE JUNGFRAU VON ORLEANS.
	9	Der Herbsttag (Iffland).
	11	Scherz und Ernst (Stoll).
		WALLENSTEINS LAGER.
	14	DIE RAÜBER (Schiller).
	16	Cervantes' Porträt.
	18	DER NEFFE ALS ONKEL (Schiller, after Picard).
	21	DIE BRAUT VON MESSINA.
	23	DER NEFFE ALS ONKEL.
	25	Scherz und Ernst.
		Der Dorfbarbier.
	28	MARIA STUART (Schiller).
	30	DIE JUNGFRAU VON ORLEANS.
June	1	Cervantes' Porträt.
		Scherz und Ernst.
	4	*Iphigenia in Tauris* (Gluck).
	6	DIE FREMDE AUS ANDROS (Terence–Einsiedel).

(A season in Lauchstädt, from 11th June to 11th August, and one in Rudolstadt, from 16th August to 10th September, followed, with similar repertoires, and the company returned to Weimar for the winter season, opening on 17th September.)

SELECT BIBLIOGRAPHY

LIST OF CONTRACTIONS

The following contractions have been used:
D.N.L.—Kürschners Deutsche Nationalliteratur (followed by number of volume in the series).
D.L.—Deutsche Literatur, Sammlung literarischer Kunst- und Kulturdenk-mäler in Entwicklungsreihen.
S.G.T.G.—Schriften der Gesellschaft für Theatergeschichte.
T.F.—Theatralische Forschungen.

GENERAL WORKS

(a) History of literature

K. Goedeke, *Grundriss zur Geschichte der deutschen Dichtung*, III and IV.
Reallexikon der deutschen Literaturgeschichte, ed. P. Merker and W. Stammler, 4 vols. (Berlin, 1925–31.)
H. Hettner, *Geschichte der deutschen Literatur im 18. Jahrhundert*, 7. Auflage, mit einem bibliographischen Anhang herausgegeben von E. A. Boucke, 4 vols. (Braunschweig, 1926.)
In 'Epochen der Literatur', ed. Julius Petersen:
Vol. II, P. Hankamer, *Deutsche Gegenreformation und deutsches Barock*. (Stuttgart, 1935.) Vol. III, F. J. Schneider, *Die deutsche Dichtung zwischen Barock und Klassizismus, 1700–1785*. (Stuttgart, 1924.) Vol. IV, F. Schultz, *Klassik und Romantik der Deutschen, I*. (Stuttgart, 1935.)
Kuno Francke, *Die Kulturwerte der deutschen Literatur*, Vol. II, 'Von der Reforma-tion bis zur Aufklärung'. (Berlin, 1923.)
E. Franz, *Deutsche Klassik und Reformation*. (Halle, 1937.)
F. Gundolf, *Shakespeare und der deutsche Geist*, 2. Auflage. (Berlin, 1914.)
A. Köster, *Die deutsche Literatur der Aufklärungszeit*. (Heidelberg, 1925.)
L. M. Price, *English-German literary influences*. (Berkeley, 1919.)
M. B. and L. M. Price, *The publication of English literature in Germany in the eighteenth century*. (Berkeley, 1934.)

(b) History of drama

R. F. Arnold (with five collaborators), *Das deutsche Drama*. (München, 1925.)
H. Bulthaupt, *Dramaturgie des Schauspiels, I*, 13. Auflage. (Oldenburg and Leipzig, 1912.)
K. Holl, *Geschichte des deutschen Lustspiels*. (Leipzig, 1923.)
A. Nicoll, *A history of early eighteenth-century drama (1700–1750)*. (Cambridge, 1925.)
A. Nicoll, *A history of late eighteenth-century drama (1750–1800)*. (Cambridge, 1927.)
A. Nicoll, *British drama*. (London, 1925.)

(c) Theatrical history

H. Calm, *Kulturbilder aus der deutschen Theatergeschichte.* (Leipzig, 1925.)

E. Devrient, *Geschichte der deutschen Schauspielkunst,* ed. W. Stuhlfeld. (Berlin and Zürich, 1929.)

A. Eloesser, *Aus der grossen Zeit des deutschen Theaters, Schauspieler-Memoiren.* (München, 1911.)

L. Fernbach, *Der wohl unterrichtete Theaterfreund.* (Berlin, 1830.)

H. Kindermann, *Theatergeschichte der Goethezeit.* (Vienna, 1948.)

W. Klara, *Schauspielkostüm und Schauspieldarstellung. Entwicklungsfragen des deutschen Theaters im 18. Jahrhundert.* (Berlin, 1931—S.G.T.G. 43.)

R. Lothar, *Das Wiener Burgtheater.* (Leipzig, Berlin and Vienna, 1899.)

S. Nestriepke, *Das Theater im Wandel der Zeiten.* (Berlin, 1928.)

H. Oberländer, *Die geistige Entwicklung der deutschen Schauspielkunst im 18. Jahrhundert.* (Hamburg, 1898—T.F. 15.)

J. Petersen, *Das deutsche Nationaltheater (Fünf Vorträge).* (Leipzig and Berlin, 1919.)

R. E. Prutz, *Vorlesungen über die Geschichte des deutschen Theaters.* (Berlin, 1847.)

C. Schäffer and C. Hartmann, *Die königlichen Theater in Berlin, statistischer Überblick auf die Tätigkeit und die Personal-Verhältnisse 1786–1885.* (Berlin, 1886.)

C. H. Schmidt, *Chronologie des deutschen Theaters* (1775)—neu herausgegeben von P. Legband. (Berlin, 1902—S.G.T.G. 1.)

J. F. Schütze, *Hamburgische Theatergeschichte.* (Hamburg, 1794.)

(d) Sociology of the theatre and dramatic theory

Julius Bab, *Das Theater im Lichte der Soziologie.* (Leipzig, 1931.)

Leo Balet, *Die Verbürgerlichung der deutschen Kunst, Literatur und Musik im 18. Jahrhundert.* (Leiden, 1936.)

K. Brombacher, *Der deutsche Bürger im Literaturspiegel von Lessing bis Sternheim.* (München, 1920.)

F. Brüggemann, *Der Kampf um die bürgerliche Welt- und Lebensanschauung in der deutschen Literatur des 18. Jahrhunderts,* in 'Deutsche Vierteljahrsschrift für Literaturwissenschaft und Geistesgeschichte', 3, 1925.

W. McNeile Dixon, *Tragedy.* (London, 1924.)

Gustav Freytag, *Die Technik des Dramas.* (Leipzig, 1863.)

L. W. Kahn, *Social ideals in German literature, 1770–1830.* (New York, 1938.)

J. Körner, *Tragik und Tragödie,* in 'Preussische Jahrbücher', 225, 1931.

T. Komisarjevsky, *The theatre and a changing civilisation.* (London, 1935.)

A. Kutscher, *Die Elemente des Theaters.* (Düsseldorf, 1932.)

G. von Lukács, *Zur Soziologie des modernen Dramas,* in 'Archiv für Sozialwissenschaft und Sozialpolitik', 38, 1914.

K. S. Pinson, *Pietism as a factor in the rise of German nationalism.* (New York, 1934.)

L. L. Schücking, *Die Soziologie der literarischen Geschmacksbildung.* (München, 1923. English London, 1944.)

L. L. Schücking and Walther Ebisch, *Bibliographie zur Geschichte des literarischen Geschmacks in England,* in 'Anglia', 1939.

J. E. Spenlé, *La pensée allemande de Luther à Nietzsche.* (Paris, 1934.)

H. Ulmann, *Das deutsche Bürgertum in deutschen Tragödien des 18. und 19. Jahrhunderts.* (Elberfeld, 1923.)

Select Bibliography

Verhandlungen des 7. deutschen Soziologentages in Berlin. Untergruppe für Soziologie der Kunst. (Tübingen, 1931.)

K. Viëtor, *Programm einer Literatursoziologie,* in 'Volk im Werden', 1934, Heft 1.

W. Witte, *The sociological approach to literature,* in 'Modern Language Review', 36, 1941.

CHAPTER I: THE SITUATION IN 1700

Anna Baesecke, *Das Schauspiel der englischen Komödianten.* (Halle, 1935.)

Mary Beare, *The German popular play ATIS and the Venetian opera.* (Cambridge, 1938.)

W. Creizenach, *Die Schauspiele der englischen Komödianten.* (Berlin and Stuttgart, 1889—D.N.L. 23.)

W. Creizenach, *Geschichte des neueren Dramas III.* (Halle, 1903.)

W. Flemming, *Geschichte des Jesuitentheaters in den Landen deutscher Zunge.* (Berlin, 1923—S.G.T.G. 32.)

W. Flemming, *Barockdrama:* 1, *Das schlesische Kunstdrama;* 2, *Das Ordensdrama;* 3, *Das Schauspiel der Wanderbühne;* 4, *Die deutsche Barockkomödie;* 5, *Die Oper;* 6, *Oratorium und Festspiel.* (Leipzig, 1930-33, D.L., Barockdrama.)

C. F. Flögel, *Geschichte der komischen Literatur.* (Leipzig, 1884—87). *Geschichte des Groteske-Komischen.* (Leipzig, 1788.)

F. Geffken, *Der erste Streit über die Zulässigkeit des Schaupiels. Die ältesten Hamburger Opern. Der Streit über die Sittlichkeit des Schauspiels im Jahre 1767*—in 'Zeitschrift des Vereins für Hamburgische Geschichte', Vol. III.

R. Genée, *Lehr- und Wanderjahre des deutschen Schauspiels.* (Berlin, 1882.)

Carl Heine, *J. Velten.* (Halle, 1887.)

Carl Heine, *Das Schauspiel der deutschen Wanderbühne vor Gottsched.* (Halle, 1889.)

F. Homeyer, *Stranitzkys Drama vom heiligen Nepomuk.* (Berlin, 1907—Palaestra 62.)

H. Kindermann, *Die Commedia dell' arte und das deutsche Volkstheater.* (Leipzig, 1938.)

Kathleen M. Lea, *Italian popular comedy,* 2 vols. (Oxford, 1934.)

J. Möser, *Harlekin, oder Verteidigung des Groteske-Komischen,* 1761, in 'Vermischte Schriften', ed. Nicolai (Berlin und Stettin, 1797.)

H. Netzle, *Das süddeutsche Wander-Marionettentheater.* (München, 1938.)

R. Pascal, *The stage of the Englische Komödianten, three problems.* ('Modern Language Review', 35, 1940.)

Sybil Rosenfeld, *Wandering players and drama in the provinces, 1660-1765.* (Cambridge, 1939.)

CHAPTER II. (a) GOTTSCHED

G. Behrmann, *Timoleon, der Bürgerfreund.* (Hamburg, 1741); *Die Horazier.* (Hamburg, 1751.)

F. Brüggemann, *Gottscheds Lebens- und Kunstreform.* (Leipzig, 1935—D.L., Aufklärung 3.)

F. Brüggemann, *Die bürgerliche Gemeinschaftskultur der 40er Jahre,* 2. Teil, Drama. (Leipzig, 1938—D.L., Aufklärung 6.)

T. W. Danzel, *Gottsched und seine Zeit.* (2nd ed. 1855.)

J. C. Gottsched, *Gesammelte Schriften,* ed. E. Reichel, 1-4. (Berlin, 1902-12.) *Der sterbende Cato.* (Reprint, Reclam.)

L. A. V. Gottschedin, *Die Pietisterei im Fischbeinrock.* (Reprint in D.L., Aufklärung 3, Leipzig, 1935.) *Das Testament.* (Reprint in D.L., Aufklärung 6, Leipzig, 1933.)

Max Koch, *Gottsched und die Reform der deutschen Literatur im 18. Jahrhundert.* (Hamburg, 1887.)

Caroline Neuber, *Ein deutsches Vorspiel.* (Reprint in 'Deutsche Literaturdenkmale des 18. und 19. Jahrhunderts', 63, Leipzig, 1897.)

Caroline Neuber, *Das Schäferfest.* (Reprint in D.L., Aufklärung 3.)

F. J. von Reden-Esbeck, *Caroline Neuber und ihre Zeitgenossen.* (Leipzig, 1881.)

E. Reichel, *Gottsched*, 2 vols. (Berlin, 1908, 1912.)

G. Waniek, *Gottsched und die deutsche Literatur seiner Zeit.* (Leipzig, 1897.)

(b) THE REGULAR THEATRE

J. W. von Brawe, *Der Freigeist*, 1757. (Reprint in D.L., Aufklärung 8, Leipzig, 1934.) *Brutus.* (Reprint in D.N.L. 72.)

J. F. von Cronegk, *Olint und Sophronia.* (Reprint in D.N.L. 72.)

C. F. Gellert, *Lustspiele*, in 'Schriften', 3. Teil (Carlsruhe, 1774). *Die zärtlichen Schwestern.* (Reprint in D.L., Aufklärung 6.)

F. Heitmüller, *Hamburgische Dramatiker zur Zeit Gottscheds und ihre Beziehungen zu ihm.* (Wandsbeck, 1890.)

J. Minor, *C. F. Weisse.* (Innsbruck, 1880.)   Introduction to *Lessings Jugendfreunde.* (D.N.L. 72.)

T. J. Quistorp, *Der Hypochondrist.* (Reprint in D.L., Aufklärung 6.)

A. Sauer, *J. W. von Brawe.* (Strassburg, 1878.)

J. E. Schlegel, *Aesthetische und dramaturgische Schriften*, ed. J. L. v. Antoniewicz. (Stuttgart 1887—Deutsche Literaturdenkmale 26.)

J. E. Schlegel, *Canut.* (Reprint in D.L., Aufklärung 6.)

J. E. Schlegel, *Werke*, 5 vols., ed. J. H. Schlegel. (Copenhagen and Leipzig, 1761–70.)

B. Aikin-Sneath, *Comedy in Germany in the first half of the eighteenth century.* (Oxford, 1936.)

Elizabeth M. Wilkinson, *J. E. Schlegel.* (Oxford, 1945.)

CHAPTER III. (a) THE THEATRE IN THE AGE OF LESSING

J. C. Brandes, *Meine Lebensgeschichte*, reprint ed. W. Francke. (München, 1923.)

J. A. Christ, *Erinnerungen*, ed. R. Schirmer. (München and Leipzig, 1912.)

H. Devrient, *J. F. Schönemann.* (Hamburg and Leipzig, 1895—T.F. 11.)

B. Litzmann, *F. L. Schröder*, I and II. (Hamburg and Leipzig, 1890–94.) *Der grosse Schröder.* (Berlin and Leipzig, n.d.—'Das Theater', Vol. I.)

J. F. Löwen, *Geschichte des deutschen Theaters*, ed. H. Stümke. (Berlin, 1903.)

J. G. Robertson, *Lessing's dramatic theory, being an introduction to and commentary on his Hamburgische Dramaturgie.* (Cambridge, 1939.)

J. F. Schütze, *Hamburgische Theatergeschichte.* (Hamburg, 1794.)

R. Thiele, *Die Theaterzettel der sogenannten Hamburgischen Entreprise (1767–69).* (Erfurt, 1895.)

H. Uhde, *Konrad Ekhof*, in R. Gottschalls 'Neuer Plutarch'. (Leipzig, 1876.)

Select Bibliography

(b) THE ENLIGHTENMENT. LESSING AS CRITIC

F. Brüggemann, *Das Weltbild der deutschen Aufklärung.* (Leipzig, 1930—D.L., Aufklärung 2.)

E. Cassirer, *Die Philosophie der Aufklärung.* (Tübingen, 1932.)

W. Dilthey, *Leibniz und sein Zeitalter. Friedrich der Grosse und sein Zeitalter,* in 'Gesammelte Schriften' III. (Leipzig, 1927.)

W. Dilthey, *Aufklärung. Der deutsche Idealismus,* in 'Gesammelte Schriften' IV. (Leipzig, 1921.)

H. R. G. Günther, *Psychologie des deutschen Pietismus* in 'Deutsche Vierteljahrs-schrift für Literaturwissenschaft und Geistesgeschichte' 4, 1926.

W. H. Lecky, *History of European rationalism.* (2nd ed., London, 1865.)

P. Hazard, *La crise de la conscience européenne.* (Paris, 1935.)

La pensée européenne de Montesquieu à Lessing, 3 vols. (Paris, 1946–48.)

C. A. Moore, *Shaftesbury and the ethical poets in England, 1700–1760,* in P.M.L.A. 31, 1916, pp. 264–325.

Lessing, *Sämtliche Werke,* ed. J. Petersen, etc. (Bong & Co.)

W. Mahrholz, *Der deutsche Pietismus.* (Berlin, 1919.)

R. Petsch, *Lessings Briefwechsel mit Mendelssohn und Nicolai über das Trauerspiel* (Leipzig, 1910.)

Erich Schmidt, *Lessing,* 2 vols., 3rd ed. (Berlin, 1909.)

H. Schöffler, *Protestantismus und Literatur.* (Leipzig, 1922.)

Leslie Stephen, *English literature and society in the eighteenth century.* (London, 1904.) *English thought in the eighteenth century,* II. (London, 1876.)

E. Troeltsch, *Epochen und Typen der Sozialphilosophie des Christentums; Leibniz und die Anfänge des Pietismus,* in 'Gesammelte Werke' IV. (Tübingen, 1925.)

R. Unger, *Hamann und die Aufklärung,* I. (Halle, 1925.)

O. Walzel, *Lessings Begriff des Tragischen; Das bürgerliche Drama,* in 'Vom Geistes-leben alter und neuer Zeit'. (Leipzig, 1922.)

CHAPTER IV. THE PLAYS OF LESSING'S MATURITY

E. Bernbaum, *The drama of sensibility, 1696–1780.* (Boston and London, 1915.)

J. Block, *Lessing und das bürgerliche Trauerspiel,* in 'Zeitschrift für den deutschen Unterricht', 18, 1904.

F. Brüggemann, *Lessings Bürgerdramen und der Subjektivismus als Problem,* in 'Jahrbuch des freien deutschen Hochstifts'. (1926.)

F. Brüggemann, *Das Drama des Gegeneinander in den 6oer Jahren.* (Leipzig, 1938—D.L., Aufklärung 12.)

J. Clivio, *Lessing und das Problem der Tragödie.* (Zürich and Leipzig, 1928.)

W. Dilthey, *Das Erlebnis und die Dichtung.* (Leipzig and Berlin, 1906.)

A. Eloesser, *Das bürgerliche Drama.* (Berlin, 1898.)

G. Kettner, *Lessings Dramen im Lichte ihrer und unserer Zeit.* (Berlin, 1904.)

G. Lanson, *Nivelle de la Chaussée et la comédie larmoyante.* (Paris, 1887.)

C. L. Martini, *Rhynsolt und Sapphira,* in D.L., Aufklärung 8.

J. G. B. Pfeil, *Lucie Woodvil,* in D.L., Aufklärung 8.

H. Selver, *Die Auffassung des Bürgers im deutschen bürgerlichen Drama des 18. Jahr-bunderts.* (Leipzig, 1931.)

Select Bibliography

R. Unger, *Von Nathan zu Faust. Zur Geschichte des Ideendramas*, in 'Gesammelte Studien', II. (Berlin, 1929.)

A. W. Ward, *Introduction to The London Merchant and Fatal Curiosity*, in Collected Papers, IV. (Cambridge, 1921.)

C. F. Weisse, Reprints: *Richard III* (D.L.N. 72); *Krispus, Rosemunde, Die Befreiung von Theben, Atreus und Thyest* (D.L., Aufklärung 12).

W. Wetz, *Die Anfänge der ernsten bürgerlichen Dichtung.* (1885.)

CHAPTER V. THE THEATRE OF THE 'SEVENTIES

J. C. Brandes, *Sämtliche dramatische Schriften*, 8 vols. (Hamburg, 1790–91.)

F. Brüggemann, *Die Aufnahme Shakespeares auf der Bühne der Aufklärung in den 6oer und 7oer Jahren.* (Leipzig, 1937—D.L., Aufklärung 11.)

J. J. Engel, *Schriften.* (Berlin, 1801–6). *Die Apotheke*, reprint in D.L., Aufklärung 10.

R. Genée, *Geschichte des Shakespeareschen Dramas in Deutschland.* (Leipzig, 1870.)

F. W. Gotter, *Die Dorfgala,* reprint in D.L., Aufklärung 10.

W. Hill, *Die deutschen Theaterzeitschriften des 18. Jahrhunderts.* (Weimar, 1915.)

R. Hodermann, *Geschichte des Gothaischen Hoftheaters 1775–79.* (Hamburg and Leipzig, 1894—T.F. 9.)

B. Litzmann, *Schröder und Gotter.* (Hamburg and Leipzig, 1887.)

F. L. W. Meyer, *F. L. Schröder.* (Hamburg, 1819.)

J. B. Michaelis, *Der Einspruch*, reprint in D.L., Aufklärung 10.

R. Pascal, *Shakespeare in Germany, 1740–1815.* (Cambridge, 1937.)

R. Schlösser, *F. W. Gotter.* (Hamburg and Leipzig, 1894—T.F. 10.) *Vom Hamburger Nationaltheater zur Gothaer Hofbühne.* (Hamburg and Leipzig, 1895—T.F. 13.)

F. L. Schröder, *Beitrag zur deutschen Schaubühne*, 3 vols. (Berlin, 1786–90.)

F. L. Schröder, *Dramatische Werke*, ed. E. v. Bülow. (Berlin, 1831.)

F. L. Schröder, *Hamlet* (stage version), in D.L., Aufklärung 11.

E. L. Stahl, *Shakespeare und das deutsche Theater.* (Stuttgart, 1947.)

G. Stephanie d. Jüngere, *Macbeth* (stage version), in D.L., Aufklärung 11.

H. A. O. Reichard, *Theaterkalender.* (Gotha, 1775–94.) *Theaterjournal für Deutschland.* (Gotha, 1777–84.)

C. F. Weisse, *Der Teufel ist los*, reprint in D.N.L. 72; *Der Dorfbalbier*, reprint in D.L., Aufklärung 10; *Romeo und Julie*, reprint in D.L., Aufklärung 11.

M. Wieland, *König Lear*, in D.L., Aufklärung 11.

CHAPTER VI. THE LITERARY DRAMA OF THE 'SEVENTIES

J. M. Babo, *Otto von Wittelsbach*, reprint in D.N.L. 138.

O. Brahm, *Das deutsche Ritterdrama.* (Strassburg, 1880.)

M. Enzinger, *Die Entwicklung des Wiener Theaters, Stoffe und Motive.* (Berlin, 1918–19 —S.G.T.G. 28–9.)

C. Fleischlen, *O. H. von Gemmingen.* (Stuttgart, 1890.)

O. H. von Gemmingen, *Der deutsche Hausvater*, reprint in D.N.L. 139.

K. F. Hensler, *Das Donauweibchen*, reprint in D.N.L. 138.

G. Keferstein, *Bürgertum und Bürgerlichkeit bei Goethe.* (Weimar, 1933.)

Select Bibliography

H. Kindermann, *Die Entwicklung der Sturm- und Drangbewegung.* (Vienna, 1925.) *Lenz und die deutsche Romantik.* (Vienna, 1925.) *Der Kampf um das soziale Ord-nungsgefüge.* (Leipzig, 1939—D.L., Irrationalismus 8.)

H. A. Korff, *Geist der Goethezeit, I, Sturm und Drang.* (Leipzig, 1923.)

W. Martini, *Die Technik der Jugenddramen Goethes.* (Weimar, 1932.)

J. M. R. Lenz, *Gesammelte Schriften,* ed. F. Blei. (München, 1909–13.) *Briefe von und an J. M. R. Lenz,* ed. Freye and Stammler. (Leipzig, 1918.) *Anmer-kungen übers Theater,* ed. T. Friedrich. (1908—Probefahrten 13.)

S. Melchinger, *Dramaturgie des Sturms und Drangs.* (Gotha, 1929.)

A. Nollau, *Das literarische Publikum des jungen Goethe.* (Weimar, 1935.)

O. Rommel, *Barocktradition im österreichisch-bayrischen Volkstheater,* 6 vols. (Leipzig, 1935–39—D.L.)

E. Schmidt, *Lenz und Klinger.* (Berlin, 1878.)

Clara Stockmeyer, *Soziale Probleme im Drama des Sturmes und Dranges.* (Frankfurt a. M., 1922.)

Stürmer und Dränger, ed. A. Sauer, D.N.L.

Sturm und Drang, ed. K. Freye. (Bong & Co., n.d.)

J. A. von Törring, *Agnes Bernauerin,* in D.N.L., 138.

A. M. Wagner, *Gerstenberg und der Sturm und Drang. Gerstenberg als Typus der Übergangszeit.* (Heidelberg, 1920–24).

H. L. Wagner, *Gesammelte Werke,* ed. L. Hirschberg. (Potsdam, 1923.) *Die Reue nach der Tat,* reprint in D.L., Irrationalismus 8.

K. Viëtor, *Der junge Goethe.* (Leipzig, 1930.)

O. Zollinger, *Merciers Beziehungen zur deutschen Literatur,* in 'Zeitschrift für franzö-sische Sprache und Literatur', 25, 1903.

CHAPTER VII. (*a*) THE YOUNG SCHILLER

L. Bellermann, *Schillers Dramen,* 2 vols. (Berlin, 1888–91.)

K. Berger, *Schiller,* 2 vols. (München, 1905–9.)

P. Böckmann, *Die innere Form in Schillers Dramen,* in 'Dichtung und Volkstum', 1934.

H. H. Borcherdt, *Schiller, seine geistige und künstlerische Entwicklung.* (Leipzig, 1929.)

R. Buchwald, *Schiller I, Der junge Schiller.* (Leipzig, 1937.)

G. Fricke, *Die Problematik der Tragödie bei Schiller,* in 'Jahrbuch des freien deutschen Hochstifts', 1930.

F. Jonas, *Schillers Briefe,* 7 vols. (Stuttgart, 1892–6.)

J. Petersen, *Schillers Gespräche.* (Leipzig, 1911.)

J. Petersen, *Schiller und die Bühne.* (Berlin, 1904.)

B. v. Wiese, *Die Dramen Schillers, Politik und Tragödie.* (Leipzig, 1938.)

W. Witte, *Schiller.* (Oxford, 1949.)

(*b*) THE THEATRE OF THE 'EIGHTIES

A. W. Iffland, *Über meine theatralische Laufbahn,* ed. H. Holstein. (Heilbronn, 1886—Deutsche Literaturdenkmale 24.)

A. W. Iffland, *Die Jäger,* reprint in D.N.L. 139. *Die Hagestolzen,* reprint in D.N.L. 139. *Briefe an seine Schwester Louise und andere Verwandte,* ed. L. Geiger. (Berlin, 1904—S.G.T.G. 5.)

Select Bibliography

Journal aller Journale, I–VII. (Hamburg, 1786–7.)

M. Knudsen, *Heinrich Beck*. (Hamburg and Leipzig, 1912—T.F. 24.)

W. Koffka, *Iffland und Dalberg*. (Leipzig, 1865.)

A. v. Kotzebue, *Menschenhass und Reue. Die Indianer in England. Die deutschen Kleinstädter*, reprints in D.N.L. 139.

M. Martersteig, *Die Protokolle des Mannheimer Nationaltheaters unter Dalberg aus den Jahren 1781 bis 1789*. (Mannheim, 1890.)

F. L. Schmidt, *Denkwürdigkeiten*, ed. H. Uhde, 2 vols. (Hamburg, 1875.)

F. L. Schröder, *Das Porträt der Mutter*, reprint in D.N.L. 139.

A. Stiehler, *Das Ifflandische Rührstück*. (Hamburg and Leipzig, 1898—T.F. 16.)

CHAPTER VIII. THE EARLY BLANK-VERSE DRAMAS OF GOETHE AND SCHILLER

Barker Fairley, *Goethe as revealed in his poetry*. (London, 1932.) *A study of Goethe*. (Oxford, 1947.)

F. Gundolf, *Goethe*. (Berlin, 1918.)

H. A. Korff, *Geist der Goethezeit, II, Klassik*. (Leipzig, 1930.)

Günther Müller, *Kleine Goethe-Biographie*. (Bonn, 1947.)

R. Peacock, *Goethe's version of poetic drama*, in 'Proceedings of the English Goethe Society', N.S. 16, 1947.

W. Rehm, *Griechentum und Goethezeit*. (Leipzig, 1936.)

H. Trevelyan, *Goethe and the Greeks*. (Cambridge, 1941.)

C. E. Vaughan, *Types of tragic drama*. (London, 1908.) *The Romantic Revolt*. (London, 1907.)

K. Viëtor, *Goethe, Dichtung, Wissenschaft, Weltbild*. (Bern, 1949.)

CHAPTER IX. THE WEIMAR COURT THEATRE

C. A. H. Burkhardt, *Das Repertoire des Weimarischen Theaters unter Goethes Leitung, 1791–1817*. (Hamburg and Leipzig, 1891—T.F. 1.)

A. Doebber, *Lauchstädt und Weimar, eine theaterbaugeschichtliche Studie*. (Berlin, 1908.)

Eduard Genast, *Aus Weimars klassischer und nachklassischer Zeit, Erinnerungen eines alten Schauspielers*, ed. R. Kohlrausch. 4th ed. (Stuttgart, 1905.)

H. H. Houben, *Hier Zensur, wer dort*. 2nd ed. (Leipzig, 1918.)

Karoline Jagemann, *Erinnerungen*, ed. E. v. Bamberg. (Dresden, 1926.)

A. Köster, *Schiller als Dramaturg*. (Berlin, 1891.)

B. T. Satori-Neumann, *Die Frühzeit des Weimarischen Hoftheaters unter Goethes Leitung*. (Berlin, 1922—S.G.T.G. 31.)

E. Pasqué, *Goethes Theaterleitung in Weimar*, 2 vols. (Leipzig, 1863.)

E. Scharrer-Santen, *Die Weimarische Dramaturgie*. (Berlin and Leipzig, 1927.)

L. Schrickel, *Geschichte des Weimarer Theaters*. (Weimar, 1928.)

J. Wahle, *Das Weimarer Hoftheater unter Goethes Leitung*. (Weimar, 1892—Schriften der Goethe-Gesellschaft, 6.)

A. Weichberger, *Goethe und das Komödienhaus in Weimar, 1779-1825*. (Leipzig, 1928—T.F. 39.)

A. Hennings, *Bemerkungen über Weimar*, in 'Der Genius der Zeit', Vol. 20, May-December 1800.

Select Bibliography

CHAPTER X. SCHILLER'S CLASSICAL PLAYS AND GOETHE'S FAUST

Schiller:

K. Cunningham, *Schiller und die französische Klassik*. (Bonn, 1939.)

E. Heusermann, *Schillers Dramen*. (Leipzig and Berlin, 1915.)

H. H. Houben, *Damals in Weimar. Erinnerungen von und an Johanna Schopenhauer*. (Leipzig, 1924.)

E. Lerch, *Lessing, Goethe, Schiller und die französische Klassik*. (Mainz, 1948.)

R. Petsch, *Freiheit und Notwendigkeit in Schillers Dramen*. (München, 1905.)

H. Schneider, *Vom Wallenstein zum Demetrius*. (Stuttgart, 1933.)

W. Spengler, *Das Drama Schillers, seine Genesis*. (Leipzig, 1932.)

Faust—a few suggestions from the immense literature:

K. Burdach, *Das religiöse Problem in Goethes Faust*, in 'Euphorion', Goetheheft I, 1932.

V. Hehn, *Gedanken über Goethe* (1887.)

G. Lukács, *Goethe und seine Zeit*. (Bern, 1947.)

G. Santayana, *Three philosophical poets*. (Harvard, 1910.)

F. M. Stawell and G. Lowes Dickinson, *Goethe and Faust*. (London, 1928.)

B. v. Wiese, *Die deutsche Tragödie von Lessing bis Hebbel*, 2 vols. (Hamburg, 1948.)

G. Witkowski, *Goethes Faust*, 2 vols. (Leiden, 1936.)

CHAPTER XI. THEATRE, DRAMA AND PUBLIC AT THE DEATH OF SCHILLER

E. Gross, *Die ältere Romantik und das Theater*. (Hamburg and Leipzig, 1910—T.F. 22.)

S. Laing, *Notes of a traveller, on the social and political state of France, Prussia, Switzerland, Italy and other parts of Europe during the present century*. (London, 1842.)

S. Lublinski, *Literatur und Gesellschaft im 19. Jahrhundert*. 2 vols. (Berlin, 1899.)

M. Martersteig, *Das deutsche Theater im 19. Jahrhundert, eine kulturgeschichtliche Darstellung*. 2nd ed. (Leipzig, 1924.)

R. Weil, *Das Berliner Theaterpublikum unter A. W.Ifflands Direktion, 1796–1814*. (Berlin, 1932—S.G.T.G. 44.)

INDEX OF PLAYS

Index of Plays

Index of Plays

GENERAL INDEX